ONE TASTE

ONE TASTE

The Journals of KEN WILBER

SHAMBHALA
Boston & London
1999

SHAMBHALA PUBLICATIONS, INC.
Horticultural Hall
300 Massachusetts Avenue
Boston, Massachusetts 02115
http://www.shambhala.com

© 1999 by Ken Wilber

9 8 7 6 5 4 3 2 1

FIRST EDITION
Printed in the United States of America

⊗ This edition is printed on acid-free paper that meets the
American National Standards Institute Z39.48 Standard.
Distributed in the United States by Random House, Inc.,
and in Canada by Random House of Canada Ltd

Library of Congress Cataloging-in-Publication Data
Wilber, Ken.
One taste: the journals of Ken Wilber / by Ken Wilber.
p. cm.
ISBN 1-57062-387-2 (hardcover)
1. Wilber, Ken—Diaries. 2. Spiritual biography—United States.
3. Spiritual life. I. Title.
BL73.W55A3 1999   98-22970
191—dc21   CIP
[B]

Contents

A Note to the Reader

In the past I have strenuously resisted going public. I am not a private person, in the sense of secretive; I'm just not a public person, in the sense of seeking the limelight. Nonetheless, as one who has written extensively about the interior life, it seemed appropriate, at some point, to share mine. The following pages therefore contain a fair amount of what would ordinarily be considered private material. Still, in the last analysis, this is a philosophical more than personal journal: it deals primarily with ideas, and especially those ideas that orbit the sun of the perennial philosophy (or the common core of the word's great wisdom traditions). In one area, however, this is a very personal journal: extensive descriptions of meditation practice and various mystical states, based on my own experience. (Those who wish a more personal account in other areas might consult *Grace and Grit*.)

Because this book is idea-focused, I have taken a few liberties with the order of the entries. Some theoretical pieces were moved up, because other entries don't make sense without them. Dates are generally accurate, but in a few cases they might be off because I sometimes made notes without dating them, so I entered these wherever it seemed appropriate. Some Naropa seminars originally occurred within a few days of each other; I have spread these out (otherwise, too much academic talk in one place); the dates are therefore not always accurate, but the excerpts themselves are. In any event, it should be remembered that these journals were not primarily meant to be a record of the details of my personal life, but rather a record of further attempts to convey the perennial philosophy.

Because the theoretical entries are fairly brief and self-contained—a page or two, usually, a dozen pages at most—the ideas themselves come in bite-size chunks. If you hit an entry that doesn't interest you—one on politics, perhaps, or business, or art—you can easily skip to the next entry. If, however, you are reading these pages for the theoretical information, you should know that each entry builds on its predecessors, so skipping around is not the best idea.

If there is a theme to this journal it is that body, mind, and soul are not mutually exclusive. The desires of the flesh, the ideas of the mind, and the luminosities of the soul—all are perfect expressions of the radiant Spirit that alone inhabits the universe, sublime gestures of that Great Perfection that alone outshines the world. There is only One Taste in the entire Kosmos, and that taste is Divine, whether it appears in the flesh, in the mind, in the soul. Resting in that One Taste, transported beyond the mundane, the world arises in the purest Freedom and radiant Release, happy to infinity, lost in all eternity, and hopeless in the original face of the unrelenting mystery. From One Taste all things issue, to One Taste all things return—and in between, which is the story of this moment, there is the only the dream, and sometimes the nightmare, from which we would do well to awaken.

K.W.
Boulder, Colorado
Spring 1998

ONE TASTE

JANUARY

You could not discover the limits of the soul, even if you traveled by every path in order to do so; such is the depth of its meaning.

—HERACLITUS

Thursday, January 2, 1997

Worked all morning, research and reading, while watching the sunlight play through the falling snow. The sun is not yellow today, it is white, like the snow, so I am surrounded by white on white, alone on alone. Sheer Emptiness, soft clear light, is what it all looks like, shimmering to itself in melancholy murmurs. I am released into that Emptiness, and all is radiant on this clear light day.

Friday, January 3

A while ago—somewhere around Thanksgiving—I started writing The Integration of Science and Religion: The Union of Ancient Wisdom and Modern Knowledge.[1] The book is now done, and I'm wondering just what to do with it. I wrote it with a specific audience in mind—namely, the orthodox, conventional, mainstream world, not the new-age new-paradigm, countercultural crowd. I have no idea if I succeeded, and I'm not sure exactly what my next step should be.

---

1. Published as *The Marriage of Sense and Soul: Integrating Science and Religion.*

I need to figure out a way to do this type of intense work and still have some sort of social life. Every time Balzac had an orgasm, he used to say, "There goes another book." I seem to have it exactly backwards.

After Treya's death—it's been eight years this month—I didn't date for a year or so. I've since had a few very nice relationships, but nothing quite right. I wonder . . .

Saturday, January 4

Some students have invited me to a "rave"—an all-night dance party with techno music and—ahem—certain illegal substances. The kids—and these really are kids, twentysomethings—use small amounts of Ecstasy, a drug that enhances empathy and group rapport. The atmosphere is communal, asexual or perhaps androgynous, and gentle but intense—with, for lack of a better term, a type of spiritual background. The music (e.g., Moby and Prodigy) generally lacks words—that is, lacks a referential nature, so the symbolic mind is not engaged—and this allows, on occasion, little glimmers of the supramental, not to mention huge doses of the inframental.

Well, whatever disapproving parents may say about all that, I find it infinitely preferable to what we used to do at our dances, which was, basically, drink a six-pack of beer and throw up on your date. And as for baby-boomer parents cluck-clucking about illegal substances, ah, gimme me a break.

Still, I think I'll pass on the rave. But more power to 'em, I say.

Tuesday, January 7

This weekend is the "Ken Wilber Conference" in San Francisco. I'm told it's sold out and they're looking for a bigger place to hold it. I'm not sure whether that's good or bad.

Roger [Walsh][2] will be one of the main presenters. I wonder if he will tell his Neil Armstrong joke, which seems to be the funniest thing anybody can ever remember hearing:

---

2. All bracketed interpolations were added for publication; all parentheses are in the original journals. All footnotes were added for publication.

When Neil Armstrong set foot on the moon, his first words were, "One small step for a man, one giant leap for mankind." The next thing he said was, "Good luck, Mr. Gorsky." The little-known story behind those words: When Armstrong was a young boy, he overheard a heated argument coming from the neighbor's bedroom window. Mrs. Gorsky screamed at Mr. Gorsky, "You'll get oral sex when that little boy next door walks on the moon."

Wednesday, January 8

Got another letter from a woman who read my foreword to Frances's book [*Shadows of the Sacred: Seeing Through Spiritual Illusions*, by Frances Vaughan]. I've received so many letters from women who relate directly to the issues raised in it.

The foreword begins, "Frances Vaughan is the wisest of the Wise Women I know. Such a wonderful concept: the woman who is wise, the woman who has more wisdom, perhaps, than you or I, the woman who brings a special knowledge, a graceful touch, a healing presence, to her every encounter, for whom beauty is a mode of knowing and openness a special strength—a woman who sees so much more, and touches so much more, and reaches out with care, and tells us that it will be all right, this woman who is wise, this woman who sees more.

"Frances is such a one: the woman who brings wisdom into the world, and does not simply flee the world for wisdom somewhere else. The woman who teaches individuality, but set in its larger and deeper contexts of communion: communion with others, with body, with Spirit, with one's own higher Self: the Spirit that manifests its very being in relationships. And that is how I think of Frances most often: the wise woman who teaches sane and sincere relationship, the woman who sets us in our deeper contexts, this wise woman whom I am proud to know."

Today's letter (from a woman therapist) talks at length about the historical tradition of the Wise Woman, and the importance of uniting psychotherapy with spirituality. I couldn't agree more. From the last part of the foreword:

"In the type of practice that Frances (and a handful of others) are attempting to forge, we see the emergence of what is so crucial: some sense of the spiritual and transpersonal, some sense of the Mystery of the Deep, some context beyond the isolated me, that touches each and every one of us, and lifts us from our troubled and mortal selves, this contracted coil, and delivers us into the hands of the timeless and very Divine, and gracefully releases us from ourselves: where openness melts defenses and relationship grounds sanity, where compassion outpaces the hardened heart and care outshines despair, this opening to the Divine that Frances teaches each of us.

"One of Frances's clients once told her that she (Frances) had helped to midwife her soul, deliver her soul. I think that somehow says it all. To midwife the Divine—already present in each, but perhaps not shining brightly; already given to each, but perhaps not noticed well; already caring for the world, but perhaps forgotten in all the rush: this opening to the Divine that Frances teaches each of us.

"Let us both, you and I, take the hand of the Wise Woman, and walk with her through the land of our own soul, and listen quietly to the tale she has to tell. And know that a surer pair of hands we are not likely to find in this lifetime."

Thursday, January 9

Fame in this country is a religion that demands human sacrifice, a religion to which I do not wish to belong. You start to take yourself so seriously—I saw it happening to me, after I had written my first book at the age of 23. I'd give lectures or seminars, people would tell me how amazingly great I was, and sooner or later, you believe them. You end up exactly with what Oscar Levant said to George Gershwin: "Tell me, George, if you had it to do all over again, would you still fall in love with yourself?"

After about a year of that, I decided I could either teach what I had written yesterday, or write something new. So I stopped going to conferences, I stopped teaching, I stopped giving interviews.

For the next twenty years, I stuck to that plan with virtually no exceptions. And yet here I am, thinking about taking Science and Religion straight to the biggest mainstream publishers and really going for it. I think I am seriously deranged.

Tuesday, January 14

Frank Visser, my Dutch translator, has come from the Netherlands to say hi, after stopping by the kw conference in San Francisco. Frank translated <u>The Atman Project</u> and <u>A Brief History of Everything</u>. I hear he's very good.

"In this field, what's the hot topic in Europe?"

"How <u>regressive</u> so many of the American approaches to spirituality are. The schools that confuse bodily feeling with spiritual awareness, bioenergetics, experiential this and that, ecopsychology, feelings and more feelings, the regressive therapies, the whole lot. I have written a paper about it. Don't you agree that you Americans are insane for regression?"

"I'm afraid so. Mostly because it's something <u>anybody</u> can do—growth is hard, regression is easy."

"It's your pre/trans fallacy all over the place."

Frank is referring to an essay I wrote, almost two decades ago, called "The Pre/Trans Fallacy." The idea is simple: since both <u>pre</u>-rational and <u>trans</u>-rational are <u>non</u>-rational, they are easily confused. And then one of two very unpleasant things happens: either you <u>reduce</u> genuine, trans-rational, spiritual realities to infantile, prerational states; or you <u>elevate</u> childish, prerational sentiments to transcendental glory. In the first case you deny spiritual realities altogether, since you think they are all infantile rubbish. In the second case, you end up glorifying childish myth and preverbal impulse. You are so intent on transcending rationality, which is fine, that you go overboard and champion <u>anything</u> that is not rational, including much that is frankly prerational, regressive, downhill.

And Frank is right; much of what is being called a "spiritual renaissance" in this country is really a prerational slide—narcissistic, self-centered, self-glorifying, self-promoting.

"We Europeans find it alarming."

Wednesday, January 15

Read all morning, part of the seemingly unending research for volume 2 of the Kosmos trilogy (<u>Sex, God, and Gender</u>).[3] The relation between men and women: the agony and the ecstasy. And it tends to drive both

---

3. Volume 1 is *Sex, Ecology, Spirituality* (Shambhala, 1995); volume 2 is tentatively titled *Sex, God, and Gender: The Ecology of Men and Women*, which I am now working on; volume 3 is outlined, and is tentatively subtitled *The Spirit of Post/Modernity.*

sides insane. I expect to see a Bret Harte update: The Outcasts of Testosterone Flat. Take Aldous Huxley's quip: "It's a law of nature. Man minus woman equals pig. Woman minus man equals lunatic." Or Gloria Steinem: "A woman without a man is like a fish without a bicycle." Woody Allen: "God gave males a penis and a brain, but only enough blood to operate one at a time." Billy Crystal: "A woman needs a reason to make love, a man needs a place."

Volume 1 was eight hundred pages, so will be volume 2. "Another damned thick square book! Always scribble, scribble, scribble, eh, Mr. Gibbon?"

Friday, January 17

Got a letter from Alex Grey, whose book Sacred Mirrors: The Visionary Art of Alex Grey I wrote a foreword for. In the letter, Alex reminds me of the conversation we had at my house, when we were talking about the nature of genuine art: "The purpose of truly transcendent art is to express something you are not yet, but that you can become."

The foreword I did for Alex's book stresses the theme that all of us possess the eye of flesh, the eye of mind, and the eye of spirit. We can classify art in terms of which eye it mostly relies on. Realism and naturalism, for example, rely mostly on the eye of flesh; abstract, conceptual, and surrealistic art rely mostly on the eye of mind; and certain great works of spiritual art—Tibetan thangkas, for example—rely on the eye of contemplation, the eye of spirit.

Each of these eyes sees a different world—the world of material objects, of mental ideas, of spiritual realities. And each eye can paint what it sees. The higher the eye, the deeper the art.

Alex is representative of those rare artists who paint with the eye of contemplation, the eye of spirit. This type of art is not symbolic or metaphorical; it is a direct depiction of realities, but realities that cannot be seen with the eye of flesh or the eye of mind, only with the eye of spirit. And the point of this art is not simple viewing but transformation: it represents higher or deeper realities available to all of us if we continue to grow and evolve. And that is why "the purpose of truly transcendent art is to express something you are not yet, but that you can become."

Wednesday, January 22

Going mainstream. This is all Tony Schwartz's fault.

I first met Tony when he was doing <u>What Really Matters: Searching for Wisdom in America</u>. Tony's is one of the great stories: an accomplished journalist—he had worked for the <u>New York Times</u>, <u>New York</u> magazine, had done almost a dozen <u>Newsweek</u> cover stories—and he had just finished coauthoring Donald Trump's <u>The Art of the Deal</u>, which promptly perched on top of the <u>Times</u> bestseller list and tossed Tony into the big time of megabucks, glamour, and glitz. Being immersed in Trump's extravagant world let Tony know that, even if he had all that material wealth, it somehow wouldn't touch the really important issues in life. So, with the money he made on the Trump book, Tony spent the next five years on his own search for wisdom, crisscrossing this country and talking to over 200 psychologists, philosophers, mystics, gurus, therapists, and teachers of all sorts. He devoted a chapter in his book to my work, and we became best of friends.

After Tony finished <u>What Really Matters</u>, and having a family to support, he took on the co-writing of Michael Eisner's autobiography, essentially doing the same job for the head of Disney that he had done for the Donald. But there the similarities ended. As Tony explains it, Trump is simply Trump: what you see is what you get; the book was fairly straightforward, if demanding. But Michael Eisner is a considerably different story, involving the entire Walt Disney empire—theme parks, movies, books, towns, television—not to mention such sideshows as Jeffrey Katzenberg and Michael Ovitz. Tony has now spent over three years on this project.

What Tony wants to do next is work on an <u>integral</u> approach to human growth and transformation, as he summarized it in <u>What Really Matters</u> and as he finds outlined in my work (but not only mine). He is determined to take this integral message to a larger audience, and this has made me more sensitive to the fact that, to some degree at least, I need to do the same thing. Yes, this is definitely all Tony's fault.

Thursday, January 23

Finished Christopher Isherwood's thousand-page diary (volume one!), and I have been deeply depressed for almost a week. Many reasons.

Isherwood represents for me several very important strands of life, all rolled into one. First, there is the whole Vedanta Society connection, and that includes, in various ways, Aldous Huxley, Gerald Heard, and Thomas Mann (the latter, loosely, but significantly). Isherwood, working with Swami Prabhavananda (cf. My Guru and His Disciple), produced some of the first, and certainly the most readable, translations of the Bhagavad Gita, Patanjali's Yoga Sutras, and my favorite, Shankara's classic The Crest Jewel of Discrimination.

So as early as 1941, Christopher is writing in his diary, "To try to annihilate your ego, to let the Real Self walk about in you, using your legs and arms, your brain and your voice. It's fantastically difficult—and yet, what else is life for?" This would also let him understand something that the purely Descended religions—from ecology to Gaia worship to ecopsychology—utterly fail to understand: "Whenever a movement has its objectives within time, it always resorts to violence." This deeply spiritual strand in Christopher was thankfully given a little spice of biting humor; he was determined to live his life "with passion, with sincere involvement, and with heartfelt hostility."

But Isherwood was always struggling, in his own way, for an integral approach that united spirituality with this life, probably because, as he put it, sex and spirit were both very strong in him and yet often apparently antagonistic. I love his honest struggle to stay with both, even in extremes.

Most people know Isherwood, even if they don't know it, because he was the lead male figure in Cabaret, which was based on one of his short stories in Goodbye to Berlin ("Sally Bowles," based loosely on singer Jean Ross, whom Isherwood met in 1931 Berlin). Michael York plays Christopher, and Liza Minnelli earned an Oscar for her role as Sally. The writing is brilliant, as Virginia Woolf must have known when she made this entry in her diary: "Isherwood and I met on the doorstep. He is slip of a wild boy. That young man, said W. Maugham, 'holds the future of the English novel in his hands.' "

The story "Sally Bowles" (the last name, incidentally, is from Paul Bowles—musical composer, translator of Sartre—"No Exit" is Bowles—and writer's writer, The Sheltering Sky being his most famous; Isherwood admired his work and named Sally after him) was also the basis of the earlier Broadway play I Am a Camera, which was made into a movie starring Julie Harris. The title comes from a famous passage in the book, often quoted, usually misunderstood: "I am a camera with its shutter open, quite passive, recording, not thinking. Recording the man shaving at the window opposite and the woman in the kimono washing her hair. Some day, all this will have to be developed, carefully printed, fixed." At this point, Isherwood was only vaguely aware of the great teachings, East and West, about the real Self as pure choiceless Witness, but you can see it shining through (it is quite similar to Emerson's famous "transparent eyeball": "All mean egotism vanishes. I become a transparent eyeball; I am nothing; I see all"). Critics jumped on Isherwood for this detachment, lack of care, etc. But this misses the nature of that state, as Isherwood himself pointed out: "The idea that I was a person very divorced from what was going on around me is quite false." The true Witness allows whatever arises to arise—passion, calm, involvement, detachment, heartfelt hostility, it doesn't matter. But the notion that it is a deathly divorce from life is silly.

Isherwood, anyway, was certainly not divorced. In fact, one of his best friends at the time, and through most of his life, W. H. Auden—already destined to be one of the two or three greatest poets of the century—had gone to Berlin in the late 1920s, mostly in search of the decadent sex, and Auden convinced Christopher to join him there. Both of them were gay, and the famous boy bars—particularly the Cosy Corner—kept Isherwood and Auden bound to Berlin for several years. Wild sex, especially as a young man—well, there's another strand.

(Isherwood has become something of a hero for present-day gays, mostly because of his unflinching acceptance of his homosexuality, an admiration I share. So did E. M. Forster; his very touching, and very gay, novel Maurice, which Forster understandably felt reluctant to publish during his life, he left to Christopher. We of today tend to forget that, until just recent times in most countries, "being homosexual" was a crime punishable by imprisonment and sometimes death. England was particularly barbaric in its stance, as the wretched cautionary tale of Alan Turing ought to remind us—Turing, who cracked the Enigma secret code machine of the Nazis and rendered Hitler's every move transparent to the Allies, a stunning display of brilliance that arguably did more to win the war than any other single act, and for which he was awarded, upon discovery of his homosexuality, with imprisonment and forced hormone injections to correct his "disease." He committed suicide shortly thereafter.)

Adolf Hitler made his Munich beer-hall putsch in 1923, was jailed, wrote Mein Kampf. By 1929, economic devastation and desperation gave the National Socialists mass support, and, astonishingly, by 1934, with the death of Hindenburg, Hitler united the offices of President and Chancellor to become Führer of all Germany.

Isherwood arrives in Berlin in 1929, and stays until 1933—exactly the hot period for this, probably the most shocking period in Western history, the ascendancy of a lunacy never seen before or since. And he records what he sees. "Here it is rather like living in Hell. Everybody is absolutely at the last gasp, hanging on with their eyelids. We are under martial law. Nobody in England can have even the remotest idea of what it is like. There are wagon-loads of police at every corner to sit on any attempt at a demonstration. You can scarcely get along the street for beggars. . . ."

Germany, the brightest of philosophical lights in the West, heir to Greece, and it had all come to this: a madman disguised as a house painter from Austria. And so now, today, one cannot think of the greats—Kant, Hegel, Spinoza, Marx, Fichte, Freud, Nietzsche, Einstein, Schopenhauer, Leibniz, Schelling—the whole Germanic sphere—without thinking, at some point, of Auschwitz and Treblinka, Sorbibor and Dachau, Bergen-Belsen and Chelmno. My God, they have names, as if they were human.

But the causal linking of Germany's transcendental tradition with the death camps, which is quite common in American postmodern cluck-clucking about meta-narratives, is simply cheap and vulgar, not to mention wrong. What happened in Germany is, among a million other causes, a classic case of the pre/trans fallacy. In fact, the entire German tradition is a study in the pre/trans fallacy, producing now a Hegel, now a Hitler. Precisely because the German tradition strove so nobly and so mightily for Geist and Spirit (which is to its everlasting credit), it was open more intensely to confusing prerational bodily and emotional enthusiasms with transrational insight and awareness. Blood and soil, return to nature, and noble savages flourished under the banner of a Romantic return to spirit, a recapture of the lost Ground, a return of the hidden God, a revelation written in blood and etched in the flesh of those who would stand in the way of this ethnic-blood purity, and the gas chambers waited as the silent womb of the Great Mother, who always rules over such proceedings, to receive all of those who corrupted this purity. It was not the rationality or the transrationality of Germany that undid her, but her reactivated prerational impulses that brought the fortress tumbling down.

But that's another strand: God and the Devil together in Berlin in 1933, and Isherwood was there.

Then there's the whole Huxley connection. Aldous Huxley was probably the last—and this is part of my depression—was probably the last author who could write intensely, deeply, and philosophically about mystical and transcendental topics . . . and be taken seriously by the intelligentsia, the media, the Manhattan Inc. crowd, the liberal insiders, the avant-garde—the last author who could write about transcendental topics and have it considered hip, hot, happening. Liberals hate Spirit, basically, and conservatives think Spirit means their own fundamentalist mythic God—they are both way off the mark, and both of them would today find Huxley largely incomprehensible. Who could write The Perennial Philosophy now and get it enthusiastically reviewed outside of California? Today's "spirituality" is mostly (1) fundamentalist revivals, (2) new age narcissism, (3) mythic regression, (4) web-of-life subtle reductionism, (5) flatland holism. Huxley and Heard and Isherwood and even Mann would have found the lot of them drearily tiresome.

Gerald Heard (author of several brilliant books, including The Five Ages of Man—which was the basis for Jean Huston's very perceptive Life-Force—and himself quite instrumental in the founding and flourishing of the Vedanta Society) introduced Isherwood to Huxley not long after Christopher had settled, more or less permanently, in Los Angeles, earning his living by writing scripts, as Huxley (and Tennessee Williams and William Faulkner and F. Scott Fitzgerald) sometimes did (those were the days!); they remained friends until Huxley's death in 1963. It was in L.A. that the Vedanta Society was formed (in one of whose temples, I believe, Adi Da had his first major breakthrough). It would form one of the three or four major currents by which Eastern wisdom would gain strong entrance to this country.

If Christopher was its literary voice, Huxley provided its sheer brain power. As Isherwood and almost everybody else commented, Aldous

was not much of a novelist; his characters are cardboard. I always liked
his own explanation for this: "I have almost no ideas about myself and
don't like having them—avoid having them—on principle even—and
only improvise them, when somebody like you asks to know them. . . ."
So he wrote novels about ideas instead, although he was aware of the
grave risks involved. "Not only must you write about people who have
ideas to express—0.01 percent of the human race. Hence the real, the
congenital novelists don't write such books. But then I never pretended
to be a congenital novelist."

Instead, he played with ideas in a dazzling way, bright and brilliant
and sometimes breathtaking. And liberating. As Sir Isaiah Berlin put it
in his memoirs, "As men of letters—led by Voltaire, the head of the
profession—rescued many oppressed human beings in the eighteenth
century; as Byron or George Sand, Ibsen, Baudelaire, Nietzsche, Wilde
and Gide and perhaps even Wells or Russell have done since, so members of my generation were assisted to find themselves by novelists,
poets, and critics concerned with the central problems of their day." Sir
Isaiah places Huxley with Ezra Pound and J. B. S. Haldane as among
the major emancipators of his time.

Sybille Bedford, one of Huxley's biographers, gives another take on
this great emancipatory tradition: it involved "a number of extraordinarily and diversely gifted individuals whose influence . . . had been
tremendous. Their common denominator was an intense desire to acquire, to advance, and to disseminate knowledge—a wish to improve
the lot as well as the administration of humankind, an assumption of
responsibility—*l'intelligence oblige*—and a passion, no tamer word will
do, for truth."

This was a time when such things even made sense, let alone mattered.
That is to say, this was before my generation, whose humanities profes-
sors decided that they could not assist anybody in creating anything,
and so devoted themselves, in a fit of resentment, to tearing down instead, leaving only the deconstructionist's Cheshire-cat smile hanging in
midair; and they are shocked, shocked, that anybody could ever have a
passion for truth, since, as they happily misinterpret Foucault, truth is
nothing but thinly concealed power—thus attempting to ensure that
none of their students seek truth either, lest they actually find it and
begin producing real works that shine with depth and glory.

Precisely because Huxley was plugged into the transcendental, his prose had power to liberate. You have to know that there actually is a transcendental something, if you are going to free anybody from anything—if there is no beyond-the-given, there is no freedom from the given, and liberation is futile. Today's postmodern writers, who hug the given, stick to the obvious, cling to the shadows, celebrate the surface, have nowhere else to go, and so emancipation is the last of what they offer . . . or you get.

No wonder that one of Aldous's best friends for several decades was Krishnamurti (the sage on whom I cut my spiritual teeth). Krishnamurti was a supreme liberator, at least on occasion, and in books such as Freedom from the Known, this extraordinary sage pointed to the power of nondual choiceless awareness to liberate one from the binding tortures of space, time, death, and duality. When Huxley's house (and library) burned down, the first books he asked to be replaced were Krishnamurti's Commentaries on Living.

Yehudi Menuhin wrote of Aldous: "He was scientist and artist in one—standing for all we most need in a fragmented world where each of us carries a distorting splinter out of some great shattered universal mirror. He made it his mission to restore these fragments and, at least in his presence, men were whole again. To know where each splinter might belong one must have some conception of the whole, and only a mind such as Aldous's, cleansed of personal vanity, noticing and recording everything, and exploiting nothing, could achieve so broad a purpose."

To the Huxley-like emancipators I would add, of course, Thomas Mann, whom I became obsessed with for several years, reading all I could by and about him. He writes his first novel, Buddenbrooks, at age 25 and gets the Nobel for it. Who could write The Magic Mountain today and even get it published? And is not "Death in Venice" perhaps the most perfect short story ever penned? Mann, too, had contact with the Vedanta Society when he moved to California. Robert Musil, Proust, and Mann are my favorite unrelentingly intelligent authors of this century. "Which remarkably enough, does not get anyone anywhere"— Musil.

Mann first supported the retro-Romantic and reactionary fascist movements in Germany—volkish blood and soil and the "soul" of Germany—and then turned away in shock and disgust to embrace humanistic rational pluralism, become the clearest and loudest anti-Nazi voice coming from a German, and perhaps the greatest humanist novelist of the century. He made a profound study of interior life—Freud, Nietzsche, Schelling, Schopenhauer, mysticism—but precisely because of his previous slide into prerational fascism, he is always at pains to differentiate prerational regression from transrational glory. His is one of the great and precious voices of this century; he belongs so clearly in that pantheon of those who helped to emancipate, to one degree or another, untold numbers of sensitive souls.

So that's another strand: the great tradition of emancipatory writing, of intellectual light in the service of liberation—helping to undo repression, thwart power, and shun shallowness, quaint as all that sounds to this year's ears. Today that noble tradition is reduced to rational scientists, such as the good Carl Sagan, trying to beat back Elvis sightings and UFO abductions, but it is so much nobler than all of that, and speaks to so much that is higher and deeper and truer in us all. That emancipatory tradition died, I fear, with Huxley.

All those strands, rolled into one. So Christopher Isherwood is sort of my "six degrees of Kevin Bacon." You can get from Isherwood to everything that's important in six moves or less.

But lord, it's so sad, because so few want to make those moves. And I am so depressed reading his diaries and being reminded of it daily.

Friday, January 24

Rented Bound, which I had already seen in a theatre; it's superb. Jennifer Tilly, Gina Gershon, Joe Pantoliano—two lesbians who do Joe in, but in fingernail-biting (and finger-removing) tension. The movie is shot in a sensual noir fashion, one of my favorite cinematic atmospheres. They're not really that similar, but it made me think of the opening credits to Seven, which were brilliantly shot. Several critics snootily dismissed Seven beginning to end (well, the entire city did seem to lack overhead lights), so I was glad to see the opening credits get the International Design Award for excellence. The designer, Kyle Cooper, described them as "bleak yet playful bookends for the feel-bad movie of the year."

I have the strangest feeling that the writing and publication of Science and Religion will be the bleak yet playful bookends of this year. Whether it's going to be "feel-bad" remains to be seen.

Saturday, January 25

Date with a woman, who shall go nameless, it didn't quite work out. Turns out that most of her relationships are very short-lived. One of her marriages lasted only a few months. I mean, I've got food in my refrigerator older than that.

Monday, January 27

Sam [Bercholz] rushed The Eye of Spirit out in time for the kw conference. My copies arrived today, a little late; but, as usual, Shambhala has done a beautiful job. In some ways this is one of my favorite books, but I'm not sure how well it will do.

Jack's generous foreword. Jack [Crittenden] and I go back a long way, to the early Lincoln days, when he came to visit me after reading The Spectrum of Consciousness. He wanted to start a journal, ReVision, and I helped get it up and running. We're no longer associated with that journal, but Jack and I have remained fast friends. He's a brilliant theorist, superb writer. He and Patricia now have three teenage sons, hard to believe. He's published Beyond Individualism (Oxford University Press) and is now working, with varying seriousness, on two or three other books, which he's sandwiching in between his teaching chores at Arizona State.

Jack does a great job explaining the meaning of "integral" and the lamentable, fragmented nature of so much of what is called "knowledge" in today's world. I've already received numerous comments on Jack's piece, along the lines of, "Oh, now I see what you're trying to do in all your writing." Thank god somebody can explain it.

[Several subsequent entries refer to Jack's foreword. For reference, a few excerpts:

Wilber's approach is the opposite of eclecticism. He has provided a coherent and consistent vision that seamlessly weaves together truth-claims from such fields as physics and biology; the eco-sciences; chaos theory and the systems sciences; medicine, neuro-physiology, biochemistry; art, poetry, and aesthetics in general; developmental psychology and a spectrum of psychotherapeutic endeavors, from Freud to Jung to Piaget; the Great Chain theorists from Plato and Plotinus in the West to Shankara and Nagarjuna in the East; the modernists from Descartes and Locke to Kant; the Idealists from Schelling to Hegel; the postmodernists from Foucault and Derrida to Taylor and Habermas; the major hermeneutic tradition, Dilthey to Heidegger to Gadamer; the social systems theorists from Comte and Marx to Parsons and Luhmann; the contemplative and mystical schools of the great meditative traditions, East and West, in the world's major religious traditions. All of this is just a sampling. Is it any wonder, then, that those who focus narrowly on one particular field might take offense when that field is not presented as the linchpin of the Kosmos?

In other words, to the critics the stakes are enormous, and it is not choosing sides at this point if I suggest that the critics who have focused on their pet points in Wilber's method are attacking a particular tree in the forest of his presentation. But if we look instead at the forest, and if his approach is generally valid, it honors and incorporates more truth than any other system in history.

How so? What is his actual method? In working with any field, Wilber simply backs up to a level of abstraction at which the various conflicting approaches actually agree with one another. Take, for example, the world's great religious traditions: Do they all agree that Jesus is God? No. So we must jettison that. Do they all agree that there is a God? That depends on the meaning of "God." Do they all agree on God, if by "God" we mean a Spirit that is in many ways *unqualifiable*, from the Buddhists' Emptiness to the Jewish mystery of the Divine? Yes, that works as a generalization—what Wilber calls an "orienting generalization" or "sturdy conclusion."

Wilber likewise approaches all the other fields of human knowledge: art to poetry, empiricism to hermeneutics, psychoanalysis to meditation, evolutionary theory to idealism. In every case he assembles a series of sturdy and reliable, not to say irrefutable, orienting generalizations. He is not worried, nor should his readers be, about whether *other* fields would accept the conclusions of any given field; in short, don't worry, for example, if empiricist conclusions do not match religious conclusions. Instead, simply assemble all the orienting conclusions as if each field had incredibly important truths to tell us. This is exactly Wilber's first step in his integrative method—a type of phenomenology of all human knowledge conducted at the level of orienting generalizations. In other words, assemble all of the truths that each field believes it has to offer humanity. For the moment, simply assume they are indeed true.

Wilber then arranges these truths into chains or networks of interlocking conclusions. At this point Wilber veers sharply from a method of mere eclecticism and into a systematic vision. For the second step in Wilber's method is to take all of the truths or orienting generalizations assembled in the first step and then pose this question: What coherent system would in fact *incorporate the greatest number of these truths*?

The system presented in *Sex, Ecology, Spirituality* (and clearly and simply summarized in the following pages) is, Wilber claims, the system that incorporates the greatest number of orienting generalizations from the greatest number of fields of human inquiry. Thus, if it holds up, Wilber's vision incorporates and honors, it integrates, more truth than any other system in history.

The general idea is straightforward. It is not which theorist is right and which is wrong. His idea is that everyone is basically right, and he wants to figure out how that can be so. "I don't believe," Wilber says, "that any human mind is capable of 100 percent error. So instead of asking which approach is right and which is wrong, we assume each approach is true but partial, and then try to figure out how to fit these partial truths together, how to integrate them— not how to pick one and get rid of the others."

The third step in Wilber's overall approach is the development of a new type of *critical theory*. Once Wilber has the overall scheme that incorporates the greatest number of orienting generalizations, he then uses that scheme to criticize the partiality of narrower approaches, even though he has included the basic truths from those approaches. He criticizes not their truths, but their partial nature.

In his integral vision, therefore, is a clue to both of the extreme reactions to Wilber's work—that is, to the claims that it is some of the most significant work ever published as well as to the chorus of angry indignation and attack. The angry criticisms are coming, almost without exception, from theorists who feel that their own field is the only true field, that their own method is the only valid method. Wilber has not been believably criticized for misunderstanding or misrepresenting any of the fields of knowledge that he includes; he is attacked, instead, for including fields that a particular critic does not believe are important or for goring that critic's own ox (no offense to vegetarians). Freudians have never said that Wilber fails to understand Freud; they say that he shouldn't include mysticism. Structuralists and post-structuralists have never said that Wilber fails to understand their fields; they say that he shouldn't include all those nasty other fields. And so forth. The attack always has the same form: How dare you say my field isn't the only true field!

Regardless of what is decided, the stakes, as I said, are enormous. I asked Wilber how he himself thought of his work. "I'd like to think of it as one of the first believable world philosophies, a genuine embrace of East and West, North and South." Which is interesting, inasmuch Huston Smith (author of *The World's Religions* and subject of Bill Moyers's highly acclaimed television series *The Wisdom of Faith*) recently stated, "No one—not even Jung—has done as much as Wilber to open Western psychology to the durable insights of the world's wisdom traditions. Slowly but surely, book by book, Ken Wilber is laying the foundations for a genuine East/West integration."

At the same time, Ken adds, "People shouldn't take it too seriously. It's just orienting generalizations. It leaves all the details to be filled in any way you like." In short, Wilber is not offering a conceptual straightjacket. Indeed, it is just the opposite: "I hope I'm showing that there is more room in the Kosmos than you might have suspected."

There isn't much room, however, for those who want to preserve their fiefdoms by narrowing the Kosmos to one particular field—to wit, their own—while ignoring the truths from other fields. "You can't honor various methods and fields," Wilber adds, "without showing how they fit together. That is how to make a genuine world philosophy." Wilber is showing exactly that "fit." Otherwise, as he says, we have heaps, not wholes, and we really aren't honoring anything.

Tuesday, January 28

Dental appointment. All the dentists in Boulder are "holistic." They can't fill a cavity but they're good for your soul. Your teeth rot, but apparently your spirit prospers.

Wednesday, January 29

It dawns on me that, for Science and Religion, I am going to have to get an agent, which I haven't had in years. For the past decade I've settled into a comfortable working relationship with Shambhala Publications, run by my long-time friend Sam Bercholz. But Sam understands that I want to go with a more mainstream publisher this time, and so, with his blessings, I am going to head out into the big bad world of commercial publishing.

So where do you find agents, anyway? Agent World? Agents Are Us? We Be Agents?

Thursday, January 30

Tomorrow is my birthday. But it's "Ken Wilber's" birthday, not the birthday of my Original Face, the great Unborn, the vast expanse of Emptiness untouched by date or duration, tense or time. This infinite ocean of Ease, this vast expanse of Freedom, this lucid sea of Stillness, is what I am in the deepest part of me, the infinite intersection where I am not, and Spirit only is.

There is no birthday for the great Unborn, for that which never comes to be, but is the Suchness of all that is, radiant to infinity. There is no celebration for the timeless moment, which is prior to history and its lies, time and its ugly terrors, duration and its drudgery. There are no gifts for the great Uncreate, the Source of all that is, the boundless Sea of Serenity that lines the entire Kosmos. There is no song for Always Already, the infinite Freedom gloriously beyond both birth and death altogether.

For every sentient being can truly say: in essence I am timeless, in essence I am All—the lines in my face are the cracks in the cosmic egg, supernovas swirl in my heart, galaxies pulse through my veins, stars light up the neurons of my night. . . . And who will sing birthday songs to that? Who will celebrate the vast expanse that sings its songs unheralded in the stillness of the night?

FEBRUARY

All the Buddhas and all sentient beings are nothing but One Spirit, beside which nothing exists. This Spirit, which is without beginning, is unborn and indestructible. It is not green or yellow, and has neither form nor appearance. It does not belong to the categories of things which exist or do not exist, nor can it be thought of in terms of new or old. It is neither long nor short, big nor small, for it transcends all limits, measures, names, traces, and comparisons. Only awake to the One Spirit.

—ZEN MASTER HUANG PO

Saturday, February 1

Worked all morning, went shopping, got groceries. There are two pigeons living under my roof, nestled in a large air vent that comes from my clothes dryer. I took the screen off the vent so they could get in during the winter; they like the warm air that comes off the dryer. So today I notice there are now three of them—they just had a bambino. People should mate for life, like pigeons, penguins, and Catholics. Except, of course, pigeons never get their marriages miraculously annulled.

Sunday, February 2

Got a copy of Andrew Harvey's The Essential Gay Mystics, a book for which I was glad to write a short blurb ["Andrew Harvey has pulled together some of the most passionate and touching works in all of mystical literature, and as it happens, the authors are all gay. But the words speak for themselves: that is, the Divine directly speaks through the words in this volume, words that flowed through gay hearts and gay minds and gay love, but words which speak profoundly, eloquently, gorgeously, to the same Divine in all of us. A mystic is not one who sees God as an object, but one who is immersed in God as an atmosphere, and the works collected here are a radiant testament to that all-encompassing condition. Harvey has given us a cornucopia of mystical wisdom, tender as tears and gentle as fog, but also passionately ablaze with the relentless fire of the very Divine."]

Before he started work on this book (whose author notice states, with characteristic charm, "Andrew attended Oxford, and at age twenty-one received England's highest academic honor, becoming the youngest Fellow of All Soul's College in its history. A prolific writer, Harvey is the author of over ten books, including *Journey to Ladakh*. He collaborated with Sogyal Rinpoche on the best-selling *Tibetan Book of Living and Dying*. Based now in Paris, Harvey is the subject of a 1993 BBC documentary, 'The Making of a Mystic' "), Andrew and his soon-to-be husband, Eryk, stopped by my house, along with Alec Tsoucatos, to say hi. I made them pasta and we ate it out on the balcony, overlooking the Denver plains.

As a Romantic, Andrew is bound to alternate between idealizing and loathing the lost lover, so he has gone through his love-Mother-Meera, hate-Mother-Meera phase, but is now, it seems, quite happily married to Eryk, from whom, he says, he has learned more about true love than from anybody else. I hope this works for him; he seems genuinely happy.

Tuesday, February 4

I'm worried about Huston's health [Huston Smith]. I sometimes feel that he will live another decade or two, then I worry he won't live out the year. Ever since Treya's death, I have tried to tell people how I feel about them before they are gone, before it's too late. Treya and I had the chance to do that, but I saw what it did to those who did not.

The amazing thing about Huston is that he was working on the perennial philosophy long before most people had even heard of it. Years before it became fashionable—multicultural wisdom traditions, the world's religious heritage, the celebration of spiritual diversity and spiritual unity—Huston was doing the work.

His body is almost transparent now, like a thin, beautiful, translucent tissue. The last time I saw him he was very frail and fragile, but radiant. I have the deep suspicion that if you turn off the lights, he might faintly glow.

Dearest Huston,

It was wonderful seeing you. But when you said, when asked about your health, "The citadel is crumbling," it had a profound effect on me, which has lingered to this day. I wanted to write and tell you about it.

The more that Emptiness saturates my being, the more my life takes on a strange "double-entry" type of awareness. On the one hand, everything that happens—every single thing, from the very best to the very worst—is the equal radiance of the Divine. I simply cannot tell the difference between them. It is a mystery, this: that pain and happiness are equal in this awareness, that the most wretched soul and the most divine are equal in this radiance, that the setting sun and the rising sun bring equal joy, that nothing moves at all, in this splendor of the All-pervading. And when, in touch with that all-pervasiveness, I hear that the citadel of dearest Huston is crumbling, it is simply as it is, just so, and all is still right, and all is still well, and all is still good, and all still radiates the unending glory that we all are.

The other side of this Emptiness—the other part of the "double-entry"—is that, in addition to (or alongside of) the constant radiance of this moment, all the little moments are all the more themselves, somehow. Sadness is even sadder; happiness is happier; pleasure is more intense; pain hurts even more. I laugh louder and cry harder. Precisely because it is all the purest Emptiness, each relative phenomenon is allowed to be itself even more intensely, because it no longer contends with the Divine, but simply expresses It.

And on _that_ side of the double-entry—where pain is more painful (because it is Empty), and where sadness is much sadder (because it is Empty)—when I hear that the citadel of dearest Huston is crumbling, I am overcome with a sadness that I do not know how to convey.

You have meant so much to so many, you have come with the voices of angels to remind us who we are, you have come with the light of God to shine upon our faces and force us to remember, you have come as a beacon radiating in the darkest night of our confused and wretched souls, you have come as our own deepest being to never let us forget. And you have done this consistently, and with integrity, and with brilliance, and with humility and courage and care, and you have left, and are still leaving, a path in which we all will follow, and we will do so with more gratitude and respect and love than my words will ever be able to convey.

So, you see, I have become a Divine schizophrenic. I am always, simultaneously, of two minds. Steeped in Emptiness, it is all exactly as it should be, a stunning gesture of the Great Perfection. And—at precisely the same time, in precisely the same perception—I am reduced to tears at the thought of you leaving us, and it is simply intolerable, it is radically unacceptable, I will rage against the dying of that light until I can rage no longer, and my voice is ragged with futile screams against the insult of samsara. And yet, just that is nirvana; not theoretically, but just so, like this, right now: Emptiness. Both perceptions are simultaneous; I know I don't have to tell you about this; it is so in your case, I know.

And so, on the side of the double-entry that rages against the crumbling of the citadel, I just wanted to tell you, as deeply as I could, what you have meant to all of us. And to me, specifically, my entire career has marched, step by step, with you never out of the picture. From that glorious letter you wrote to a young 25-year-old, praising his first book, to your agreement to sign on with ReVision (I told Jack Crittenden that I wouldn't feel comfortable doing the journal unless Huston came aboard), to giving the eulogy at Treya's ceremony, which reduced me to tears and made me pretty much incoherent. On this side of the double-entry, I know I will not do well when the citadel crumbles.

Now you must forgive me for prematurely burying you, and speaking as if your demise were imminent; God willing, it will be decades before we will all gather together to actually speak out loud these types of words as your ashes return to the cosmic dance and your soul returns to where it never left. But, as I warned you, "the citadel is crumbling" sent such a sadness rushing through me, I wanted to err on the side of getting these words to you now, even if decades too soon. Perhaps because of Treya, I am more sensitive than most to the "bubble bursting" at just the damnedest times, expected or not.

So do forgive me for delivering my eulogy to you; at the same time, I always liked the derivation of "eulogy"—*eu*: true, *logy*: story—the true story. I send back to you the biggest portion that I can manage of that love that you have freely given to us all and called us all to incarnate. Your own love, God's love—you have taught us that they are the same—I offer back to you, my mentor, my guide, my friend, the man I am least likely ever to forget.

Yours always,

Ken

Sunday, February 9

Right before I began work on <u>Sex, Ecology, Spirituality</u> [SES], several teachers at The Naropa Institute in Boulder asked me if I would meet with them and their students. I generally decline offers to lecture or teach, which is too bad, because I enjoy it, but in this case we hit upon a compromise. I would simply invite the students to come to my house—in three or four shifts, thirty to fifty students each shift—and we would discuss any topics they wanted for as long as they wanted. During my three-year hermitage [working on SES] these seminars were canceled, but this year I agreed to start them up again. As long as the students come to my house, I can pretend to keep my "no public teaching" record clean—you know, I'm not lecturing, I'm just having a few students over to chat.

So today we had another seminar. I've agreed to do these seminars perhaps twice a month, more or less indefinitely. Somebody suggested we start videotaping these, and perhaps we will.

Monday, February 10

By last week, the blurbs for <u>Science and Religion</u> had all arrived, from some very kind people who took pity on me. I assembled these into a package, with a blustery braggadocio letter, and sent it off to all the agents recommended to me by various friends and publishers. I have now heard back from all of them. The whole idea is funny. I am in effect doing an auction among a half-dozen agents, the winner of which will then auction my book among a half-dozen publishers, the winner of which will then publish the book.

It's also slightly awkward, because several of these agents are involved with flamboyant new-age writers. I appreciate the work of some of these writers, but in too many cases, it seems to me, the spirit offered is prerational and narcissistic, not transrational and divine. These writers, finding God and Goddess absent in the modern world, have decided to take their place—and their agents are anxious to get 15% of God. Already I have the feeling that this is much more than I bargained for.

Tuesday, February 11

A SPIRITUALITY THAT TRANSFORMS

Hal Blacker, the editor of *What Is Enlightenment?*, has described the topic of this issue of the magazine in the following way:

> We intend to explore a sensitive question, but one which needs to be addressed—the superficiality which pervades so much of the current spiritual exploration and discourse in the West, particularly in the United States. All too often, in the translation of the mystical traditions from the East (and elsewhere) into the American idiom, their profound depth is flattened out, their radical demand is diluted, and their potential for revolutionary transformation is squelched. How this occurs often seems to be subtle, since the *words* of the teachings are often the same. Yet through an apparent sleight of hand involving, perhaps, their context and therefore ultimately their meaning, the message of the greatest teachings often seems to become transmuted from the roar of the fire of liberation into something more closely resembling the soothing burble of a California hot tub. While there are exceptions, the radical implications of the greatest teachings are thereby often lost. We wish to investigate this dilution of spirituality in the West, and inquire into its causes and consequences.

I would like to take Hal's statement and unpack its basic points, commenting on them as best I can, because taken together, those points highlight the very heart and soul of a crisis in American spirituality.

TRANSLATION VERSUS TRANSFORMATION

In a series of books (e.g., *A Sociable God, Up from Eden, The Eye of Spirit*), I have tried to show that religion itself has always performed two very important, but very different, functions. One, it acts as a way of creating *meaning* for the separate self: it offers myths and stories and tales and narratives and rituals and revivals that, taken together, help the separate self make sense of, and endure, the slings and arrows of outrageous fortune. This function of religion does not usually or necessarily change the level of consciousness in a person; it does not deliver radical transformation. Nor does it deliver a shattering liberation from the separate self altogether. Rather, it consoles the self, fortifies the self, defends the self, promotes the self. As long as the separate self believes the myths, performs the rituals, mouths the prayers, or embraces the dogma, then the self, it is fervently believed, will be "saved"—either now in the glory of being God-saved or Goddess-favored, or in an afterlife that ensures eternal wonderment.

But two, religion has also served—in a usually very, very small minority—the function of radical transformation and liberation. This function of religion does not fortify the separate self, but utterly shatters it—not consolation but devastation, not entrenchment but emptiness, not complacency but explosion, not comfort but revolution—in short, not a conventional bolstering of consciousness but a radical transmutation and transformation at the deepest seat of consciousness itself.

There are several different ways that we can state these two important functions of religion. The first function—that of creating meaning for the self—is a type of *horizontal* movement; the second function—that of transcending the self—is a type of *vertical* movement (higher or deeper, depending on your metaphor). The first I have named *translation;* the second, *transformation.*

With translation, the self is simply given a new way to think or feel about reality. The self is given a new belief—perhaps holistic instead of atomistic, perhaps forgiveness instead of blame, perhaps relational instead of analytic. The self then learns to translate its world and its being in the terms of this new belief or new language or new-paradigm, and this new and enchanting translation acts, at least temporarily, to alleviate or diminish the terror inherent in the heart of the separate self.

But with transformation, the very process of translation itself is challenged, witnessed, undermined, and eventually dismantled. With typical *translation,* the self (or subject) is given a new way to think about the world (or objects); but with radical *transformation,* the self itself is inquired into, looked into, grabbed by its throat, and literally throttled to death.

Put it one last way: with horizontal translation—which is by far the most prevalent, widespread, and widely shared function of religion—the self is, at least temporarily, made happy in its grasping, made content in its enslavement, made complacent in the face of the screaming terror that is in fact its innermost condition. With translation, the self goes sleepy into the world, stumbles numbed and near-sighted into the nightmare of samsara, is given a map laced with morphine with which to face the world. And this, indeed, is the common condition of a religious humanity, precisely the condition that the radical or transformative spiritual realizers have come to challenge and to finally undo.

For authentic transformation is not a matter of belief but of the death of the believer; not a matter of translating the world but of transforming the world; not a matter of finding solace but of finding infinity on the other side of death. The self is not made content; the self is made toast.

Now, although I have obviously been favoring transformation and belittling translation, the fact is that, on the whole, both of these functions are incredibly important and altogether indispensable. Individuals are not, for the most part, born enlightened. They are born in a world of sin and suffering, hope and fear, desire and despair. They are born as a self ready and eager to contract; a self rife with hunger, thirst, tears, and terror. And they begin, quite early on, to learn various ways to translate their world, to make sense of it, to give meaning to it, and to defend themselves against the terror and the torture never lurking far beneath the happy surface of the separate self.

And as much as we, as you and I, might wish to transcend mere translation and find an authentic transformation, nonetheless translation itself is an absolutely necessary and crucial function for the greater part of our lives. Those who cannot translate adequately, with a fair amount of integrity and accuracy, fall quickly into severe neurosis or even psychosis: the world *ceases to make sense*—the boundaries between the self and the world are not transcended but instead begin to crumble. This is not breakthrough but breakdown; not transcendence but disaster.

But at some point in our maturation process, translation itself, no matter how adequate or confident, simply ceases to console. No new beliefs, no new-paradigm, no new myths, no new ideas, will staunch the encroaching anguish. Not a new belief for the self, but the transcendence of the self altogether, is the only path that avails.

Still, the number of individuals who are ready for such a path is, always has been, and likely always will be, a very small minority. For most people, any sort of religious belief will fall instead into the category of consolation: it will be a new horizontal translation that fashions some sort of meaning in the midst of the monstrous world. And religion has always served, for the most part, this first function, and served it well.

I therefore also use the word *legitimacy* to describe this first function (the horizontal translation and creation of meaning for the separate self). And much of religion's important service is to *provide legitimacy* to the self—legitimacy to its beliefs, its paradigms, its worldviews, and its way in the world. This function of religion to provide a legitimacy for the self and its beliefs—no matter how temporary, relative, nontransformative, or illusory—has nonetheless been the single greatest and most important function of the world's religious traditions. The capacity of a religion to provide horizontal meaning, legitimacy, and sanction for the self and its beliefs—*that function of religion has historically been the single greatest "social glue" that any culture has.*

And one does not tamper easily, or lightly, with the basic glue that holds societies together. Because more often than not, when that glue dissolves—when that translation dissolves—the result, as we were saying, is not breakthrough but breakdown, not liberation but social chaos. (We will return to this crucial point in a moment.)

Where translative religion offers *legitimacy,* transformative religion offers *authenticity.* For those few individuals who are ready—that is, sick with the suffering of the separate self, and no longer able to embrace the legitimate worldview—then a transformative opening to true authenticity, true enlightenment, true liberation, calls more and more insistently. And, depending upon your capacity for suffering, you will sooner or later answer the call of authenticity, of transformation, of liberation on the lost horizon of infinity.

Transformative spirituality does not seek to bolster or legitimate any present worldview at all, but rather to provide true authenticity by shattering what the world takes as legitimate. Legitimate consciousness is sanctioned by the consensus, adopted by the herd mentality, embraced by the culture and the counterculture both, promoted by the separate self as *the* way to make sense of this world. But authentic consciousness quickly shakes all of that off its back, and settles instead into a glance that sees only a radiant infinity in the heart of all souls, and breathes into its lungs only the atmosphere of an eternity too simple to believe.

Transformative spirituality, authentic spirituality, is therefore revolutionary. It does not legitimate the world, it breaks the world; it does not console the world, it shatters it. And it does not render the self content, it renders it undone.

And those facts lead to several conclusions.

WHO ACTUALLY WANTS TO TRANSFORM?

It is a fairly common belief that the East is simply awash in transformative and authentic spirituality, but that the West—both historically and in today's "new-age"—has nothing much more than various types of horizontal, translative, merely legitimate and therefore tepid spirituality. And while there is some truth to that, the actual situation is much gloomier, for both the East and the West alike.

First, although it is generally true that the East has produced a greater number of authentic realizers, nonetheless, the actual percentage of the Eastern population that is engaged in authentic transformative spirituality is, and always has been, pitifully small. I once asked Katagiri Roshi, with whom I had my first breakthrough (hopefully, not a breakdown), how many truly great Ch'an and Zen masters there have historically been. Without hesitating, he said, "Maybe one thousand altogether." I asked another Zen master how many truly enlightened—deeply enlightened—Japanese Zen masters there were alive today, and he said, "Not more than a dozen."

Let us simply assume, for the sake of argument, that those are vaguely accurate answers. Run the numbers. Even if we say there were only one billion Chinese over the course of history (an extremely low estimate), that still means that only one thousand out of one billion had graduated into an authentic, transformative spirituality. For those of you without a calculator, that's 0.0000001 of the total population. (Even if we say a million instead of a thousand, that is still only 0.001 of the population—a pitiful drop in the bucket.)

And that means, unmistakably, that the rest of the population were (and are) involved in, at best, various types of horizontal, translative, merely legitimate religion: they were involved in magical practices, mythical beliefs, egoic petitionary prayer, magical rituals, and so on—in other words, translative ways to give meaning to the separate self, a translative function that was, as we were saying, the major social glue of the Chinese (and all other) cultures to date.

Thus, without in any way belittling the truly stunning contributions of the glorious Eastern traditions, the point is fairly straightforward: radical transformative spirituality is extremely rare, anywhere in history, and anywhere in the world. (The numbers for the West are even more depressing. I rest my case.)

So, although we can very rightly lament the very small number of individuals in the West who are today involved in a truly authentic and radically transformative spiritual realization, let us not make the false argument of claiming that it has otherwise been *dramatically* different in earlier times or in different cultures. It has on occasion been a *little* better than we see here, now, in the West, but the fact remains: authentic spirituality is an incredibly rare bird, anywhere, at any time, at any place. So let us start from the unarguable fact that vertical, transformative authentic spirituality is one of the most precious jewels in the entire human tradition—precisely because, like all precious jewels, it is incredibly rare.

Second, even though you and I might deeply believe that the most important function we can perform is to offer authentic transformative spirituality, the fact is, much of what we have to do, in our capacity to bring decent spirituality into the world, is actually to offer more *benign and helpful modes of translation*. In other words, even if we ourselves are practicing, or offering, authentic transformative spirituality, nonetheless much of what we must *first* do is provide most people with a more adequate way to translate their condition. *We must start with*

*helpful translations, before we can effectively offer authentic trans-
formations.*

The reason is that if translation is too quickly, or too abruptly, or too
ineptly taken away from an individual (or a culture), the result, once
again, is not breakthrough but breakdown, not release but collapse. Let
me give two quick examples here.

When Chögyam Trungpa Rinpoche, a great (though controversial)
Tibetan master, first came to this country, he was renowned for always
saying, when asked the meaning of Vajrayana, "There is only Ati." In
other words, there is only the enlightened mind wherever you look. The
ego, samsara, maya, and illusion—all of them do not have to be gotten
rid of, because none of them actually exist: There is only Ati, there is
only Spirit, there is only God, there is only nondual Consciousness anywhere in existence.

Virtually nobody got it—nobody was ready for this radical and authentic realization of always-already truth—and so Trungpa eventually
introduced a whole series of "lesser" practices leading up to this radical
and ultimate "no practice." He introduced the Nine Yanas as the foundation of practice—in other words, he introduced nine stages or levels
of practice, culminating in the ultimate "no practice" of always-already
Ati.

Many of these practices were simply translative, and some were what
we might call "lesser transformative" practices: miniature transformations that made the bodymind more susceptible to radical, already-
accomplished enlightenment. These translative and lesser practices issued forth in the "perfect practice" of no-practice—or the radical,
instantaneous, authentic realization that, from the very beginning, there
is only Ati. So even though ultimate transformation was the prior goal
and ever-present ground, Trungpa had to introduce translative and
lesser practices in order to prepare people for the obviousness of what
is.

Exactly the same thing happened with Adi Da, another influential
(and equally controversial) adept (although this time, American-born).
He originally taught nothing but "the path of understanding": not a
way to attain enlightenment, but an inquiry into why you want to attain
enlightenment in the first place. The very desire to seek spiritual enlightenment is in fact nothing but the grasping tendency of the ego itself, and

thus the very search for enlightenment prevents it. The "perfect practice" is therefore not to search for enlightenment but to inquire into the
motive for seeking itself. You obviously seek in order to avoid the present, and yet the present alone holds the answer: to seek forever is to
miss the point forever. You always already *are* enlightened Spirit, and
therefore to *seek* Spirit is simply to deny Spirit. You can no more attain
Spirit than you can attain your feet or acquire your lungs.

Nobody got it. And so Adi Da, exactly like Trungpa, introduced a
whole series of translative and lesser transformative practices—seven
stages of practice, in fact—leading up to the point that you could dispense with seeking altogether, there to stand open to the always-already
truth of your own eternal and timeless condition, which was completely
and totally present from the start, but which was brutally ignored in the
frenzied desire to seek.

Now, whatever you might think of those two adepts, the fact remains:
they performed perhaps the first two great *experiments* in this country
on how to introduce the notion that "There is only Spirit"—and thus
seeking Spirit is exactly what prevents realization. And they both found
that, however much we might be alive to Spirit, alive to the radical *transformative* truth of this moment, nonetheless *translative* and lesser transformative practices are almost always a prerequisite for that final and
ultimate transformation.

My second point, then, is that in addition to offering authentic and
radical transformation, we must still be sensitive to, and caring of, the
numerous beneficial modes of lesser and translative practices. This more
generous stance therefore calls for an "integral approach" to overall
transformation, an approach that honors and incorporates many lesser
transformative and translative practices—covering the physical, emotional, mental, cultural, and communal aspects of the human being—in
preparation for, and as an expression of, the ultimate transformation
into the always-already present state.

And so, even as we rightly criticize merely translative religion (and all
the lesser forms of transformation), let us also realize that an integral
approach to spirituality combines the best of horizontal and vertical,
translative and transformative, legitimate and authentic—and thus let
us focus our efforts on a balanced and sane overview of the human
situation.

WISDOM AND COMPASSION

But isn't this view of mine terribly elitist? Good heavens, I hope so. When you go to a basketball game, do you want to see me or Michael Jordan play basketball? When you listen to pop music, who are you willing to pay money in order to hear? Me or Bruce Springsteen? When you read great literature, who would you rather spend an evening reading, me or Tolstoy? When you pay sixty-four million dollars for a painting, will that be a painting by me or by Van Gogh?

All excellence is elitist. And that includes spiritual excellence as well. But spiritual excellence is an elitism to which all are invited. We go first to the great masters—to Padmasambhava, to Saint Teresa of Ávila, to Gautama Buddha, to Lady Tsogyal, to Emerson, Eckhart, Maimonides, Shankara, Sri Ramana Maharshi, Bodhidharma, Garab Dorje. But their message is *always* the same: let this consciousness be in you which is in me. You start elitist, always; you end up egalitarian, always.

But in between, there is the angry wisdom that shouts from the heart: we must, all of us, keep our eye on the radical and ultimate transformative goal. And so any sort of integral or authentic spirituality will also, always, involve a critical, intense, and occasionally polemical shout from the transformative camp to the merely translative camp.

If we use the percentages of Chinese Ch'an as a simple blanket example, this means that if 0.0000001 of the population is actually involved in genuine or authentic spirituality, then 0.99999999 of the population is involved in nontransformative, nonauthentic, merely translative or horizontal belief systems. And that means, yes, that the vast, vast majority of "spiritual seekers" in this country (as elsewhere) are involved in much less than authentic occasions. It has always been so; it is still so now. This country is no exception.

But in today's America, this is much more disturbing, because this vast majority of horizontal spiritual adherents often claim to be representing the leading edge of spiritual transformation, the "new-paradigm" that will change the world, the "great transformation" of which they are the vanguard. But more often than not, they are not deeply transformative at all; they are merely but aggressively translative—they do not offer effective means to utterly dismantle the self, but merely ways for the self to think differently. Not ways to transform, but merely

new ways to translate. In fact, what most of them offer is not a practice
or a series of practices; not *sadhana* or *satsang* or *shikan-taza* or yoga.
What most of them offer is simply the suggestion: read my book on the
new-paradigm. This is deeply disturbed, and deeply disturbing.

Thus, the authentic spiritual camps have the heart and soul of the
great transformative traditions, and yet they will always do two things
at once: appreciate and engage the lesser and translative practices (upon
which their own successes usually depend), but also issue a thundering
shout from the heart that translation alone is not enough.

And therefore, all of those for whom authentic transformation has
deeply unseated their souls must, I believe, wrestle with the profound
moral obligation to shout from the heart—perhaps quietly and gently,
with tears of reluctance; perhaps with fierce fire and angry wisdom; perhaps with slow and careful analysis; perhaps by unshakable public example—but *authenticity* always and absolutely carries a *demand* and
duty: you must speak out, to the best of your ability, and shake the
spiritual tree, and shine your headlights into the eyes of the complacent.
You must let that radical realization rumble through your veins and
rattle those around you.

Alas, if you fail to do so, you are betraying your own authenticity.
You are hiding your true estate. You don't want to upset others because
you don't want to upset your self. You are acting in bad faith, the taste
of a bad infinity.

Because, you see, the alarming fact is that any realization of depth
carries a terrible burden: Those who are allowed to see are simultaneously saddled with the obligation to *communicate* that vision in no uncertain terms: that is the bargain. You were allowed to see the truth
under the agreement that you would communicate it to others (that is
the ultimate meaning of the bodhisattva vow). And therefore, if you
have seen, you simply must speak out. Speak out with compassion, or
speak out with angry wisdom, or speak out with skillful means, but
speak out you must.

And this is truly a terrible burden, a horrible burden, because in any
case there is no room for timidity. The fact that you might be wrong is
simply no excuse: You might be right in your communication, and you
might be wrong, but that doesn't matter. What does matter, as Kierkegaard so rudely reminded us, is that only by investing and speaking your

vision with *passion,* can the truth, one way or another, finally penetrate the reluctance of the world. If you are right, or if you are wrong, it is only your passion that will force either to be discovered. It is your duty to promote that discovery—either way—and therefore it is your duty to speak your truth with whatever passion and courage you can find in your heart. You must shout, in whatever way you can.

The vulgar world is already shouting, and with such a raucous rancor that truer voices can scarcely be heard at all. The materialistic world is already full of advertisements and allure, screams of enticement and cries of commerce, wails of welcome and whoops of come hither. I don't mean to be harsh here, and we must honor all lesser engagements. Nonetheless, you must have noticed that the word "soul" is now the hottest item in the title of book sales—but all "soul" really means, in most of these books, is simply the ego in drag. "Soul" has come to denote, in this feeding frenzy of translative grasping, not that which is timeless in you but that which most loudly thrashes around in time, and thus "care of the soul" incomprehensibly means nothing much more than focusing intensely on your ardently separate self. Likewise, "spiritual" is on everybody's lips, but usually all it really means is any intense egoic feeling, just as "heart" has come to mean any sincere sentiment of the self-contraction.

All of this, truly, is just the same ole translative game, dressed up and gone to town. And even that would be more than acceptable were it not for the alarming fact that all of that translative jockeying is aggressively called "transformation," when all it is, of course, is a new series of frisky translations. In other words, there seems to be, alas, a deep hypocrisy hidden in the game of taking any new translation and calling it the great transformation. And the world at large—East or West, North or South—is, and always has been, for the most part, perfectly deaf to this calamity.

And so: given the measure of your own authentic realization, you were actually thinking about *gently whispering* into the ear of that near-deaf world? No, my friend, you must shout. Shout from the heart of what you have seen, shout however you can.

But not indiscriminately. Let us proceed carefully with this transformative shout. Let small pockets of radically transformative spirituality, authentic spirituality, focus their efforts, and transform their students.

And let these pockets slowly, carefully, responsibly, humbly, begin to spread their influence, embracing an *absolute tolerance* for all views, but attempting nonetheless to advocate a true and authentic and integral spirituality—by example, by radiance, by obvious release, by unmistakable liberation. Let those pockets of transformation gently persuade the world and its reluctant selves, and challenge their legitimacy, and challenge their limiting translations, and offer an awakening in the face of the numbness that haunts the world at large.

Let it start right here, right now, with us—with you and with me—and with our commitment to breathe into infinity until infinity alone is the only statement that the world will recognize. Let a radical realization shine from our faces, and roar from our hearts, and thunder from our brains—this simple fact, this obvious fact: that you, in the very immediateness of your present awareness, are in fact the entire world, in all its frost and fever, in all its glories and its grace, in all its triumphs and its tears. You do not see the sun, you are the sun; you do not hear the rain, you are the rain; you do not feel the earth, you are the earth. And in that simple, clear, unmistakable regard, translation has ceased in all domains, and you have transformed into the very Heart of the Kosmos itself—and there, right there, very simply, very quietly, it is all undone.

Wonder and remorse will then be alien to you, and self and others will be alien to you, and outside and inside will have no meaning at all. And in that obvious shock of recognition—where my Master is my Self, and that Self is the Kosmos at large, and the Kosmos is my Soul—you will walk very gently into the fog of this world, and transform it entirely by doing nothing at all.

And then, and then, and only then—you will finally, clearly, carefully and with compassion, write on the tombstone of a self that never even existed: There is only Ati.

Wednesday, February 12

I have finally settled on Kim Witherspoon as an agent (protégée of my old acquaintance John Brockman). We have chosen the top seven "mainstream" publishers we are hoping for: Random House, Simon and Schuster, Doubleday, Bantam, Broadway, Riverhead/Putnam, Harper SanFran. Kim sent the book out to all of them today. So we wait.

Friday, February 14

Well, pretty good news. All seven publishers got back to Kim within forty-eight hours. She says the book is "red hot," but in the publishing world of hype and holler, you have to wonder what that actually means. "Here's what's happening. Ann Godoff, the head editor at Random House—she's our first choice—wants to make a preemptive bid."

"How much?"

"I don't know; I'm guessing around $500,000."

"Good lord. Well, the problem is, I promised the other publishers they could get in on the bidding. I feel kind of odd leaving them out."

"They want in, especially since all fourteen of your books are still in print. It looks like we're headed into an auction, and it could get pretty wild. It would be a good idea for you to come to New York."

"Um, okay."

"Soon."

"Um, okay."

"Like next week."

"Um, okay."

Friday, February 21—Boulder—New York

Early morning, on a plane to New York, rushing to the mainstream. I'm deeply ambivalent: Of course I want the book to do well; I hope it's a mega-best-seller—I just don't want to be a part of it. I'm not even sure if I packed all the right clothes. I need something that won't clash with reluctance.

I will split my stay between Tony Schwartz's house and a downtown hotel. I'm looking forward to seeing Tony and his family—wife Deborah and two adorable daughters, Emily and Kate, just in their teens. But for the auction, I need to be in the thick of it, and a hotel in midtown Manhattan will be best. "Fasten your seatbelts, it's going to be a bumpy night."

Sunday, February 23—New York

Tony and Deborah have the most beautiful house. It's in Riverdale, an anomalously posh section of the Bronx just north of Manhattan. I arrive

on Friday, have a few days to relax before the auction, which begins tomorrow. The first night they forgot to show me where the thermostat was, and, this being winter in New York, I was properly freezing to death, and spent most of the night trying to get their two dogs to jump into bed with me for some warmth, Eskimo-style. "Come on, you can do it, you can do it, jump right up, right here, that's a good dog." But the little rats had been totally trained to never get on beds, and the most I could do is get one of them to come halfway on board; she insisted on keeping her hind legs on the floor, thus never technically committing a foul. They must train these dogs with cattle prods.

So, tomorrow it starts.

Tuesday, February 25—New York

Tony pulled some strings and got me into the Four Seasons Hotel—the only hotel in the Western hemisphere, I note, designed by I. M. Pei. It's exquisite.

Meetings all day long yesterday and today. All of the publishers kindly consented to meet me at the restaurant here at the Four Seasons. They each were scheduled for two-hour presentations, starting at ten and going till six. I sat at the same table each day, all day, drinking tomato juice, trying to impress them as they tried to impress me. I hate tomato juice.

Kim and I knew early on that there was a buzz starting about the book, and it continued. Alice Mayhew, grand dame of Simon and Schuster, editor of All the President's Men, etc., said she definitely wanted it. Phyllis Grann, head of Putnam, publisher of Tom Clancy, etc., said, "This is the first nonfiction book I really want to publish." I am slightly flabbergasted by these reactions. What's going on? There are larger currents afloat here, I think, and my book is getting caught up in them. By the time Ann Godoff and I meet—she was the last meeting, late today—the first thing she said was, "In my professional career I've never seen a buzz like this on a nonfiction book."

"Good grief." And we talk for an hour or two. What I like about Ann, even more than the nice comment, is that when I say I will do nothing to promote the book, she says, "No problem," whereas the other publishers were visibly appalled at my lack of interest in the marketing end of the deal.

"Listen, Ann, we really do have to see what the other publishers are going to do. But please try to keep Random House in the game."

"Don't worry."

Wednesday, February 26—New York

The auction began this morning, and almost immediately we ran into something of a catastrophe. Kim began reading the various bids to me, over the phone. By one P.M., the bidding was approaching $400,000. Random House's top bid, however, was $200,000, which meant they were definitely out of the running. I was totally taken aback. What's going on here?

What we didn't know was that Harry Evans, head of Random House, looked at the book—just this morning, right as the auction was getting under way—and decided that anything over $200,000 was too much for an academic work. (Personally, I think he's right.)

This meant a difficult decision. Although I could use the money, I have decided—and Kim strongly agrees—that the only house that can really do what I want for this particular book is Random House. In the middle of the proceedings I tell Kim my decision and she immediately calls off the auction, which shocks pretty much everybody.

But I am very glad to have Random House, and very glad to have Ann. Wonder who will tell her.

Thursday, February 27—New York

I meet with Ann in her office. She has just finished ushering James Hillman's The Soul's Code to #1 on the Times best-seller list, no small feat. And her Midnight in the Garden of Good and Evil is the best-seller of the decade. I sent her flowers late yesterday; they're on her desk.

"Harry's around here somewhere. You should meet him."

In comes Harry, short, sharp, bright, and rambling. Harry is a leading contender to get the Eisner book, so it's funny that I'm staying with Tony. Both of our editors might be in this room right now.

"Ken Wilber, it's fine to meet you! Ann, when . . . when . . . when is the last time we've seen a buzz like this on a nonfiction book?"

"Never, Harry."

"That's right, never. We're very happy about this."

We chat for a few moments, and then Harry vanishes as quickly as he had materialized.

Ann and I talk for an hour or two—I like her enormously—and I return to the Four Seasons. Her comment about the book's buzz gave me one of those warm glows, but she probably says that to all the boys.

It has been a swift five months, almost to the day, since I started writing Science and Religion. And now, suddenly, it all seems over.

MARCH

Our normal waking consciousness is but one special type of consciousness, while all about it, parted from it by the filmiest of screens, there lie potential forms of consciousness entirely different. We may go through life without suspecting their existence, but apply the requisite stimulus and at a touch they are there in all their completeness. . . . There is a continuum of cosmic consciousness, against which our individuality builds but accidental fences, and into which our several minds plunge as into a mother-sea or reservoir.

No account of the universe in its totality can be final which leaves these other forms of consciousness quite disregarded.

—WILLIAM JAMES

Monday, March 3—New York—Boulder

On the plane, back to Boulder, back to a life that seems somehow far away from itself.

Is this a topic whose time has truly come? The integration of science and religion? Or have I just written a clever book that temporarily impressed a few people and will otherwise go as quickly as it came? Publication date is set for early 1998; we'll find out soon enough.

Tuesday, March 4—Boulder

Worked all morning, went grocery shopping, paid bills, watched two videos. Atom Egoyan's Family Viewing, one of his first, and quirkily brilliant. All of Egoyan's films are fascinating; his Exotica is a truly stunning film. I keep hoping he'll break out soon. And Hal Hartley's Amateur, my favorite of his (also Simple Men and Unbelievable Truth). Hartley's films are all so slyly funny.

There is light snow falling now, dancing with the sunlight shining off the ground. I feel enfolded in some sort of luminous cosmic blanket, lightly.

Wednesday, March 5

Science and Religion opens with a quick summary of the perennial philosophy, or the common core of the world's great wisdom traditions. They all maintain, in their various ways, that there are different levels or dimensions of existence, stretching from matter to living body to symbolic mind to subtle soul to causal and nondual spirit. Matter, body, and mind we moderns have no problem accepting; but soul and spirit? Where is the proof that soul and spirit actually exist? The answer, it seems, involves direct spiritual experience—repeatable, reproducible, confirmable. This, anyway, is what Science and Religion attempts to demonstrate.

[See figure 1. This is the so-called Great Chain of Being, although that is something of a misnomer. Each senior level transcends and includes, or enfolds and embraces, its juniors, so this is really the Great Nest of Being. For this reason it is more accurately called, not a hierarchy, but a holarchy, a series of nested spheres.]

The cross-cultural evidence is massive and overwhelming: it appears that human awareness and identity can span the entire spectrum of consciousness, from matter to body to mind to soul to spirit. There appears to be an actual development or evolution of consciousness along that extraordinary continuum. At each level, what we consider to be our "self" changes dramatically. When consciousness is identified with the vital body, we have the bodyego or bodyself—we are identified with our impulses, our feelings, our immediate bodily sensations. When consciousness identifies with the mind, we have the ego—the conceptual, mental, narrative sense of self, involving the taking of roles and the following of rules. When consciousness identifies with the subtle level, we have the soul—a supra-individual sense of self that begins to breathe an atmosphere beyond the conventional and mundane. And when con-

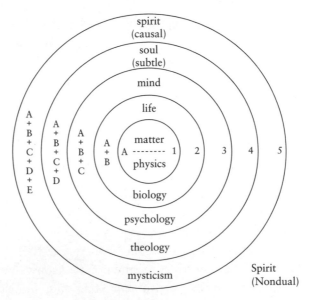

FIGURE 1. *The Great Nest of Being. Spirit is both the highest level (causal) and the nondual Ground of all levels.*

sciousness evolves even further, and identifies with nondual reality, we have Spirit itself, the Goal and Ground of the entire Nest of Being.

The evidence for this Great Spectrum is grounded at every point in direct experience that can be confirmed or rejected by any who adequately follow the interior experiments in consciousness. These experiments, generally known as meditation or contemplation, cannot be dismissed on the ground that they are "merely subjective" or "interior" apprehensions—after all, mathematics is "merely subjective" and "interior," but we don't dismiss that as unreal or illusory or meaningless. Just so, the contemplative sciences have amassed an extraordinary amount of phenomenological data—direct experiences—relating to the subtle and causal, or soul and spirit, levels. And if you want to know if this data is real, all you have to do is follow the experiment—contemplation—and see for yourself. Of those who adequately do so, the majority report a simple conclusion: you are directly introduced to your True Self, your Real Condition, your Original Face, and it is none other than Spirit itself.

Thursday, March 6

Read all morning (new historicism, cultural studies, critical legal studies, new-paradigm), most of it very disappointing, and poorly written to boot. I don't mind if most theoretical writers can't turn a phrase like William James. When Whitehead was asked, "Why don't you write more clearly?," he replied, "Because I don't think more clearly." Fine, no problem. It's the sense you get that so few are even trying. . . .

Friday, March 7

Mail bag from Shambhala, containing last month's letters. About one-fourth of the mail I get is still from Grace and Grit: Spirituality and Healing in the Life and Death of Treya Killam Wilber; to date I've received over eight hundred letters. Many of these I try to respond to, however briefly, because they are always so deeply moving.[4] When I first wrote Grace and Grit, I thought that the intense mail would last for a year or so and then perhaps fade out. But it has been continuous; I get dozens of the most agonizing letters a month. But I have also come to realize that this will be a part of my life indefinitely, and that is fine. So once each month, I go through the letters.

> Dear Ken,
> My name is ―― and I just finished reading Grace and Grit. I had been diagnosed with Breast Cancer in February and a friend from Zurich sent me and my husband your book. At first I felt it would be too depressing to read, but I became curious about it and began. Sometimes it was too sad for me to read and I would put it down. However, I continued to read it and at some point I no longer felt

---

4. When it became apparent that I might publish these journals, I thought about deleting these letters—they are so painfully personal. But because they are an indelible part of my life, I decided to leave them in, with one editorial change: I have deleted, from the letters, most of the congratulatory praise for the book's author, simply because publishing that would be more than ordinarily self-serving. It is simply understood that most of the people who write me about G&G are grateful, but it is their stories, not their gratitude, that I hope these letters most convey.

afraid to read it. On the contrary, I felt supported by it. I appreciated your honesty in sharing what it was like being a support person
and I also loved getting to know Treya. She was a remarkable and
wonderful role model. I do believe I have learned more about love,
compassion and forgiveness from this book than from anything else
I have read.

Your book gave me another chance to cry and reconnect with
myself. Thank you.

Love,
———

Dear Mr. Wilber,
I want to thank you for your book Grace and Grit. I bought it for
Christmas 1994, after my wife died in September. She had a terrible
Non Hodgin Lymphom.

Over one Year she was in hospital for getting chemo therapie.
My wife came from Laos and lived in Thailand since thirty years.
About six years I had a wonderful time of marriage with her.

She was a Buddhist.

I stopped my working and stayed with her in hospital. All day
and night I was beside her. By this time I didn't know your book.
But today I can find a lot of truth in your words.

My wife died in hospital, because she could not leave her bed
anymore. I was very sad about this situation, but we were forced to
stay. I would be happy if I could bring her back home. But it was
impossible.

As she died in the afternoon a great storm and strong rain came
up. And I saw a great grey cloud going upstairs from her body and
drifting away out of the opened window. After twenty minutes the
storm was over.

Then one week later I brought her body back to Thailand. I
didn't cremate her in Germany. An inner voice told me—bring her
back home—and I did so.

Since last weeks I studied your book nearly six or seven times.

And every time I find something more for my spirit. And I hope
many people will read your books and try to change something in
their lives.

You have written a great book. It will be one of the important books of my life. I can read it again and again. And for this I must thank you so much.

Greetings,

———

The stories are so moving, they just tear your heart out; that dear man, taking his wife back to Thailand. Here's an easier one from a young man:

Dear Ken,
I have just finished reading Grace and Grit. In a way, I feel that I know Treya, or perhaps I should say that I feel her. I would like to share with you my experience on finishing the book.

As I read the last two chapters, I could feel the tears coming. I don't know why I waited to the end to cry but I did. Then, just as I finished the last page, I really cried, and my whole body started shaking uncontrollably. I thought to myself, "What's happening here?," and got up and walked around the house, as if movement would somehow give me understanding. About this time, I was also struck with the realization of how precious life is, and I had a strong desire to rush upstairs and awaken my sleeping parents so that I could tell them how much I loved them. Something held me back, perhaps my ego, perhaps the late hour—I do not know—but I do know that I shall not look at them the same way again.

Then I sat down again, and just sat quietly for a few minutes. No tears now, just quiet. And a sense of peace.

I'm very grateful to you, Ken, and to Treya, for sharing your special gift with me. The message of the book, my message, is Life, and Love.

Peace,

———

Dear Ken,
Last August I was diagnosed with breast cancer. I had segmental surgery, lymph node dissection and a three week treatment. I am in constant relationship with cancer on all levels. Several weeks ago a

friend told me of your book and I knew I had to read it. It was a scary thought because, after all, I knew the ending.

"But," I thought, "she had some other kind of more serious cancer." How's that for denial? The fact is, I have the same kind of terrible cancer Treya had. The truth is this book has been at moments terrifying, but totally freeing.

As I read Treya's writings and your reflections I heard my own voice and those of people I know who love me as well. The same self-abuse, the same "I can do it, thank you very much" way of being. And my friends and family puzzled over how I could not see how beautiful I am, how much they love me, and how accomplished they believe me to be. I too have struggled for years with the question of "What's my work, my purpose here?" I too have a willingness to let go and trying to live in the knowing that living is not a reward and death is not a punishment.

I thank you, praise you and bless you for your courage and honesty in writing Grace and Grit. I offer the enclosed music a gift back to you. May you continue to be healed and blessed.

Peace,
———

I have received many letters from women who say expressly how much they identified with Treya—that her concerns and issues were exactly the ones they were wrestling with in their own lives. And often people just want to tell their story, share it with me, whether it has anything to do with cancer or not.

Dear Mr. Wilber,
Greetings from Poland.

I have just read your book Grace and Grit, and I am still under the influence of it. I have been touched by the book to the bottom of my heart. I haven't experienced similar feelings for many years.

Many years ago I was interested in Freud's theory of psychoanalysis but when I became a mother I had to change my interests. Although I was very busy taking care of my children and working as a teacher, I have always tried to perceive the other people near by me. But I am very unhappy because of my unsuccessful personal life and sometimes I ask the question "Why me?" The answer is "Why not?"—I have found it also in your book. I would like to live the fullness of life, like your Treya, but it is so difficult. Her life was so unusual that it seems to be unreal. Sometimes I feel it was a dream only, not a book written by you.

I have just started looking for my daemon and I think I have to change something in my life. I have made some notes about your other books and also about the other authors and philosophers you wrote about in your book.

At the end of the letter I want to say that the book about your wife, Treya, and you is for me the most beautiful book about love and sacrifice. I am very happy I have read it.

If the letter reached you I would be very pleased.

With best summer wishes from Poland.

Yours sincerely,

———

Dear Mr. Wilber,

I just finished Grace and Grit. I identified so much with Treya. She was struggling with so many of the same things that I have been struggling with—trying to find her daemon, exploring spirituality and creativity, being vs. doing, masculine vs. feminine, excessive self-criticism—these are the major issues in my life. I was completely taken over by the book when I was reading it, and I don't believe it will ever leave me. Your openness about your and Treya's feelings was very courageous and poignant. The admiration I grew to have for both of you, combined with your openness about your weaknesses, was a good lesson for me in learning not to be so hard on myself. Thank you. I was impressed with Treya's acceptance and transcendence of her cancer and its implications. It was an impetus for me to put more energy into my meditation practice. The words that kept coming into my mind when reading Grace and Grit were "devastating" and "beautiful," it was devastatingly beautiful. I just wanted to say thanks.

With appreciation and affection,

———

Dear Ken,
My husband and I have been reading the book Grace and Grit. It is
so full of love and emotions and also very educational. When we
read the book we get lumps in our throats and can barely continue
reading it with our teary eyes. If I may say, the love that is expressed
in so genuine. My husband's sister is undergoing chemotherapy and
it is helping us understand what she is feeling and experiencing.

Sincerely,
___

It has surprised me how many letters I get from couples who read the
book aloud to each other. I think because I quoted extensively from
Treya's journals—letting her speak for herself—couples like to take
turns reading each part. I didn't expect this would happen, but it is very
moving to think of lovers using our experience, and Treya's death, to
express their love for each other in life—and not waiting until it's too
late to say the dear things that need to be said now.

Dear Ken,
I am writing to you, even though I don't know if you'll receive this
or if in fact you do read unsolicited mail, to thank you from the
bottom of my heart for writing Grace and Grit. I was, and still am
some 10 days after finishing it, so moved and touched by your courage and love to write so deeply and honestly about your time together with Treya. How you must miss her physical presence and
yet paradoxically how can you miss someone who is so completely
with you in that immersion of love?
    I, too, know of that love. I met ——— in 1988 and a year after we
married she was diagnosed with an almost crippling case of Lyme
disease. It took me about a year of being a round the clock support
person to realize I desperately needed help, which I found in a wonderful therapist who I still see regularly today. Some five years later
my wife has recovered from most of her debilitating symptoms except her back pain which still keeps her lying down a good half to
two-thirds of her waking hours. We, too, have become very familiar
with all the levels that a disease resides in and all the levels of healing that can take place. And likewise our anger and outrage at our

new-age–thinking friends who could say such things as "Oh, you have a pain in your back, what are you trying to avoid?" Enough of this, Ken, really all I wanted to say is thank you and God Bless you for sharing with me and the world your incredible and continuing love story. When I finished it I cried like I haven't cried in many, many years with such deep and sad and heart-opening sobs and tears.

With my love and gratitude,

——

Dear Ken,
With fullest of hearts, I write to you thanks for living your story of Grace and Grit with such candor, love, honesty, and acceptance. I have set your book down a few days ago, and the story runs through my being, so powerful, even many years after her passing. The experience for me has been one of those lovely mystical events that opens me up in new and better ways (not without a few floods!), changing me once again. I feel such a kinship with Treya because our life paths have crossed in so many ways, so I could relate to her intimately. Would I choose the same choices? Would a noble soul within me be revealed by such a devastating disease?

Though I never knew her in life, I am so very grateful to you for showing her to me in such clear ways. Her struggle with and eventually accepting the unacceptable, to continue on to her physical death in "passionate equanimity" (a perfect term for me to embrace) mixed with her utter humanity, moved me immeasurably. I feel such a longing for female role models to be inspired by, so many spiritual teachers are male and for me somehow there is a gap in understanding. Treya's story spoke to me in my words, and bless you for allowing her to tell her own story, in her own words, and never once speak for her.

I was also very touched, very moved by your process, your struggle, your acceptance in serving her, totally loving her. Your devotion to her, even after death in those 24 hours—I am really so blown away—tears—I have never known such a love. Though I have always imagined such depth, for whatever luck, karma, destiny or unconscious choices I have not experienced what the two of you found. However, just the fact that you and Treya found that kind of love feels so good to me! I'm not completely crazy! It does exist. Yes. It does.

When you write a book, it's strange that you let so many people into your soul and you may not ever meet them or hear from them. I just wanted you to know that you helped me, affected me by living your story. Thank you with all my heart.

Love,
___

Dear Ken,
Last year I was diagnosed with advanced metastatic breast cancer. A friend of mine said I had to read this book, Grace and Grit, but when I asked how it ended, he said, "She died." I was afraid of the book for a long time.

But having finished it, I wanted to thank you and Treya from the bottom of my heart. I know I might die, too, but somehow following Treya's story has made me unafraid. I feel free of fear, for the first time. I had two strong experiences, satori I guess, just from reading your descriptions of higher awareness. When Treya died in the book, I felt like I died, so now I don't have to worry.

Thank you again so very, very, very much. I do think I will die and I do think Treya will be there for me.

Sincerely,
___

I feel I am with these people, and they with me. Suffering is a constant reminder of the pain of being human, but also one of the most elemental ways that we all connect with each other, because we all suffer terribly at some point. Suffering is not just "negative"; it is a bond through which we all touch each other. Suffering, truly, is the first grace.

Dear Ken,
Grace and Grit pretty much stopped my life. I had to finish it, or should I say, consume it before I could do much else. When I read the first few chapters, I sat down and sobbed uncontrollably for quite some time. It is hard for me now to capture the intensity I felt.

I was totally overwhelmed as if a torrent of blocked emotion had been released and was flooding my body. You know the kind of sobs that start way down in your gut and rattle your whole being. I was touched so deeply. I found Grace and Grit to be the most beautiful love story I have ever read. I sobbed for your joy and for your loss, bliss that I have only glimpsed, pain that I am not sure I can imagine. And, I sobbed for the sense of joy and loss it triggered in me.

My joy sprang from knowing that it is possible to experience the kind of connection you so beautifully reveal, that sacred love is real and not just some crazy fantasy and that a man of your intellectual depth and intensity is capable of such profound emotional connection. I suppose, because of my father, a brilliant man who has never really inhabited his body (pretty much cut off at the neck), I have always separated these things. As sobs racked my body, for the first time in my life I really got in the fabric of my being that it is possible to connect mind and body and heart in a deeply felt connection.

I grieved, for while I have had fleeting glimpses of this type of connection, I have never experienced it with a man who was willing or able to maintain that level of intensity beyond the briefest encounter. And, even more so, because it is my deepest heart's desire and I had, after years of holding hope in my heart, stopped believing it was possible.

Once again, your words brought me back to what I knew to be True at the deepest level; that it really is OK for me not to settle for anything less than the depth I desire and that this is possible!

I understand that you are something of a recluse, but I hope someday we can meet. With much respect, admiration, and love,

——

Dear Ken Wilber,

I am fourteen years old. Since I was a little girl I have been very afraid of dying. I read Treya's story, and ever since, I have not been afraid to die. I wanted to tell you this.

Sincerely,

——

Treya's journals were truly extraordinary. As I went through them some time after her death, I was struck by one amazing fact: there were no secrets in them. Oh, they were very intimate and very personal, but nothing Treya hadn't shared with me or somebody. She simply had no split between her public and private selves—they were basically identical. With Treya, you knew exactly what she was thinking and feeling—she simply never lied or shaded the truth. This enormous integrity was what people found absolutely compelling, and irresistibly attractive, about her. I think this honesty comes across in the book, and people respond gratefully for getting her uncompromisingly honest account of living—and dying—with a terrible disease. Many of them write to me in an attempt to thank Treya, and that is fine with me; and they say nice things about me, in an attempt to praise Treya, and that's okay, too.

It's funny, though. I had planned to destroy Treya's journals when she died, and I decided that I would not read them first. Even though, as I later found out, there were no secrets in them, Treya cherished her time alone when she wrote in her journal, and I was determined not to violate that by reading them. Curious as I might be, I was very clear about this. Nobody was ever going to see her journals.

And then, twenty-four hours before she died—and right before I carried her up the stairs for the last time—she pointed toward her journals and said, very simply, "You'll need those."

A week earlier she had asked me to write of our ordeal—she was diagnosed with breast cancer ten days after we were married. She hoped, she said, that all the lessons we had learned the hard way would help others. I promised her I would write the book. And so, "You'll need those" meant, you'll need my journals if you are going to give a full account of what transpired. I knew then that I would read them, all of them, first page to last, and I did, with more difficulty than I can record.

The last entry in those journals—ten notebooks in all—the very last entry was: "It takes grace, yes!—and grit."

Saturday, March 8

Joyce Nielsen is the author of Sex and Gender in Society, which is probably the single best text on feminism. It is thorough, fair, comprehensive, judicious. Nielsen is one of my favorite feminist writers, along with Janet

Chafetz, Carol Gilligan, Martha Nussbaum. . . . It never really dawned on me that she teaches at the University of Colorado, Boulder.

I get home today and there's a message on the machine: "If this is the Ken Wilber who wrote Sex, Ecology, Spirituality, and I'm pretty sure it is, I'd like to talk to you. I teach sociology at the University of Colorado, and I use Sex, Ecology, Spirituality as a textbook for my advanced graduate seminar. I was wondering if you could come and talk with us. Please call me at. . . ."

I pick up the phone and call her number, get her machine. "If this is the Joyce Nielsen who wrote Sex and Gender in Society, and I'm pretty sure it is, I'm a real fan. . . ." I'm assuming she'll call back.

Sunday, March 9

It's taken almost a week for any sort of meditative awareness to return, including lucid dreaming. The entire time I was in New York I lost all access to pure witnessing, and I had no subject permanence during the dream and deep sleep state. That is, I was not conscious during the dreaming and deep sleep state—a consciousness, a kind of current, that has been with me off and on for the last three or four years.

This constant consciousness through all states—waking, dreaming, and sleeping—tends to occur after many years of meditating; in my case, about twenty-five years. The signs are very simple: you are conscious during the waking state, and then, as you fall asleep and start to dream, you still remain conscious of the dreaming. This is similar to lucid dreaming, but with a slight difference: usually, in lucid dreaming, you start to manipulate the dream—you choose to dream of sex orgies or great food or flying over mountains or whatnot. But with constant witnessing consciousness, there is no desire to change anything that arises: you simply and innocently witness it. It's a choiceless awareness, a mirrorlike awareness, which equally and impartially reflects whatever arises. So you remain conscious during the dream state, witnessing it, not changing it (although you can if you want; usually you don't want).[5]

---

5. I call this "pellucid dreaming" to distinguish it from lucid dreaming. Throughout many entries I simply use the well-known term "lucid dreaming." Nonetheless, I almost always mean pellucid dreaming. I also refer to pellucid deep sleep, or tacit witnessing in the deep dreamless state.

Then, as you pass into deep, dreamless sleep, you still remain conscious, but now you are aware of nothing but vast pure emptiness, with no content whatsoever. But "aware of" is not quite right, since there is no duality here. It's more like, there is simply pure consciousness itself, without qualities or contents or subjects or objects, a vast pure emptiness that is not "nothing" but is still unqualifiable.

Then, as you come out of the deep sleep state, you see the mind and the dream state arise and take form. That is, out of causal emptiness there arises the subtle mind (dreams, images, symbols, concepts, visions, forms), and you witness this emergence. The dream state continues for a while, and then, as you begin to wake up, you can see the entire gross realm, the physical realm—your body, the bed, the room, the physical universe, nature—arise directly out of the subtle mind state.

In other words, you have just taken a tour of the Great Chain of Being—gross body to subtle mind to causal spirit—in both its ascending and descending movements (evolution and involution). As you fall asleep, you pass from gross body (waking) to subtle mind (dreaming) to causal emptiness (deep sleep)—that's evolution or ascent—and then, as you awaken, you move down from causal to subtle to gross—that's involution or descent. Everybody moves through this cycle every twenty-four hours. But with constant consciousness or unbroken witnessing, you remain aware during all these changes of state, even into deep dreamless sleep.

Since the ego exists mostly in the gross state, with a few remnants in the subtle, then once you identify with constant consciousness—or that which exists in all three states—you break the hold of the ego, since it barely exists in the subtle and does not exist at all in causal emptiness (or in the deep sleep state, which is one type of emptiness). You cease identifying with ego, and you identify with pure formless consciousness as such, which is colorless, spaceless, timeless, formless—pure clear emptiness. You identify with nothing in particular, and therefore you can embrace absolutely everything that arises. Gone to the ego, you are one with the All.

You still have complete access to the waking-state ego, but you are no longer only that. Rather, the very deepest part of you is one with the entire Kosmos in all its radiant glory. You simply are everything that is arising moment to moment. You do not see the sky, you are the sky. You do not touch the earth, you are the earth. You do not hear the rain, you are the rain. You and the universe are what the mystics call "One Taste."

This is not poetry. This is a direct realization, as direct as a glass of cold water in the face. As a great Zen Master said upon his enlightenment: "When I heard the sound of the bell ringing, there was no bell and no I, just the ringing." And in that nondual ringing is the entire Kosmos, where subject and object become One Taste and infinity happily surrenders its secrets. As researchers from Aldous Huxley to Huston Smith have reminded us, One Taste or "cosmic consciousness"—the sense of oneness with the Ground of all creation—is the deepest core of the nearly universal consensus of the world's great wisdom traditions. One Taste is not a hallucination, fantasy, or product of a disturbed psyche, but the direct realization and testament of countless yogis, saints, and sages the world over.

It is very simple, very obvious, very clear—concrete, palpable, unmistakable.

Monday, March 10

Aldous Huxley, of course, wrote a famous book, The Perennial Philosophy, which is about the universal core of the world's great wisdom traditions. Huston Smith's Forgotten Truth is still its best introduction. I wrote an essay for the Journal of Humanistic Psychology that begins: "Known as the 'perennial philosophy'—'perennial' precisely because it shows up across cultures and across the ages with essentially similar features—this worldview has, indeed, formed the core not only of the world's great wisdom traditions, from Christianity to Judaism to Buddhism to Taoism, but also the thinking of some of the greatest philosophers, scientists, and psychologists East and West, North and South. So overwhelmingly widespread is the perennial philosophy—the details of which I will explain in a moment—that it is either the single greatest intellectual error ever to appear in humankind's history—an error so colossally widespread as to literally stagger the mind—or it is the single most accurate reflection of reality yet to appear."[6]

So what are the details of this perennial philosophy? Very simple: the Great Nest of Being, culminating in One Taste—there, in a nutshell, is the perennial philosophy.

---

6. This essay is included in chapter 1 of *The Eye of Spirit*.

This is not to say that everything about the perennial philosophy is set in concrete or etched in gold. I actually wrote a paper called "The Neo-Perennial Philosophy," pointing out that much of it needed to be updated and modernized.[7] Nonetheless, the core of the world's great wisdom traditions is a framework we ought to consult seriously and reverentially in our own attempts to understand the Kosmos.

And at its heart is the experience of One Taste—clear, obvious, unmistakable, unshakable.

Tuesday, March 11

Well, unshakable with further practice. I'm always curious what will interrupt this nondual current, what will obscure or disrupt constant consciousness, what will throw you out of the All and into the clutches of your separate self, where suffering awaits. Interestingly, in my case, one glass of wine will prevent it (that is, if I have one glass of wine, then that night I am not conscious during the dream and deep sleep state. I'm sure great yogis can drink and still remain conscious through all three states, but not me). Stress usually does not disrupt this constant current. But in New York I drank several glasses of wine most of the days there, so that alone would account for the disruption of witnessing. On the other hand, I was there to do blatant self-promotion, something that I am not good at doing gracefully—I either underdo or overdo it, mostly because it's awkward for me. So it could have been the simple fact that I was in the clutches of the egoic self-contraction for the better part of a week that virtually obliterated stable access to the Witness.

Last night it all seemed to rearrange itself. I was not lucid dreaming at first, I was just dreaming: a woman and I are sitting in front of Sri Ramana Maharshi. There is a large audience, but I don't really notice it. The woman is explaining how you practice self-inquiry, which is a practice of inquiring "Who am I?" and attempting to feel into the very source of consciousness; it is an attempt to find the pure and ever-present Witness. For some reason the woman was explaining it all wrong; she was presenting it as the result of making an effort to be aware. I looked at Ramana and said, No, there's no effort, you simply notice that you are

---

7. This essay is included in chapter 2 of *The Eye of Spirit*.

already aware, and that awareness—just as it is—is it. No effort at all. Ramana smiled, and my mind and his mind were instantly one. I started lucid dreaming at that point, but more a witnessing. That current of witnessing or constant consciousness has stayed with me now for several days and nights, which is usually the way it has been, off and on, for several years now.

It's a fascinating process. It is pure Emptiness, altogether unbounded, radiant, pure, free, limitless, beyond light and beyond bliss, radically unqualifiable. Ramana called this deep witnessing (or constant consciousness) the I-I, because it is aware of the little I or separate self. Ken Wilber is just a gross-level manifestation of what I-I really am, which is not Ken at all, but simply the All. Ken was born and will die, but I-I never enters the stream of time. I-I am the great Unborn, I-I am the mysterious Undying; the entire Kosmos exists as the simple feeling of my own Being. And every sentient being in the entire universe can make that claim, as long as they stand as the great I-I, which is no I whatsoever.

(Vedanta emphasizes the I-I, Buddhism emphasizes no I, but they are both pointing to pure, nondual, unqualifiable Emptiness—shunyata or nirguna—which is the simple suchness or thusness or isness of the entire world, and is not other than the pure, natural, spontaneous, ever-present consciousness that is your own true state right now—an unbroken nondual stream that persists through all possible changes of state, waking, dreaming, sleeping. In its pure form the Witness dissolves into everything it witnesses—the mirror-mind is one with its objects, Emptiness is one with all Form. And so, as both Vedanta and Buddhism emphasize, pure consciousness itself is nondual, empty, and finally unqualifiable.)

When meditators first start developing (or rather, noticing) this constant consciousness, they tend to go through a type of split-mind awareness. On the one hand, you are developing a capacity for strong meditative equanimity, a capacity to Witness both pain and pleasure without flinching, without either grasping or avoiding. "The perfect person," said Chuang Tzu, "employs the mind like a mirror: it accepts but does not grasp, it receives but does not keep." As this mirror-mind awareness (or constant consciousness) grows stronger, the gross waking state becomes more and more "dreamlike," in the sense that it loses its power to overwhelm you, to shake you, to make you believe that passing sensations are the only reality. Life starts to look like one great big movie, and you are the unmoved Witness watching the show. Happiness arises, you witness it; joy arises, you witness it; pain arises, you witness it; sorrow arises, you witness it. In all cases, you are the Witness, and not some passing surface wave of silly sound and fury. At the center of the cyclone, you are safe. A deep and inward peace begins to haunt you; you can no longer manufacture turmoil with quite the same conviction.

But that doesn't mean that you can't feel desire, hurt, pain, joy, happiness, suffering, or sorrow. You can still feel all of those; they just don't convince you. Again, it's like being at the movies. Sometimes you get so caught up in what is happening on screen that you forget it's just a movie. At a thriller, you might actually become frightened; at a romance, you might start crying. Then your friend leans over and says, Hey, lighten up, it's just a movie, it's not real! And you snap out of it.

Enlightenment is . . . to snap out of the movie of life. To wake up, to shake it off. You are, and always have been, at the movies, as the Witness. But when you take life seriously—when you think the movie is real—you <u>forget</u> you are the pure and free Witness and you <u>identify</u> with a little self—the ego—as if you were part of the movie you are actually watching. You identify with somebody on screen. And therefore you get frightened, and therefore you cry, and therefore you suffer altogether.

With meditation, you begin to relax in your seat and just watch the movie of life, without judging it, avoiding it, grasping it, pushing it, or pulling it. You merely Witness it: you employ the mirror-mind, you rest in simple, clear, spontaneous, effortless, ever-present consciousness.

As you persist in noticing (and relaxing into) the choiceless awareness of what is, then this consciousness will begin to extend from the waking state into the dream state—you will simply remain as choiceless awareness, as the mirror-mind, as constant consciousness, even as the dream state arises. You will notice that phenomenologically the gross world—the physical body, the sensorimotor world, and the ego built upon them—all begin to dissolve into the subtle world of imagery and vision. In any event, you remain conscious.

With further practice, that choiceless awareness will extend from the dream state even into deep dreamless sleep. And since "you" are still present (not as ego but as I-I, as pure consciousness without an object), you will find a much deeper and truer identity: you are still tacitly conscious when there are no objects, no subjects, and no contents at all—no suffering, no pain, no pleasure, no desire, no goals, no hope, no fear. There is nothing arising at all, in this pure Formless state—and yet you are, you still exist, but only as pure consciousness. There is no body, there is no ego, there is no mind—and yet you know that you exist, and so you are obviously none of those lesser states. You are only you—that is, there is nothing but pure I AMness, pure nondual Consciousness, which is so radically free, unlimited, unbounded, and unqualifiable, that strictly speaking we can only call it "Emptiness"—and that is what it "feels" like as well: an infinite Absence or Abyss, which is just another name for infinite Freedom.

Thursday, March 13

Just got off the phone with Mike Murphy (our exuberant conversations rarely last less than two hours). He and his friend Sylvia Tompkins are doing a series of projects, including a CD-ROM and a book, focusing on an integral (or balanced) spirituality—an updated, modernized version of the perennial philosophy, which is also sympathetic with my own work. Sylvia thought of putting this integral view on CD-ROM, and she and Mike eventually found themselves hooked up with James Redfield, author of The Celestine Prophecy and The Tenth Insight, who, because of his extraordinary commercial success (over fifteen million readers), would help these projects reach a much wider audience.

It looks like I will be going to San Francisco to speak to the Fetzer Institute, so I arranged to get together with Mike when I'm out there. Mike is truly amazing. Not only did he cofound Esalen Institute—ushering in the Human Potential Movement—he has remained on the forefront of psychological and spiritual development ever since. He's just finished writing The Kingdom of Shivas Irons, the avidly awaited follow-up to his classic Golf in the Kingdom. Last I heard, Clint Eastwood was going to make, and star in, the film version of Golf, along with Sean Connery. Lord, that will probably ruin Mike's life; he'll never have a quiet moment again.

Friday, March 14—Boulder—San Francisco

Early morning, on a plane, headed to San Francisco. The Fetzer Institute, founded by John Fetzer, is one of the few liberal organizations that will fund genuinely spiritual projects. Liberals and God don't get along too well, so conservatives have cornered the market on God-talk in this country. Both of those facts are unfortunate.

This is why Fetzer is largely unique—a liberal charity not frightened by Spirit. They have, for example, funded Bill Moyers's PBS series on health and meditation. Rob Lehman is now head of Fetzer, although he works closely in conjunction with a Board. My old friend Judith Skutch (publisher of A Course in Miracles) has been on the Board for a long time, and she has been instrumental in getting several other good people to join, including Frances Vaughan. Fetzer is in the process of reorganizing, and they asked me to talk with them about various directions for their future development.

So here I am, 36,000 feet above it all, about to abruptly descend into it. The Board is meeting all day Friday and Saturday; I am scheduled to speak each afternoon from around 2 to 5. The format is question and answer. I'll go directly from the plane to the meeting, which starts a few hours from now.

Saturday, March 15—San Francisco

I figured that, in order to describe a comprehensive or integral approach to transformation, I would have to spend the first hour or two outlining my general ideas, as summarized in, say, A Brief History of Everything. But when I got to the conference room, they had diagrams from Brief History on the wall, and everybody was quite conversant with all the technical terms. Then I think I went too far the other way. During the first break, I passed Roger [Walsh] in the hall—he was there as a consultant—and he whispered "Keep it simple."

Today more meetings, and I again went on in the afternoon. The questions—and my answers, or attempted answers—centered on the nature of a truly integral or holistic or comprehensive vision, and how best to implement it, or simply make it available to individuals and the culture at large.

There are many ways to explain "integral" or "holistic." The most common is that it is an approach that attempts to include and integrate matter, body, mind, soul, and spirit—attempts, that is, to include the entire Great Nest of Being. Thus, physics deals with matter, biology deals with the living body, psychology deals with the mind, theology deals with the soul, and mysticism deals with the direct experience of spirit—so an integral approach to reality would include physics, biology, psychology, theology, and mysticism (to give just a few examples). [See figure 1 on page 44.]

Although that is a good start at defining "integral," what I have tried to do in my writings is make that scheme a little more sophisticated by pointing out that each of those levels actually has at least four important aspects or dimensions. Each level can be looked at from the inside and from the outside in both individual and collective forms.

For example, your consciousness can be looked at from the inside—the subjective side, your own awareness right now—which is experienced in the first person as an "I" (all the images, impulses, concepts, and desires floating through your mind right now). You can also study consciousness in an objective, empirical, scientific fashion, in the third person as an "it" (for example, the brain contains acetylcholine, dopamine, serotonin, etc., all described in objective it-language). And both of those exist not just in singular but in plural forms—not just an "I" or an "it," but a "we." This collective form also has an inside and outside: the cultural values shared from within (e.g., morals, worldviews, cultural meaning), and the exterior concrete social forms seen from without (e.g., modes of production, technology, economic base, social institutions, information systems).

So each level in the Great Chain actually has an inside and outside in both individual and collective forms—and that gives us the four dimensions (or "four quadrants") of each level of existence. [Figure 2 gives several details of the four quadrants; the terminology will be explained as the entries proceed.]

Because both of the Right-Hand quadrants are objective it(s), they can be counted as one, so I often simplify the four dimensions to just three: I, we, and it; or first-person, second-person, and third-person. [These are also indicated in figure 2.]

There's an easy way to remember these three basic dimensions. Beauty is in the eye of the beholder, the "I" of the beholder. The Good refers to moral and ethical actions that occur between you and me, or "we." Truth usually refers to objective empirical facts, or "its." So the three

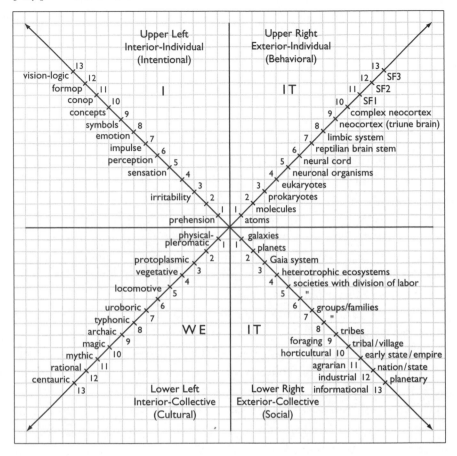

FIGURE 2. *The Four Quadrants*

basic dimensions of "I," "we," and "it" also refer to the Beautiful, the Good, and the True. Or again, art, morals, and science.

So a truly integral view would not talk just about matter, body, mind, soul, and spirit—because <u>each</u> of those levels has a dimension of art, of morals, and of science, and we need explicitly to include all of them. So, for example, we have the art of the matter/body realm (naturalism, realism), the art of the mental realm (surrealistic, conceptual, abstract), the art of the soul and spirit realm (contemplative, transformative). Likewise, we have morals that spring from the sensory realm (hedonism), from the mental realm (reciprocity, fairness, justice), and from the spiritual realm (universal love and compassion). And so on.

So putting these three <u>dimensions</u> (I, we, and it; or art, morals, and science; or Beauty, Goodness, and Truth) together with the major <u>levels</u>

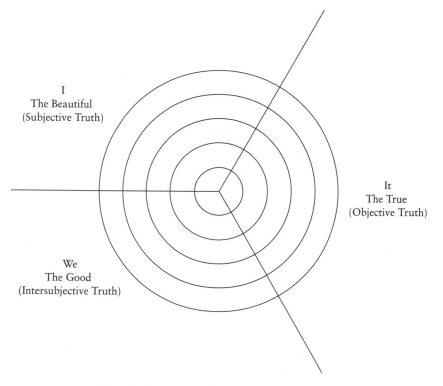

I
The Beautiful
(Subjective Truth)

It
The True
(Objective Truth)

We
The Good
(Intersubjective Truth)

FIGURE 3. *Levels of the Good, the True, and the Beautiful*

of existence (matter, body, mind, soul, and spirit) would give us a much more genuinely integral or holistic approach to reality. [See figure 3. See *The Marriage of Sense and Soul* for a further discussion of this topic.]

The Fetzer Institute wants to support and promote an integral approach to the world—in education, medicine, spirituality, scientific research, consciousness studies, and so forth. The Board members found my dimensions/levels to be useful in furthering the discussion, and for several hours the dialogue focused on these issues.

Apparently today I was doing better, since nobody whispered urgent suggestions to me in the hall.

Monday, March 17—San Francisco

Today I moved from the Inn Above Tide, in Sausalito, where Fetzer put us all up (we figured it beat the Inn Below Tide), and into the Hyatt off

Union Square in downtown San Francisco. I'm sitting here on the thirty-sixth floor, in a restaurant at the top of the hotel, overlooking the most beautiful city in America. The Golden Gate, on my left, connecting the airiness of the city to the greenness of Marin; the Bay Bridge, on the right, reaching over to unamusing Oakland; the prison Alcatraz, straight ahead, a craggy monument to male aggression.

I love San Francisco. I'd live here if I could afford it, and if the house in Boulder weren't the perfect place to do a lot of work. I'm going to spend a few days wandering around the city before I have to head back to the relentless grind of research on volume 2.

My old friend Mitch Kapor is in town; he's staying across the street at Campton Place, but he's away for a few days at a meditation retreat. Yesterday, on his way out, I asked him to stop by at Frances and Roger's, so I could introduce them. Frances and Roger are the most special couple in my life, and have been for over two decades—all my adult life, really. I still sort of think of us as a trio. My life would be so much less without them; we have all shared our greatest ups and downs, and most things in between. To my mind, they are exemplary human beings in almost every way, caring, bright, brilliant. Both have written several books of surpassing merit, and I have seen them give countless hours of what can only be called selfless service. They both absolutely die when I say this kind of stuff, but there it is.

Mitchell and I met back in the Lincoln days. He had read The Spectrum of Consciousness and came out to my house a couple of times to talk. I liked him immediately—Mitch is bitingly brilliant but it's not off-putting; there is something instantly likeable about him. He was then friends with—and the meditation teacher of—Jack Crittenden. Jack and I were in the process of setting up ReVision Journal, which we did, and which eventually took me to Boston, where both Jack and Mitch lived. Mitch, in the meantime, went back to graduate school, got a business degree from MIT, then founded Lotus software, the most successful software of its time. He eventually sold Lotus for many millions, cofounded the Electronic Frontier Foundation, and set up Kapor Enterprises. It's always nice to introduce friends, so Mitch and Frances and Roger and I spent an afternoon together, talking about this and that.

Wednesday, March 19—San Francisco

This morning I rented a car and drove out to Muir Beach, to Sam Keen's house, where Treya and I first lived together after we were married (we rented the house from him; nobody was there today). I sat on the porch for an hour, maybe two. It's still with me. She lingers still. The sadness is palpable, part of the misty atmosphere over the beach, making it hard to breathe.

For about two weeks after her death, I was in the same state of glory and grace in which she had passed. There was only radiant awareness, with no subject and no object, but everything arising just as it should, beautifully. We were together, then, I'm sure. And then the self-contraction returned, as is its wont, and I was Ken again, mostly.

I look out over the beach; scenes of our life together emerge from the clouds and come looking for me. In many ways, I always think of Treya and me together in this house. We had a few months here before cancer struck; it was the only cancer-free zone in our entire time together. So it is here that I see her whole and full, breathtakingly beautiful, a radiance that reached right into you and grabbed your soul, and spoke in words too tender too repeat. It was here that we danced and cried, made love and laughter, held on to each other as if to life itself. And it was here that those wretched words, "Terry has cancer," were first spoken by me, over the phone, to family and friends, in that first, horrible, hideous night.

But I don't think of her that much anymore, because she is a part of that which thinks. She runs in my blood and beats in my heart; she is part of me, always, so I don't have to picture her to remember her. She is on this side of my skin, not that, not out there, not away from me. Treya and I grew up together, and died together. We were always two sides of the same person. It will always be so, I think.

Thursday, March 20—San Francisco—Boulder

On the plane, back to Boulder. Had dinner with Mike Murphy and Sylvia the other night. We talked about the Integral Transformative Practice centers that he and George [Leonard] are starting. Mike's got the Stanford Center for Research in Disease Prevention on board to help document the progress and effectiveness of the integral training. This is truly important work, groundbreaking work, I think, and it will help to define an entirely new approach to psychological and spiritual transformation, one that includes the best of ancient wisdom and the brightest of modern knowledge. No surprise that once again Murphy is at the leading edge.

Friday, March 21—Boulder

Glorious morning—Boulder can be beautiful. Went shopping, restocked the refrigerator, started through the piles of mail, 62 phone messages, etc.

Finished reading The Andy Warhol Diaries. Well, now we know the speed of shallow. Actually, I came to rather like Warhol. And his art. The fruit of one branch of the tree of Duchamp, Warhol is the consummate artist of flatland. His works are all surface, bright and vigorous, alarming and electric, with absolutely nothing underneath. I don't like flatland, but I like his striking representation of it. "Surface, surface, surface was all that anyone found meaningful." Warhol is really a great forerunner of postmodernism's aggressive, virulent, unyielding shallowness.

Sunday, March 23

Sitting here on the porch, watching the sun go down. Except there is no watcher, just the sun, setting, setting. From purest Emptiness, brilliant clarity shines forth. The sound of the birds, over there. Clouds, a few, right up there. But there is no "up," no "down," no "over," and no "there"—because there is no "me" or "I" for which these directions make sense. There is just this. Simple, clear, easy, effortless, ever-present this.

I became extremely serious about meditation practice when I read the following line from the illustrious Sri Ramana Maharshi: "That which is not present in deep dreamless sleep is not real."

That is a shocking statement, because basically, there is nothing—literally nothing—in the deep dreamless state. That was his point. Ultimate reality (or Spirit), Ramana said, cannot be something that pops into consciousness and then pops out. It must be something that is constant, permanent, or, more technically, something that, being timeless, is fully present at every point in time. Therefore, ultimate reality must also be fully present in deep dreamless sleep, and anything that is not present in deep dreamless sleep is NOT ultimate reality.

This profoundly disturbed me, because I had had several kensho or satori-like experiences (glimpses of One Taste), but they were all generally confined to the waking state. Moreover, most of the things I cared for existed in the waking state. And yet clearly the waking state is not permanent. It comes and goes every twenty-four hours. And yet, according to the great sages, there is something in us that is always conscious— that is literally conscious or aware at all times and through all states, waking, dreaming, sleeping. And that ever-present awareness is Spirit in us. That underlying current of constant consciousness (or nondual awareness) is a direct and unbroken ray of pure Spirit itself. It is our connection with the Goddess, our pipeline straight to God.

Thus, if we want to realize our supreme identity with Spirit, we will have to plug ourselves into this current of constant consciousness, and follow it through all changes of state—waking, dreaming, sleeping— which will (1) strip us of an exclusive identification with any of those states (such the body, the mind, the ego, or the soul); and (2) allow us to recognize and identify with that which is constant—or timeless— through all of those states, namely, Consciousness as Such, by any other name, timeless Spirit.

I had been meditating fairly intensely for around twenty years when I came across that line from Ramana. I had studied Zen with Katagiri and Maezumi; Vajrayana with Kalu and Trungpa; Dzogchen with Pema Norbu and Chagdud; plus I had studied—sometimes briefly, sometimes for extended periods—Vedanta, TM, Kashmir Shaivism, Christian mysticism, Kabbalah, Daism, Sufism . . . , well, it's a long list. When I ran across Ramana's statement, I was on an intensive Dzogchen retreat with my primary Dzogchen teacher, Chagdud Tulku Rinpoche. Rinpoche also stressed the importance of carrying the mirror-mind into the dream and deep sleep states. I began having flashes of this constant nondual awareness, through all states, which Rinpoche confirmed. But it wasn't until a year later, during a very intense eleven-day period—in which the separate-self seemed to radically, deeply, thoroughly die—that it all seemed to come to fruition. I slept not at all during those eleven days; or rather, I was conscious for eleven days and nights, even as the body and mind went through waking, dreaming, and sleeping: I was unmoved in the midst of changes; there was no I to be moved; there was only unwavering empty consciousness, the luminous mirror-mind, the witness that was one with everything witnessed. I simply reverted to what I am, and it has been so, more or less, ever since.

The moment this constant nondual consciousness is obvious in your case, a new destiny will awaken in the midst of the manifest world. You will have discovered your own Buddha Mind, your own Godhead, your own formless, spaceless, timeless, infinite Emptiness, your own Atman that is Brahman, your Keter, Christ consciousness, radiant Shekhinah—in so many words, One Taste. It is unmistakably so. And just that is your true identity—pure Emptiness or pure unqualifiable Consciousness as Such—and thus you are released from the terror and the torment that necessarily arise when you identify with a little subject in a world of little objects.

Once you find your formless identity as Buddha-mind, as Atman, as pure Spirit or Godhead, you will take that constant, nondual, ever-present consciousness and reenter the lesser states, subtle mind and gross body, and reanimate them with radiance. You will not remain merely Formless and Empty. You will Empty yourself of Emptiness: you will pour yourself out into the mind and world, and create them in the process, and enter them all equally, but especially and particularly that specific mind and body that is called you (that is called, in my case, Ken Wilber); this lesser self will become the vehicle of the Spirit that you are.

And then all things, including your own little mind and body and feelings and thoughts, will arise in the vast Emptiness that you are, and they will self-liberate into their own true nature just as they arise, precisely because you no longer identify with any one of them, but rather let them play, let them all arise, in the Emptiness and Openness that you now are. You then will awaken as radical Freedom, and sing those songs of radiant release, beam an infinity too obvious to see, and drink an ocean of delight. You will look at the moon as part of your body and bow to the sun as part of your heart, and all of it is just so. For eternally and always, eternally and always, there is only this.

But you have not found this Freedom, or in any way attained it. It is in fact the same Freedom that has lived in the house of the pure Witness from the very start. You are merely recognizing the pure and empty Self, the radical I-I, that has been your natural awareness from the beginning and all along, but that you didn't notice because you had become lost in the intoxicating movie of life.

Monday, March 24

With the awakening of constant consciousness, you become something of a divine schizophrenic, in the popular sense of "split-minded," because you have access to <u>both</u> the Witness and the ego. You are actually "whole-minded," but it sounds like it's split, because you are aware of the constant Witness or Spirit in you, and you are also perfectly aware of the movie of life, the ego and all its ups and downs. So you still feel pain and suffering and sorrow, but they can no longer convince you of their importance—you are no longer the victim of life, but its Witness.

In fact, because you are no longer afraid of your feelings, you can engage them with much greater intensity. The movie of life becomes more vivid and vibrant, precisely because you are no longer grasping or avoiding it, and thus no longer trying to dull or dilute it. You no longer turn the volume down. You might even cry harder, laugh louder, jump higher. Choiceless awareness doesn't mean you cease to feel; it means you feel fully, feel deeply, feel to infinity itself, and laugh and cry and love until it hurts. Life jumps right off the screen, and you are one with all of it, because you don't recoil.

If you are having a dream, and you think it's real, it can get very scary. Say you are dreaming that you are tightrope walking across Niagara Falls. If you fall off, you plunge to your death. So you are walking very slowly, very carefully. Then suppose you start lucid dreaming, and you realize that it's just a dream. What do you do? Become more cautious and careful? No, you start jumping up and down on the tightrope, you do flips, you bounce around, you have a ball—precisely because you know it isn't real. When you realize it's a dream, you can afford to play.

The same thing happens when you realize that ordinary life is just a dream, just a movie, just a play. You don't become more cautious, more timid, more reserved. You start jumping up and down and doing flips, precisely because it's all a dream, it's all pure Emptiness. You don't feel less, you feel more—because you can afford to. You are no longer afraid of dying, and therefore you are not afraid of living. You become radical and wild, intense and vivid, shocking and silly. You let it all come pouring through, because it's all your dream.

Life then assumes its true intensity, its vivid luminosity, its radical effervescence. Pain is more painful and happiness is happier; joy is more joyous and sorrow is even sadder. It all comes radiantly alive to the mirror-mind, the mind that doesn't grasp or avoid, but simply witnesses the play, and therefore can afford to play, even as it watches.

What would motivate you if you saw everything as the dream of your own highest Self? What would actually move you in this playful dream world? Everything in the dream is basically fun, at some deep level, except for this: when you see your friends suffering because they think the dream is real, you want to relieve their suffering, you want them to wake up, too. Watching them suffer is not fun. And so a deep and powerful compassion arises in the heart of the awakened ones, and they seek, above all else, to awaken others—and thus relieve them from the sorrow and the pity, the torment and the pain, the terror and the anguish that comes from taking with dreadful seriousness the silly dream of life.

So you are a divine schizophrenic, you are "split-minded" in the sense that you are simultaneously in touch with both the pure Witness and the world of the ego-film. But that really means you are actually "whole-minded," because these two worlds are really not-two. The ego is just the dream of the Witness, the film that the Witness creates out of its own infinite plenitude, simply so it will have something to watch at the movies.

At that point the entire play arises within your own constant consciousness. There is no inside and no outside, no in here versus out there. The nondual universe of One Taste arises as a spontaneous gesture of your own true nature. You can taste the sun and swallow the moon, and centuries fit in the palm of your hand. The pure I-I, the great I AMness, breathes to infinity and creates a Kosmos as the Song of its very Self, and oceans of compassion fall as tears from your very own Original Face.

Last night I saw the reflection of the moon in a cool clear crystal pond, and nothing else happened at all.

Friday, March 28

A small stream, softly murmuring, runs down behind my house; you can hear it actually singing, if you listen with ears of light. The sun plays on the green leaves, sparkling emeralds each and all, and Spirit speaks in times like these, just a little louder. "I become a transparent eyeball; I am nothing, I see all." There is nothing solid here, all that is hard melts into air, all that is rigid softens to transparency, the world is diaphanous, not in appearance but essence. I disappear into the transparent show, and we are all light in light, images in images, floating effortlessly on a sea of the serene.

Nature is the outer form of Buddha, nature is the corporeal body of Christ. Take, eat, for this is my flesh; take, drink, for this is my blood. Poor dear nature, expression of the Real, impulse of the Infinite, transparent to Eternity, is merely a shining surface on an ocean of unending Spirit, dancing in the daylight of the Divine, hiding in the night of ignorance. For those who do not know the Timeless, nature is all they have; for those who do not taste Infinity, nature serves its last supper. For those in need of redemption, nature tricks you into thinking it alone is real. But for those who have found release, nature is the radiant shell in which a deeper truth resides. So it is—nature, mind, and spirit—Nirmanakaya, Sambhogakaya, and Dharmakaya—gross, subtle, and causal—are an eternal trinity in the folds of the Kosmos, never lost, never found.

Except today, where we are all light in light, and images in images, floating effortlessly on a sea of the serene.

APRIL

Now I shall tell you the nature of this absolute Witness. If you recognize it, you will be freed from the bonds of ignorance, and attain liberation.

There is a self-existent Reality, which is the basis of our consciousness of ego. That Reality is the Witness of the states of ego consciousness and of the body. That Reality is the constant Witness in all three states of consciousness—waking, dreaming, and dreamless sleep. It is your real Self. That Reality pervades the universe. It alone shines. The universe shines with Its reflected light.

Its nature is timeless awareness. It knows all things, Witnesses all things, from the ego to the body. It is the Witness of pleasure and pain and the sense-objects. This is your real Self, the Supreme Being, the Ancient. It never ceases to experience infinite release. It is unwavering. It is Spirit itself.

—SHANKARA

Wednesday, April 2

Resting as the formless Witness brings both a radical liberation and a compelling duty: liberation, in that you are free from the bondage to the world of objects, which only live and die and suffer in the process; and duty, in that, from this infinite space of release, you feel compelled to help others find the same salvation, which is their own truest Self and deepest Condition—pure Emptiness, pure Spirit, pure Godhead. The ultimate metaphysical secret is that there are no others to save; the problem is, they don't realize that, and this ignorance drives the relentless round of birth and death and untold agony.

"Ignorance," Patanjali reminds us, "is the identification of the Seer with the instruments of seeing." Instead of Witnessing the body, we identify with it. Instead of Witnessing the ego, we identify with it. Instead of Witnessing suffering, we identify with it. And yet inevitably we are controlled by that with which we identify; we are tortured by all that we have not transcended. Thus lashing ourselves to the masts of misery, we suffer the outrages of space and time and terror. As one poet expressed the message of the Buddha:

> Ye suffer from yourselves, none else compels,
> None other holds you that ye live and die
> And whir upon the wheel, and hug and kiss its spokes of
>   agony,
> Its tire of tears, its nave of nothingness.

Thursday, April 10

Alec Tsoucatos is an old friend of Treya's who has become a good friend of mine. He teaches business and economics at various colleges in the area, and every now and then leads a kw study group. He brought his group by the house to say hello, and I invited a few other friends, Kate Olson, a PBS producer, and Phil Jacobson, Director of Continuing Education at Naropa.

At some point in the evening we got into a discussion about meditation and the changes it can produce in brain waves. A young man training to be a psychiatrist asked me to get out a videotape I have of me connected to an EEG machine while I meditate. He believed none of the discussion about how meditation could profoundly alter brain waves, and he wanted "proof."

The tape shows me hooked to an EEG machine; this machine shows alpha, beta, theta, and delta waves in both left and right hemispheres. Alpha is associated with awake but relaxed awareness; beta with intense and analytic thinking; theta is normally produced only in the dream state, and sometimes in states of intense creativity; and delta is normally produced only in deep dreamless sleep. So alpha and beta are associated with the gross realm; theta with the subtle realm; and delta with the causal realm. Or, we could say, alpha and beta tend to be indicative of ego states, theta of soul states, and delta of spirit states. Delta presumably has something to do with the pure Witness, which most people experience only in deep dreamless sleep.

This video starts with me hooked up to the machine; I am in normal waking consciousness, so you can see a lot of alpha and beta activity in both hemispheres. But you can also see a large amount of delta waves; in both hemispheres the delta indicators are at maximum, presumably because of constant or stable witnessing. I then attempt to go into a type of nirvikalpa samadhi—or complete mental cessation—and within four or five seconds, all of the machine's indicators go completely to zero. It looks like whoever this is, is totally brain-dead. There is no alpha, no beta, no theta—but there is still maximum delta.

After several minutes of this, I start doing a type of mantra visualization technique—yidam meditation, which I have always maintained is predominantly a subtle-level practice—and sure enough, large amounts of theta waves immediately show up on the machine, along with maximum delta. The fact that theta, which normally occurs only in dreaming, and delta, which normally occurs only in deep sleep, are both being produced in a wide-awake subject tends to indicate a type of simultaneous presence of gross, subtle, and causal states (e.g., turiyatita). It is, in any event, attention-grabbing.

I dragged the video out and we all watched it. Sam says I make a total ass out of myself by showing this, since it seems so self-serving, so braggadocio. Probably so. But to me it's just an objective event. Too bad the test subject isn't somebody else, because the results are striking to the average viewer. It really gets their attention, and much more than my books do. It also convinced the soon-to-be psychiatrist, as it does virtually every scientific type I show it to.

I had started doing these videos—entering various types of meditation states and videotaping the corresponding brain-wave patterns on the EEG—as part of an integral approach to studying higher states and levels of consciousness (correlating what I would call Upper Left—subjective consciousness—and Upper Right—objective brain). I've found that there really are distinctively different brain-wave patterns for different types and levels of meditation. If nothing else, this could serve as a simple pilot project for more adequate and controlled studies. And, of course, Charles Alexander and the TM people are doing this type of research with much greater sophistication, and I'm a big fan of their work. Most of my friends who have seen this tape—Roger Walsh, Frances Vaughan, Mike Murphy, Tony Schwartz, Lex Hixon—have immediately seen the usefulness of this general type of research.

Anyway, people tend to get very serious after seeing this tape—serious in a good sense, I think, because it shows them that there is truly something profound going on, that primordial awareness is not just an idea you memorize but the result of actual practice that truly changes your very makeup. Some people are discouraged watching this, because they think they can't do it; but most people are encouraged, encouraged to take up an authentic spiritual practice and follow the current of constant consciousness through all three states, waking, dreaming, and deep sleep, thus finding that constant ray of Spirit that speaks to each and all in no uncertain terms.

Saturday, April 12

Sam is coming in tomorrow for a short visit. I've invited Reb Zalman Schachter-Shalomi to stop by with his wife, Eve, to meet Sam. Zalman is radiant, beautiful, blessed, sanctus. He's the spearhead of the Jewish Renewal movement, and a great scholar, especially of Kabbalah and Jewish mysticism. He's also the one who "rabbitized" Michael Lerner. Michael strikes me as a perfect spiritual descendant of Zalman—they both have the same type of twinkle in their eyes. Michael's new book, The Politics of Meaning, is a significant attempt to get liberalism and spirituality together (as is his magazine, Tikkun). But when Michael was last in Boulder he told me how disappointed he was with the book, because it had to be dramatically edited to make it more "popular" (he's happier with his previous book, Jewish Renewal).

Michael's story is a real cautionary tale about what the liberal media in this country will do to anything "spiritual." My own politics can fairly well be described as postconservative, postliberal. I'm working on several books on just this topic. Both liberalism and conservatism have their strengths and weaknesses, and we need to combine the strengths of both and jettison the weaknesses.

The main strength of liberalism is its emphasis on individual human rights. The major weakness is its rabid fear of Spirit. Modern liberalism came into being, during the Enlightenment, largely as a counterforce to mythic religion, which was fine. But liberalism committed a classic pre/ trans fallacy: it thought that all spirituality was nothing but prerational myth, and thus it tossed any and all transrational spirituality as well, which was absolutely catastrophic. (As Ronald Reagan would say, it tossed the baby with the dishes.) Liberalism attempted to kill God and replace transpersonal Spirit with egoic humanism, and as much as I am a liberal in many of my social values, that is its sorry downside, this horror of all things Divine.

One of the strengths of typical conservatism is its reliance on Spirit; one of its downsides is that this "spirit" is almost always prerational, mythic, fundamentalist, ethnocentric. As such, conservatives are a little too eager to impose their beliefs and their "family values" on you, and since they have God on their side, they feel quite confident in their agenda. Witch hunts are never far behind the more intense conservative smiles.

The trick is to take the best of both—individual rights plus a spiritual orientation—and to do so by finding liberal humanistic values plugged into a transrational, not prerational, Spirit. This spirituality is transliberal, evolutionary, and progressive, not preliberal, reactionary, and regressive.

It is also political, in the very broadest sense, in that its single major motivation—compassion—is pressed into social action. However, a postconservative, postliberal spirituality is not pressed into service as a public policy (transrational spirituality preserves the rational separation of church and state, as well as the liberal demand that the state shall neither protect nor promote a favorite version of the good life). Those who would "transform" the world by having all of us embrace their new-paradigm, or their particular God or Goddess, or their version of Gaia, or their favorite mythology—those are all, by definition, reactionary and regressive in the worst of ways: preliberal, not transliberal, and thus their particular versions of the witch hunt are never far removed from their global agenda. A truly transliberal spirituality exists instead as a cultural encouragement, a background context that neither prevents nor coerces, but rather allows, genuine spirituality to arise. [See December 10 for further discussion of this topic.]

Michael Lerner is working on this most important issue, and I support him strongly. His organization wanted to give Sex, Ecology, Spirituality its ethics award, but I don't get out much, so we are trying to work out some way for me to do a column in Tikkun. I'm not sure if I can manage it, but it is very tempting.

The cautionary tale. Michael is friends with Bill and Hillary, and his "politics of meaning" was particularly espoused by Hillary. The liberal media found out about it and had a field day. Saint Hillary, Michael was "Hillary's guru," and so on. This was very hard on Michael, and it never really let up until . . . Jean Houston stepped into take the flack. A simple visualization technique, used by thousands of therapists daily, was turned into Hillary's "channeling" Eleanor Roosevelt, whereas all she was doing was creative visualization. But anything interior is so utterly, radically, hideously alien to the liberal media that they could hardly discuss the topic without snickering or choking.

This is why Science and Religion is such a test case, as least as I see it. It is written expressly to take into account the fears of liberals, and attempts to hold their hands on what they must see as Mr. Toad's Wild Ride. The last chapter emphasizes the importance of keeping the gains of the liberal Enlightenment, and outlines a trans-liberal, not anti-liberal, view, which calls for the joining of the Enlightenment of the West (or political freedom) with the Enlightenment of the East (or spiritual freedom). Of course, by "Enlightenment of the East" I mean any truly authentic spiritual transformation, whether East or West, North or South. The point is to take the legal, political, and civil liberties of the modern West and, using that as a protective platform, allow transformative spiritual realization—and its compassion—to flourish. So I see Science and Religion, which ends on that message, as a test case on how far liberals can move in the direction of a transrational spirituality.

Sunday, April 13

Last night I had a date with a really nice woman, very beautiful, Marci Walters. We went to her favorite restaurant, Mataam Fez (Moroccan)—sat on the floor, ate with our fingers, and I tried not to drool on myself. She's a graduate student at Naropa, while holding down two jobs (working with the developmentally disabled). She's been accepted into the Peace Corps when she finishes school. She's a dedicated meditator, lifts weights, has completed over a dozen marathons and six triathlons. If I get out of line I suspect she will simply beat the crap out of me.

Wednesday, April 16

Back on typical schedule. I awaken between three and five, meditate for one or two hours, go straight to my desk and work till one or two P.M. The type of meditation I do varies, but the basic form is "the practice of the morning," or "ultimate guru yoga," where the true nature of one's own mind is the ultimate guru. The practice is: Upon waking, or upon passing from the dream state to the waking state, look directly into the mind, inquire directly into the source of consciousness itself—inquire "Who am I?" if you like, or practice looking directly into the looker. Upon inquiring into the self, the self disappears, dissolving back into radiant Emptiness, and consciousness rests as absolute Freedom, unbounded and unlimited, unborn and undying, unseen and unknown.

Within that vast Emptiness, the subtle soul arises, but you are not that. Within that vast Emptiness, the gross ego arises, but you are not that. Within that vast Emptiness, the gross body, nature, and matter all arise, but you are not those either. You are the radiant I AMness, prior to all worlds but not other to all worlds, which you embrace with a single glance, and your grace will make the sun rise, and the moon will reflect your glory, and you will not exist at all, in this vast expanse of Emptiness, that only alone is.

Thursday, April 17

In that transcendental state, delta presumably is off the wall, and if you keep some sort of access to that mirror-mind or stable witnessing as you enter the waking state, presumably delta waves would also remain operative. This seems to be the case in the videotape; but it is, at any rate, a fertile field of research.

As you "come out" of the causal or unmanifest state—the state of pure cessation, deep dreamless sleep, nirvikalpa samadhi, ayn, jnana samadhi, or pure consciousness without an object, to name a few variations on a theme—you can directly perceive the subtle and mental realms arise, and it is obvious that these subtle realms are a type of condensation or crystallization or contraction of the causal. That is, the subtle realm feels like a gesture of causal spirit, much like, if you make a fist, it is a gesture of your hand.

Likewise, if you remain witnessing, and you then come out of the subtle state—savikalpa samadhi, archetypal illumination, the dream state, creative vision, to name a few variations on that theme—you can directly perceive the gross realm arise, the realm of the physical body, matter, nature, and the gross-reflecting ego which arises in that sensorimotor world. These gross realms likewise feel like a gesture of the subtle: they feel like something the subtle is doing.

The net result of this involutionary arc—where causal spirit contracts into subtle soul, and subtle soul contracts into the gross world of ego and nature—is that the entire manifest world is a gesture of your own primordial awareness, your own Spirit, your own Godhead, your own Original Face. Each and every thing in the Kosmos is thus a manifestation of the Great Perfection, a manifestation of Primordial Purity in all its infinite delight.

Manifestation is not a sin; getting lost in manifestation is. We think that ego and nature are the only realities in the entire Kosmos, and there is our sin and our suffering. We have become lost in the gross movie of life, forgetting that the projector, the light, and the screen are all nothing but forms of the ultimate One Taste, radiant ripples on luminous Emptiness.

When you reestablish even a modest capacity for the mirror-mind or stable witnessing, and you generate a little bit of continuity between states (so you are not always losing consciousness as you pass from state to state, such as from waking to deep sleep), then it starts to become obvious that all states and levels—high or low, sacred or profane, shallow or deep—are in fact the effervescent manifestation of your own primordial Spirit. And therefore all seemingly "lesser" occasions, which the orthodox would consider "sin," become not distractions from Spirit but celebrations of Spirit's exuberant, wild, overflowing, ever-present creativity.

This is the whole point of Tantra, of course: each "defilement"—anger, envy, grasping, ignorance, jealousy—has hidden in its very heart a transcendental wisdom—clarity, equality, openness, all-accomplishing, discriminating. Tantra is based on one uncompromising insight: There is only God. There is only Spirit. There is only Goddess. There is only Tao. Not metaphorically, but literally. As Zen puts it, "That which one can deviate from is not the true Tao." You cannot deviate from It because there is only It—every "deviation" is still nothing but It. (Which is why the books purporting to tell us how we have deviated from the Goddess, or from Tao, or from the true Way, are miles off the mark.)

This is the experience of One Taste, where every single thing and event in the Kosmos, high or low, sacred or profane, has the same taste, the same flavor, and the flavor is Divine. All are gestures of God, which is to say, gestures of your own primordial Perfection, manifestations of your own radiant Emptiness, waves of your own nondual Consciousness. The entire universe will fit in the palm of your hand, you can hold the moon in two fingers, you can give the sun for Christmas presents, and nothing really happens at all.

Friday, April 18

The sunlight is playing off the remnants of snow, scattered everywhere in patches, snuggling under the dark green pines that cozy up against the house. It all arises in the luminous clearing of Emptiness, the spaciousness of Godhead, the unqualifiable expanse of All Space, which is not other than one's own choiceless awareness, moment to moment. There is just this. It blinds me into submission, takes my breath away, forces me to surrender to my own deepest state, where I am totally undone in the Beauty of it all.

That is exactly why Beauty takes on such a profound meaning. In that choiceless awareness, in the utter simplicity of One Taste, all realms— from causal formlessness to subtle luminosity to gross body, mind, and nature—take on a painful beauty, a truly painful beauty. Aesthetics takes on an entirely new importance, aesthetics in all domains—the beauty of the body, the beauty of the mind, the beauty of the soul, the beauty of spirit. When all things are seen as perfect expressions of Spirit, just as they are, all things become deeply, painfully beautiful.

Yesterday I sat in a shopping mall for hours, watching people pass by, and they were all as precious as green emeralds. The occasional joy in their voices, but more often the pain in their faces, the sadness in their eyes, the burdenous slowness of their paces—I registered none of that. I saw only the glory of green emeralds, and radiant buddhas walking everywhere, and there was no I to see any of this, but the emeralds were there just the same. The dirt on the sidewalk, the rocks in the street, the cries of the children, here and there—a paradise in a shopping mall, and who would ever have suspected?

Saturday, April 19

Just got a rather extraordinary letter from Joyce Nielsen [author of *Sex and Gender in Society*]. Six pages, single-spaced, and thoughtful from beginning to end. She refers specifically to the chapter entitled "Integral Feminism" in The Eye of Spirit. In that chapter, I point out that there are at least a dozen schools of feminism, and the only thing they all agree on is that females exist. Otherwise, they possess widely divergent views about what constitutes feminism (and females, for that matter). Using an "all-quadrant, all-level" approach, I try to show that each of these dozen schools stems from, or emphasizes, a different quadrant/level. As such, they all have something important, if limited, to tell us, and the only sane approach is an "integral feminism" that draws upon the strengths of each and jettisons their partialities. So a truly integral feminism would include all four quadrants (intentional, behavioral, social, and cultural)—each of which has preconventional, conventional, and postconventional levels, giving us a truly multidimensional feminism—not flatland, not one quadrant only, not one level only. Anyway, I try to spell this out in The Eye of Spirit, and Joyce says she is appreciative of (and mostly agrees with) this inclusiveness.

Nonetheless, Joyce feels—and here is the main difference she is writing to tell me about—that biological factors are negligible in explaining gender stratification, and worse, to even entertain such ideas, as I do, can help to bring about exactly the stratification we are trying to avoid. I understand her concern, but I do disagree. Besides, I think she is for emphasis exaggerating the role I place on biological sex differences. They are definitely important, in my opinion (that women get pregnant, for example, has an enormous influence in the productive roles of men and women in agrarian societies—and the fact of pregnancy is not itself a social construction). But I do not think that biology is the only, or even the most important, factor. In addition to the biological differences in the sexes (Upper Right), there are the social forces (Lower Right), individual differences (Upper Left), and background cultural values (Lower Left). Culturally constructed values play a tremendous role in gender stratification—I emphasize that strongly—but I refuse, with the constructivists, to reduce all other quadrants to that quadrant. All four are equally important.

Perhaps Joyce can be persuaded to look over volume 2 (Sex, God, and Gender: The Ecology of Men and Women) when I write it. I'm hoping she can help prevent me from making a total ass of myself, although this will be asking an awful lot of her.

Monday, April 21—Denver

Marci and I spent the weekend in Denver, at the Oxford Hotel, in an area called LoDo (LOwer DOwntown), deliberately modeled on SoHo. I love this place, and love this antiquated hotel. The old Union Railroad Station, eight stories high and half a block long, is right across the street. Around the corner is a branch of the Tattered Cover bookstore, which several news organizations have labeled the finest bookstore on the planet. My friend Dave Query—who was the chef on Malcolm Forbes's yacht for two years—has just opened Jax restaurant next door. There are dozens of art galleries, stores, cafés, bars, restaurants. . . . It really is like a little cross-section of SoHo.

Especially for the last five or six years, I have become fascinated with aesthetics, with beauty in any domain, which I attribute directly to meditative awareness. The great contemplative traditions did not hate this world, they strove mightily to bring beauty into it (along with compassion, clarity, and care). Think of the great Zen gardens, the exquisite illumined manuscripts of medieval mysticism, the stunning architectural beauty of everything from the Taj Mahal to Angkor Wat. The true nondual mystics are not haters of this world, but celebrators of it. Grace, said St. Thomas, perfects nature, it does not obliterate it.

Physical aesthetic beauty is simply one of the ways that Spirit shines in and through the sensorimotor world. And for many people—this was Thomas Mann's point—for many people, seeing something physically beautiful is the closest they will ever get to the Beauty of the Divine. It's a little miniature version, a little reduced version, of the infinite Beauty that is the radiant Face of God. Reduced, yes, but still a ray of the Divine. Plato's Symposium, of course, is a reminder that we can start with this ray of physical beauty and use it to climb back to a vision of the Good, the ultimate Beauty itself.

But in this country we have this sad, aggressive, puritanical, merely ascending notion that aesthetic beauty—in architecture, in people, in clothing—is somehow a sin. What a sorry notion.

The other side is equally true, of course. For many people in this country, physical beauty is all there is. We know of no higher beauty—the beauty of a mental vision, the stunning beauty of archetypal illumination, the blissful painful excruciating beauty of the true and radiant soul, the beauty beyond beauty that is the infinite unmanifest. And so we worship fashion models. And they all marry rock stars or sports figures—good lord, will the depth never cease?

I like the LoDo precisely because of the aesthetics; it's just beautiful, and therefore a beautiful reminder. Marci and I had a grand time—art galleries, bookstores, carefree cappuccinos, naked bodies in the night. Marci wanted some new makeup, and settled on Dior, so the saleswoman and I struck up a conversation about the Brit John Galliano taking over Dior instead of Jean-Paul Gaultier; I was for Jean-Paul, she for John; but then, she works there. Martinis in the Cruise Bar, huge salads at Jax. When you spend so much time at a desk, these are wonderful pleasures.

Tuesday, April 22—Boulder

Sam called and said Shambhala is planning on bringing out my collected works, starting next year. I believe they are going to release all the volumes at once. Here are the tentative contents at this point:

Vol. 1—The Spectrum of Consciousness and No Boundary
Vol. 2—The Atman Project and Up from Eden
Vol. 3—A Sociable God and Eye to Eye
Vol. 4—Transformations of Consciousness and miscellaneous papers (including intros to The Holographic Paradigm and Quantum Questions)

Sunday, April 27

Another Naropa seminar at my house. These seminars usually last for three or four hours, and follow a Q&A format. Mostly I like to hear the students' confusions, because it gives me clues to issues I need to address in my writing. They also point out problems they have with my work, which helps me clarify it.

This time the students were particularly interested in the Witness. We're videotaping these seminars now; here are a few excerpts:

· · ·

I know I've talked about witnessing awareness persisting through waking, dreaming, and deep sleep. But the Witness is fully available in any state, including your own present state of awareness right now. So I'm going to talk you into this state, or try to, using what are known as "pointing out instructions." I am not going to try to get you into a different state of consciousness, or an altered state of consciousness, or a nonordinary state. I am going to simply point out something that is already occurring in your own present, ordinary, natural state.

So let's start by just being aware of the world around us. Look out there at the sky, and just relax your mind, let your mind and the sky mingle. Notice the clouds floating by in the sky. Notice that this takes no effort on your part. Your present awareness, in which these clouds are floating, is very simple, very easy, effortless, spontaneous. You simply notice that there is an effortless awareness of the clouds. The same is true of those trees, and those birds, and those rocks. You simply and effortlessly witness them.

Look now at the sensations in your own body. You can be aware of whatever bodily feelings are present—perhaps pressure where you are sitting, perhaps warmth in your tummy, maybe tightness in your neck. But even if these feelings are tight and tense, you can easily be aware of them. These feelings arise in your present awareness, and that awareness is very simple, easy, effortless, spontaneous. You simply and effortlessly witness them.

Look at the thoughts arising in your mind. You might notice various images, symbols, concepts, desires, hopes, and fears, all spontaneously arising in your awareness. They arise, stay a bit, and pass. These thoughts and feelings arise in your present awareness, and that awareness is very simple, effortless, spontaneous. You simply and effortlessly witness them.

So notice: you can see the clouds float by, because you are not those clouds—you are the witness of those clouds. You can feel bodily feelings, because you are not those feelings—you are the witness of those feelings. You can see thoughts float by, because you are not those thoughts, you are the witness of those thoughts. Spontaneously and naturally, these things all arise, on their own, in your present effortless awareness.

So who are you? You are not objects out there, you are not feelings, you are not thoughts—you are effortlessly aware of all those, so you are not those. Who or what are you?

Say it this way to yourself: I have feelings, but I am not those feelings. Who am I? I have thoughts, but I am not those thoughts. Who am I? I have desires, but I am not those desires. Who am I?

So you push back into the source of your own awareness. You push back into the Witness, and you rest in the Witness. I am not objects, not feelings, not desires, not thoughts.

But then people usually make a big mistake. They think that if they rest in the Witness, they are going to see something, or feel something, something really neat and special. But you won't see anything. If you see something, that is just another object—another feeling, another thought, another sensation, another image. But those are all objects; those are what you are not.

No, as you rest in the Witness—realizing, I am not objects, I am not feelings, I am not thoughts—all you will notice is a sense of Freedom, a sense of Liberation, a sense of Release—release from the terrible constriction of identifying with these puny little finite objects, your little body and little mind and little ego, all of which are objects that can be seen, and thus are not the true Seer, the real Self, the pure Witness, which is what you really are.

So you won't see anything in particular. Whatever is arising is fine. Clouds float by in the sky, feelings float by in the body, thoughts float by in the mind—and you can effortlessly witness all of them. They <u>all</u> spontaneously arise in your own present, easy, effortless awareness. And this witnessing awareness is not itself anything specific you can see. It is just a vast, background sense of Freedom—or <u>pure Emptiness</u>—and in that pure Emptiness, which you are, the entire manifest world arises. You <u>are</u> that Freedom, Openness, Emptiness—and not any itty bitty thing that arises in it.

Resting in that empty, free, easy, effortless witnessing, notice that the clouds are arising in the vast space of your awareness. The clouds are arising within you—so much so, you can taste the clouds, you are one with the clouds, it is as if they are on this side of your skin, they are so close. The sky and your awareness have become one, and all things in the sky are floating effortlessly through your own awareness. You can kiss the sun, swallow the mountain, they are that close. Zen says "Swallow the Pacific Ocean in a single gulp," and that's the easiest thing in the world, when inside and outside are no longer two, when subject and object are nondual, when the looker and looked at are One Taste. You see?

MAY

A kind of waking trance I have frequently had, quite up from my boyhood, when I have been all alone. This has generally come upon me through repeating my own name two or three times to myself silently, till all at once, as it were out of the intensity of the consciousness of individuality, the individuality itself seemed to dissolve and fade away into boundless being; and this is not a confused state, but the clearest of the clearest, the surest of the surest . . . , utterly beyond words, where death was an almost laughable impossibility, the loss of personality (if so it were) seeming no extinction, but the only true life.

—ALFRED, LORD TENNYSON

Friday, May 2

The sunlight is playing with the drops of rain, turning each into colored diamonds, which explode with energy as they fall to earth. They are talking to each other as they fall, I think, but then, I know better than that.

The Eye of Spirit was the first time since Transformations of Consciousness that I could cover the field of developmental psychology and spirituality, bringing my work up to date (and comparing it with many important and recent contributions by others). It was also a chance to write even more explicitly about my own spiritual life and try to convey, once again, the radiance of always-already truth. I also included chapters on philosophy, anthropology, epistemology, meditation, and feminism, all from an integral perspective. And finally, a long essay I had written on art and its interpretation, which is perhaps my favorite single piece of all my writings. Its genesis is interesting.

I had for some time been working on "hermeneutics"—the art and science of interpretation, or how we discover the meaning of a statement, the meaning of last night's dream, the meaning of mathematics, of a work of art, a play, a movie, or anything, really. Even right now, what does this sentence mean? Meaning, you know, hermeneutics. And it's not so easy to figure out. A staggering number of factors go into our ability to understand any sort of meaning at all—and therefore to understand life, or God, or literature, or even each other. I had found a way, or so it seemed, to unite signifier (the written word), signified (its interior meaning), syntax (its formal rules), and semantics (its cultural background) into an integral view of symbolic meaning and interpretation.[8] This also led to certain specific conclusions about art and how to interpret it.

At about the same time, several previously unseen Andrew Wyeth paintings had surfaced from an anonymous art collector—which was something of a big deal—and, concomitant with the international Olympics in Atlanta, a large exhibition was planned. They asked me to write the art essay for the companion volume, and I was glad to oblige.[9] I think they asked me because they were positively sick of the standard postmodernist "theory," which embarrassingly talks about everything but the actual artwork. So I took a strange and novel approach, for an art theorist, and wrote about art.

I first gave a brief historical overview of the major schools of art and its interpretation—including representational, intentional-expressivist, symptomatic, formalist, and reception-and-response. I then tried to show that—using holons,[10] the spectrum of consciousness, and the four

8. This integral theory of semiotics is outlined in *The Eye of Spirit*, chap. 5, n. 12.
9. "How Shall We See Art?," in *Andrew Wyeth: America's Painter*, by Martha R. Severens with an essay by Ken Wilber (New York: Hudson Hill Press, 1996). Reprinted in *The Eye of Spirit*, chaps. 4 and 5.
10. A holon is a whole that is also a part of other wholes. The universe is basically composed of holons: a whole atom is part of a molecule, the whole molecule is part of a cell, the whole cell is part of an organism, the whole organism is part of an ecosystem, and so on. Holons are organized holarchically, with each higher holon transcending but including its juniors: organisms contain cells which contain molecules which contain atoms—*but not vice versa*, hence the

quadrants—all of these schools could be integrated in a very precise way. Moreover, the interpretive tools of each of them would then have a useful place in the repertoire of the integral interpretation of any piece of art.

And then the conclusion: if science gives us objective Truth, or the "it" of Spirit, and morals give us the Good, or the "we" of Spirit, then Beauty—which is in the "eye" of the beholder—helps open us to the "I" of Spirit. The essay ended:

> Think of the most beautiful person you have ever seen. Think of the exact moment you looked into his or her eyes, and for a fleeting second you were paralyzed: you couldn't take your eyes off that vision. You stared, frozen in time, caught in that beauty. Now imagine that *identical* beauty radiating from every single thing in the entire universe: every rock, every plant, every animal, every cloud, every person, every object, every mountain, every stream—even the garbage dumps and broken dreams—every single one of them, radiating that beauty. You are quietly frozen by the gentle beauty of everything that arises around you. You are released from grasping, released from time, released from avoidance, released altogether into the eye of Spirit, where you contemplate the unending beauty of the Art that is the entire World.
>
> That all-pervading Beauty is not an exercise in creative imagination. It is the actual structure of the universe. That all-pervading Beauty is in truth the very nature of the Kosmos right now. It is not something you have to imagine, because it is the actual structure of perception in all domains. If you remain in the eye of Spirit, every object is an object of radiant Beauty. If the doors of perception are cleansed, the entire Kosmos is your lost and found Beloved, the Original Face of primordial Beauty, forever, and forever, and endlessly forever. And in the face of that stunning Beauty, you will completely swoon into your own death, never to be seen or heard

hierarchy (or holoarchy). The Great Chain is also a holarchy composed of holons: spirit transcends but includes soul, which transcends but includes mind, which transcends but includes body. Each senior holon enfolds, envelops, and embraces its juniors, and this is the very nature of whole/parts, holons, and holarchy: nests of increasing wholeness and embrace.

from again, except on those tender nights when the wind gently blows through the hills and the mountains, quietly calling your name.

Monday, May 5—Denver

Marci and I spent the weekend in Denver again. Back to LoDo, back to the Oxford, back to some sort of aesthetic wonder.

I tend to follow pop culture closely—music, books, movies, fashion, fads—first, because I enjoy it; second, to spot the zeitgeist, the general cognitive structure serving as a background that organizes average or popular perception—and the only way you can spot this is by following popular culture. The broad trend now is a slow movement from modern rational to postmodern aperspectival, and nowhere can this be seen more clearly than in pop culture, especially fashion.

Giorgio Armani, for example, is pure modernist—sleek, sparse, elegant, beautiful, often in monotones. Versace and Gaultier, on the other hand, are quintessentially postmodern—wild, exuberant, pluralistic, disheveled, diversity on the verge of fragmentation, trying to find a unity, close to falling apart. The central cognitive structure of postmodernity has been called integral-aperspectival (which I also call vision-logic): "aperspectival," because no particular perspective is privileged, and "integral" because nonetheless some sort of coherence has to be found or the whole thing falls apart. This, for example, is Frank Gehry's brilliance; he is a towering genius of postmodernism; he produces stunning examples of integral-aperspectival vision: his architectural designs are a collection of curving, twisting, pluralistic pieces right on the verge of dissociating and completely flying apart, and yet they are all inevitably, miraculously brought together into an exquisitely whole and unified form—a true integral-aperspectival vision, a true "unity-in-diversity."

The problem with much of postmodernism is that it has initially been so taken with diversity, it has forgotten the unity, and so it simply falls into fragmented pieces, jerking and choking in their own isolated little worlds. This is simply the pathological form of integral-aperspectival, a pathology I call aperspectival madness—all diversity, no unity: schizophrenic fragments. And almost all of postmodernism, so far, is not much more than aperspectival madness, awaiting the emergence of the truly

great geniuses—like Gehry, but in other fields as well—who will unify the fragments, connect the unconnected, reweave the fabric of a reality ripped to shreds by the mindless diversity movements.

Well, to hell with all that. I think I'm falling in love.

Sunday, May 11—Boulder

Mother's Day, called Mom. She's such a dear, but she's infuriated with Tony Schwartz's chapter on me in What Really Matters, because Tony made some passing Freudian Oedipal comments about her. She hopes the book suffers a horrible fate and nobody ever, ever buys it. Otherwise, she's doing fine. After my visit with them last year, both Mom and Dad are now lifting weights—they're in their seventies. I took them to a gym and got them signed up, and they love it.

Got an essay from Michael Zimmerman, the great Heidegger scholar—and a wonderful man, bright, witty, sincere. He spoke at the kw conference in San Francisco last year, and I hear he was the audience favorite. The essay is "Heidegger and Wilber on the Limitations of Spiritual Deep Ecology." Michael is a sympathetic and profound ecological theorist, as evidenced in his book Radical Ecology. But he also is cognizant of the major limitations of most forms of "spiritual ecology."

From the essay: "In my opinion, Wilber achieves a great deal in his analysis of modernity, retro-romanticism, and the ecological crisis. He manages to include much of what is worthwhile in Heidegger's views about the transcendent domain, while discarding the anti-modernist sentiments that led Heidegger into such political trouble [collaborating with the Nazis]. Moreover, Wilber's view of the transcendent includes important aspects of spiritual traditions that Heidegger either rejected or adopted in truncated ways. Wilber's contention that modernists and environmentalists alike adopted the materialistic world-system of modern science allows him to conclude that nothing good will come of well-meaning efforts to 're-sacralize' nature, unless the transcendent dimension of nature, humankind, and the divine is first rediscovered and reaffirmed."

Nice as that is, today, anyway, all it does is seem to throw me into doubt and sadness. "I remain convinced that Wilber has made an enormous contribution to the contemporary discussion of the divine, nature,

and humanity. In particular, he has something important to say both to modernists and to spiritual deep ecologists: that the way beyond ecological crisis lies in solving the crisis of meaning created by the adoption of a one-dimensional materialist ontology [i.e., flatland]. Wilber makes clear that this crisis cannot be solved by a spasm of life-denying transcendentalism and otherworldly longing, but rather by developing a multi-dimensional [i.e., integral] non-dual ontology that allows room for what has so long been excluded. A truly deep spiritual ecology would acknowledge the depth dimension of reality, rather than maintaining that the material natural system—the 'web-of-life'—exhausts the infinite dimensions of the divine. Wilber is playing an important role in the process of generating such a deeply spiritual ecology."

It just makes me sad. For some reason, all I am thinking about right now is what a slim chance any of this has in making any sort of difference at all. Not just my work, but any of the truly integral writers—Zimmerman's own good work, Roger, Frances, Tony, Jack, Murph, and crew; it's just so empty out there, it seems. I am totally at home in Emptiness, but emptiness just sucks.

Monday, May 12

On the spur of the moment, Marci and I have decided to take a short vacation. I haven't had a real vacation in, well, many years. Manhattan and San Francisco were fun, but they were work, and I did anything but relax. Since I am not specifically writing now, but plowing through research reading, I don't mind, in the least, missing a few days of that.

We need a place that fits several difficult requirements. Marci and I both like sun and sand and beach. But since I spend most of my time working alone, away from people, I also want to be in the middle of a crowd, rubbing elbows and getting jostled. We also both like culture as much as nature, so we'd like an urban center close by. I don't just want to lie in the sun, I want to suck auto fumes and have people yelling at me. What fun is a vacation without a genuine possibility of getting shot at, or at least mugged? And finally, since both Marci and I spend our days studying depth, we want, as a change of pace, something utterly superficial, glitzy, shiny and vapid.

No question about it. We're on our way to South Beach, Miami.

Sunday, May 18—South Beach

Oh, this is glorious. What a riot. In our real lives, South Beach is every-thing we don't want, and less. Which is to say, it's perfect.

Actually, it's very, very beautiful. South Beach is the southern twenty blocks or so of Miami Beach; it used to be quite run down and dilapi-dated, but has, in the last decade, undergone a spectacular development, mostly under the influence of the jet set, modeling agencies, movie stars, and megabucks. Madonna owns the restaurant in the Delano Hotel; Sly Stallone owns a dance club; Michael Caine runs the Brasserie; Versace's house on Ocean Drive looks like an embassy. There are over two dozen restored Art Deco hotels, all brightest of neon and softest of pastels, all simply gorgeous. The hotels face the ocean, which is right across the street, which is pure sandy sand with no rocks or shells to tear the feet. The ocean, unlike most Atlantic Ocean water, is not cold steel gray blue, but beautiful aqua green and turquoise, and it makes me happy just to look. The ocean flickers and floats in transparency, no substance here but scintillation, luminous arising, shimmering ornaments on primordial awareness, the mind and the world are not-two, here on the edge of the earth.

We check into the Cavalier, which is the hip hotel on Ocean Drive, and it is, shall we say, way cool. Everybody in South Beach is gay, or a model, or an actor, or all three. The hotels alternate with superb and adorable restaurants, most of which have sidewalk cafés, so you can sit and watch the half-naked bodies go by. Marci, getting into the swing of things, has her navel pierced. She's now an official Gen-Xer. We alter-nate stays on the beach with restaurant sampling, bar hopping, boutique shopping, and outright gawking. We are both determined to drink a bottle of wine a day—her, hearty triathlon red; me, sissy dry white. Goodbye Witness, hello cruel world.

Each day we hit the beach around eleven A.M. and stay until around four P.M. This is truly one of the nicest beaches I've ever seen. Besides being pure sand—you can wade out forever and never hit a rock or shell—the water temperature is perfect, somewhere around eighty de-grees, so you never get chilled, no matter how long you stay in. And, as a matter of fact, I spend about three hours in the water each day, exactly up to my neck, gently bobbing up and down, tiptoes barely touching the bottom to hold me up. Marci, a champion swimmer, swims circles around me, literally. Where does that woman hide all her muscles? She's too curvaceous to be this athletic. Don't triathlon women have, like, 0% body fat? Actually, aren't they in negative fat space? Don't they like owe the world some fat?

I had fully expected to lose all access to the Witness, given our vino schedule. And for the first night and day this happened. But floating in the water has not only brought back the Witness, it seems to have facilitated the disappearance of the Witness into nondual One Taste, at least on occasion. (The Witness, or pure witnessing awareness, tends to be of the causal, since there is usually a primitive trace of subject/object duality: you equanimously Witness the world as transparent and shimmering object. But with further development, the Witness itself disappears into everything that is witnessed, subject and object become One Taste, or simple Suchness, and this is the nondual estate. In short: ego to soul to pure Witness to One Taste.) So I am utterly, pleasantly surprised, floating here in nature's blood, to be dipped into One Taste, which in this case, is nicely salty.

There is no time in this estate, though time passes through it. Clouds float by in the sky, thoughts float by in the mind, waves float by in the ocean, and I am all of that. I am looking at none of it, for there is no center around which perception is organized. It is simply that everything is arising, moment to moment, and I am all of that. I do not see the sky, I am the sky, which sees itself. I do not feel the ocean, I am the ocean, which feels itself. I do not hear the birds, I am the birds, which hear themselves. There is nothing outside of me, there is nothing inside of me, because there is no me—there is simply all of this, and it has always been so. Nothing pushes me, nothing pulls me, because there is no me—there is simply all of this, and it has always been so.

My ankle hurts from dancing last night, so there is pain, but the pain doesn't hurt me, for there is no me. There is simply pain, and it is arising just like everything else—birds, waves, clouds, thoughts. I am none of them, I am all of them, it's all the same One Taste. This is not a trance, or a lessening of consciousness, but rather an intensification of it—not subconscious but superconscious, not infra-rational but supra-rational. There is a crystal-clear awareness of everything that is arising, moment to moment, it's just not happening to anybody. This is not an out-of-the-body experience; I am not above looking down; I am not looking at all; and I am not above or below anything—I am everything. There is simply all of this, and I am that.

Most of all, One Taste is utter simplicity. With mystical experiences in the subtle and causal, there is often a sense of grandeur, of ominous awesomeness, of numinous overwhelmingness, of light and bliss and beatitude, of gratefulness and tears of joy. But not with One Taste, which is extraordinarily ordinary, and perfectly simple: just this.

I stay here, neck deep in water, for three hours. How much of it I spend as ego, as Witness, or as One Taste, I don't know. There is always the sense, with One Taste, that you have never left it, no matter how confused you get, and therefore there is never really the sense that you are entering it or leaving it. It is just so, always and forever, even now, and even unto the ends of the world.

But in this particular now, it is time for early dinner, and for the ugly business of moving this particular bodymind from one place to another. Besides, I'm sure Marci is going to get something else pierced, and no-body—ego, soul, or God—wants to miss that one.

Tuesday, May 20—South Beach

For a change of pace, we move from the Cavalier to the Casa Grande; both are fabulous. The Cavalier is hot and hip, the Casa Grande is ele-gant. But none of them are mega-hotels like a Hyatt or Four Seasons; they are, like most of the hotels in South Beach, relatively small Art Deco buildings, three or four stories high, at most, and all a type of quaint chic.

Day before we went boutique shopping—we both liked the Nicole Miller shop, but there are a dozen terrific little shops in the area. Heated discussion with the sales folks over who the hottest new designer was—I was championing Tom Ford, who has taken over the stodgy old house of Gucci and is causing a major sensation (especially for an American); his clothes, for both men and women, are stunning, sexy, sleek, and elegant. They, the fools, were for Galliano. Marci likes Isaac Mizrahi, because we saw Unzipped and she thought he was adorable (and has "fun fun colors"). It's too bad Hollywood has made Armani a cliché, because there's still nothing like him; he's a modernist genius, bulwark against the goofier elements of postmodernism in La Croix, Gaultier, Versace, Dolce & Gabbana, although many of their designs I definitely like. But postmodernism has yet to produce its genius in fashion, the way it has in architecture with Gehry, although Gaultier verges on it; and who knows, Galliano or McQueen might yet pull it off. Great dinner—some sort of fish, can't remember exactly, why I don't know—oh yes, the wine.

Then last night, we were standing in front of Versace's house, and we met a really nice couple, struck up a conversation, and all went to dinner together. In the course of the evening it became obvious that the woman—these people were very bright and perceptive but somewhat conservative—was going to get a tattoo. The more she drank, the more certain she became.

We went to the same place that pierced Marci's navel. I guess it's sort of an all-purpose body mutilation store. Disfigurations Are Us, I suppose. Marci was hilariously egging the woman on: "Oh look at this great American eagle," pointing to an image the size of a dinner plate. I started getting nervous for the woman. "Oh gee, look at this nice little heart"—about the size of a pea. She settled on the heart, and two minutes later, done.

Monday back on the beach, but this time, no Witness and no One Taste, just a slightly hungover ego. But the water is exquisite, and we eat sandwiches and drink beer and fry in the sun on this largely topless beach. Marci is not only going topless, she is getting more and more into the spirit of South Beach, which is to say, no spirit at all, just bright and shiny and down and dirty. That night, she decides to have both nipples pierced. I give a very serious let's-be-responsible speech, and then we both rush right over to Mutilations Are Us. A hundred dollars later—and a few images I will not soon forget—and Marci's got two nipple rings, which look sorta like two towel holders coming at me. (Every time I tell this to baby boomers, they get alarmed, disgusted, or slightly nauseous; every Gen-Xer says, "Cool!")

We fly back tomorrow, but it's been a scream. And Marci is a wonderful traveling companion. She never gets angry, she's genuinely happy and delighted with life, she's very sincere but not in the least serious. On the plane, looking down, I watch the ocean shimmering in Emptiness, a wonderful dream vacation—literally, a dream.

Sunday, May 25—Boulder

Another Naropa seminar. Topics the students raised included compassion versus idiot compassion, the pre/trans fallacy, meditation and neurosis, the startling anger of several theorists when you try to bring up an integral view. . . . A few excerpts:

STUDENT: I was discussing an integral view with some other students, and they said that because I was making judgments I was showing a real lack of compassion. I didn't think I was.

KW: Yes, there is probably more confusion about this issue than any other in spiritual circles. Basically, most of the trouble comes from confusing compassion with idiot compassion, which are the terms Trungpa Rinpoche used for this crucial distinction. We in this country—and especially in new-age circles—have a type of tepid egalitarianism and political correctness that says no view is really any better than another, and therefore all views are to be cherished equally, as a sign of rich diversity. If we don't make any judgments about better or worse, then we are showing real compassion. So we have judgmental versus compassionate, and that is the common understanding.

But, you see, that stance is a massive self-contradiction. On the one hand, it says that all views are equally part of a rich diversity, and thus no view is better than another. On the other hand, it strongly claims that this view itself is <u>better</u> than the alternatives. So this "compassion" states that no view is better than another, <u>except its own view</u>, which is <u>superior</u> in a world where nothing is supposed to be superior at all. It is a ranking that denies ranking and a judgment that all judgments are bad. So, although it is often truly well-intentioned, it's nonetheless a type of hypocrisy, because it is strongly doing that which it condemns in everybody else.

That hypocrisy has nothing to do with real compassion; in fact, that is idiot compassion. Idiot compassion thinks it is being kind, but it's really being very cruel. If you have an alcoholic friend and you know that one more drink might kill him, and yet he begs you for a drink, does real compassion say that you should give it to him? After all, to be kind you should give him what he wants, right? Who are you to impose your views on him, right? Giving him the drink would therefore show compassion, yes? No. Absolutely not.

Real compassion includes wisdom and so it makes <u>judgments</u> of care and concern: it says some things are good, and some things are bad, and I will choose to act only on those things that are informed by wisdom and care. Giving a severe alcoholic a case of whiskey because he wants it and you want to be "kind" is not being kind at all. It is showing idiot compassion, not real compassion.

Zen calls this the difference between "grandmother Zen" and "real Zen." In order to awaken from the dream of samsara, the ego itself must be really kicked around, often severely. Otherwise you will simply continue to play your favorite games. Grandmother Zen doesn't challenge you. In order to be "kind," grandmother Zen will let you sleep a little late if you want, and stop meditating early if you don't like how it's going, and allow you to wallow in you. But real Zen uses a very big stick, and lots of loud yelling, and there are occasionally broken bones and certainly shattered egos. Real compassion kicks butt and takes names, and it is not pleasant on certain days. If you are not ready for this fire, then find a new-age, sweetness-and-light, soft-speaking, perpetually smiling teacher, and learn to relabel your ego with spiritual-sounding terms. But stay away from those who practice real compassion, because they will fry your ass, my friend. What most people mean by "compassion" is: please be nice to my ego. Well, your ego is your own worst enemy, and anybody being nice to it is not being compassionate to you.

Now maybe you and I aren't accomplished masters, and so maybe we don't always know what is real compassion and what is not. But we must <u>start</u> to try to learn to exercise real compassion instead of idiot compassion. We need to learn to make <u>qualitative distinctions</u>. These are hierarchical judgments that involve the ranking of values. If you don't like hierarchy, well, fine, that is <u>your</u> hierarchy: you hierarchically value nonhierarchies more than you value hierarchies. That's fine with me, just be honest enough to correctly label what you are really doing. If you don't like value rankings and want to avoid them, then fine, <u>that</u> is your value ranking—you rank nonranking as better than ranking— and that itself is a ranking, <u>your</u> ranking. At least be honest about this. The fact is, ranking is unavoidable in values, so at least do it consciously, honestly, and above board, and stop this hypocritical stance that you are being "nonjudgmental," which itself is a colossal judgment.

STUDENT: But isn't choiceless awareness without judgments?

KW: Choiceless awareness accepts absolutely <u>everything</u> that arises, including <u>both</u> judging and not judging. You see, nonjudgmental is itself a <u>choice</u> between two opposites—judging versus not judging—which is why "nonjudgmental" is not at all the same as choiceless awareness. Choiceless awareness is the absolute mirror that effortlessly reflects whatever arises—it does <u>not</u> try to chose not-judging versus judging.

Choiceless awareness really refers to what the Buddhists call <u>absolute</u> *bodhichitta*, or Emptiness; whereas making judgments is referred to as <u>relative</u> *bodhichitta*, or compassion. This means real compassion, not idiot compassion, and real compassion uses wisdom to make judgments! <u>So in neither case</u>, absolute or relative, is "nonjudgmental" a wise stance. In the absolute, we rest in Emptiness, which doesn't care if we make judgments or not, since both arise equally in pure Emptiness. In the relative, we make judgments based on wisdom and compassion, and that means judgments based on qualitative distinctions, value rankings, and depth.

So when you hear somebody saying they are being "nonranking" and "nonjudgmental," run! We need to learn to <u>consciously</u> make qualitative distinctions. We need to make judgments, based on degrees of depth. Idiot compassion has nearly destroyed this field, and made genuine spiritual progress difficult indeed.

STUDENT: These people jumped all over me for making qualitative judgments, and they were really sanctimonious. . . .

KW: Well, you know, there is a big difference between making qualitative judgments and being obnoxious. So my advice, when you run into this, is to first check your own attitude and check your own motivation. It does no good for us to also get sanctimonious. You know, we have the real compassion and those schmucks have the idiot compassion. We can all get caught in this; I know I do. It's judgment bereft of skillful means, and that's just obnoxious. So watch out for that. But you said you were attacked because you were talking about the importance of a more integral view?

STUDENT: Yes.

KW: That's a special problem. A good rule of thumb is that people are not going to expand their present views or outlooks by much more than 5% at any given time. So if you are trying to push a very big picture at them, they are probably going to shut down, and maybe get angry, and then start calling you names—you lack compassion, you're arrogant, etc. If you keep pushing, then at that point it really is your problem. Maybe your ego is enjoying shoving this down their throats. I know I've done that on occasion, and it helps nothing. Anyway, if you are really trying to help—real compassion—then don't put more in the spoon than can be swallowed, yes?

Also, remember that belief systems are not merely beliefs—they are the home of the ego, the home of the self-contraction. Even a holistic belief, like the web-of-life, <u>always</u> houses the ego, because beliefs are merely <u>mental</u> forms, and if the <u>supramental</u> has not been discovered, then any and all mental constructions house a tenacious ego. When you challenge any belief system, the separate-self experiences that as a death threat and a death seizure, and this will engage all its survival instincts. You are not just discussing the truth or falsity of a theory—you are engaged in a life and death struggle. Whenever we do this, we're dealing with a cornered rat—in others and in ourselves, so watch out.

STUDENT: Why is idiot compassion so popular?

KW: Oh, because it does not threaten anything. It's rampant in so many spiritual circles because the ego does not fundamentally want to be challenged. It wants grandmother Zen. So the ego will pay big money for a weekend workshop that will "empower" the ego, tell it that it is really God or Goddess, give it a new concept to think about and call "spirit," plug it into the "web-of-life" and promise ultimate unity from that merely mental idea. In fact, the huge market in spiritual books in this country is basically motivated by one intense drive: the boomers want to be told that their ego is God, their self-contraction is Spirit. The self-contraction is simply relabeled "sacred" and grandmother Zen smiles on all.

But I don't think any of those approaches are bad or mean-spirited or anything like that at all. I just think they are a little bit confused. I think that because they don't have a very comprehensive map of the Kosmos, they get a little sidetracked in their noble search. So the hope is that a more integral view will help clear up some of this confusion.

STUDENT: Why is an integral view so threatening to so many people?

KW: Well, it almost always demands much more than a 5% expansion of beliefs, and few will follow that.

STUDENT: I was shocked at the anger that came up at me.

KW: Yes, that's unfortunate. I used to think that if you took approach A, approach B, and approach C, and showed how all of them are equally important, they would all be very grateful and thank you profusely. In fact, A and B and C all tend to get very annoyed with you, because you have just demonstrated that their field is not the only important field in existence. As soon as you show that Freud, Piaget, and Buddha are all important for understanding consciousness, Buddhists will say, Why are you trashing Buddhism? As soon as you show that gross-realm nature, subtle-level soul, and transcendental spirit are all important, ecologists will say, Why do you hate nature?

Of course, let me add, some people might react negatively to an integral view because it's wrong! I mean, it's possible that those of us who believe in a more integral view might simply be mistaken, and so of course sane and rational people will react negatively to it. So we always have to keep that possibility in mind. It's not automatic that they are threatened because we're right and they're wrong—it could be the other way around.

Tuesday, May 27

Worked all morning, reading, reading, reading. Marci and I went grocery shopping and then worked out together. The family that pumps iron together . . . stays together? Ends up in the emergency room together?

Wednesday, May 28

The tenth anniversary issue of the Noetic Sciences Review recently came out. For it, they asked me to write a summary and overview of the last decade of consciousness studies. They followed this with responses by Alwyn Scott, Duane Elgin, Jeanne Achterberg, Peter Russell, and Will Keepin. The responses were all very thoughtful and perceptive, and I think the entire issue was quite well done, thanks largely to the efforts of the executive editor, Barbara McNeill, and managing/associate editors David Johnson, Carol Guion, Christian de Quincey, and Keith Thompson.

The editors introduce the discussion: "In a special overview of the field of consciousness studies for our tenth anniversary Review, Wilber outlines 12 key components of a truly integral approach to this most challenging topic of our times." And, well, that's more or less what I tried to do—outline a dozen different fields of consciousness studies, all of which need to be brought together in an integral view. I summarized the twelve main schools: cognitive science, introspectionism, neuropsychology, individual psychotherapy, social psychology, clinical psychiatry, developmental psychology, psychosomatic medicine, nonordinary states of consciousness, Eastern and contemplative traditions, quantum consciousness approaches, and subtle energies research. The point was:

"What I have observed in the field of consciousness studies (as elsewhere), is that consciousness researchers tend to choose one or two of those approaches very early in their careers, usually under the influence of a significant mentor, organization, or academic department. And, human nature being what it is, it is then extremely difficult for them to embrace, or sometimes even acknowledge, the existence of the other approaches. Evidence that supports their position is avidly accumulated; evidence that does not is ignored, devalued, or explained away.

"But what if, instead, we make the following assumption: the human mind is incapable of producing 100 percent error. In other words, nobody is smart enough to be wrong all the time.

"That would mean, very simply, that each of those dozen approaches cannot contain only error; put positively, each of them has something extremely important and valuable to say. And that means, inescapably, that we will measure our progress toward a truly integral orientation based precisely on our capacity to include, synthesize, and integrate all twelve of those important approaches. It is clearly a daunting challenge; but it is equally clear that anything less than that simply cannot claim the adjective 'integral.' "

After a long discussion of that theme, the essay concludes:

"How far down this integral path are we? In the last decade, although there have been some significant exceptions, we have mostly had twelve pieces all claiming to be the whole pie.

"In a series of books (particularly *The Eye of Spirit*), I have attempted to outline one version of an integral theory of consciousness that explicitly includes those twelve major approaches. But what is important is not my particular version of an integral view, but rather that we all begin to enter into this extraordinary dialogue about the possibility of an integral approach in general, an approach that—we can say this in several different ways—integrates the hard-headed with the soft-hearted, the natural sciences with the noetic sciences, objective realities with subjective realities, the empirical with the transcendental.

"And so let us hope that a decade from now somebody might spot a great mega-trend in consciousness studies—namely, the truly integral—and let it start right now with all of us who share this concern for holism, for embrace, for synthesizing, for integrating: let this outreach start with us, right here, right now.

"Is a genuinely integral theory of consciousness even possible? Well, that would be my question to you all, and that would be my challenge. How big is our umbrella? How wide and how deep can we throw our net of good will? How many voices will we allow in this chorus of consciousness? How many faces of the Divine will smile on our endeavor? How many colors will we genuinely acknowledge in our rainbow coalition?

"And when we pause from all this research, and put theory temporarily to rest, and when we relax into the primordial ground of our own intrinsic awareness, what will we find therein? When the joy of the robin sings on a clear morning dawn, where is our consciousness then? When the sunlight beams from the glory of a snow-capped mountain, where is consciousness then? In the place that time forgot, in this eternal moment without date or duration, in the secret cave of the heart where time touches eternity and space cries out for infinity, when the raindrop pulses on the temple roof, and announces the beauty of the Divine with every single beat, when the moonlight reflects in a simple dewdrop to remind us who and what we are, and when in the entire universe there is nothing but the sound of a lonely waterfall somewhere in the mists, gently calling your name—where is consciousness then?"

Thursday, May 29

The world arises quietly this morning, shimmering on a radiant sea of transparent Emptiness. There is only this, vast, open, empty, clear, nakedly luminous. All questions dissolve in this single Answer, all doubts resolve in this single Shout, all worries are a ripple on this Sea of equanimity.

This One Taste is compatible with any and all worlds, but, paradoxically, it is happiest when it sings of holistic embrace. Which is why the whole point of an integral theory of consciousness is to include and integrate all levels in all quadrants—or simply all levels in the Big Three of I, we, and it; or first-person, second-person, and third-person accounts of consciousness.

We have a huge war now raging between the first-person or introspective accounts (which emphasize the immediate introspection of the mind's contents as they display themselves to your own awareness) and the third-person or objective/scientific accounts (which seek to translate all of consciousness into objective entities or "its" disclosed by empirical science). Both of them overlook the importance of second-person accounts—the intersubjective domain of linguistic structures, moral contexts, shared semantics, and cultural backgrounds, without which neither "I" nor "it" can be recognized in the first place. On the other hand, the humanities and cultural studies emphasize nothing but cultural backgrounds, as they attempt to reduce all subjective awareness (of "I") and all objective knowledge (of "its") to nothing but cultural constructions (of "we").

All three of those approaches are wrong, because all three are right—partially right, that is, and all three need to be brought equally to the integrative table. I am aware of nobody taking a similar integral approach (embracing equally first-, second-, and third-person realms), except, of course, the smartest man on the face of the planet, Jürgen Habermas. But Habermas doesn't allow for any of the transrational, transpersonal domains, so he is all-quadrant but not all-level, or so it seems to me.

At any rate, I specifically spelled out this approach in The Eye of Spirit and more technically in "An Integral Theory of Consciousness," which was published by the Journal of Consciousness Studies. This is an exceptional journal, only been out four years, and yet it has already become the central focal point for these important discussions, involving luminaries such as John Searle, Daniel Dennett, Francisco Varela, John Eccles, Roger Penrose, David Chalmers, the Churchlands, etc. The front cover of this particular issue says: "Taxonomy or Taxidermy?," which is very clever: is consciousness to be accepted and categorized as real (taxonomy) or is it dead meat (fit only for taxidermy)?

Saturday, May 31

In meditation this morning, instead of resting in choiceless, clear, ever-present awareness—a standard "nonpractice"—I did an old yabyum tantra visualization (technically, anuttaratantra yoga)—"old," because I used to do this a lot—which involves the transformation of sexual energy into radiant bliss and compassionate embrace. These are all mostly subtle-level practices (they start at psychic, lead to subtle, and occasionally dissolve into causal. Rarely do they reach nondual One Taste or *sahaja*, but they are exemplary exercises for the development of the psychic-to-subtle domains). The standard core of this type of practice is summarized as "Bliss cognizing Emptiness arises as compassion."

It goes like this. In meditation, you visualize yourself in sexual union with your consort. You visualize yourself and your consort as a god or goddess, angel or bodhisattva, buddha or saint—whatever works as a symbol of your deepest or highest nature. But you must visualize very intensely and very clearly you and your consort as transparent radiant divinities, making love. You actually become sexually aroused, and you coordinate this with breathing: on the in-breath, you breathe Light down the front of the body to the genitals, seat of Life; on the out-breath, you breathe Life up the back of the body—up the spine—into Light at and above the crown of the head. (This is just another version of involution/evolution, or the higher entering into the lower, and then the lower returning to the higher, forming a great circle of descending and ascending energy. If you are doing this with an actual partner, you can coordinate breathing.)

Any pleasure that is generated in the genital region is, with the out-breath, directed up the spine and released into the Light at the crown of the head—you simply breathe any pleasure in the body directly into and above the crown of the head, the home of infinite Light and Release. Then, on the in-breath, you directly breathe Light down and into the body—especially down the frontal line of the body, face to throat to chest to stomach to the base of the genitals. And so the cycle goes, bringing heavenly Light down and into earthly Life, and then returning Life to Light—thus uniting downward Agape and upward Eros, Descending and Ascending, Compassion and Wisdom, with every breath you take.

As your entire bodymind becomes full with circulating pleasure-bliss, you simply but directly take any bliss that is present and use it to meditate on Emptiness—or on the absolute Mystery of existence, or on the simple Transparency of the world, or on God as unqualifiable expanse—whatever works for you. In practice, a simple way to do this is to rest as I-I—rest as the great Seer which cannot itself be seen, the pure Witness that is completely open and empty. And then, resting as I-I, allow bliss to expand into that open and empty space that you now are—allow bliss to expand and fill the infinity of the I-I that you are. The sky of your awareness becomes filled with the bliss of the divine union that you are.

When you are in this state of the spacious bliss of I AMness, and you are full to infinity, with no desires and no wants, allow a gentle, small, ripple of a thought to arise: I vow to liberate all sentient beings into this free and open space. And with that, a ripple of compassion arises out of this vast ocean of bliss. That compassion is literally composed of this infinite empty bliss, it is made of it, as waves are of the ocean. Compassion is infinite empty bliss in action.

And so: bliss cognizing emptiness arises as compassion—in other words, bliss recognizing and reconnecting with its own divine ground (spirit or emptiness) is moved to extend this liberating and ecstatic grace to all beings, and so it arises as compassion in the service of others.

I get out of bed, make breakfast, go back to work.

JUNE

Why are you unhappy?
Because 99.9 percent
Of everything you think
And of everything you do,
Is for yourself—
And there isn't one.
        —WEI WU WEI

Sunday, June 1

T George Harris and Kate Olson just stopped by. Kate, a producer for the "Jim Lehrer News Hour" on PBS, is largely responsible for getting some very good spiritual segments on the air, such as those on Father Thomas Keating, the Dalai Lama, etc. Kate is a wonderful person—very bright, attractive, dedicated to spiritual practice—so we hang out whenever we can.

T George is in the process of trying to start up a national magazine on spirituality. I suppose if anybody can do it, he can. He was responsible for starting Psychology Today, which, as long as he was running it, was an extraordinary publication. It seemed that everybody was reading it; it was a real lifeline to so many of us. That was twenty years ago; I still have many of my copies. George then started American Health magazine, and now he's working on Spirituality and Health. He's in his seventies, and, like Huston Smith, a real role model for not letting age intimidate you.

We sit out on the balcony, overlooking the plains, and begin to nibble lunch. The standard discussion that T George and I have is about how to make the magazine accessible and popular, but also include some real depth and sophistication. It's a standard commercial dilemma—the more depth in the product, the smaller the audience, usually. My lame contribution is to layer the magazine, with many departments simple and accessible, but several that are advanced and demanding. Lame, because how do you actually do that? Anyway, George is still working on getting funding; he says right now he's negotiating with Time Warner. I hope something comes of it, because we really need a national forum for an authentic spirituality.

So we have a long discussion focused on the pre/trans fallacy. The pre/trans fallacy—which was introduced in The Atman Project and elaborated in an essay called "The Pre/Trans Fallacy" (included in Eye to Eye)—is a simple concept. It says that because both pre-rational and trans-rational are non-rational, they are easily confused. And then one of two very unfortunate things happens: either mature, spiritual, transrational states get reduced to infantile, prerational states; or infantile, narcissistic, prerational states get elevated to transrational glory. Reductionism and elevationism. Freud was a typical reductionist, who tried to reduce profound nondual mystical states to primary narcissism and infantile oceanic fusion: The Future of an Illusion. And Jung was a typical elevationist, who often took prerational myth and elevated it to transcendental greatness.

(A myth is a story that, for the most part, is always taken to be literally and concretely true by its believers: Moses really did part the Red Sea, Jesus really was born of a biological virgin, etc. When, on the other hand, myth is consciously used in an allegorical, symbolic, or interpretive fashion, it is actually drawing on higher cognitive faculties, reason to vision-logic, and, in that mode, occasionally stands open to transpersonal glimmers. Unless otherwise specified, when I refer to myth, I mean concrete-literal myths, which are generally prerational.)

It used to be that the real threats to genuine spiritual studies were the reductionists, but an even greater threat has surfaced from the new-age movement, namely, the elevationists. These folks, with many good and decent intentions, nonetheless take some rather infantile, childish, egocentric states and, simply because they are "nonrational," relabel them "sacred" or "spiritual," which is definitely a problem.

Real growth goes from prerational to rational to transrational; from subconscious to self-conscious to superconscious; from preconventional to conventional to postconventional; from prepersonal to personal to transpersonal; from id to ego to God. But under confusion of the pre/trans fallacy, pre is often getting elevated to trans, and a narcissistic immersion is taking the place of the demanding process of genuine growth and transformation.

Alas, it seems to me, much of the "spiritual renaissance" supposedly sweeping this country is really a case of prerational regression, not transrational growth. This is deeply worrisome. Prerational acting out is being confused with transrational awareness; preverbal feeling and impulse are being elevated to transverbal insight; premoral ego-license is confused with transmoral Self; preconventional nature is promoted to postconventional Spirit; prerational id is confused with transrational God.

This entire package of "Spirit" is being sold by publishers and book clubs at an astonishing rate. But the notion that we are entering a genuinely "integral culture" or a "spiritual renewal" is a little bit dubious, I'm afraid. William Irwin Thompson estimated that about 80% of this "spiritual" renaissance was prerational, and less than 20% was transrational. I tend to agree, but it's really much worse than that. My own analysis indicates that the truly transrational is less than 1% of the population.[11] Studies consistently show that the percentage of those reaching the highest stages of <u>personal</u> development is less than 5%—imagine how fewer there are that go <u>even further</u> into the realms of <u>transpersonal</u> development!

In any event, this is a marketing nightmare, and this is what T George and Kate and I discuss. If the majority of the "spiritual market" is drawn to prerational magic and myth, how do you reach the small group who are involved in genuine, laborious, demanding, transrational spiritual practice? This is very difficult, because both markets are referred to as "spiritual," but these two camps really don't get along very well—one is mostly translative, the other is mostly transformative, and they generally disapprove of each other—so how do you put them into one magazine

---

11. See *The Eye of Spirit*, chapters 9 and 10, for an extended discussion of this theme.

without alienating them both? More than that, a large portion of those involved in prerational pursuits genuinely wish to open themselves to authentic, transpersonal, transrational states, so it's very important to make room for everybody. T George is alive to this issue, which is good, because this is going to be <u>the</u> marketing difficulty for boomer spirituality.

Monday, June 2

Early morning, the orange sun is slowly rising, shining forth in empty luminous clarity. The mind and the sky are one, the sun is rising in the vast space of primordial awareness, and there is <u>just this</u>. Yasutani Roshi once said, speaking of satori, that it was the most precious realization in the world, because all the great philosophers had tried to understand ultimate reality but had failed to do so, yet with satori or awakening all of your deepest questions are finally answered: it's <u>just this</u>.

Tuesday, June 3

And we worry about the state of art in the postmodern world? From the magazine 5280:

"When '60 Minutes' aired a report on the ridiculous world of postmodern art, Morely Safer noted an eight-foot ashtray—filled with real cigarette and cigar butts—as one of the most outrageous examples of what passes for art these days. As a postscript, Safer noted that the piece was recently purchased by the Denver Art Museum for $60,000."

And we worry about business ethics in today's world? Reported in <u>Men's Health</u>:

"Quality to Exhibit at Work: *Best*: Loyalty. In a recent survey of chief executives, 86 percent of them said they valued that attribute the most in their subordinates. *Worst*: Integrity. Only 3 percent valued that the most."

Wednesday, June 4

Worked all morning; decided to go jogging down behind my house. If you remain as the Witness while you run, you don't move, the ground does. You, as the Witness, are immobile—more precisely, you have no qualities at all, no traits, no motion and no commotion, as you rest in the vast Emptiness that you are. You are aware of movement, therefore you as the Witness are not movement. So when you run, it actually feels as if you are not moving at all—the Witness is free of motion <u>and</u> stillness—so the ground simply moves along. It's like you're sitting in a movie theater, never moving from your seat, and yet seeing the entire scenery move around you.

(This is easy to do when you're driving down the highway. You can simply sit back, relax, and <u>pretend</u> that you are not moving, only the scenery is. This is often enough to flip people into the actual Witness, at which point you will simply rest as choiceless awareness, watching the world go by, and you won't move at all. This <u>motionless</u> center of your own pure awareness is in fact the <u>center</u> of the <u>entire</u> Kosmos, the eye or I-I of the Kosmic cyclone. This motionless center—there is only one in the entire world and it is identical in all beings, the circle whose center is everywhere and whose circumference, nowhere—is also the center of gravity of your soul.)

This is why Zen will say, "A man in New York drinks vodka, a man in Los Angeles gets drunk." The <u>same</u> Big Mind is timelessly, spacelessly, present in both places. So drinking in New York and getting drunk in L.A. are the same to the motionless, <u>spaceless</u> Witness. This is why Zen will say, "Without moving, go to New York." The answer: "I'm already there."

As the Witness, I-I do not move through time, time moves through me. Just as clouds float through the sky, time floats through the open space of my primordial awareness, and I-I remain untouched by time and space and their complaints. Eternity does not mean living forever in time—a rather horrible notion—but living in the <u>timeless</u> moment, prior to time and its turmoils altogether. Likewise, infinity does not mean a really big space, it means completely <u>spaceless</u>. As the Witness, I-I am spaceless; as the Witness, I-I am timeless. I-I live in eternity and inhabit infinity, simply because the Witness is free of time and space. And <u>that</u> is why I can drink vodka in New York and get drunk in L.A.

So this morning I went jogging, and nothing moved at all, except the scenery in the movie of my life.

Thursday, June 5

As scholars from Ananda Coomaraswamy to Huston Smith have pointed out, the core of the perennial philosophy is the Great Chain of Being, the Great Nest of Being. But it is now apparent that there are at least four major inadequacies to the Great Chain as it was traditionally conceived, and in order to bring it into the modern and postmodern world—and develop a truly integral approach—these shortcomings need to be carefully addressed.

The Great Chain is traditionally given as matter, body, mind, soul, and spirit [figure 1, page 44]. Many traditions subdivide this considerably. For example, the soul is often divided into psychic and subtle levels, and spirit into causal and nondual. An expanded Great Nest would therefore include: matter, body, mind, soul (psychic and subtle), and spirit (causal and nondual).

That is fine. But those levels are supposed to include all of reality. Yet as stated, they mostly apply to just the Upper Left quadrant (the spectrum of interior consciousness)—and that's the first inadequacy. Thus, as I have often tried to point out, each of the vertical levels of the Great Chain needs to be differentiated into four horizontal dimensions (the four quadrants). So in addition to the subjective spectrum of consciousness, we need to add objective correlates (the Upper Right quadrant), intersubjective cultural backgrounds (Lower Left quadrant), and collective social systems (Lower Right) [see figures 1, 2, and 3]. Otherwise the Great Chain cannot withstand the blistering critiques that modernity has (correctly) leveled at it.

For example, the great traditions rarely understood that states of consciousness (Upper Left) have correlates in the organic brain (Upper Right), a fact that has revolutionized our understanding of psychopharmacology, psychiatry, and consciousness studies. Likewise, the traditions evidenced little understanding that individual awareness (Upper Left) is profoundly molded by both its background cultural worldviews (Lower Left) and the modes of techno-economic production (Lower Right) in which it finds itself. This left the Great Nest open to devastating critiques from modern biological science, from Marxists, and from cultural and historical studies, among others, all of which demonstrated that consciousness is not merely a disembodied, transcendental noumenon, but is deeply embedded in contexts of objective facts, cultural backgrounds, and social structures. The Great Chain theorists had no believable response to these charges (precisely because they were deficient in these areas). Only as body, mind, soul, and spirit are differentiated into the four quadrants (or simply the Big Three), can these objections be handled.[12]

The second inadequacy is that the level of mind itself needs to be subdivided in the light of its early development. Here the contributions of Western psychology are decisive. To put it in a nutshell, the mind itself has at least four major stages of growth: magic (2–5 yrs), mythic (6–11 yrs), rational (11 onward), and integral-aperspectival or vision-logic (adulthood, if then).

If we put all this evidence together, drawing on the East and West alike, then a more complete Great Nest of Being would include these ten spheres, each of which enfolds its predecessor(s) in a development that is envelopment:

1. Sensorimotor—the physical body, the material level, the physiosphere.
2. Emotional-sexual—biological drives, sensations, perceptions, feelings; life energy, élan vital, libido, prana, bioenergy.
3. Magic—the early form of the mind ("preop," or early symbols and concepts), where subject and object are poorly differentiated. It is marked by egocentrism, artificialism, animism, anthropocentrism, and word magic. Because inside and outside are poorly differentiated, physical objects are imbued with human egoic intentions. Likewise, the narcissistic ego believes that it can directly and magically alter the world (Saturday morning children's cartoons are largely of the magical structure: superheroes can move mountains just by a glance; they can fly, melt steel, zap enemies, and otherwise push the world around by sheer magical power). It short, because subject and object are not yet clearly differentiated, the magical ego treats the world as an extension of itself and imbues the world with its own egoic traits. Narcissism and egocentrism rule.
4. Mythic—an intermediate level of mind ("conop," or the concrete rule/role mind), where magical power is shifted from the ego to a

12. See *The Marriage of Sense and Soul* for a discussion of this topic.

host of mythic gods and goddesses; if the ego cannot miraculously alter the world at will, the gods and goddesses can. In magic, the ego _itself_ always has the power to perform miracles; in myth, the power to perform miracles is always possessed by a great Other, in a very _concrete-literal_ way (e.g., Jehovah really did part the Red Sea). Thus magic uses _rituals_ to display its own miraculous power; myth uses _prayer_ in an attempt to get the god or goddess to perform the miracle for it. Myth is nonetheless the beginning realization that the ego cannot itself magically push the world around; it is thus a lessening of narcissism, a diminution of egocentrism.

5. _Rational_—a highly differentiated function of the mind ("formop," or formal reflexive) that dispenses with concrete-literal myths and attempts instead to secure its needs through evidence and understanding. Neither egocentric magic nor mythic god figures are going to miraculously intervene in the course of Kosmic events just to satisfy your egoic desires. If you want something from the Kosmos, you are going to have to understand it on its own terms, following its own evidence; the birth of a truly scientific attitude, another lessening of narcissism.

6. _Vision-logic_—the highest function of the gross-realm mind; a synthesizing, unifying mode of cognition. Vision-logic does not achieve unity by ignoring differences but embracing them—it is integral-aperspectival—it finds universal pluralism and unity-in-diversity.

7. _Psychic_—the beginning of the transpersonal, supra-individual, or spiritual realms. This level is often marked by an intense mystical union with the entire gross realm—the realm of nature, Gaia, the World Soul. The home of _nature mysticism._

8. _Subtle_—the subtle realm proper is the home, not of gross-realm mythological god and goddess figures focused on your ego, but of directly cognized, vividly intense, and ontologically real Forms of your own Divinity. The home of genuine _deity mysticism._

9. _Causal_—the causal realm per se, the formless unmanifest, nirvikalpa, nirvana, pure Emptiness, the Abyss, ayn. The root of the Witness. The home of _formless mysticism._

10. _Nondual_—this is both the highest _Goal_ of all stages, and the ever-present _Ground_ of all stages. The union of Emptiness and Form,

Spirit and World, Nirvana and Samsara—One Taste, sahaja samadhi, turiyatita. The home of integral or <u>nondual mysticism</u>.

That is a much more complete Great Chain or spectrum of consciousness (a more complete Upper Left quadrant).[13] Each of those levels actually has four dimensions or four quadrants, but even on its own, this
more complete Great Nest allows us to do several important things at
once:

- Stop elevating magic and mythic to psychic and subtle. This elevation of magical narcissism to transcendental awareness is perhaps
  the single defining characteristic of much of the new-age movement,
  however well intentioned it often is.
- Stop confusing mythological stories with direct and immediate
  transpersonal awareness. This elevation of myth to subtle illumination is common in countercultural spirituality.
- Stop confusing magical indissociation with holistic vision-logic. This
  elevation of magical cognition, which <u>confuses</u> whole and part, to
  the status of vision-logic, which <u>integrates</u> whole and part, is prevalent in eco-primitivism (or the belief that foraging tribes integrated
  self, culture, and nature, whereas—as theorists from Lenski to Habermas to Gebser have pointed out—they actually failed to clearly
  differentiate them in the first place).
- Stop confusing the biosphere, bioenergy, and prana (level 2) with
  the World Soul (level 7). This elevation of ecology to World Soul is
  often one of the defining characteristics of ecopsychology, ecofeminism, and deep ecology. (It often joins the previous confusion—that
  of magic with vision-logic—to recommend a retro-embrace of foraging or horticultural worldviews).

---

13. For this simplified account, I am not distinguishing between basic structures,
    transition structures (such as worldviews), or self-fulcrums. See the November
    16 entry for a short overview, and *The Eye of Spirit* for a detailed presentation.
    At the same time, this simple summary is more than adequate for the following
    discussion. Incidentally, the levels themselves are defined by the basic structures
    of each level (sensorimotor, rule/role cognition, formal reflexive, vision-logic,
    etc.). Each of those levels has a particular worldview (magic, mythic, rational,
    existential, etc.), and I often use those more accessible terms to describe the
    level itself. But basic structures and worldviews should not be confused. See
    November 16.

Those examples could be multiplied almost indefinitely. Suffice it to say that, with a more complete Great Holarchy of Being, we can in fact spot the regressive nature of many movements. Thus the great wisdom traditions, when complemented by Western psychology, help us to move forward, not backward.

Here is the problem, correctable by Western developmental psychology: In the traditional depiction of the Great Chain (e.g., matter, body, mind, psychic, subtle, causal, and nondual), the "mind" level almost always meant the logical or rational faculty, and anything nonrational had to be placed on the higher, transrational levels because the early prerational stages of development were poorly understood. These early, prerational levels can be grasped only by an intense investigation of infant and child development, an almost exclusive contribution of the modern West.

In other words, the traditional Great Nest (in Christianity, Hinduism, Buddhism, Sufism, Taoism, paganism, Goddess worship, etc.) was—and most definitely still is—open to massive pre/trans fallacies, because it has no way to differentiate magic and mythic from psychic and subtle— they all get placed in the transpersonal/transrational domain. This unfortunate confusion was responsible, in no small measure, for the Western Enlightenment's complete and total rejection of spirituality, since so much of it (and the Great Chain) was obviously full of dogmatic magic and myth. The West officially tossed the bathwater of prerationality, but it also, unfortunately, tossed the transrational baby with it.

The third inadequacy: Because the traditional Great Chain theorists had a poor understanding of the early, infantile, prerational stages of human development, they likewise failed to grasp the types of psychopathologies that often stem from complications at these early stages. In particular, psychosis can often stem from problems at stages 1–2; borderline and narcissistic disorders, stages 2–3; and psychoneurosis, stages 3–4.[14]

Western depth psychology has amassed compelling evidence for these pathologies and their genesis, and the Great Chain needs desperately to be supplemented with these findings. As it is, every time the Great Chain

---

14. See *Transformations of Consciousness* for a discussion of the spectrum of psychopathology. See September 10, note 17, for the role of neurophysiology.

theorists were confronted with a case of mental madness—and lacking an understanding of the prerational stages—they were <u>forced</u> to assume it was a wild descent of transrational God, whereas it was, more often than not, a frightening resurgence of prerational id. These poor deranged people were rarely God-intoxicated, they were borderline basket cases. Treating them as God-realized is right up there with sacred cows—and did <u>nothing</u> to assuage modernity's suspicion that <u>all</u> of spirituality is a nut case. If babbling idiots and cows are enlightened, why listen to Eckhart and Teresa and Rumi, either?

The fourth inadequacy in the traditional Great Chain is its lack of understanding of evolution, an understanding that is also a rather exclusive contribution of the modern West. The funny thing—as many theorists have pointed out—is that if you tilt the Great Chain on its side and let it unfold in time—instead of being statically given all at once, as traditionally thought—you have the outlines of evolution itself. Plotinus temporalized = evolution.

In other words, evolution to date—starting with the Big Bang—has unfolded approximately three-fifths of the Great Chain, in precisely the order predicted—insentient matter to living bodies to conceptual mind (or physiosphere to biosphere to noosphere). All that is required is to see that the Great Chain does not exist fully given and statically unchanging, but rather evolves or develops over great periods of time, with each of the higher levels emerging through (not from) the lower. And the fact is, despite the bluff of western biologists, nobody really understands how higher stages emerge in evolution—<u>unless</u> we assume it is via Eros, or Spirit-in-action.

Evolution in the <u>cultural</u> domain is, of course, a politically incorrect topic, which almost certainly means it is true. Numerous theorists have come around to this view. In recent times, cultural evolution has been championed, in various ways, by Jürgen Habermas, Gerald Heard, Michael Murphy, W. G. Runciman, Sisirkumar Ghose, Alastair Taylor, Gerhard Lenski, Jean Houston, Duane Elgin, Jay Earley, Daniel Dennett, Robert Bellah, Erwin Laszlo, Kishore Gandhi, and Jean Gebser, to name a few. The pioneering work of Jean Gebser is paradigmatic for the lot: he sees cultural worldviews evolving—to use his words—from <u>archaic</u> to <u>magic</u> to <u>mythic</u> to <u>mental</u> to <u>integral</u>. Sound familiar?

The point is that, once the Great Chain is plugged into an evolution-ary and developmental view, it can happily coexist with much of the God of the modern West, namely, evolution.[15] Moreover, it raises the stunning possibility: if evolution has thus far unfolded the first three-fifths of the Great Chain, isn't it likely that it will continue in the coming years and unfold the higher two-fifths? If that is so, God lies down the road, not up it; Spirit is found by going forward, not backward; the Garden of Eden lies in our future, not our past.

Those are four inadequacies of the Great Chain of Being that have thoroughly prevented it from being accepted by modernity (it doesn't cover the four quadrants; doesn't take early, prerational development into account, and thus is open to massive pre/trans fallacies; doesn't understand early pathologies; doesn't grasp evolution). Conversely, repairing those deficiencies can—and I believe will—make the Great Holarchy fully compatible with modern research, evidence, and infor-mation, thus uniting the best of ancient wisdom with the brightest of modern knowledge—and this is precisely the essence of the integral ap-proach.

I can't help but think of Huston here. The Great Chain is his legacy, the one idea that he has fought the hardest to introduce into the modern world. But if the Great Chain is indeed to survive, it will have to be in this refurbished and reconstructed and integral form.

Friday, June 6

Outlining the Great Nest [in the above entry], it dawns on me, yet again, how tiresome it is to write of the levels of consciousness in third-person it-language. Useful (and necessary) as that is, it is rather beside the point. I'm going to write a piece—I think I'll call it "Anamnesis"—where each level is described from within, in first-person I-language: not what each level looks like, but what the world looks like from each level.

Saturday, June 7

Worked all morning, went grocery shopping, lifted weights. Back at my desk, and I see my little fox friend. He has taken to living under my

---

15. For an extensive discussion of this theme, see *The Marriage of Sense and Soul*.

porch, so I toss him eggs every now and then. A few months ago I found out he has a girlfriend, because I was working and they both came up and sat down outside my window—I looked up and they were staring at me. They were adorable; they looked like twins. I haven't seen her lately, though, I wonder where she is.

Sunday, June 8

This morning, only vast Emptiness.
I-I is only, alone with the Alone, all in All.
Fullness pushes me out of existence,
radiance blinds me to the things of this world,
I see only infinite Freedom,
which means I see nothing at all.
There is a struggle to reanimate the soul,
to crank consciousness down and into the subtle,
to pull it down into ego and body,
and thus get out of bed at all.
But the Freedom is still there,
in this little twilight dawn,
and Release inhabits even
the smallest moves to make manifest
this glorious Estate.

Thursday, June 12

Interview with Scott Warren. Scott is a graduate student with Michael Mahoney, author of the superb Human Change Process (and literally hundreds of other publications of exceptional merit). Scott is also a dedicated Zen practitioner and transpersonal psychologist, so I agreed to meet with him. A few excerpts:

SW: What's your typical day like? What's your schedule?
KW: I wake up around three or four A.M., meditate for one or two hours, and I'm at my desk around five or six. I work pretty much non-stop until around two P.M. Then I lift weights for an hour or so. I run errands, and eat dinner around five. I then go out, usually to a movie,

or watch a movie at home, hang out with friends, or do correspondence and light reading, make phone calls, go to bed around ten. If I'm seeing somebody, we spend evenings together.

sw: When you say work until two, what is the work like?

kw: Well, this depends on whether I'm researching or writing. If I'm researching, it's plain old-fashioned homework—you just read and read and read. I usually try to go through two to four books a day, which means I skim through them very quickly, making a few notes where necessary. If I find a really important book, then I'll slow down and spend a week or more with it, taking extensive notes. Really good books I'll read three or four times.

When I'm writing, it's a little different. I work at a very intense pace, in some sort of altered state, where I seem to process information at a frightening rate. I'll sometimes put in fifteen-hour days. In any event it's truly exhausting, physically exhausting, which is the main reason I took up weightlifting.

sw: How long does it take to write a book?

kw: My usual pattern of writing is, I read hundreds of books during the year, and a book forms in my head—I write the book in my head. Then I sit down and enter it on computer, which usually takes a month or two, maybe three.

sw: So all these books took a few months to write?

kw: Yes, except Sex, Ecology, Spirituality. That book took me three years, really excruciating years. But the amount of actual writing time itself was still fairly short, several months.

sw: Why excruciating? What happened?

kw: Well, if you think about a book like The Spectrum of Consciousness or The Atman Project, those were difficult books to conceive because you're trying to fit together dozens of different schools of psychology. But those books only covered the Upper Left quadrant. In SES I was trying to pull together dozens of disciplines in all four quadrants, and this was a seemingly unending nightmare. So I really closed in on myself, and for three years I lived exactly the type of life that many people think I live all the time—namely, I really became a hermit. In fact, apart from grocery shopping and such, I saw exactly four people in three years. It turned out to be very close to a traditional three-year silent retreat. It was by far the most difficult voluntary thing I've ever done.

sw: Didn't you go nuts?

kw: The worst part came about seven months into the retreat. I found that what I missed most was not sex, and not talking, but skin contact—simple human touch. I ached for simple touching, I had what I started calling 'skin hunger.' My whole body seemed to ache with skin hunger, and for about three or four months, each day when I finished work, I would sit down and just start crying. I'd cry for about half an hour. It just really hurt. But what can you do in these cases except witness it? So eventually a type of meditative equanimity started to develop toward this skin hunger, and I found that this very deep need seemed to burn away, at least to some degree, precisely because of the awareness I was forced to give it. After that, my own meditation took a quantum leap forward—it was shortly thereafter that I started having glimpses of constant consciousness, or a mirrorlike awareness that continued into the dream state and the deep sleep state. All this of came about, I think, because I was not allowed to act on this skin hunger, I was forced to be aware of it, to bring consciousness to it, to witness it and not merely act it out. This skin hunger is a very primitive type of grasping, a very deep type of desire, of subjective identity, and by witnessing it, making it an object, I ceased identifying with it, I transcended it to some degree, and that released my own consciousness from this most ancient of biological drives. But it was a very rocky roller-coaster ride for a while.

sw: Okay, some theoretical questions. Based on extensive cross-cultural references, you have divided transpersonal or spiritual development into four higher waves or realms, which you call psychic (which centers on the gross waking state), subtle (which centers on the subtle dream state), causal (which centers on the deep formless state), and nondual (which integrates all of them). This also gives four different types of spiritual experience: nature mysticism, deity mysticism, formless mysticism, and nondual mysticism.

kw: That's basically correct, yes. But the idea is to bring all of them into awareness, so that a basic wakefulness and choiceless awareness pervades all realms of life—waking, dreaming, sleeping—at which point you are known, appropriately enough, as an Awakened One, which really means, very ordinary, just this.

sw: Many of the transpersonal and spiritual therapists I know use your material in a very rational way. They say that the only thing they have to do is memorize your higher stages. They don't think they need to take up a spiritual practice, like Zen or yoga or centering prayer, because you've already given all the results.

kw: They don't practice because of me? Good lord, that is exactly the opposite of what I intended. I constantly emphasize that you have to take up a practice, an injunction, to actually see and understand these higher stages of development. Tell me you're kidding.

sw: Seriously, they think that memorizing your stages is all they need in order to be a good transpersonal therapist.

kw: Well, I couldn't disagree more. That's like saying, I have drawn a nice map of the Bahamas, and so now you don't need to actually go to the Bahamas for your vacation, you can just sit in your living room and look at the map. This is horrible. You cannot be a tour guide of the Bahamas if you have never been there.

sw: The common practice, when you find it, seems to be a type of bodily focusing and sensory awareness. This sensory body awareness seems to be confused with spiritual awareness.

kw: Yes, that's very common, and it is a mistake. Sensory body awareness is very important, but it is not the same as spiritual awareness. To begin with, nondual or spiritual awareness is "bodymind dropped"—that is, you cease identifying exclusively with the bodymind and its thoughts and feelings. Those are still present and fully functioning, but in addition to those, you find a more expansive identity with all of manifestation—and focusing on your body will definitely not cover that.

sw: These therapists say that experiential bodily focusing results in the same state as enlightenment.

kw: Yikes. It's true that meditation often starts with bodily awareness—following the breath, focusing on various bodily sensations and feelings—but it never simply stays there. Meditative awareness—the capacity to evenly witness or give bare attention to whatever arises—eventually extends from a few minutes to several hours, and, during intensives, for most of the day. Once you can stabilize witnessing for most of the day, that mirrorlike meditative awareness will then extend into the dream state and something like lucid dreams, and from there it will extend into deep dreamless sleep, so that one will finally discover turiya, the "fourth state," which is the pure Witness above and beyond the three states of waking, dreaming, and sleeping, and then turiyatita— "beyond the fourth," which means One Taste, or the ever-present awareness or constant consciousness or basic wakefulness or choiceless awareness that transcends and includes all possible states and is therefore confined to none. This is not a Witness but a Nondual consciousness that is not other than radical Spirit itself. To say that all of this is found in waking, experiential, bodily focusing is wildly off the mark. Likewise, you find none of this constant consciousness in the writings of deep ecology, ecofeminism, neopaganism, Jungian, web-of-life, ecopsychology, or new-paradigm theorists—which means, whatever else they are doing—and I'm a fan of much of their work—they are not dealing with constant consciousness, mirror awareness, or ever-present nondual Spirit.

sw: Well, that's my next question. Another common approach to spiritual therapy is a type of systems theory thinking, or Gaia thinking, or ecopsychology, or web-of-life theories, and so on. The idea is that if you begin to think holistically, you will get better. And the final idea is that Gaia or the web-of-life is Spirit itself.

kw: But, you see, the web-of-life is just a concept, just a thought. Ultimate reality is not that thought, it is the Witness of that thought. Inquire into this Witness. Who is aware of both analytic and holistic concepts? Who or what in you right now is aware of all those theories? The answer, you see, lies in the direction of this Witness, not in the direction of all those objects of thought. Whether they are right or wrong is beside the point. The point is the Self, the Witness, which itself is actually pure Emptiness. If an analytic concept arises, we witness that; if a holistic concept arises, we witness that. The ultimate reality is in the Witness, not in the concepts, right or wrong. As long as you are trying to work at the level of thoughts and concepts and ideas and images, you will never get it.

sw: Pure consciousness is pure Emptiness?

kw: Yes, radical consciousness is unqualifiable, which can be metaphorically indicated by saying that pure consciousness is pure Emptiness. But I repeat, Emptiness is not a concept, it is a simple and direct awareness. Look, right now you can see various colors—that tree is green, the earth over there is red, the sky is blue. You can see color, so your awareness itself is colorless. It's like the cornea of your eye, which is clear—if the cornea were red, you wouldn't be able to see red. You can see red because the cornea is "red-less" or colorless. Just so, your present consciousness sees color and is therefore itself <u>colorless</u>. You can see space, so your present consciousness is <u>spaceless</u>. You are aware of time, because your consciousness is <u>timeless</u>. You see form, your consciousness is <u>formless</u>.

So your basic, immediate consciousness—not the objects of consciousness, but consciousness itself, the witnessing awareness—is colorless, formless, spaceless, timeless. In other words, your basic and primordial awareness is unqualifiable. It is <u>empty</u> of form, color, space, and time. Your consciousness, right now, is pure Emptiness, and yet an Emptiness in which the entire universe is arising. The blue sky exists in your consciousness, right now. The red earth exists in your consciousness, right now. The form of that tree exists in your consciousness, right now. Time is flowing by in your consciousness, right now.

So the entire world of Form is arising in your own Formless awareness right now. In other words, Emptiness and Form are not-two. They are both One Taste in this moment. And you are That. Truly. Emptiness and Consciousness are just two names for the same reality, which is this vast Openness and Freedom in which the entire universe is arising moment to moment, an Emptiness that is your own primordial Awareness right now, and an Emptiness that by any other name is radical Spirit itself.

And then—as an entirely separate issue—there is the question of what the <u>manifest</u> world is actually like. I happen to believe it is an interwoven network of interpenetrating processes or holons, which is indeed a type of holistic model. But we decide the truth of that model—and the truth of the manifest world—by investigating the manifest world. We decide the truth of Spirit by investigating the inward I-I. That they are eventually not-two is correct, but the <u>only</u> way you can find that reality is by following the inward I-I, not by running around in the objective world looking for the web-of-life. If you do that, you will miss the mark. If you do that forever, you will miss the mark forever.

sw: So what do you think the role of a spiritual therapist should be? We've talked about the ones that don't seem to work—memorizing the higher stages without practicing them, confusing body sensory awareness with spiritual awareness, confusing web-of-life and ecopsychology theories with direct spiritual consciousness. What would work?

KW: I have what I think is a fantastic idea, [laughing] so of course I can't get anybody interested in it. In medicine we have the wonderful concept of a General Practitioner or GP. These are your basic family doctors. They are trained in general medicine, but not in specialized medicine. They can't do brain surgery, or make intricate differential diagnoses, or perform lab work—but they know specialists who can, and they are trained to refer you to these specialists should you need it.

I think a spiritual therapist should be like a GP of the spirit. They should have at least a theoretical familiarity with all levels of the spectrum of consciousness—matter, body, mind (magic, mythic, rational, and integral-aperspectival), soul (psychic and subtle), and spirit (causal and nondual). They should be familiar with the types of pathologies that can occur at each of those levels. They should be trained in the general lower techniques of bodily focusing and mental interpretation. They should know how to deal with persona, shadow, and ego problems. And they should themselves have a specific higher or contemplative practice. But they should also be trained to spot specific pathologies from the entire spectrum of consciousness, low to high—and for the ones that they cannot handle themselves, they should refer their clients to specialists—maybe in Zen, vipassana, t'ai chi, Vedanta, TM, Christian centering prayer, Sufi zikr, Jewish hitbodedut, the Diamond Approach, yoga—at the upper end—and at the lower end, weightlifting, aerobics, nutritional counseling, Rolfing, bioenergetics, whatever. The point is, they wouldn't try to do the brain surgery themselves. Their primary responsibilities are: first, to practice general psychotherapy and some transpersonal therapy with the client; second, to recommend specialists if needed; and third, to help coordinate all of the client's various tools of transformation. But they can't actually do all the therapies themselves. As it is now, too many transpersonal and spiritual therapists think they can and should do it all themselves, which is unfortunate for their clients. So that's my stupid idea, which nobody seems to like.

Friday, June 13

Went to see Children of the Revolution, mostly because of Judy Davis, who is quite amazing. She was hysterical in Woody Allen's Husbands and Wives, brilliant as Madame George Sand in Impromptu—to name a few. Children of the Revolution is a black comedy that succeeds modestly, despite an uneven style that veers between Strictly Ballroom and Daniel. But Davis is riveting. What I like about the script is the way it captures the fact that Marxism/Leninism was a religion, a fundamentalist bible-thumping religion, for millions and millions of people around the world. It was, in fact, the first truly great modern religion—that is, a religion that tried to make scientific materialism, gross-realm naturalism, and flatland holism into an emancipatory God. The God of the Right Hand world, the God and Goddess of Flatland. In this regard, it was a forerunner of many purely Descended and flatland religious movements in today's world, including much of deep ecology, ecofeminism, Gaia worship, neopaganism, and web-of-life revivals. The flatter the religion, the more intense the fanaticism.

Saturday, June 14

"My problems start when the smarter bears and the dumber visitors intersect."—Yosemite Park official Steve Thompson.

Sunday, June 15

Random House asked for a literary title for Science and Religion (and could I use the words "soul" or "spirit" or some such?). Oh well. Thinking of Oscar Wilde's great quote ["There is nothing that will cure the senses but the soul, and nothing that will cure the soul but the senses"], I suggested several variations on Sense and Soul, and they finally settled on The Marriage of Sense and Soul: Integrating Science and Religion. So there it is. So much for my diatribes against the commodification of the words "soul" and "spirit"—I'm now guilty as charged.

Tuesday, June 17

For almost twenty years, I've done hatha yoga as my main physical exercise. Five years ago, I also began weightlifting, which has been an extraordinary help in writing, meditation, and immune system health—a true testament to integral practice. I'm forty-eight, and I don't ever remember being this comfortable in the body.

Which makes it all the easier to transcend. That is, my experience is that when the bodymind is strong and healthy—not ascetically starved and despised—it is all the easier to drop it, transcend it, let it go. Precisely because the bodymind is running smoothly, with no distracting glitches, it doesn't hold awareness obsessively circling around it. You can more easily forget it and slip into Witnessing or even One Taste.

Of course, neither the ego nor the body is left behind in higher states. They are still present, still functioning, still serving their conventional purposes. If somebody calls your name, you will respond. You know where your body starts and where it stops—this is not borderline or psychotic indissociation. It's just that your identity is no longer exclusively confined to these lesser vehicles. When these vehicles are functioning smoothly, and not being the squeaky wheel that demands the oil of your awareness, your awareness is free to settle into deeper and higher domains. Of course, you can do this under almost any circumstances, but a strong glitch-free bodymind makes it all the easier to drop, and thus find it floating on the ocean of infinity that is its true abode.

Wednesday, June 18

Speaking of integral practice, this is certain to be the "next big thing" on the spiritual circuit; but this "fad," for one, is going to last, at least among that 1% who are serious about transformation.

There are many ways to talk about integral practice. "Integral yoga" was a term first used by Aurobindo (and his student Chaudhuri), where it specifically meant a practice that unites both the ascending and descending currents in the human being—not just a transformation of consciousness, but of the body as well. (Which makes it all the sadder that the California Institute of Integral Studies, founded by Chaudhuri, today has little if any integral practice, which is why I cannot, at this time, recommend CIIS to students.) Mike Murphy's Future of the Body is an excellent compendium of an integral view, as is Tony Schwartz's What Really Matters. I outline my own integral approach in The Eye of Spirit. Murphy and Leonard's The Life We Are Given is a practical guide to one type of integral practice, and is highly recommended.

But anybody can put together their own integral practice. The idea is to simultaneously exercise all the major levels and dimensions of the human bodymind—physical, emotional, mental, social, cultural, spiritual. To give several examples, going around the quadrants, we have the following levels and capacities, with some representative practices from each:

UPPER RIGHT QUADRANT
(INDIVIDUAL, OBJECTIVE, BEHAVIORAL)

Physical
DIET: Pritikin, Ornish, Atkins; vitamins, hormones
STRUCTURAL: weightlifting, aerobics, hiking, Rolfing, etc.

Neurological
PHARMACOLOGICAL: various medications/drugs, where appropriate
BRAIN/MIND MACHINES: to help induce theta and delta states of consciousness

UPPER LEFT QUADRANT
(INDIVIDUAL, SUBJECTIVE, INTENTIONAL)

Emotional
BREATH: t'ai chi, yoga, bioenergetics, circulation of prana or feeling-energy, qi gong
SEX: tantric sexual communion, self-transcending whole-bodied sexuality

Mental
THERAPY: psychotherapy, cognitive therapy, shadow work
VISION: adopting a conscious philosophy of life, visualization, affirmations

Spiritual
PSYCHIC (shaman/yogi): shamanic, nature mysticism, beginning tantric
SUBTLE (saint): deity yoga, yidam, contemplative prayer, advanced tantric
CAUSAL (sage): vipassana, self-inquiry, bare attention, witnessing
NONDUAL (siddha): Dzogchen, Mahamudra, Shaivism, Zen, etc.

LOWER RIGHT QUADRANT
(SOCIAL, INTEROBJECTIVE)

Systems: exercising responsibilities to Gaia, nature, biosphere, and geopolitical infrastructures at all levels

Institutional: exercising educational, political, and civic duties to family, town, state, nation, world

LOWER LEFT QUADRANT
(CULTURAL, INTERSUBJECTIVE)

Relationships: with family, friends, sentient beings in general; making relationships part of one's growth, decentering the self
Community Service: volunteer work, homeless shelters, hospice, etc.
Morals: engaging the intersubjective world of the Good, practicing compassion in relation to all sentient beings

The general idea of integral practice is clear enough: Pick a basic practice from each category, or from as many categories as pragmatically possible, and practice them concurrently—"all-level, all-quadrant." The more categories engaged, the more effective they all become (because they are all intimately related as aspects of your own being). Practice them diligently, and coordinate your integral efforts to unfold the various potentials of the bodymind—until the bodymind itself unfolds in Emptiness, and the entire journey is a misty memory from a trip that never even occurred.

Friday, June 20

Books, just out, by friends, keep arriving. M. Scott Peck—everybody calls him "Scotty"—sends Denial of the Soul. "I don't pick up too many causes," his letter says, "but the euthanasia or assisted suicide issue is of great concern to me." His point is that the euthanasia movement, which seems so sensible and rational, often hides a glib denial of the lessons that can be learned from conscious death and dying. He's a supporter of the hospice movement, as am I, where the standard procedure is to almost completely eliminate pain (with medication that does not dull the mind), so the individual can face death consciously, with family and loved ones present. I strongly agree.

Michael Crichton has signed his novel Airframe: "For the next time you want some airplane reading." This is very funny, and has its genesis here: after I read his Travels, where he ends one chapter by saying that he sat on the beach in Hawaii and read Wilber, I sent him a copy of

SES, that 800-page monster, inscribed "For the next time you're on the beach." About the only thing that two-ton book would be good for on the beach is beating a shark to death should one attack, and reading it there would be about as much fun as . . . reading Airframe while flying, hence the inscription. (Airframe is about the literally one-million ways a plane can fall out of the sky.)

A pre-pub copy of Mike Murphy's The Kingdom of Shivas Irons arrives. It's wonderful, a rip-roaring read. I can't believe Murphy is slipping this massive amount of mysticism into the golf section of every Barnes and Noble bookstore in the country—not just a little hint every now and then, but page after page of it. John Updike called Golf in the Kingdom "A golf classic if any exists in our day," and it looks like Shivas Irons is going to pick right up where that left off. I'm really happy for him. All of this helps to break up the topsoil of the rocky inhospitality of pragmatic America to transcendental concerns.

Surya Das's Awakening the Buddha Within, and it's really quite good. Those of us who followed its writing were a little worried that it was a bit disconnected, but Surya really pulled it together.

It's been a while since I've seen Surya. He, Sharon Salzberg, Mitch Kapor, and Mitch's son, Adam, stayed at my house last summer for a four-day visit. I have a lot of respect for what Surya is trying to do—make Tibetan Dzogchen accessible to American culture, which upsets both most Americans and most Tibetans.

It looks like the book is off to a great start, with everybody from Richard Gere to Alan Dershowitz lining up behind it. One Spirit Book Club and Tommy Boy Records are co-sponsoring some of its promotion. Tommy Boy was founded by Tom Silverman when he was still a boy (hence the name), but now we call him Tommy Man. He and his girl Friday, Susan Pivar (a meditation student of Sam's), stopped by the house recently for an afternoon; Tom and I spent much of our time trading weightlifting training tips. He's set up a branch of Tommy Boy—Upaya—to help get a spiritual orientation out to a larger pop audience. He's the one getting Deepak on MTV, Andrew Weil on tape, etc. This got him featured in W's "The God Rush: Is the new spirituality in New York and Hollywood a godsend—or just divine madness?" Tom and Susan know I'm skeptical about the possibility of doing "pop spirituality" without its becoming thin and diluted, but it's certainly worth a try, and it can always serve to whet the appetite in a large and hungry audience.

Tuesday, June 24

There are four or five major obstacles to an integral orientation and integral practice. I'm not talking about mainstream—atheistic liberals and fundamentalist conservatives—both of whom will ignore integral spirituality anyway. I'm talking about threats from within the avant-garde, countercultural, alternative spiritual community itself.

The first obstacle, as I see it anyway, is from the merely translative camps, who focus on new ideas or new-paradigms about reality. Some of these concepts and ideas are truly important, and I often agree with them; but learning a new concept will not get you to nondual constant consciousness; only intense and prolonged practice will. This translative camp includes many aspects of systems theory, ecopsychology, ecofeminism, the web-of-life theorists, neopaganism, astrology and neo-astrology, deep ecology, and Goddess/Gaia worship. There are some wonderful exceptions, but most of those approaches are largely trapped in the gross sensorimotor world, the descended world of flatland, and they simply offer new ways to <u>translate</u> that world, not ways to <u>transform</u> consciousness into subtle, causal, and nondual domains. At best they access the psychic level of nature mysticism and the World Soul, which is wonderful, but is nonetheless only the beginning of the transpersonal realms.

Of course, they often say that these higher realms deny and repress the earth, but that only applies to <u>pathologies</u> of the higher states; the normal higher states <u>transcend and include</u> the lower, so that Spirit transcends and includes nature, not denies it. It is true, however, that certain spiritual paths do in fact repress the lower domains, and those paths constitute the <u>second</u> major obstacle to a balanced or integral practice. This threat can be introduced in the following way.

During the great <u>axial period</u> (roughly sixth century BCE), the growing tip of an evolving humanity made a monumental breakthrough: certain pioneering sages—Parmenides, Krishna, Jesus of Nazareth, Gautama Buddha, Lao Tzu—found that they could follow consciousness <u>to its source</u>, at which point a psychic-level <u>communion</u> with Spirit and a subtle-level <u>union</u> with Spirit gives way to a causal-level <u>identity</u> with Spirit: the Atman that is Brahman, I and the Father are One, the separate self dissolves in Emptiness, consciousness finds the unqualifiable One. This breakthrough—from the highest <u>Forms</u> of consciousness (subtle level) to pure <u>Formless</u> consciousness (causal level)—was a stunning achievement, the greatest mutation in consciousness up to that time, and the power of which set in motion virtually every one of the world's major wisdom traditions that still flourish to this day.

(It only confuses things to bring gender politics into this particular issue. The causal level is a genuine state attainable by either sex; it is itself <u>gender-neutral</u>. The cornering of this state by males during the axial period was unfortunate by today's standards and unavoidable by yesterday's. The agrarian structure itself selects the male value sphere, on average, for non-home enterprises, including intense religious retreats, where most of these breakthroughs occurred. We of the industrial and postindustrial social structure, which does not necessitate this type of gender stratification, can begin to equalize access to these domains without having to call men dirty names as a prelude.)

The great <u>downside</u> of these axial discoveries was that, in their rush to find the Formless beyond the world of Form, they generally came to despise the entire world of Form itself. The aim was to find a nirvana divorced from samsara, a heaven that is not of this earth, a kingdom that is not of this world, a One that excludes the Many. The paradigm, the exemplar, of these axial approaches was nirvikalpa samadhi, ayn, nirodh—in other words, pure cessation, pure formless absorption. The goal, in short, was the causal or unmanifest state. The path was purely Ascending and otherworldly, and almost everything identified with "this world"—sex, money, nature, flesh, desire—was pronounced sin, ignorance, illusion.

In a sense, there is a fair amount of truth to that. If you are <u>only</u> after the things of this sensory world, then you will not discover higher or deeper realities. But if you go overboard and deny or repress this world, you will never find the Nondual, the radical estate that includes <u>both</u> the One and the Many, otherworldly and this-worldly, Ascending and Descending, Emptiness and Form, Nirvana and Samsara, as equal gestures of One Taste.

The great axial age began around the sixth century BCE in both East and West. The advanced religions of that period were all dominated by yogic withdrawal, purely ascending practices, life-denial, asceticism, bodily renunciation, and the "way up." They were, almost without exception, deeply dualistic: spirit divorced from body, nirvana separate from samsara, formless at war with form. But by the second century CE, the limitations of a causal and dualistic nirvana were becoming quite apparent, and the growing-tip (or most-advanced) consciousness began a great movement beyond the causal unmanifest, a movement that would transcend yet include the causal Abyss. Spirit, in other words, began to recognize its own pure Nondual condition, and it first did so, most especially, in two extraordinary souls, Nagarjuna in the East and Plotinus in the West.

"That which is Form is not other than Emptiness, that which is Emptiness is not other than Form," is perhaps the most famous summary of this Nondual breakthrough (the quote is from The Heart Sutra, said to summarize the entire essence of Mahayana Buddhism, a revolution set in motion largely by Nagarjuna). Nirvana and Samsara, the One and the Many, Ascending and Descending, Wisdom and Compassion, the Witness and everything witnessed—these are all not-two or nondual. But that nonduality is not an idea or a concept; it is a direct realization. If it is made into a concept, or something merely believed in, then all you get is a sharp whack from the Zen master's stick. For this reason, nonduality is often referred to as "not-two, not-one" (just to make sure we don't turn it into a merely conceptual monism, web-of-life theory, or flatland holism).

The point was clear enough: what was taken by the merely Ascending paths to be defilements, sins, or illusions were now seen as radiant gestures of Spirit itself. As Plotinus put it, the Many are not apart from One, the Many are a manifestation of the One (not as a theory you think about with the eye of mind, but as something you directly perceive with the eye of contemplation). Thus one's spiritual practice was not to deny all things manifest, but rather to "bring everything to the path." According to Tantra, another flower of the Nondual revolution, even the worst sin contains, hidden in its depths, the radiance of its own wisdom and salvation. In the center of anger is clarity; in the middle of lust is compassion; in the heart of fear is freedom.

It all rested on a simple principle: the higher transcends and includes the lower, not transcends and denies it. Spirit transcends and includes soul, which transcends and includes mind, which transcends and includes body, which transcends and includes matter. And therefore all levels are to be included, transformed, taken up and embraced in the true spiritual path. This is essentially the same Great Chain of the ascending schools, but now it was understood, not as a map of the escape route from the prison of the flesh, but as the diagram of the eternal embrace of all manifestation by the Spirit from whence it issued.

So began the extraordinary Nondual revolution. In the West, the great Neoplatonic tradition would carry it bravely forward, but it was everywhere resisted by the Church, which had officially pledged allegiance to the Ascending path, for my kingdom is not of this world, and render unto Caesar. . . . But for those with eyes to see and souls to hear, the Neoplatonic current blazed a trail of Nonduality across the first and second millennia. When it was realized that the Great Nest actually unfolded or developed in time, the Neoplatonic tradition directly fueled the great Idealist vision of Fichte, Schelling, and Hegel (which saw the entire universe as a product of Spiritual development and evolutionary unfolding—a product of Spirit-in-action), although all that remains today of that stunning vision is the scientific theory of evolution, a true but pale and anemic and sickly little child of its towering parents.

In the East, the Nondual revolution gave rise to Mahayana Buddhism, Vedanta, neo-Confucianism, Kashmir Shaivism, and Vajrayana Buddhism—all of which can loosely be summarized as "Tantra." The great flowering of the nondual Tantra especially occurred from the eighth to the eleventh centuries in India, and from there it spread (beginning as early as the sixth) to Tibet, China, Korea, and Japan. When it was also understood in the East that the Great Chain did indeed unfold or evolve over time, the great Aurobindo expounded the notion with an unequaled genius.

We are today at an auspicious moment in history, where these two great Nondual currents, in their evolutionary and integral form, are starting to come together. The Neoplatonic and Idealist currents of the West, appropriately combined with the West's scientific understanding of evolution, are being integrated with the East's great Nondual and Tantric schools, also with their own strong developmental orientation.

The result is the general <u>integral approach,</u> now involving, in its various forms, hundreds of researchers around the world. To this mix the modern integral approach also brings a commitment to depth psychology—a virtually exclusive discovery of the modern West—and a desire to allow excellence to shine from every level, every dimension, every quadrant, every domain in the human and divine estate. This integral approach is in its infancy, but growing at an exhilarating rate.

If the first obstacle to the integral approach is flatland (or the merely Descended schools), the second obstacle, as I started to say, is the reverse error, the merely Ascending path. This approach—remnant from the axial age—includes Theravadin Buddhism, some forms of Vedanta (that rest in nirvikalpa or jnana samadhi, and don't push through to sahaja), many forms of asthanga and hatha yoga (when they aim only for mental cessation). Again, it's not that these approaches are wrong; they simply need to be supplemented with the Path of Descent in order to take a more Nondual stance.

A third obstacle is the "spiritual bypass" school, which imagines that if you find Spirit or Goddess or your Higher Self, everything else will magically take care of itself. Job, work, relationships, family, community, money, food, and sex will all cease their annoying habits. The despairingly sad thing is, it usually takes ten or twenty years to discover that this is definitely not the case, and then, where has your life gone? So the first half of your life is spent somewhat misguided, the second, bitter.

This spiritual bypass approach can be very tricky, especially—and ironically—if you are dealing with the very highest Nondual schools. One Taste is an <u>ever-present</u> consciousness (it is the natural and spontaneous mind in its present state: if you are aware of this page right now, you have 100% of this ultimate consciousness fully present). Precisely because One Taste is "always already" present, many people can gain a quick but extremely powerful glimpse of this ultimate state if an accomplished teacher carefully points it out to them. And, in fact, many of the great Nondual schools, such as Dzogchen and Vedanta, have entire texts devoted to these "pointing out instructions" [see April 27 for an example].

Once students get a strong hit of this always-already awareness, certain unfortunate things can happen. On the one hand, they are, in some profound ways, liberated from the binding nature of the lower levels of the bodymind. On the other hand, that doesn't mean these lower levels cease to have their own needs or problems, relative though they may be. You can be in One Taste consciousness and still get cancer, still fail at a marriage, still lose a job, still be a jerk. Reaching a higher stage in development does <u>not</u> mean the lower levels go away (Buddhas still have to eat), nor do you automatically master the lower levels (enlightenment will not automatically let you run a four-minute mile). In fact, it often means the opposite, because you might start to neglect or even ignore the lower levels, imagining that they are now no longer necessary for your well-being, whereas in fact they are the means of expression of your well-being and the vehicles of Spirit that you now are. Neglecting these vehicles is "spiritocide"—you are neglecting to death your own sacred manifestations.

It gets worse. In order to pass through the oral stage of psychosexual development, you don't have to become a great chef. In order to discover the transverbal, you do not have to be Shakespeare. In other words, you absolutely do <u>not</u> have to develop perfect mastery of a lower stage before you can move to a higher stage—all that is required is a certain vague competency. But this means that you can arrive at some very high stages of development and <u>still have all sorts of problems at various lower stages</u>. And simply plugging into the higher stage is <u>not</u> necessarily going to make those lower problems go away.[16]

This becomes a bit of a nightmare with the always-already schools, because once you get a strong glimpse of One Taste, you can lose all motivation to fix those holes in your psychological basement. You might have a deep and painful neurosis, but you no longer care, because you are no longer identified with the bodymind. There is a certain truth to that. But that attitude, nonetheless, is a profound violation of the bodhisattva vow, the vow to communicate One Taste to sentient beings in a way that can liberate all. You might be happy not to work on your neurotic crap, but everybody around you can see that you are a neurotic jerk, and therefore when you announce you are really in One Taste, all

---

16. For further discussion of this topic, see the entries for November 16 and December 18.

they will remember is to avoid that state at all costs. You might be happy in your One Taste, but you are failing miserably to communicate it in any form that can be heard, precisely because you have not worked on all the lesser vehicles through which you must communicate your understanding. Of course, it is one thing if you are being offensive because you are engaged in angry wisdom or dharma combat, quite another if you are simply being a neurotic creep. One Taste does not communicate with anything, because it is everything. Rather, it is your soul and mind and body, your words and actions and deeds, that will communicate your Estate, and if those are messed up, lots of luck.

Again, it's not that the One-Taste or sahaja schools are wrong. They are plugged into the highest estate imaginable, but they need to be complemented with an understanding that work also can (and needs to) be done on the lower levels and lesser stages (including psychotherapy, diet and exercise, relationships, livelihood, etc.) in order for a truly integral orientation to emerge. In this way only can a person communicate One Taste to all sentient beings, who themselves live mostly on lower domains and respond most readily to healthy messages addressed to those domains, not higher messages strained through neurotic and fractured lower realms.

The last major obstacle to an integral approach, as I see it, is the new-age epidemic, which . . . oh, well. Elevates magic and myth to psychic and subtle, confuses ego and Self, glorifies prerational as transrational, confuses preconventional wish-fulfillment with postconventional wisdom, grabs its self and calls it God. I wish them well, but . . . May they get their wishes quickly granted, so they can find out how truly unsatisfying they really are.

So those are the major obstacles to a nondual integral approach, as I see them: Descended flatland and its merely translative schools; the solely Ascending paths with their distaste for this world; spiritual bypassing; One-Taste sufficiency that leaves schmucks as it finds them; and new-age elevationism. If we add the conventional world at large—both liberal atheists and conservative mythic fundamentalists—that's a half-dozen roadblocks to integral self-realization, which only means, Spirit has certainly not yet tired of this round of the Kosmic Game of Hide and Seek, for it is content to continue hiding in just the damnedest places.

Thursday, June 26

Ram Dass is doing better, and there is hope that a fair amount of recovery will occur. The last time I saw him was at Roger's fiftieth birthday party. Frances and I had planned this party as our present to Roger on his half-century milestone. We thought the best thing we could give him was a gathering of those who love him dearly. Roger is eminently lovable. Huston Smith, Stan and Christina Grof, Jack Kornfield, Jim Fadiman, Miles Vich, Bryan Wittine, John O'Neil, Robert McDermott, Keith Thompson, Philip Moffet, Ram Dass . . . over fifty people, and we held it at Campton Place, off Union Square in San Francisco.

Ram Dass and I sat together with Roger and Frances, and he was full of life, full of spirit. Then, when I was in New York, Frances leaves a message on Tony's machine: Ram Dass has had a major stroke; his body is almost completely paralyzed; he can't move or speak. Frances is audibly shaken; she and Roger and Ram Dass had become especially close in the last few years. But Ram Dass is now speaking some, and with two years or so of therapy, might make a reasonable recovery. I'm praying he can indeed make this grist for the mill. I also know, from painful experience, that no matter how strong and seemingly unshakable one's spiritual realization, life can yank the rug right out from under you when you're not looking, and, more embarrassingly, when you are.

Saturday, June 28—Denver

Dinner in Denver with two of my best friends in the area, Warren Bellows and Willy Kent, and I'm sad that they are moving. To Sonoma County, right north of San Francisco. I met Warren through Treya; they had met at Findhorn. I describe Warren in Grace and Grit; he was the only non–family member present at Treya's death. It was really Warren and I who took care of her those last few weeks, and he was an absolute godsend. His longtime lover, Willy, is a gifted physician; I love them both. Warren tends to be more spiritually oriented, especially in his acupuncture practice, and Willy is more the skeptical scientist; I have strong affinities with both camps, so we've always enjoyed hanging out together. I've never had a homosexual experience, but I've always been comfortable in gay culture, probably because of the aesthetics. Straight males are, on average, aesthetically challenged.

"You really are sad they're leaving, aren't you?" Marci asked.

"Yes, of course. Why would you even ask that?"

"Well, you know, I thought you'd just make your brainwaves go to zero and not worry about it."

"Emptiness means you care more, not less. I'm very sad."

"Yes, I know. I'm glad."

Monday, June 30

Emptiness alone, only and all, with an edge of extremely faint yet luminous bliss. That is how the subtle feels when it emerges from the causal. So it was early this morning. As the gross body then emerges from this subtle luminous bliss, it's hard to tell, at first, exactly where its boundaries are. You have a body, you know that, but the body seems like the entire material universe. Then the bedroom solidifies, and slowly, very slowly, your awareness accepts the conventions of the gross realm, which dictate that <u>this</u> body is <u>inside</u> this room. And so it is. And so you get up. And so goes involution, yet again.

But the Emptiness remains, always.

JULY

*See! I am God; see I am in all things; see! I do all things; see!
I never lift mine hands off my work, nor ever shall, without
end; see! I lead all things to the end I ordained it to from
without beginning, by the same Might, Wisdom, and Love
whereby I made it. How should anything be amiss?*
—Dame Julian of Norwich

Tuesday, July 1

ANAMNESIS, OR THE PSYCHOANALYSIS OF GOD

1

Push pull crash . . . push pull crash . . . push pull crash . . . push pull
crash . . . push pull crash . . . push pull crash . . . push pull crash . . .
push pull crash . . . push pull crash . . . push pull crash . . . push pull
crash . . . push pull crash . . . push pull crash . . . push pull crash . . .
push pull crash . . . push pull crash . . . push pull crash . . . push pull
crash . . . push pull crash . . . push pull crash . . . push pull crash . . .
push pull crash . . . push pull crash . . . push pull crash . . . push pull
crash . . .

2

> Yearning, yearning.
> Hunger, thirst, hunger here.
> Swallowing, to swallow.

Must have, must have, must have.
Move toward, run away.
Fear, fear, fear, here.
Anger, rage, explode, swallow, grasping hard, terror.

3

I see, hear, feel. I am not alone. There are others here, of my blood, and we are one, against the others.

Nature sleeps with us, and rises with us, and we are sometimes bright, sometimes frightened, by this power over us. Our strong desire is not strong enough, many times. Earth, air, fire, water, follow no course, sometimes they help, many times they hurt.

Life is short, following the way of all blood on earth. There are others here, some are bright, some are dark. Those of my blood are with me. Those who are not, are not. Death is with us, and we put death on those who are not.

Family is of blood, and is with us. I am four in this family. Eighteen suns have brought me here. Now the moon is putting death on me. The moon, the snake, the water, they are one.

All things touch all things. There is no separation here on earth. To touch a thing is to be that thing; to eat a thing is to be that thing. We do not touch that of the other, we do not eat that of the other. Life is on this side, of our blood. Death is on that side, of the other. We do not touch the other, we do not eat that of the other. Now the moon is putting death on me, because the snake, the moon, and the water are one. When the snake bit, the moon entered me, and now death is entering me.

I have learned these things, from those who know. My family goes on, our blood mixed with this earth.

4

Boy and girl together are killed, we roast them and eat them carefully, for they are of the Mother. Blood is of the Mother, and we offer blood to Her, which comes back as our food.

I am Tiamat, of the fifth house, planter of the seeds that were brought to us by ancestors in the days before time began. My blood is of the Mother, my bones are of the Mother, my heart beats with the time calling us to Mother. My body mixes with earth, which is the Mother.

Few understand Mother. She is Life, her blood makes life. We offer her blood, the boy and girl are killed together, which we eat for the Mother, or else the seeds will not bring forth. Each four moon season, we sacrifice for Mother, which comes back as our food. If we do not sacrifice, we all will perish. I, Tiamat, know this, from the ancestors who brought us the seeds, in the days before time began.

5

My father's father descended from the Creator, whose abode is not here, but Heaven, and His ways we cannot know. In our city, the priests have means to contact our Father, but my family does not understand them. My father's father understood the Father, for they were kin, but we have forgotten. It does not matter, our lives are in His hands. There are many gods and goddesses, and He is just the sometimes leader of them all, though we do not know how.

The priests tell us that there was a time that our ancestors walked with the Creator, but then something terrible happened. We pray twice daily to be returned to before the mistake. I pray very hard, but the last time I prayed hard, my sister died anyway. My uncle said I must pray harder, so something must be wrong with me.

I am being trained to be a potter, because I am very good with my hands, and I see things about making. My brother was a potter; my other brother plows. One of my sisters died; they will not tell me what happened to my other sister.

We are fortunate, for we have a strong house. This is because my father's father was descended from the Creator. Also, in the blood fight that took this city from the others, our family fought well, and so we have this house.

The day of sacrifice is the best day, because everything comes from the Creator and we must give some of it back. My family sacrifices beautiful birds, which we raise for this. There are dark rumors about what goes on in the Temple, but I don't believe them. We see the sacrifices here, with the birds. The blood of the bird returns to the earth. Blood is the life we are given, so we give it back. To eat a thing is to be that thing, so after the bird is blessed by the priest, we eat it, because now it is food of the gods, and the gods are in it. So in this way we become strong, and the elements leave us alone. And yet, the last time I prayed for my sister, she died anyway, so there must be something wrong with me.

6

This world makes sense, obviously. And I am constantly struggling with those who want to hide the light of rationality under some obscure basket of deceit. UFOs, astrology, alchemy, astral travel, Eastern mysticism. . . . What a mess.

Most of these people, however well intentioned, don't seem to realize that they are living in a relatively safe and protected world precisely because of rational science and its fruits of medicine, dentistry, physics, economic production and abundance, the extension of average life span from thirty years to seventy years. The critics condemn that which shelters them. I've been an electrical engineer for over three decades, because it works, it is verifiable, it betters human lives. There is a real world out there, with real truth in it, and real hard work required to dig it out. You can't just contemplate your navel and hope to find out anything worth anything.

The fortress of science, is how I think of it. It will stand forever, constantly updated. That is, as long as the antirational inmates don't take over the hospital.

Perhaps I shouldn't get angry, but I do. Ever since my son died last year in an automobile accident, things have been a little rough. But running to a pie-in-the-sky God does no good at all. We human beings, for good or ill, are the only gods in existence, the only force of rational intention and good will. And we will save ourselves if we can be saved at all. The Bible is right about one thing: the truth will set you free. And science is the only path of discovering truth. What else could there be?

I'm not worried, anyway. Oh, once in a while, I can't sleep, you know. I lie awake and stare into the darkness, and wonder.

7

All things are related to all things. When I first had that realization, perhaps when I was a young girl, maybe fourteen or so, it completely changed my life! I would later learn names for this—holism and so on— but at the time, all I knew was that all things were related to, connected to, all things. Twenty years, two husbands, no kids, three jobs, and one National Book Award later, I still believe this firmly!

My book, To Re-weave the Web, is a detailed account of this holistic view, based not only on all the late-breaking scientific discoveries—and oh there are so many! from chaos theory to quantum physics to complexity theories and systems theory, my head just spins, it's so exciting!—but also we have the holism of the indigenous peoples the world over, who knew all this stuff way before modern science stumbled onto it. The Great Goddess returns! Gaia is alive! All things are related to all things.

This is wondrous, isn't it? Now that science is catching up with this holistic interwoven view—why, I was writing about this years ago!—I am looked upon as something of a forerunner. So I have become a heroine, imagine that! I've been asked to be on this board and that, serve on this journal and that, go to this conference and that. Me! Imagine that!

Oh, I forgot. Not just the indigenous beliefs, but Eastern mysticism, too. All saying the same thing, about the web-of-life, all things and all things and all of that and so on. So I don't see why those Zen people keep annoying me and asking if I meditate. What difference does it make?, I keep asking them. If you believe that everything is connected to everything, what else is there? You do it your way, which is meditation, and I do it my way, which is called holistic thinking. They said, that was just an idea and could I show them this oneness right now? And that made no sense to me at all. They're just being obnoxious, I think, like they know it all. Imagine that!

8

The hike through the mountain with my fiancé was everything I wanted. Madly in love, slightly crazed, we both were babbling fools. More like children, but it didn't matter. For an hour John had dutifully carried the picnic basket on his back, kidding all the time that it was only fitting that he should carry the food of the CEO of Digital Data Corporation, and I said, No, it's only fitting for a love slave, and that would be you. And I wasn't even finished with the sentence when suddenly I disappeared, and there was only the vista in front of me, and John, and this body . . . but no me, or no I, or . . . well, I'm not sure. I was one with all of this scenery, one with the mountain, one with the sky, it was exhila-rating, a little scary, but mostly completely peaceful, like coming home. I've never really told anyone about it, because on Monday I was back at the office, running Digital, and who would have believed me anyway?

It never happened again. I sometimes read about things like this, one-ness and whatnot, cosmic consciousness, but none of the words sound right for what happened to me. I hear that some people can stay in this state constantly, but I don't see how, I really doubt it. You'd lose all sense of orientation, I think. Anyway, it came and went. The more I think about it, the more I think it might have been something like a small seizure. It didn't seem like it at the time, but now it does. After all, what else could it be, seriously?

9

It was just the other day, I can still remember it as if it's happening right now, vivid, electric, weird. I was sitting alone, at home, and it's late, around midnight maybe. I have the distinct feeling that somebody or something is in the house—you know that feeling? Well at first it really scared me, I was really scared. I finally got up the nerve to go through the house, checked it really well. I sit back down and it happens.

This really intense fireball, I don't what else to call it, simply material-ized right there in front of me, right there in the living room. I know this sounds crazy, but this has never happened to me before, I don't see things, you know? But it wasn't just an electrical thing. I know this sounds crazy, but it was alive. Well, I'll just say it: it was Love. It was a living fire of Love and Light. I know this as sure as I'm sitting here. It sort of moved from in front of me to on top of my head, then back in front of me, then on top of my head. When it sits on top of my head my whole spine begins to vibrate, and shooting currents run up it, right to the top. Pretty crazy, huh? And then as soon as I knew that this was Love, it just disappeared, just like that. It just went away, but it scared the daylights out of me. But then it didn't, I mean it didn't scare me. It made me feel completely safe, I've never really felt like that.

I've heard about, you know, that light at the end of the tunnel? Except I wasn't dead. But I know what I know, and I know that Love is some-where out there. My entire body feels different somehow. My spine hurts, like somebody plugged it into the wall socket, I don't know exactly. But the truth is out there. I know that. Oh, and I know I've started praying, just to say thanks.

10

Nature retreats before its God, Light finds it own Abode. That's all I keep thinking as I enter into this extraordinary vastness. I am going in and up, in and up, in and up, and I have ceased to have any bodily feelings at all. In fact, I don't even know where my body is, or if I even have one. I know only shimmering sheaths of luminous bliss, each giving way to the next, each softer and yet stronger, brighter and yet fainter, more intense yet harder to see.

Above all, I am Full. I am full to infinity, in this ocean of light. I am full to infinity, in this ocean of bliss. I am full to infinity, in this ocean of love. I cannot conceive of wanting something, desiring something, grasping after anything. I can contain no more than is already here, full to infinity. I am beyond myself, beyond this world, beyond pain and suffering and self and same, and I know this is the home of God, and I know that I am in God's Presence. I am one with Presence, it is obvious. I am one with God, it is certain. I am one with Spirit, it is given. I shall never want again, for Grace abounds, here in the luminous mist of infinity.

Around the edges of this love-bliss there are tender tears, the faint reminders that I have so wanted this, so longed for this, so desperately yearned for this—to be saturated to the ends of the universe, to be full and free and final. All the years, all the lifetimes, searching for only this, searching and suffering and screaming for only this. And so the tender tears stand at the edge of my infinity, reminding me.

Out of this Light and Love, all things issue forth, of this I am now certain, for this I have seen with the eye of my own true soul. Into this Light and Love, all things will return, of this I am now certain, for this I have seen with the eye of my own true soul. And I have returned with a message: Peace be unto you, my human brothers and sisters; and peace be unto you, my animal brothers and sisters; and peace be unto you, my inanimate brothers and sisters—for all is well, and all is well, and all manner of things shall be well. We are all of the same Light and Love, of this I am now certain, for this I have seen with the eye of my own true soul.

11

Exactly how long I was Light, I cannot say. How long Form existed, I cannot say. How long I have been neither, I cannot say.

On the other side of Light, the Abyss. On the other side of Love, the Abyss. How long, I cannot say.

I once was a rock, I remember that, and push pull crash, I remember that. I roamed the universe of myself in slumbering abandon, and truth be told, it was humorous, always.

I once was a plant, then an animal, and thirst and hunger, I remember that. I ran toward, and ran away from, the forms of my own lust. I wandered driven, starving, dying. But truth be told, it was humorous, always.

I once awoke as human beings, and entered into the school of my own becoming. I first worshipped myself in the form of my other, I worshipped my slumbering self. I moved toward my own skin, dear nature, and I approached me now with wonder, now with terror, and did unending trembling and ritual pleading to deal with the terror I induced by my own sleep. But truth be told, it was humorous, always.

I once awoke as human beings in search of me as heavenly other, in my own form as misty mythic mystery, still asleep, but barely. I sacrificed aspects of my still slumbering self in order to appease the terror that my own twilight still evoked. But to awaken all at once, you see, would have ended the game right there. And truth be told, it was humorous, always, even as I cut into myself.

I soon awoke as human beings who, in striving to be a light unto themselves, were dimly on the trail of the Light that I am, even in my otherness. In one great move I stopped looking for me out there. In one great move, I awoke to a consciousness of light. In one great move, I turned within, or began to, and I could sense that this game was getting old, because I was now on the trail of I. Truth be told, it was humorous, even as it was starting to end.

And then one day, sitting alone as my otherness, I saw myself as a ball of Light and Love, and knew the Great Awakening was upon me.

In the next move in the school of myself, I entered into Me, as that Love and Light itself, and I was with I to infinity. And this I recognized altogether, in a whisper of breath that embraced all space, and a flash of Light that contained all time.

And then, the Abyss beyond all beyonds. Some would call it radical Freedom, infinite Release, ultimate Liberation, the great Redemption, boundless Being. I wouldn't know, for there is no I to know, in any form, sacred or profane, and so there is only this radical Formlessness, which remains its own remark. It is not bliss, it is not God, it is not love. It is not holistic, it is not Goddess, it is not interwoven anything. It is not infinite, it is not eternal, it is not any conception or object or state whatsoever. I-I am not light, am not love, am not spirit, am not bliss. I-I am not bound, am not free, am not ignorant, am not liberated.

But this much can be said: where there is not this Emptiness, there is only suffering.

All this I remember, in the school of myself. All this I have seen, in the history of my own discovery. All this I sing of now, to the audience of myself. All this I promise to others, who are the forms of my own slumbering. All this others will also see, as they awaken from their otherness and return their slumbering selves to the Awake-ness that has always existed, undiminished and untorn, in the heart of what they are.

Exactly how long I was Light, I cannot say. How long Form existed, I cannot say. How long I have been neither, I cannot say.

On the other side of Light, the Abyss. On the other side of Love, the Abyss. How long, I cannot say.

But I know I will empty even this Emptiness, and therefore create a Kosmos, and therefore incarnate as the world of Form, and enter with Wakefulness the children of my own Awareness.

12

Around the sea of Emptiness, a faint edge of bliss.
From the sea of Emptiness, a flicker of compassion.
Subtle illuminations fill the space of awareness,
As radiant forms coalesce in consciousness.
A world is taking shape,

A universe is being born.
I-I breathe out the subtlest patterns,
Which crystallize into the densest forms,
With physical colors, things, objects, processes,
That rush upon awareness in the darkness of its night,
To arise as glorious sun, radiant reminder of its source,
And slumbering earth, abode of the offspring of Spirit.

13

The phone rings and I run to pick it up. "Yes?"

"Hi, it's Marci."

"Hi, sweetie. What's up?"

"I think we should go on a vacation, spur of the moment. Just do it."

"Um, well, I've got all this work, you know, it's sorta . . ."

"Come on, it won't kill you to take a few days off."

"Okay, okay. We've never been to South Beach, and we wanted to give it a try, so we might as well do it now, yes?"

"Yes!"

Two weeks later, here we are, in South Beach, Miami, of all places. And resting in the ocean, dipped into the sea, I find glimmers of One Taste everywhere.

Emptiness, clarity, and care, are the names of this present moment, exactly as it is arising, now and now and now. The bodies of Buddha, the hands of Christ, the faces of Krishna, the breasts of the Goddess, the aspects of this very moment. I know that all of that is somehow tied to a pledge that I have made, deep in the heart of my very soul, how or where or when exactly, does not really matter. It is just that, for those who remember the course of their own consciousness—from mineral to plant to animal, from magic to mythic to mental to supramental, from body to ego to soul to Emptiness to radical One Taste—there is an extra duty asked of them, and that is to communicate what they have seen, and what they have remembered, and what they have found—what each I has found in the school of I as it returns to itself, shining and free, empty and bright, called and caring, just so, and again, just so.

And truth be told, it was humorous, always.

14

Marci is swimming. I finish my Coke and my sandwich. It is noon. The sky is clear, the ocean is blue, the waves surge freely on the beach, wetting the soft white sand.

Wednesday, July 2

Read all morning, answered a few urgent phone messages, spent an hour unpacking and shelving the weekly shipment of books that arrived. Books, really, who needs them? People think that being awakened means you understand everything, but it really means the opposite. It means you don't understand anything. It is, all of it, a total Mystery, a baffling babbling of unending nonsense.

Enlightenment is <u>not</u> "omniscience" but "ascience"—not all-knowing but not-knowing—the utter release from the cramp of knowledge, which is always of the world of form, when all you are in truth is formless. Not the cloud of knowing, but the cloud of unknowing. Not divine knowledge, but divine ignorance. The Seer <u>cannot</u> be seen; the Knower <u>cannot</u> be known; the Witness <u>cannot</u> be witnessed. What you are, therefore, is just a free fall in divine ignorance, a vast Freedom from all things known and seen and heard and felt, an infinity of Freedom on the other side of knowledge, an eternity of Release on the other side of time.

Knowledge is mandatory in the conventional, relative world, and I am glad to unpack those particular books and try to communicate through them, because of certain vows and duties that operate in that world. But all of it, truly, is just a series of ornaments on primordial awareness, a pattern of reflections in the empty mirror. Ken Wilber is just a scab on my Original Face, and this morning I flick it off like a tiny insect, and disappear back into the infinite space that is my true abode.

But that infinite space is impulsive. It sings its songs of manifestation, it dances the dance of creation. Out of sheerest purest gossamer nothingness, now and now and forever now, this majestic world arises, a wink and a nod from the radiant Abyss. So I finish unpacking the books, and go on about the morning's business.

Friday, July 4

Got a copy of the Association for Transpersonal Psychology Newsletter, and find this notice: "The American Medical Writers Association of

New England has given its Award in Excellence in Medical Communication to the Textbook of Transpersonal Psychiatry and Psychology (Basic Books, 1996) by psychiatrists Bruce Scotton, Allan Chinen, and John Battista."

They deserve it; they did an absolutely first-rate job on that book. They asked me to do a foreword for it, and I was glad to, with an added bonus for all of us: I sat down to write the piece, got carried away, and fifty pages later had what I thought was a terrific article—but a horrible foreword, massively too long. No way they could use it. So I then wrote a properly short, four-page foreword—which worked just fine—and the long essay became one of my favorite pieces, called "The Integral Vision," which is now the Introduction to The Eye of Spirit. So everybody got something out of my ineptitude.

But more than that, to have the very conservative New England medical establishment give an award to a book on spiritual and transpersonal psychiatry is extraordinary, truly amazing. In what amounts to a political act, medical psychiatry in this country determines which states of consciousness are "real" and which are "pathological," "sick," "illusory." And what do you know, it looks like God is no longer a mental disease.

Saturday, July 5

Perhaps a few explanatory notes to "Anamnesis." In it, I tried to describe what each major level of consciousness looks like from within, from the inside, from the first-person or "I" point of view. Since, in academic writing, you are always forced to speak in objective it-language, I wanted to speak, for a change, in I-language. Of course, one of the main reasons academic religious writers stick to objective it-language is that it relieves them of the burden of having to transform consciousness (the I) in order to see any of this. Instead of going to Bermuda, they read books about Bermuda and discuss the books! Very strange.

For the lower levels (up through section 9), I created short stories to represent what the world looks like at each level. Starting with section 10, the entries are phenomenological: entering the various states, recording the experience. I ended up rather arbitrarily with 14 sections to "Anamnesis," and since I usually use ten major levels of consciousness, the correlations are as follows:

· Section 1 is the sensorimotor world (level 1), the world of matter and physics. My treatment is not very imaginative, but there it is.

· Section 2 is the pranic or emotional-sexual world (level 2). Also not that imaginative, but obvious enough.

· Section 3 is the magical world (level 3). In magical-animistic cognition, subjects with similar predicates are often equated, and wholes are conflated with parts, so that condensation and displacement rule. Still, it is in its own way one of the more beautiful worldviews, and its laws of metaphor (equating items with similar agency) and metonym (equating items with similar communion) are important roots of language and still expressly inhabit poetry; it's easy to see how Romantics get confused about its actual contours.

· Sections 4 and 5 are the mythic world (level 4), divided into horticultural mythology (section 4), which is often matrifocal, and agrarian mythology (section 5), which is almost always patrifocal (patriarchal). Historically, the shift from the previous magical/foraging to mythological/horticultural occurred when planting was discovered. In horticultural societies, planting is done with a simple digging stick or hand-held hoe; because the physical demands are modest, pregnant women can participate, and up to 80% of foodstuffs in horticultural societies were produced by females. Consequently, around one-third of all horticultural societies had female-only deities (the Great Mother); about one-third had male and female deities; and about one-third, male-only deities. (With a few maritime exceptions, wherever you find a Great Mother society, it has a horticultural base.) When it was discovered that an animal could pull a large and heavy plow, much more planting could be done, but the work was physically harsh and demanding (women who participate in heavy physical plowing have a significantly higher rate of miscarriage; it is to their Darwinian advantage not to plow). Consequently, almost the entire food production was done by males, and—accordingly—over 90% of agrarian societies have predominantly male deities.

What was particularly striking about the matrifocal horticultural societies was the sporadic practice of human sacrifice. The Great Earth Mother demanded blood to bring forth new crops, and, as scholars such as Joseph Campbell have documented, "a fury for sacrifice" marked the rise of many matrifocal horticultural societies around the world (starting around 10,000 BCE). Although sacrifice in some cases intensified in later cultures, it appears certain to have begun here. I have used a particularly graphic and well-documented example from Campbell, where a young boy and girl are killed while copulating, their bodies roasted and eaten. This blood-and-body earth worship is typical of Great Mother religion.

The rise of patrifocal agrarian societies was often marked by a sharp break with human sacrifice, but a retention of many of its themes in symbolic or reduced form (as in the Catholic Mass—"Take, eat, this is my body; take, drink, this is my blood"). The patriarchal mythic religions saw themselves as more ethical than the previous earth-worshipping pagan religions, largely because of the banning of human sacrifice.

This overall mythic level is one that Jungian psychology often confuses with transrational spiritual domains. It has its own haunting beauty, but it is prerational, not transrational. Nonetheless, we still have a type of access to all of these early levels, and, when properly subsumed, they offer a great deal of vitality and imaginative richness. But my overall point is that neither horticultural nor agrarian mythology—nor mythology in general—can serve as genuine, transrational, spiritual guides for the modern and postmodern world.

• Section 6 is the rational world (level 5). The capacity for rational-perspectivism and pluralism brings such an increase in the good, the true, and the beautiful—brings such an increase in the light of understanding—no wonder they almost immediately called it "the Enlightenment." But there is also much hubris with rationality; only occasionally, with tragedy, does wonder and remorse break through.

• Section 7 is vision-logic or the integral-aperspectival world (level 6). In this story I went a little bit overboard; I was playing off the typical new-age new-paradigm exuberance, which takes the important truths of vision-logic and holism, but then injects them with a number of confusions: systems theory is not disclosing the same "web of life" that the magical world sees (systems theorists do not think that the volcano is exploding because it is personally mad at them); holistic thinking is not the same as Eastern contemplation (the former is mental, the latter is supramental); Gaia is not the same as the Goddess (the former is finite, the latter, infinite). In general, the woman in this story is falling prey to the fallacies that often dog the new-age new-paradigm agenda: a flatland holism (Right Hand only), retro-Romantic, purely Descended, biocentric, numerous pre/trans fallacies, etc. [I call this the "415 Paradigm," since its epicenter is the Bay Area and such institutions as CIIS. I have been a sharp critic of the 415 Paradigm, and many of its believers have responded with vehemence. See September 23 for an elaboration and critique of this view.] But the higher truth concealed in all this is indeed that of vision-logic and the integral-aperspectival view.

• Section 8 is one type of experience at the <u>psychic</u> level (level 7); specifically, this is a classic example of cosmic consciousness, or the temporary feeling of oneness with the entire gross realm. Notice that it is not permanent, and it does not involve the higher subtle or causal realms—in other words, it is a classic case of <u>nature mysticism</u>. This is the highest type of mysticism generally recognized by deep ecologists, ecopsychologists, neopagans, ecofeminists, Gaiasophists, and Great Mother worshippers, although it is the lowest of the mystical spheres, that of the World Soul or Eco-Noetic Self. Nonetheless, it is a profound and powerful dimension of consciousness, one glimpse of which can alter a life irrevocably.

The <u>tone</u> of experience at the psychic level (of nature mysticism) is almost always one of complete <u>reverence</u>; a sense of the <u>awesomeness</u> of existence; and a sense of the <u>insignificance</u> of humans in general and me in particular.

• Section 9 is another type of experience at the <u>psychic</u> level (level 7), pursued on <u>the path of shaman/yogis</u>, namely, the awakening of the psychic currents known as kundalini. These currents begin with the etheric body (the emotional-sexual body), but usually become conscious at the psychic level (as in this story) and persist into the subtle. This person has a kundalini awakening and, unable to contain it, sees it as an external other, which only slowly returns to the currents of his own bodymind. These types of psychic experiences are often the gateway to the next level, the subtle; and in kundalini yoga, the practitioner rides these bodily currents to their source in the sahasrara, the radiance of light at and beyond the crown of the head (epitome of the high subtle).

The <u>tone</u> of these experiences often starts reverential (when the sacred force is externalized as a Great Other), but eventually becomes one of <u>power</u> and <u>empowerment</u> (when the sacred force is realized to be an internal current of one's own bodymind). Traditionally, it is said that at this level the power can easily be misused, a type of Darth Vader, Castaneda move.

• Section 10 is a typical experience at the subtle level (level 8), pursued on the path of saints. The gross realm is temporarily left behind, so much so that it is often not even recognized. The energy currents of the bodymind return to their origin in the subtle (and especially the sahasrara, the infinity of Light and Bliss that is Above all gross orientation, a "saintly" stance often symbolized as a halo of light around the head). In these types of meditation, the sensation is always "in and up," in a literal, not metaphorical, sense. The Light and Bliss that is infinitely Above is directly experienced as such; this is the Form of Deity, which is one's own deepest Structure. This is the Sambhogakaya, the home of deity mysticism, the union of God and soul.

The tone of these experiences is usually ecstatic, visionary, apocalyptic, peaceful, and prophetic.

• Section 11 is the causal level (level 9), pursued on the path of sages. This is the home (the root source) of the Witness, of consciousness without an object, of pure cessation, classical nirvana and nirvikalpa, ayn, the unmanifest, the Formless, the great Unborn, Godhead, Urgrund, Dharmakaya, pure Emptiness. Where the psychic involves the communion of soul and God, and the subtle involves the union of soul and God, the causal is the identity of soul and God in prior Godhead. That is, when consciousness ascends to the infinity of subtle Light and Bliss Above (which is the subtle realm), at some point it "falls" into the causal Heart, and the separate-self sense is finally undone in radical Emptiness, nirguna Brahman, or unqualifiable Godhead. (The causal Heart, on the right, is not to be confused with the heart chakra, which is a subtle-level energy center of love on the central meridian; the former is pure Emptiness or absolute bodhichitta, the latter is compassion, or relative bodhichitta; cf. Sri Ramana Maharshi.)

With all lesser mystical states, there is always the sense of entering or leaving the state, always the sense of something different happening (seeing Light, feeling Love, knowing Deity, finding peace, etc.). But at some point in those ascending or descending currents—which are all gross or subtle experiences—there comes a sudden Witnessing of anything and everything that arises, and one no longer is moved to search for experiences of any variety at all. One moves off the line of ascent and descent (which, in itself, is samsara), and stands Free as the Witness-ing Heart. Instead of chasing after objects—sacred or profane, high or low, earthly or heavenly—one simply rests as the mirror-mind in which all objects are equally and impartially reflected. One is no longer moving up to the infinite Light above, or down to the vital Life below—one is simply Witnessing any and all movements. This is a stepping off of the Great Circle of Ascent (Eros) and Descent (Agape), and, although both those movements are perfectly embraced by the Witness, they no longer motivate consciousness itself. As consciousness—as the empty Wit-ness—one is the Unmoved Mover.

The centers of the gross-vital Life below (i.e., the lower chakras) are themselves a condensation of the subtle Light above (the higher chak-ras), and the highest chakra itself (the sahasrara) is simply the manifest reflection of the Unmanifest—it shines by the power of the causal Heart, even though the causal Heart is not itself Light (or any other manifest quality). In other words, all ascending and descending currents have their ultimate root source in the causal Heart, which itself is none of those currents—which is why the Witness can impartially witness all of manifestation, itself being free of the entire show.

(The Witness itself, however, inherently possesses the last remnant of separation, self, and duality, present as the tension between the Witness and everything witnessed, the tension—and the separation—between the unmanifest and the manifest, nirvana and samsara, emptiness and form; this final duality will dissolve when the causal Witness itself dis-solves into nondual One Taste, where Emptiness embraces all Form, nirvana and samsara are not-two, and the Witness is everything wit-nessed).

I chose, in this section, to include a recollection of past stages of growth. Just as an individual with a near-death experience might "see" a review of his or her entire life, so upon causal death, one might "see" a review of the entire sweep of cosmic history, which is the history of the unfolding of one's deepest Self. (Such an experience, when I was twenty-seven, was the basis of Up from Eden). This "review" does not itself take place in the causal—nothing exists in the causal—but rather, on either side of it (going in or coming out).

The tone of the causal is stone. It is unmoved and unmovable; a great mountain of the unmanifest; but also a sense of vastness, freedom, spaciousness, release, liberation. Also—and this is rather hard to convey—none of those "tones" has a sense of being an experience. Experiences come and go, but the empty Mirror is the vast space in which all experiences come and go, and is not itself experiential in the least.

· Section 12 is the descent from the causal to the subtle, or the beginning of involution, emanation, or manifestation itself. Sections 1–11 are the story of the ascent or evolution of consciousness, from matter to body to mind to soul to causal spirit. But once consciousness returns to its root source in the causal Heart, then descent or involution can consciously begin, moving from spirit to soul to mind to body to matter. Of course, variations on this cycle are occurring constantly, and it's a thoroughly nested affair (evolution and involution are occurring with each breath, and even with each microsecond. It's just that, at the point of return to the causal Heart, the entire cycle can be investigated consciously and deliberately, thus penetrating and undoing its power to fascinate.) Sections 12–14 are a very short version of the involution story, told from the perspective of this particular bodymind (i.e., kw).

Most people "experience" this transition each night when they move from deep sleep (one version of the causal) to the dream state (one version of the subtle), but they can't remember it. One of the aims of meditation is to render all these transitions conscious and thus become transparent to Source of the movement itself.

· Section 13 is the continuation of descent, moving from the subtle to the gross, completing the circle of evolution and involution (what Plotinus called reflux and efflux). When there is continuity of consciousness through all three major realms or states (causal, subtle, gross), in ascending and descending arcs, then the One Condition and One Taste of all realms becomes shockingly, simply obvious.

The tone of One Taste—and the path of the siddhas—is traditionally described in one of two ways, both of which tend to confuse people. The first is a tone of utter boredom, a great big yawn in the face of the entire world. The reason is that, because One Taste is the taste of absolutely everything in existence, then tasting One Taste, you have tasted it all. Been there, seen That. And thus it is traditional in, for example, Dzogchen Buddhism, to picture the Adept as looking infinitely bored.

The second is a tone that is <u>flippant</u>, almost wise-ass, and certainly irreverent. When Bodhidharma was asked the nature of reality, he said, "Vast Emptiness, nothing holy, nothing sacred." Nothing, in other words, that can't be made fun of. When <u>all</u> things are seen to be <u>equally</u> Spirit, there is no room for piety. Where the psychic shaman/yogi embodies great power, where the subtle saint embodies peaceful radiance, where the causal sage embodies stony equanimity, the nondual siddha embodies limitless humor. A great laughter returns, a lightness surrounds all acts. Needless to say, not everybody with a sense of humor is established in One Taste; humor is usually egoically driven. It's just that, when nothing is sacred, everything is taken lightly.

· What both of those tones have in common is a relentless ordinariness, nothing special. It is <u>just this</u>, nothing more (section 14).

Sunday, July 6

Phil Jacobson—his full name is Philip Rubinov-Jacobson, an old and honorable Russian Jewish name—has just returned from a month in Vienna with Ernst Fuchs, founder of the Vienna School of Fantastic Realism and major heir of Salvador Dali. Because I've written fairly extensively on art and aesthetics, I have often been contacted by artists from around the world, who send me their material and ask for help in getting it promoted. So I have for some time being trying to think of how to help with this situation. It seemed that a good place to start would be to create a type of clearinghouse—a modern museum—for transpersonal or spiritual art. I thought Phil would make a good project coordinator for this museum, and he agreed. The question has been where to locate it, and how to fund it.

Off Phil goes to Vienna. Fuchs, it turns out, has also been thinking about a museum for spiritual art, and when Phil mentions our similar idea, Fuchs gets so excited that they go into Vienna and Fuchs buys a building to house it! Fuchs is now looking for a castle to buy in which the artists themselves could actually work, while the Vienna building will house the archives, information exchange network, etc. Right now, it looks like Phil will spend about six months in Vienna getting the museum up and running, and then he will return to the States, set up a branch outlet here, and divide his time between the States and Europe.

The house in Vienna is actually a baroque palace, apparently quite beautiful, very large. And the castle—they are now in the process of buying it—is Franz Josef's summer castle. This is astonishing. If it works out—and the devil, of course, is in the details—this could be a real boon to transpersonal artists around the world.[17]

Tuesday, July 8

Raindrops are beating, a large puddle is forming, there on the balcony. It all floats in Emptiness, in purest Transparency, with no one here to watch it. If there is an I, it is all that is arising, right now and right now and right now. My lungs are the sky; those mountains are my teeth; the soft clouds are my skin; the thunder is my heart beating time to the timeless; the rain itself, the tears of our collective estate, here where nothing is really happening at all.

Wednesday, July 9

Sam and his daughter, Sara, arrived. It's always wonderful to see a little girl that you have known all her life suddenly show up a young woman. Sara is now eighteen, and simply beautiful. She's very bright, with a sharp and keen intellect, and she wants to get her degree in, of all things, philosophy.

"Sara wanted to talk to you about where to go to college."

"Yes," she said, "whether here, at a place like Sarah Lawrence or Brown, or perhaps in Canada, or somewhere else."

"The problem with a humanities education in the States is that my generation has made it a very dicey game, I'm ashamed to say. Extreme postmodernism is the mood, and the problem with extreme postmodernism is that in many ways it's driven by nihilism and narcissism. In other words, it believes in nothing but itself. Too many present-day treatises in the humanities are simply boomers attempting to demonstrate their moral superiority by condemning all previous works of art, science, literature, and philosophy. So cultural studies have often been turned into,

17. As of this writing, the Transpersonal and Spiritual Art Museum is still going forward. Those interested can contact Phil Jacobson in care of Shambhala Publications.

basically, self-esteem therapy for boomers, a way to promote themselves at the expense of all who came before."

Harsh words, but I recalled a recent article in lingua franca: The Review of Academic Life, by Professor Frank Lentricchia, where he exposes the epidemic of nihilism and narcissism now parading as literary and cultural studies in American universities. It "stems from the sense that one is morally superior to the writers that one is supposedly describing. This posturing of superiority," he says, treats everything that came before it as "a cesspool that literary critics will expose for mankind's benefit." Then he nails it: "The fundamental message is self-righteous, and it takes this form: 'T. S. Eliot is a homophobe and I am not. Therefore, I am a better person than Eliot.' To which the proper response is: 'But T. S. Eliot could really write, and you can't.' " No wonder Lentricchia concludes his survey of the present state of humanities in America: "It is impossible, this much is clear, to exaggerate the heroic self-inflation of academic literary and cultural criticism." Ouch.

"Are there any good points about the postmodern movements?" Sara wondered.

"Oh, definitely. I'm criticizing the extremists. But postmodernism in general has introduced what I think are three very important truths: constructivism, contextualism, and pluralism. Constructivism means that the world we perceive is not simply given to us, it is partially constructed by us. Many—not all—of the things we thought were universal givens are really socially and historically constructed, and thus they vary from culture to culture. Contextualism points out that meaning is context-dependent. For example, the 'bark of a dog' and the 'bark of a tree'—the word 'bark' means something entirely different in each phrase—the context determines the meaning. This gives interpretation (also called hermeneutics) a central place in our understanding of the world, because we do not simply perceive the world, we interpret it. And pluralism means that, precisely because meaning and interpretation are context-dependent—and there are always multiple contexts—then we should privilege no single context in our quest for understanding. (This is also referred to as integral-aperspectival, vision-logic, or network-logic.)

"So those three truths are the core of the various postmodern movements, and I strongly support those core truths. In that sense, I am definitely a postmodernist. The problem is, as with any movement, you can take these truths and blow them all out of proportion, at which point they become self-contradictory and self-defeating. So the extreme postmodernists do not just say that some truths are socially constructed and relative, they say all truths are, so there is no such thing as universal truth. But they are claiming that their truth is in fact universal. So they exempt themselves from the charges they level at everybody else—and again we see the narcissism underlying their nihilism."

"I see," Sara said, "so it's not so much postmodernism as extreme postmodernism we want to avoid."

"In my opinion, yes. Unfortunately, the extremists have a dominant hand in the humanities departments of most American universities today." Another recollection from a recent article, this one by Richard A. Posner in The New Republic: "The postmodern left is defined by its opposition to the values, the beliefs, and the culture of the 'West,' the 'West' being conceived as the domain of nondisabled heterosexual white males of European extraction and their east Asian and west Asian 'imitators,' such as the Japanese (Hitler's 'honorary Aryans') and the Jews. The postmodern left is radically multiculturalist, but it is more, for the 'West' that it denigrates is not historically specific; it encompasses liberalism, capitalism, individualism, the Enlightenment, logic, science, the values associated with the Judeo-Christian tradition, the concept of personal merit, and the possibility of objective knowledge." In other words, a nihilistic rejection of everything except its own worth: nihilism, narcissism. And the melancholy conclusion: "The postmodern left is well ensconced in American universities."

"So where can you get a good humanities education?" Sara asked, naturally concerned.

"Well, one good professor can turn almost any university into a worthwhile experience. There are plenty in the States, so shop around."

"I've thought about several universities in Canada, such as Victoria."

Sam jumped back in. "There's always Cambridge and Oxford."

"What do you think, Sara?"

"I'm visiting London this year, so maybe I'll check them out."

"The great advantage of a place like Oxford or Cambridge is that you can help to design and create your own curriculum, so you can turn it into a genuine multicultural education, studying the best of both West and East, North and South, without getting caught up in massive ideological agendas and the silliness of extreme postmodernism. We're slowly moving in this direction in the States, but in the meantime . . ."

Thursday, July 10

Sam is putting together a project that sounds exceptional; I've signed on as a consultant. It's a documentary called Pilgrimage, consisting of six one-hour segments. Each segment is by, and about, one person making a pilgrimage to a major religious site. So far the six are: Sri Lanka for Hinduism, Bodhgaya for Buddhism, Greenland for Inuit, Konya for Islamic dervishes, Australia for the Aboriginal tradition, and Jerusalem for Christianity/Judaism/Islam. This film will be distributed all over the world, through various television, satellite, cable, and theater outlets.

Rudy Wurlitzer is the main screenwriter, and Philip Glass has signed on to do the music. The idea of the series is to avoid the "anthropological tourism" of a National Geographic special, and aim instead for a combination of subjective journey with objective pilgrimage site. Each person will share their own hopes, fears, desires, worries, as they make their way to the particular shrine. So it will combine a rich, luscious photography of the objective site with a very personal account of spiritual seeking. And above all, the idea is to show each of the great traditions, not as a relic of the diminished past, but as an invitation to take up a genuine spiritual practice and thus open oneself to the glory of a greater tomorrow.

Friday, July 11

Party for Alex Grey at my house, with Marci, Sam, Sara, Tammi, Kate, Phil, etc. Alex is a remarkable person. It's not just that he's a brilliant and pioneering painter. He has a heart of gold and a gentleness that indicates not weakness but great strength. He also has the capacity to offer almost ecstatic praise of others, which is painfully rare in our culture of irony.

I had known that Alex had, for quite some time, been working on a book about art; he surprised me by pulling out a first draft. An accompanying volume contained dozens of his stunning artworks. Sam made an offer to publish both volumes, and Alex was simply stupefied. He could hardly talk.

I'm so glad for Alex. I think he's right on the verge of major international recognition. If only all parties could be this fun _and_ this rewarding.

Saturday, July 12

There is an ecopsychology conference coming up at Naropa. Ecopsychology has some wonderful points to recommend it. Among other things, it attempts to heal the dissociation between the knowing human subject and objective nature known; it seeks to end a certain arrogant anthropocentrism; it wishes to protect the environment, not as an "Other" but as part of our deepest Self; it sees human neurosis embedded in the (avoidable) fragmentation of organism and environment; it seeks to cure many of our major ills by healing this (arrogant) split between human and nature.

All of that is to ecopsychology's great credit. But my concern is that ecopsychology, in attempting to be a truly holistic approach, actually falls into the merely Descended world of flatland (or "flatland holism"), which is exactly the charge leveled by Michael Zimmerman [see May 11]. Here are my concerns (and this really applies to virtually all forms of eco-philosophy—deep ecology, ecofeminism, neopaganism, neoastrology, ecopsychology):

1. At its best, ecopsychology deals beautifully with the World Soul, Gaia, or the Eco-Noetic Self, by whatever name (level 7). In other words, at its best it is a genuine nature mysticism of the gross realm. But it leaves out and completely ignores the deity mysticism of the subtle realm, the formless mysticism of the causal realm, and the integral mysticism of the nondual. (Some Buddhists seem drawn to ecopsychology, but they should realize that it deals only with the Nirmanakaya, and leaves out the Sambhogakaya, the Dharmakaya, and the Svabhavikakaya.)

2. Although at its best it aims for the World Soul or Eco-Noetic Self, the bulk of ecopsychology, under a pre/trans fallacy, confuses the biosphere (level 2) with the World Soul (level 7). It doesn't appear to understand that the World Soul is that which _transcends_ the physiosphere (matter), the biosphere (life), and the noosphere (mind)—and therefore

can include and integrate all of them. Instead, it simply tries to reduce everything to the biosphere (what many critics have called eco-fascism).

3. Even those ecopsychologists who grasp the actual nature of the World Soul generally lack an interior technology of transformation—that is, they lack any sort of injunction, exemplar, or paradigm for genuinely transforming consciousness to the level of the World Soul. They champion a goal without a path. Lacking such, ecopsychology, even at its best, tends to degenerate into flatland maps and systems theory—mere mental concepts without the power to take you to the transmental.

4. The magical structure of foraging tribes is often confused with, and elevated to, the holistic embrace of vision-logic, and thus a regressive eco-primitivism is coupled with flatland systems theory, and this is often presented as a "new-paradigm," which is, let us say, problematic.

In short, only a few of the ecopsychology approaches seem to grasp the nature of the World Soul or Eco-Noetic Self, and of those that do, few have a reproducible technique for actually getting you there. Almost all ecopsychology, under the pre/trans fallacy, confuses the biosphere with the World Soul, which collapses the interior dimensions of consciousness, prevents people from taking up truly transformative practices, fosters regression to mere sensory-vital life, and champions a descended and flatland view, which itself is a prime contributor to ecological despoliation.

These criticisms were raised in Sex, Ecology, Spirituality, in a series of lengthy endnotes, and again in Brief History. But most eco-philosophers have chosen to ignore these criticisms, and have done so by focusing on two trivial points in SES involving interpretations of Emerson and Plotinus. With Emerson, in one long quote I deleted the word "nature" with an ellipsis, because Emerson uses that word in at least three different ways, which later becomes quite obvious (I included the source of the original quote so scholars could check it for themselves; nonetheless, I freely confess I should have done so more explicitly). With Plotinus, I indicated that all translations were from William Inge unless otherwise mentioned, then I gave "the Divine-in-Us departs to the Divine-in-All," which is actually Karl Jaspers's translation, not Inge's, and I failed to note this. Those were minor but regrettable errors, and they were corrected in all subsequent printings, although neither of them altered the conclusions in the slightest.

Alas, to this day, when many eco-theorists discuss SES, all they talk about is how I "distorted" Emerson and Plotinus (a spurious charge I exhaustively answered in The Eye of Spirit, chapter 11, endnotes 1, 2, and 3), and as evidence they point to nothing but those few trivialities. The sad thing is, this allows them to ignore not just my substantial and major criticisms, but those that Emerson and Plotinus themselves leveled against nature mysticism (and would therefore level against almost all forms of present-day ecopsychology, deep ecology, ecofeminism, and neopaganism).

Here, from The Eye of Spirit, is a summary of the widely accepted interpretation of Emerson's view: (1) nature is not Spirit but a symbol of Spirit (or a manifestation of Spirit); (2) sensory awareness in itself does not reveal Spirit but obscures it; (3) an Ascending (or transcendental) current is required to disclose Spirit; (4) Spirit is understood only as nature is transcended (i.e., Spirit is immanent in nature, but fully discloses itself only in a transcendence of nature—in short, Spirit transcends but includes nature). Those points are uncontested by Emerson scholars.

As far as those points go, Plotinus would have completely agreed. So forget my critique of those eco-movements: both Emerson and Plotinus would condemn—as true but partial and therefore not genuinely holistic—virtually all forms of ecopsychology, Gaia worship, neopaganism, deep ecology, and ecofeminism. My criticisms are simply fleshing out theirs. But all of these rather damning critiques, many eco-philosophers try to avoid by focusing on how SES "distorts" these pioneers.

The major reason I mention this is that ecopsychology, as a profound attempt to grasp the World Soul, could—if it pursued its venture more consistently—take its worthy spiritual project even deeper, into the genuinely transpersonal domains of subtle, causal, and nondual occasions. But in order to do so it must relinquish its grasp on the gross sensorimotor world as if that were the only major reality in the Kosmos. There are deeper domains, higher affairs, wider perceptions—gross to subtle to causal to nondual—awaiting those who penetrate the World Soul and find its Witness, and from there, One Taste.

At that point, the glorious promise of the eco-philosophies could be fulfilled and completed, resting in the One Taste that has often been their own admirable intuition from the start.

Tuesday, July 15

Good lord, Gianni Versace was shot to death early this morning, right outside his house in South Beach. At first it was thought that it might be due to his alleged connections with the Mafia—it's been rumored for years that he was laundering money for the mob. But now it looks like it was Andrew Cunanan, a serial gay murderer.

In the world of pop culture, this is a great loss, and it's sad he had to die so senselessly. There are no happy deaths; but many are redeemed in a moment of transcendence, or clarity, or care, or suffering carried with grace. But poor Versace, two bullets to the head, no grace, no glory, just sudden darkness.

It's especially sad because Versace—in addition to his electrifying effect on fashion—was instrumental in the renovation of South Beach. So much so that, as one TV commentator put it, Versace's house had become "the most famous house on the most famous drive in the most famous vacation spot in the world." Well, a little hyperbole never hurt anybody. But Versace managed to unite the worlds of entertainment and fashion—"frock and roll"—and his loss is truly lamentable.

At the same time, I can't help but be reminded how shallow pop culture is, was, and probably always will be. When gross-realm aesthetics are consciously plugged into subtle or causal depth, then sensory display in fashion and form becomes a rich expression of Spirit instead of a pitiful substitute for it. But such is popular culture—a sea of substitute gratifications, attempts to wring a pleasure from the body that can be found only in the fullness of Spirit—a sea of desires yearning for infinity, an ocean of itches eager for the All, finding instead a pathetic trickle of passing temporal release—an orgasm here, fifteen minutes of fame there, a sleek fashion here, a sneeze of cocaine there, all packaged by the purveyors of glossy glitzy shiny surfaces, one of whom was brutally murdered today.

It's very eerie watching the coverage on TV, because Versace was shot on exactly the place Marci and I stood to admire his house—directly on the steps outside of the iron gate. The place where we were standing is now a small puddle of blood.

Saturday, July 19

Roger and Frances arrived for a few days' visit, on their way to Fetzer, where Frances has organized a conference on "Spiritual Intelligence."

Tony is coming tomorrow, to decompress from Eisner and Aspen, so it's a bit crowded around here, but pleasantly so.

Monday, July 21

Roger and Frances left for Fetzer, leaving Tony and me. For several years Tony has been a practitioner and an advocate of the Diamond Approach, a method of psychospiritual growth founded by Hameed Ali. In fact, Tony gave the Diamond Approach one of his highest ratings in What Really Matters. But it now appears that, while he continues to appreciate that approach, he is also having a few second thoughts.

(I wrote a thirteen-page critique of the Diamond Approach in The Eye of Spirit [chapter 11, note 11]. I believe that the approach is very important and a major step forward in the integration of psychology and spirituality. But it also contains several pre/trans fallacies that render it dangerously unstable, and I said so strongly in the critique. Tony has come to a similar position.)

To put it in a very simplified form, the Diamond Approach maintains that we all start out, as infants, basically in touch with our spiritual Essence, but the process of growing up represses or chokes off this Essence. This repression of Essence leaves us with various 'holes' in our being—various symptoms and defenses and distresses. Using psychological techniques to undo this repression allows us to recontact the lost Essence, and thus bring a spiritual awareness into our lives. The Diamond Approach therefore seeks to unite psychotherapy and spirituality in one system. It is now enjoying a surging popularity.

"But you think that the Diamond Approach is caught in a pre/trans fallacy," Tony said.

"Yes, definitely. It confuses pre-egoic impulse with trans-egoic Essence, just because both are non-egoic. That's a classic mistake."

"But they would say something like this. You can tell by watching young children when they play that they are really in touch with Essential Joy. They are spontaneous, alive, vibrant, and glowing with pure joy. But then as they grow up, they start to lose touch with that pure joy, they . . ."

"Just a second. You've already loaded the argument by using the word 'pure' in front of 'joy.' Who says this is pure joy, meaning pure spiritual joy? It's not pure, and it's not spiritual. It's just impulsive. There is a big difference."

"Why?"

"As you know, a crucial watershed in psychological development occurs somewhere around ages five to seven, when young children learn to take the role of other. There is a series of famous experiments that show this. If you take a ball colored green on one side and red on the other, put the green side facing the child, and ask him, 'What color are you looking at?,' he will correctly say green. But if you ask him, 'What color am I looking at?,' he will say green, even though you are looking at red. He cannot put himself in your shoes, he cannot take the role of other."

"Yes, I know. And around age seven, children will get the answer right. They can start to take the role of other."

"Yes, meaning that the child has moved from an egocentric to a sociocentric capacity—from me to we—from narcissism to social sharing, to taking the role of others and including others. This is a huge transformation in consciousness—also known as the shift from preconventional to conventional awareness. And then finally, around adolescence, there occurs a shift from conventional to postconventional awareness, which means that awareness is no longer trapped and limited to my group or my tribe or my nation, but rather opens to a universal, global, worldcentric awareness, where all people are treated with justice and fairness, regardless of race, sex, religion, or creed. And, as you know, in my system this global worldcentric awareness is the gateway to genuine spiritual states."

"Yes," said Tony. "So how does this apply to the Diamond Approach?"

"Well, to use your example, the Diamond Approach confuses preconventional, narcissistic, egocentric joy with postconventional, worldcentric, spiritual joy. It confuses pre and trans."

"But what exactly is the difference?" Tony asked.

"Joy is not spiritual joy until it can take the joy of others into account. Joy that is confined solely to your own ego may be joy, but it is not spiritual joy or essence of joy or anything like that at all. It is self-centered, self-absorbed, self-glorifying—and if that is your idea of Spirit, somebody is in deep trouble."

"So joy would what? develop into higher forms?"

"Yes, that's right. Like most traits, joy grows and evolves—or develops—from preconventional to conventional to postconventional to spiritual forms."

"What would joy at the conventional level look like?"

"When most people are happy, it's not really fun until you can share it with someone, especially someone you love, a mate or a friend. It's the joy not just of 'me' but of 'we'—not egocentric but sociocentric. You aren't happy if just you are happy—you want your family and friends to be happy, and you suffer if they aren't. In fact, at this level, if your joy remains locked in the self-absorbed mode, there is probably some deep pathology."

"And joy at the postconventional level?"

"As your consciousness grows and evolves into global and worldcentric modes, you can no longer be truly happy without at least the thought of extending this happiness and joy to all others. You become idealistic in the best sense of the word, wishing to relieve the suffering of—and extend happiness to—all people—not just your family, or your friends, or your tribe, your religion, your nation (those are all sociocentric and ethnocentric), but rather to all peoples, regardless of race or sex or creed. At least to some degree, you realize that you are not deeply and truly happy if somebody, somewhere, is suffering. The thought of others suffering starts to disturb your awareness, just a little at first, then a lot—a nagging thought that rains on your parade and keeps you from rejoicing, and you begin to act, to whatever degree you are moved, to try to better the lot of humankind, with whatever talents and resources you have. Your happiness is not truly happy until all others can share in that joy."

"Using your words," said Tony, "that would begin to open to the genuine spiritual modes of happiness, extended to all sentient beings. Like the bodhisattva vow."

"Yes, I think so. And that is where we start to see Essential Joy, or true spiritual Joy—and not at the narcissistic and egocentric stage! Confusing these two is a nightmare, really, and is itself deeply narcissistic. It is a travesty that these narcissistic modes are being elevated to spiritual glory."

"Okay. But you do acknowledge that the young child's joy can be repressed and choked off?"

"Oh, definitely, absolutely. Of course you can seal out the joy of child-hood, but it's a preconventional joy, not a postconventional joy."

"And your point has always been that sealing out the former makes it less likely the latter will emerge," Tony added.

"Exactly. If you step on an acorn, you are going to damage it, and it will have a hard time growing into the oak that it might be. But what you are hurting and repressing is the acorn—you are <u>not</u> repressing or stepping on the oak, because that hasn't emerged yet—there aren't any leaves, branches, roots, etc., to step on. So you can definitely repress or damage joy at <u>any</u> of its stages of growth, and this will make it less likely that Essential Joy will emerge later in development. But that Essence is an <u>emergent</u> that comes down, not a <u>recontacted</u> infantile state coming back up. It is God descending, not id arising."

"Yes, I agree," he said. "But the proponents of the Diamond Approach would say that they have the experiential data to prove they are right. When you do the Diamond work, you start by feeling or experiencing any 'hole' that you might have—any empty feeling, bored feeling, agitated feeling, whatever. When you relax your defenses and simply feel into this hole, then sooner or later the corresponding Essence will emerge, and the hole will 'fill up' with a positive warmth and wisdom. That shows, they say, that you are <u>recontacting</u> the Essence that was repressed while growing up."

"It shows nothing of the sort. There are two very different things going on here, and they have thoroughly confused them. To begin with, if you repress a preconventional impulse—say, early joy—then that repression is a wall that seals off not only the lower impulses trying to come up, but the higher impulses trying to come down. In other words, a strong repression against id will also tend to block out God, simply because both id and God can threaten the ego, and a defense against one helps defend against the other. Thus, if you relax the wall of repression—a repression first created against a <u>lower</u> impulse when you were perhaps two or three years old—you can simultaneously open yourself to the descent of a <u>higher</u> impulse, which itself was <u>never</u> repressed in the past but is now <u>emerging</u> for the first time. Essence is an emergent, not an infantile regurgitation. There is a timeless feeling about Essence, which gives it a sense of being recontacted, which is true enough, but it is a recontacting of the depth of the timeless present, not a dredging up of an infantile past. By relaxing and disarming the repression against preconventional impulses, you can more easily open yourself to postconventional and spiritual modes. But to confuse the two is a classic pre/trans fallacy."

Tuesday, July 22

"I still think," Tony picked up the conversation, "that the Diamond Approach is a useful path, but it definitely seems caught in these pre/trans fallacies. I've also begun to worry that for all its talk of healing early childhood traumas, it doesn't go very far in actually reaching these early traumas, let alone healing them. And this problem applies to virtually all spiritual approaches to growth, as far as I can tell."

"How so?" I asked.

"You were saying that relaxing the defenses meant to keep the id from coming up can allow Spirit to come down."

"Yes. There are other, separate defenses that are often put up against Spirit, and they need to be addressed on their own. But yes, the early defenses against a lower impulse also tend to seal out the higher, and regression in service of transcendence is then necessary."

"Going back and undoing these early defenses so higher growth can proceed. I totally agree. The problem is that very few approaches go back far enough, or efficiently enough, to genuinely relax and undo these primitive defenses and repressions. I don't think the Diamond Approach does. And most forms of spiritual growth don't even address this issue, so they don't either."

"True. About the only schools that deal effectively with these early traumas are object relations—such as Kernberg—and self psychology—such as Kohut—and the similar approaches of Masterson, Stone, and so on. The Diamond Approach draws on these sources for theoretical understanding, which is great, but it doesn't really use any of the powerful tools of these approaches, which is too bad."

"That's right. So the loosening of early defenses that occurs is very short-lived. I once finished an intense period of Diamond work, and I was in a state of essential Joy for two hours—it was wonderful. Then it faded. Never happened since. It's like you open the doors, and they snap back like a rubber band. The Diamond Approach is powerful enough to stretch the rubber band for a short period, but it always snaps back," Tony concluded.

"And just as you said, Tony, virtually all forms of spiritual growth don't even address this issue—don't even try to understand and undo these early defenses—and so they don't stretch the rubber band at all. The result is that your own individual bodymind cannot really become a spacious vehicle for Spirit. Your being is too tight, too enclosed, too defended, too sealed off to open fully to the Divine."

"In your system," Tony said, "the Diamond Approach deals with mostly levels 7 and 8, the soul levels."

"Yes, I think so. Which itself is pretty impressive. And Hameed at least takes into account the extensive theoretical work that has been done on levels 1, 2, and 3—the early object relations and primitive defenses. But, as we were saying, the Diamond Approach doesn't seem to have the tools to actually reach and repair these early lesions in awareness. But I'm very encouraged that they are aware of the extensive research that has been done on the early levels, and I applaud this in my review."

I then told Tony about my idea of "spiritual GPs"—full-spectrum therapists who, even if they can't themselves perform all types of therapy, are trained to spot problems coming from any and all levels of the spectrum of consciousness, and can therefore refer their clients to therapists, spiritual teachers, analysts, yogis, psychotherapists, etc., who focus on the particular level(s) where the client is having a problem.

Tony responded with a typical Tonyism: "I once asked Hameed what he did when students in the Diamond Approach really needed psychotherapy, and he said, 'Oh, when they need it, we recommend a therapist.' I said, 'But they all need it.' And they do."

Wednesday, July 23

Got an e-mail from Leo Burke in Beijing. Leo heads the team at Motorola responsible for the development of some twenty thousand managers worldwide. Business management is one of the last areas that I have addressed, and Leo helped spark this interest when, two years ago, he sent an arresting fax, brilliant in its analysis of the state of business in the world today. They're using Sex, Ecology, Spirituality in their courses at Motorola University. Since Leo's fax, I have been more open to the correspondence coming to me from business people around the world, and I expect that interest will accelerate with the publication of volume 2, which deals specifically with the techno-economic base of social evolution—"business" in the broad sense.

Leo writes that "My own journey at this point is interesting. At a meeting on Friday at the Santa Fe Institute I posed the questions, 'What role do institutions of commerce, especially multinational corporations, play in the evolution of our species? And what potential, if any, does business have to support a vision of humanity that integrates spirit, mind, and body on individual, organizational, and societal levels?' There were no answers forthcoming, but asking the questions in a business context is a small step forward. Yet any exercise of considering such questions is quite limp without the questioners having a fundamental commitment to their own transformation. Ultimately, of course, this is a commitment not to incremental self-improvement, but to genuine self-transcendence."

Amen.

Tuesday, July 29

Roger is now involved in a national debate on astrology. I'm loving this, because so far I've been the only one to draw intense fire from the new-age new-paradigm crowd, and now Roger is going to get both barrels. This is great.

Bless their hearts, but what so many new-agers do not seem to understand is that there are not <u>two</u> major groups in this country—the rational (which they distrust) versus the nonrational (which they champion). Rather, there are <u>three</u> major groups—the prerational, the rational, and the transrational. And, again bless their hearts, the vast majority of new-age approaches tend to slide into the prerational camp. To make matters worse, the transrational camp—including Roger—actually has more in common with the rational than with the prerational (although the aim, of course, is to integrate all three).

So the new-age coterie is surprised, hurt, and angered when a genuine transrational mystic—such as Roger—starts criticizing them, because all us "nonrational mystics" are supposed to be in the same boat, fighting the rational, conventional, antispiritual types. But the trans-rational mystics are fighting, most strongly, pre-rational regression, and then mere rationality, attempting to open both to a genuine transrational approach.

Well, Roger has now stepped directly in the line of fire. He's going public with his attack on astrology. Roger maintains that he has come to his conclusion—namely, that virtually all of traditional astrology is somewhere in the neighborhood of bunk—by systematically reviewing the massive amount of carefully controlled studies done on the topic. He wants to write a book with the title The Scam of the Century or The Rip-Off of the Ages or something like that [but has since decided against it].

So Noetic Sciences Review has invited Roger and Will Keepin to debate this topic in its pages. Will is a very intelligent writer, with a felicitous style and thoughtful presentation. Trained as a physicist and originally viewing astrology as totally bonkers, he came late to a strong belief in its validity, based on the same claim Roger makes: the evidence itself led him to this conclusion. So eloquent is Will on this topic, he is the feature theorist in Life magazine's cover story on astrology, where he convinced the journalist of its truth. This promises to be a great match. Really, this is the closest thing this field gets to a thrilla in Manila.

I'm getting the papers as they're written, and here's where it stands so far. Roger opened round 1 with a summary of research to date: "Most people are surprised to learn just how much experimental research has been conducted on astrology. Well over one hundred studies are available, some of them done by astrologers or in collaboration with astrologers. Taken together they constitute a body of research of sufficient quality and quantity to provide a powerful assessment of the validity of astrological claims."

What has been found? Roger asks. Quoting from his paper:

> Researchers have studied five capacities that astrologers claim are essential if astrology is to be considered legitimate.
> • The first group of studies examined the degree of agreement between astrologers in judging the same birth charts. The results are striking! *There is virtually no agreement whatsoever between different astrologers' interpretations of the same chart.* This was a

consistent finding across studies, including those using expert astrologers, those run by astrologers themselves, and those run by astrologers and scientists in collaboration.

· This finding alone is devastating and virtually destroys any claim for reliability or validity of astrological readings. As one critic concluded, "If astrologers can't even agree on what a birth chart *means* then their entire practice is reduced to absurdity."

· Subjects of astrological readings are unable to pick their own readings from other randomly chosen profiles. In other words, subjects are just as likely to think that another person's profile is as accurate a description of them as their own.

· Studies of over 3,000 astrological predictions showed that they fared no better than chance or guesses.

· Over three dozen studies show that astrologers' readings do not match or correlate at better than chance levels with well-validated psychometric tests of personality. This failure occurred even when the astrologers were highly esteemed experts, helped design the study, regarded the study as good measures of their skills, and rated their confidence in their readings as high.

· Astrologers usually claim that whole chart readings are more accurate than individual factors. However, the research finds no support for the accuracy of either individual factors or whole chart readings.

"In short," Roger concludes, "research finds no support whatsoever for the reliability or validity of astrological readings."

Oooooooh, great opening shots! Some skull-crunching punches. We might have had a total knockout were it not for the rather extraordinary Gauquelin studies. Starting in the 1950s, French researcher Michel Gauquelin began a several-decades-long exhaustive analysis of statistical data relating to astrology. "To his surprise," Roger points out, "analysis did reveal small but significant correlations between eminence in various professional fields and the position of certain planets at birth. For example, eminent scientists, journalists, and athletes were likely to have the planets Saturn, Jupiter, and Mars, respectively, just over the horizon or at the zenith of the sky at the time of their birth."

Oooooh, a big opening here, and Will moves right in. He begins by pointing out that several skeptical scientific organizations have tried to refute the Gauquelin studies, to no avail. Hans Eysenck, the highly respected statistical psychologist, has summarized what this means: "Emotionally, I would prefer the Gauquelin results not to hold, but rationally, I must accept that they do. . . . We can find no valid major criticism of their conclusions, methods, or statistics. They cannot be wished away because they are unpalatable or not in accord with the laws of present-day science. . . . Perhaps the time has come to state quite unequivocally that a new science is in the process of being born."

Wow! Great left hook, as round 1 closes. Astonishingly, Roger doesn't even blink. He opens round 2 by straightforwardly accepting the general results of the Gauquelin studies. But it's all in the interpretation, he says:

"First, Gauquelin's patterns do not fit traditional astrological patterns." In other words, if this is true, and since the Gauquelin study is the only major study that has shown validity, then if we are to agree with its findings, we must also jettison most of traditional astrology, because there was little if any support found for that. "Second, Gauquelin's findings apply *only* to eminent people. People who do not attain eminence—in other words, the vast majority of us—show no correlation with planetary birth position." Again, traditional astrology takes a huge hit. "Third, the correlations are *extremely* small, about 0.05, meaning that they account for less than 1% of variability." This means that, for example, eminent athletes are only 5% more likely to have Mars in position. Whatever the effect, it is clearly very weak. Roger maintains that "this is far, far too small to be of any value whatsoever for astrological readings or predictions."

Ooooooh. This is where it stands at the end of round 2. Whatever else may be said, traditional astrology has taken a very bad beating. The only studies either side can come up with that unequivocally command respect are Gauquelin's. But according to those results, a good deal of traditional astrological claims do not hold up at all. Will maintains that some of them do, although both agree that sun-sign astrology and newspaper astrology are kaput. But Roger comes back with a strong right jab: "You [Will] imply that Gauquelin's findings support traditional Western-applied astrology, whereas I argue for several reasons that his findings offer no comfort whatsoever to the specific claims of traditional astrology. Indeed, apart from a few very general principles, which you quote him to support (e.g., the meridian is important), Gauquelin himself was very clear that his findings did *not* fit traditional astrological patterns." Roger then makes what is probably a safe conclusion, at least at this point: "I emphasize the absolute necessity of differentiating clearly between Gauquelin findings and traditional astrology"—because there is strong evidence for the former, little for the latter.

But even the Gauquelin astral associations that hold are very, very weak. According to Roger, fatally so. But Will maintains that, even if small, these influences are a fact, which Roger does not contest, and so they must be explained. Drawing on a few of my ideas, Will suggests a way to do so. "The implications [of the Gauquelin studies] are dumbfounding. Borrowing on Wilber's concepts, astrology points toward a vast 'holarchy' which not only unifies the physiosphere, biosphere, and noosphere, as Wilber calls for, but does so in a larger celestial context that 'transcends but includes' the Gaian system. By going deeper within, we indeed discover a wider beyond: a living 'Kosmic' holarchy in which the Earth is but one among many higher planetary 'superholons.' Astrological transits correspond to the effects of these celestial superholons as they 'limit the indeterminacy' of their junior holons, i.e., they modify the probability structures of terrestrial events. The entire process is not mechanistically causal, but is more likely a unitive process that unfolds holographically at multiple holonic levels simultaneously—thereby giving rise to observed temporal correlations."

Will uses each of my terms accurately, which is impressive; and I find his theory plausible. However, I think there is another explanation, within the same "wilber" framework, that makes more sense.

The question is, are we working with upward or downward causation? That is, are these weak astral influences generated at the level of the World Soul ("celestial superholons"), and then imposed on the junior holons of individual human beings—by "downward causation" or "downward influence"—as Will maintains? Or are they operating merely at the physical level—exerted by physical planets on the physical human body—and from there have a mild "upward influence" on the emergence of higher levels, including the emotions and the mind? I strongly suspect the latter, for several reasons.

First, these influences, as both Roger and Will note, are very, very weak. This is often a tip-off to upward influence, not downward influence. Downward influence is often very strong, almost causal. For example, when the senior-holon "I" decides to move my junior-holon arm, all of the molecules in my arm get right up and move. Five percent of them don't move, they all bloody well move.

Second, there is that fascinating point that Gauquelin's astral associations do not hold with Caesarean or induced deliveries. Any Kosmic superholon that can't override a C-section is not much of a superholon.

Third, these astral associations occur only for people of eminence. This is extremely telling—and, I think, the crucial point—and it is very hard to account for if the influences are stemming from the level of the World Soul. If the World Soul or Kosmic superholon is happily modifying the probability of the lower holons, why does it do so only for the prominent and powerful and famous?

But these astral associations with eminence make sense if they are emanating from the physical level and exerting their relatively weak upward influence on the higher levels of emotion and mind (and character traits), because only the strongest of these already weak forces would be expected to have any observable influence at all. That is, only the really strong influences manage to persist through the dampening that occurs with upward influence: the lower has to struggle very hard to override—or decisively influence—the higher. For the average person, who is presumably not getting a huge dose of what are already very weak astral forces, these tepid influences would wash out entirely.

At the close of round 3, I'd have to say that Roger has delivered a devastating blow to most of typical astrology. I myself, who have remained agnostic on this topic for quite some time, find many of his arguments compelling. And Will agrees that sun-sign astrology, newspaper astrology, and outer planet astrology are dead meat. So it's a clean knockout to all those forms of typical astrology.

Both agree, however, that Gauquelin astral associations are real, but very weak: 0.05 is simply not much to write home about. However, as Will (and Eysenck) point out, this anomaly is devastating to any worldview that cannot accommodate it. Both Will and I agree that, at least at this point, only some sort of holonic (or holarchical) conception can do so. I used to think that this explanation would come from the level of the World Soul (or psychic-level superholon), but I now think that the most likely explanation involves physical-level interaction—merely physical planets on physical human bodies—and this is carried, via upward influence <u>during development</u>, to the higher levels of emotion and mind (possibly through gravitational/hormonal interaction, or geomagnetic/neuronal interaction, or some combination thereof), with only the strongest of the relatively weak forces surviving in observable forms as eminence in various fields.

My sun sign is Aquarius, although I'm trying to have it legally changed. Let's see what my horoscope says for today. "The beautiful creature I'm spying on seems to be turning into a bliss addict. The ambiance here is lush and sensual. The air is saturated with juicy pheromones. Yet there's also an unmistakably *sacred* feeling. It's not out of the question to speculate that Aquarius is poised to break all previous records for Spiritual Growth While under the Influence of Lust."

I take it back, I believe everything about sun signs.

AUGUST

What is the world? An eternal poem,
out of which the spirit of Godhead shines and glows,
the wine of wisdom foams and sparkles,
the sound of love speaks to us.
—HUGO VON HOFMANNSTHAL

The new spirit, as it becomes more conscious, is increasingly
capable of transforming the moments of contemplation into
one moment, into a permanent vision.
—PIET MONDRIAN

Saturday, August 2

"Hi Ken, it's Frances."

"Oh, hi, Frances. Now that Roger is off to his month-long meditation retreat, are you enjoying your breathing space?"

"Things are too busy around here. I just got back from the annual Association for Transpersonal Psychology conference."

"They asked you to give the closing address."

"Yes. I arrived the day before and mingled with old friends, which was nice, very nostalgic. My first conference there was thirty-two years ago! It was big event in my life; it really changed my life. Huston Smith, Jim Fadiman, the original crew. Anyway, one person came up to me and I was so glad to meet her after all these years. It was Laura Huxley."

"You're kidding."

"She must be in her eighties, very small and petite, but very lively. She told me how much she liked my work, I told her how much I admired hers, it was very nice."

"How'd the speech go?"

"I did it on creativity, it was fine."

"I'll bet it was better than fine."

"Creativity can be a way for people to connect with their own spiritual intelligence, so I talked about that. It was fine."

"How's the World Forum coming along?"

The State of the World Forum is a rather remarkable organization founded by James Garrison and Mikhail Gorbachev, and has included Desmond Tutu, Elie Wiesel, James Baker, Jehan Sadat, Ted Turner, among hundreds of others. This year's Forum will be held November 4–9 in San Francisco. Frances was asked to put together the session on "Intelligence and Evolution," which she divided into three subsessions: Human Intelligence and Evolution, Practice and Inner Work, and Legacy of Wisdom. She has assembled a stellar cast of participants for the first two, but the last one—which was meant to be a panel of elders discussing the importance of tradition and legacy—is not proceeding smoothly.

"Everything is going fine except the Legacy of Wisdom. Some of the participants, like Ram Dass, are ill, and others, like Huston, are wisely choosing not to come. They have too much wisdom to be part of a show on wisdom, so I'm stuck!"

Frances will pull it off, though, she always does.

Sunday, August 3

People typically feel trapped by life, trapped by the universe, because they imagine that they are actually in the universe, and therefore the universe can squish them like a bug. This is not true. You are not in the universe; the universe is in you.

The typical orientation is this: my consciousness is in my body (mostly in my head); my body is in this room; this room is in the surrounding space, the universe itself. That is true from the viewpoint of the ego, but utterly false from the viewpoint of the Self.

If I rest as the Witness, the formless I-I, it becomes obvious that, right now, I am not in my body, my body is IN my awareness. I am aware of my body, therefore I am not my body. I am the pure Witness in which my body is now arising. I am not in my body, my body is in my consciousness. Therefore, be consciousness.

If I rest as the Witness, the formless I-I, it becomes obvious that, right now, I am not in this house, this house is IN my awareness. I am the pure Witness in which this house is now arising. I am not in this house, this house is in my consciousness. Therefore, be consciousness.

If I look outside this house, to the surrounding area—perhaps a large stretch of earth, a big patch of sky, other houses, roads and cars—if I look, in short, at the universe in front of me—and if I rest as the Witness, the formless I-I, it becomes obvious that, right now, I am not in the universe, the universe is IN my awareness. I am the pure Witness in which this universe is now arising. I am not in the universe, the universe is in my consciousness. Therefore, be consciousness.

It is true that the physical matter of your body is inside the matter of the house, and the matter of the house is inside the matter of the universe. But you are not merely matter or physicality. You are also Consciousness as Such, of which matter is merely the outer skin. The ego adopts the viewpoint of matter, and therefore is constantly trapped by matter—trapped and tortured by the physics of pain. But pain, too, arises in your consciousness, and you can either be in pain, or find pain in you, so that you surround pain, are bigger than pain, transcend pain, as you rest in the vast expanse of pure Emptiness that you deeply and truly are.

So what do I see? If I contract as ego, it appears that I am confined in the body, which is confined in the house, which is confined in the large universe around it. But if I rest as the Witness—the vast, open, empty consciousness—it becomes obvious that I am not in the body, the body is in me; I am not in this house, the house is in me; I am not in the universe, the universe is in me. All of them are arising in the vast, open, empty, pure, luminous Space of primordial Consciousness, right now and right now and forever right now.

Therefore, be Consciousness.

Monday, August 4

Mitch is just back from the Spiritual Intelligence conference, organized by Frances, held at Fetzer. He thought it was interesting and useful in many ways, but could have benefited from a little more critical and skeptical attitude. Frances knew that Mitch—our glorious skeptic, as Kate

Olson calls him—felt this way, so on the last day she invited him to voice his concerns.

"So how did it go?" I asked over the phone.

"Stan Grof was there. He was talking about his latest book, The Cosmic Game. He said you helped with it."

"Not really. Only a little. He sent me the manuscript, and it became apparent that there were really two books mixed together in it, so I suggested separating them, which works much better, I think. He did so, and now SUNY is publishing the first one. It's really an exceptionally important work, and yet another version of the Great Chain of Being, this time developed with modern techniques. Anyway, how did the last day go, with your skepticism and all?"

"A few of us got on the topic of UFO abductions, and some people simply did not want to have their beliefs questioned. One person said, 'There are over ten thousand reported abductions each year. Do you think all of these people are just making this up?' 'Well, sure,' I replied. It didn't go over too well."

"I can imagine."

"I'm sometimes too skeptical, but some of these people seem to lack the capacity entirely. It's too bad, because this field is crazy enough without UFO abductions getting tossed in. And if you don't believe them, they think you are sick, or antispiritual, or whatever. But the fact that ten thousand people claim to have been abducted is the last place you would look for corroborating evidence."

"I agree," I said. "Last year alone there were a reported fifteen hundred Elvis sightings. So I suppose that means Elvis is alive and well and making all these visits. This is not evidence."

Mitch and I said goodbye, after making some plans for his visit.

UFO abductions. I saw John Mack on a talk show with several "abductees." It was painfully obvious what was happening. These people had all been "abducted," given a physical exam, subjected to the ubiquitous anal probe, and had sperm or ovum collected from them. And then—this was the primal scene, the dark heart of the hallucination— they had been shown their sons and daughters, produced by a cross-fertilization between their sperm/ovum and the aliens'. These people, in other words, were the fathers and mothers of the new race that would populate the earth. And right there the staggering narcissism becomes perhaps too obvious. I really don't mean to be cruel, but all you keep thinking is, if these folks are the parents of the new race, we're in deep trouble. Sort of like your parents being first cousins.

When people have a memory or an experience of being "abducted," I don't doubt the experience seems absolutely real to them (most would pass a lie detector test). And it is real, as an experience, as phenomenology, but not as ontology, not as an objective reality. So there's the phenomenology (or the experience itself), and there is how you interpret the experience. And for that interpretation—as with all interpretation—you need to draw on the total web of available evidence, which is exactly what the believers in these experiences are not doing. Especially Mack, it seems.

Do any UFO experiences represent higher realities? It's theoretically possible that some of these experiences are stemming from the psychic or subtle level of consciousness (levels 7 and 8), and that, precisely because these people do not directly grow and evolve into these levels, they experience them as an "other." Instead of their own deeper and higher luminous nature, they project it outwardly as an alien form. Even if that is true, these people are still in the grips of a dissociative pathology. In either case, this is nothing to brag about.

The giveaway, as usual, is the narcissism. The comedian Dennis Miller nailed it: "Only man is a narcissistic enough species to think that a highly evolved alien life force would travel across billions and billions of light-years—a group of aliens so intelligent, so insouciant, so utterly above it all, they feel no need whatsoever to equip their spacecraft with windows so that they can gaze out on all that celestial beauty—but then immediately upon landing, their first impulse is to get in some hick's ass with a flashlight."

What do people really want when they think about UFOs? What are they yearning for at the thought of something extraterrestrial? Why, they want something bigger than themselves. They want to know that, in the entire, wild, extraordinary Kosmos, there is something other than their meager egos.

Well, there is.

Tuesday, August 5

Just this greets me this morning; just this, its own remark; just this, there is no other; just this, the sound of one hand clapping—the sound, that is, of One Taste. The subtle and causal can be so overwhelmingly numinous and holy; One Taste is so pitifully obvious and simple.

Maureen Silos sent me her doctoral dissertation, "Economics Education and the Politics of Knowledge in the Caribbean"—she just got her Ph.D. from UCLA. Maureen and I began corresponding last year, when she wrote that she was applying my work "to issues of Third World development." I put her in touch with, among others, Michael McDermott, who is doing similar work in Swaziland. Maureen was born and raised in the Caribbean; as a black woman she is uniquely situated to address these difficult, delicate, seemingly intractable problems. She had originally contacted me in mild exasperation at the anti-evolutionary, implicitly reactionary stance of her supposedly "liberal" and "progressive" advisory committee—a stance that is, in fact, the norm in postmodern flatland, and especially in its universities, where an allegiance to a tepid egalitarianism (maintained only by an intellectual elite!) actually has the effect of discouraging interior consciousness development, individual as well as cultural, which alone can alleviate so many of these distresses.

Maureen tackles these issues head on, based in part on my work, but going quite beyond that with her own additions and applications. The results are impressive. She begins by pointing out that "Evolution is taboo in anthropology and progressive circles of the social sciences, [due to] a particular reaction within progressive circles in the West to social Darwinism, colonialism, racism, the holocaust, and assorted ideas that rank human beings as essentially inferior or superior. Even though the reaction is understandable, the result is disastrous for social theory because we now face a massive hostility to cultural evolution."

I'll say. She continues: "The social origins of the wholesale rejection of the notion of cultural evolution by Western progressive social theorists is something that Caribbean and other Third World scholars have to be aware of when we adopt these ideas, because this position, even though very well intended, creates 'the extremely bizarre situation of driving a virulent wedge right through the middle of the Kosmos: everything nonhuman operates by evolution; everything human does not.' What I try to do therefore is to distinguish between the valid and invalid aspects of the notion of cultural evolution, because this is the only approach that offers me the opportunity to understand the *nature* of the clash between worldviews in the Caribbean *and* to argue for a vertical dimension of cultural and consciousness development based on the evolutionary model of the contemplative traditions of both the East and the West."

Excellent. Maureen continues: "The idea of the evolution of cultures, consciousness, and worldviews is necessary because without it there seems to be no alternative to the idea that with the emergence of liberal democratic industrialized Western societies humankind has reached the end of history. And that is unacceptable to me. Is there something better possible and how do we get from here to there?" Touché. Her point is that, contrary to the prevailing flatland postmodern view, not only is cultural evolution not an ethnocentric or eurocentric notion, it is the only way out of the hidden ethnocentrism of most "progressive" circles of Western social science, which in fact discourage the cultural evolution that alone would transcend the ethnocentrism. In other words, although they nobly desire to alleviate oppression, the anti-cultural-evolutionists are part of the very disease they so aggressively denounce.

But we must distinguish between valid and invalid theories of cultural evolution, and here Maureen outlines some of my work: "So to make the case for cultural evolution, for ways of being in the world and ways of knowing in the world that are higher and better than the current hegemonic model, we need 'a set of tenets that can explain *both* advance and regression, good news and bad news, the ups and downs of an evolutionary thrust that is nonetheless as active in humans as it is in the rest of the Kosmos.' Wilber discusses five of these tenets in his book *The Eye of Spirit*. These are: the dialectic of progress, the distinction between differentiation and dissociation, the difference between transcendence and repression, the difference between natural hierarchy and pathological hierarchy, and the fact that higher structures can be hijacked by lower impulses."

Maureen then proceeds through a smart, occasionally brilliant analysis of the cultural conditions and future of the Caribbean. She says that "This quarter I am teaching two courses at UCLA, one on the 'Sociology of Education' and one on 'Identity, Agency, and Social Transformation in the African Diaspora.' The latter is based on your work. The students really like it. But some have a problem with the fact that you hardly mention Islam or African philosophy. The emphasis on Eastern religions is a bit frustrating. . . ."

Good point. I need to emphasize more explicitly that I have drawn on African and Islamic religion, especially Sufism and core African shamanism. My tendency in the past has been to simplify by presenting "the best of the West"—summarized mostly by the Neoplatonists—and "the best of the East"—summarized mostly by India (Hinduism and Buddhism). But it clearly wouldn't hurt to be more specific about the many different sources I have in fact drawn upon.

"I have set myself the task to place African thought within your schema in such a way that it does not reinforce racism nor lapse into romanticizing pre-colonial Africa"—in other words, steering between repression, on the one hand, and regression, on the other—how to avoid both of those is a major theme of my work. "My first attempt to do this publicly is a lecture that I will give entitled 'Religion, Spirituality, and Social Transformation in the African Diaspora.' I am a bit nervous about it because it is going to be very critical of attempts to ground an African-American identity in ancient Egyptian thought. I will also argue for an evolutionary view of consciousness and spirituality and how this relates to social transformation." That is one brave soul.

"My next project is a postdoctoral fellowship with the UCLA Center for Pacific Rim Studies, where I will replicate my Caribbean project for the emerging economies of East Asia, in an ongoing attempt to theorize the complex relationship between cultural context (consciousness) and economic prowess. I hope to visit Indonesia, Taiwan, and Malaysia in 1998 to interview faculty in the departments of economics, businessmen/women, and policy makers."

Godspeed, Maureen Silos.

Wednesday, August 6

William S. Burroughs died. With his death, the Beat triumvirate—Kerouac, Ginsberg, Burroughs—is no more.

Ginsberg ended up a student of Trungpa Rinpoche; we ran into each other every now and then, particularly in connection with Naropa, whose new library building was named after him. Every time he saw me he would ask if he could rub my shaved head; I always said yes, he always rubbed away happily. What I liked most about Allen was not his poetry—blasphemy, I realize—but watching him read his poetry, which was an unending delight. He was a contorting vortex of playful energy; bliss packaged, bound, and offered to the audience, generously.

What I loved about the Beats was not their writing but their theater—the theater of themselves, of course, but done with a bravura unusual even for the sixties. Their lives were an unending drama of sometimes hilarious, sometimes grotesque, performance art—starting most conspicuously with Burroughs accidentally killing his wife while attempting to shoot a glass off her head; running through Kerouac's hideous death agony as a wasted alcoholic; ending with Ginsberg's embrace of a religion whose central aim is to undermine egoic performance, and which, if successfully practiced, would erase his raison d'être.

It was a show the likes of which we will not again soon see. Along with the death of Timothy Leary—and Ram Dass's stroke—I fear my generation is now officially beginning its death watch. The last few years have seen a rash of fiftieth birthdays—and the beginning wave of deaths. It's now a long, slow glide path to that final exit, at least for this time around. And will we find the great Unborn, the womb of saints and sages and bodhisattvas, or we will find only ourselves?

Sunday, August 10

Very early in the morning, maybe 3 A.M. Surfing the subtle—riding the boundary between the causal formless of deep sleep and the subtle form of the dream state. Out of pure, infinite, formless blackness—yet alive, and tacitly conscious, a radiantly clear emptiness—arises the most subtle form, sometimes a luminous blue-white billowing cloud, sometimes an infinite impulse of faintest bliss. Strange that such bliss is actually a step down. At the same time, it simply coexists with Emptiness; it is the Form of Emptiness at that point.

But behind it all, and all along, there is <u>just this</u>.

Tuesday, August 12

Naropa seminar. This time the dominant theme, raised by several students, was the rampant anti-intellectualism that you usually find at many spiritual and countercultural institutions. "Experiential" is contrasted to "intellectual"; the former is valued, the latter, denigrated. If you start to give an intellectual explanation of anything, you are, as one student put it, "nearly crucified on the spot." This is because you are supposed to be experiential, not intellectual, abstract, or conceptual. You are supposed to come from the heart, not from the head; you are supposed to center in the body, not in the mind. Experiential is spiritual, which is good; intellectual is the ego, which is analytic and divisive and "like way totally bad."

All of which, I responded, is a complete misunderstanding of both experiential and spiritual. A few excerpts:

KW: We were talking about experiential. Experience is basically just another word for awareness. If I experience my body, it means I am aware of my body. You can indeed be aware of your body, but you can also be aware of your mind—you can right now notice all the thoughts and ideas and images floating in front of the mind's inward eye. You can, in other words, experience your mind, be aware of your mind. And it's very important to be able to experience your mind directly, cleanly, intensely, because only by bringing awareness to the mind can you begin to transcend the mind and be free of its limitations. When that begins to happen, usually in meditation or contemplation, you can have even higher experiences, spiritual experiences, mystical experiences—satori, kensho, samadhi, unio mystica, and so on. You can, we might say, be aware of spirit, experience spirit, although in a more nondual manner.

So you can experience body, mind, and spirit. All of those are experiential. So perhaps you can begin to understand why it is a grave error to reduce experiential to just the body, to just bodily sensations, feelings, emotions, impulses, and so on. This is a very unfortunate reductionism. It denies the higher experiential realities of the mind and spirit: it denies intellect and buddhi, higher mental vision and imagery and dreams, higher rational discrimination and perspectivism and moral depth, higher formless awareness and deeply contemplative states—all are denied or reduced.

The body, you see, is basically narcissistic and egocentric. Bodily feelings are just about your body, period. The body's sensations cannot take the role of other—that's a mental capacity—and therefore the body's sensory awareness cannot enter into care and compassion and ethical discourse and I-thou spirituality—all of those demand a cognitive, mental, intellectual awareness. To the extent you "stay in your body" and are "anti-intellectual," then you stay in the orbit of your own narcissism.

So that's the first mistake in this "experiential versus intellectual" prejudice—all of the experiential modes are reduced to bodily experiences only, which is the essence of egocentrism. The second mistake is to then reduce spiritual experiences to bodily experiences. The idea is that if you stay focused in your body, focused in your feelings, that these are the direct door to spirituality, because they transcend the mind. But bodily sensations and feelings and emotions are not transrational, they are prerational. By staying only in the body, you are not beyond the mind, you are beneath it. You are not transcending, you are regressing— becoming more and more narcissistic and egocentric, focusing on your own feelings. And this, if anything, prevents actual spiritual experiences, because genuine spirituality is "bodymind dropped"—that is, you cease identifying exclusively with both the feelings of the body and the thoughts of the mind, and this you cannot do if you merely "stay in the body."

So anytime you hear somebody tell you to be "experiential" instead of "intellectual," you can almost be certain they are making these two simple but crucial mistakes. They are taking the experiences of body, mind, and spirit and claiming that only the body experiences are real—the lowest of the experiential domains!—and then they are reducing spiritual experiences to bodily experiences. Both are extremely unfortunate.

But the thing is, it's even worse than that. Although we can accurately speak of bodily, mental, and spiritual experiences, the fact is, the very highest spiritual states are not even experiences. Experiences, by their very nature, are temporary; they come, stay a bit, and pass. But the Witness is not an experience. It is aware of experiences, but is not itself experiential in the least. The Witness is the vast openness and freedom in which experiences arise, and through which experiences pass. But the Witness itself never enters the stream of time—it is aware of time—and thus it never enters the stream of experiences.

So even here, to say that Spirit is experiential (versus intellectual) is still to completely distort Spirit, because Spirit is not a passing experience but the formless Witness of all experience. To remain stuck in experiences is to remain ignorant of Spirit.

STUDENT: But the body does contain "felt meanings" that are important.

KW: Oh, definitely, and they need to be integrated with the mind and spirit. But to call those bodily sensations alone "spirituality" is a travesty.

STUDENT: Why is that so popular?

KW: Because everybody already has that bodily capacity available. You've had access to body awareness since you were a child. Anybody can experience the body, so you have a high success rate with "body focusing work." But if you were giving a workshop on "Let's contact nirvikalpa samadhi"—a true spiritual state—that takes the average person five years or more. That's not going to be a popular weekend workshop! So you can't easily market these genuine transpersonal realms, you can only market quick altered states that come and go, or simple bodily experiences that everybody can already tap into fairly easily.

Likewise, if you are an institution that relies on student money to survive, you are not going to make much money if you specialize in genuine subtle and causal and nondual states of consciousness—you can't afford to wait five and ten years for these things to come to fruition and you get paid! So there is a hidden but intense pressure to offer these lesser, even regressive states, call that "spirituality," and plug ahead. With this approach, you have a chance of close to a 100% success rate, because pretty much everybody can locate some sort of feeling or bodily emotion or bodily awareness, whereas very few can demonstrate satori on the spot. So everybody feels good, everybody is being "experiential" and "coming from the heart" and "not coming from the nasty intellect" and so everybody is being "spiritual." Oy vey.

STUDENT: Is there no use for bodily awareness?

KW: Oh, I don't want to give that impression. There is a very important role in contacting the body, which perhaps we can explain this way. In the course of human growth and development, consciousness begins identified largely with the body—with the vital and sensorimotor domain. Starting around age 2 or 3, the mind begins to emerge, and by age 6 or 7, consciousness begins to identify with the expanded perspective offered by the mind. The sensory body, recall, is preconventional and egocentric, because it cannot take the role of other. But with the emergence of the mind, consciousness can switch from egocentric to sociocentric modes of awareness—that is, evolve from me to we. The mind transcends and includes the body, so the mind can be aware of both "me" and "we."

But if there is pathology—and here Freud's contributions are pivotal—then the mind does not just transcend and include the body, it represses the body, denies the body, alienates and dissociates the body. More specifically, some mental concept or idea or superego represses or denies some bodily feeling, impulse, or instinct, often sex or aggression, or sometimes just bodily vitality in general. And that repression of the body by the mind produces various types of neurosis, emotional illness, bodily alienation, and life numbness.

So one of the first things you do in therapy—in "uncovering therapies"—is to relax the repression barrier and allow yourself to feel your body, feel your feelings, feel your emotions, and try to understand why you repressed them in the first place. You then befriend these lost feelings and reintegrate them with the mental-ego to form a more wholesome and accurate self-image.

Now the fact that you have recontacted the body and its feelings, and this has made you feel alive, vibrant, radiant—this is terrific, this is what is supposed to happen. You are recontacting your organic roots, your élan vital. But many people then erroneously conclude that the bodily feelings themselves are somehow a higher reality than the mental-ego, which is absolutely incorrect. They believe this because they feel so much better after having recontacted the body. But we need to recontact the body, not because it is a higher reality, but because it is a lower one being terribly mistreated by a higher. So we temporarily regress to the bodily sensations that were alienated—"regression" simply means moving to a lower level in the hierarchy of consciousness—and we reintegrate those lost feelings. This is regression in the service of a higher growth.

So the result of that higher growth is then the integration of the mind and the body—I call that the centaur, where human mind and animal body are one. But many body therapists completely confuse this integrated mind-and-body union with just the body itself. You find this confusion in writers like Alexander Lowen and Ida Rolf and Stanley

Keleman. They frequently elevate the body to the status of the centaur (or mind-and-body integrated unit), and you can tell they do this because there is virtually no discussion of the mind per se, the mind as mind—no discussion of rational ethics, of perspectivism, of postconventional morality, of mutual understanding, and so on. What they call the bodymind union is really just a bunch of deep bodily sensations. This is a miniature pre/trans fallacy—it confuses postconventional centaur with preconventional body—and this confusion marks most of the body therapy schools.

At any rate, both therapy and meditation often begin with the body and with body awareness, because most people are indeed out of touch with their roots. But neither effective therapy nor authentic meditation remains at the level of bodily awareness. In effective therapy, you eventually must move to cognitive and mental experience and begin to understand why you repressed the body and certain of its feelings in the first place. It is only as you cease to act out your alienated impulses on a bodily level and convert them into mental insight that therapy advances.

Likewise with genuine meditation. Although it often starts with bodily awareness—focusing on the breath, on bodily sensations, and so on—it soon moves to an investigation of mental experience and the mind stream itself. It moves from the gross body and sensorimotor world to the mental and subtle world. It is only by investigating the subtle contractions in the mind stream—and especially the subtle contraction known as the separate-self sense—that one's identity can expand from the bodymind to Spirit itself. One's personal identity with the organism is subsumed by an identity with the All.

So the body is never left behind. It is transcended and included by the mind, which is transcended and included by Spirit. The body is the foundation and the roots and the starting point. But if you merely stay there, you will totally sabotage mind and Spirit. You will get the Nirmanakaya (form body), but not the Sambhogakaya (subtle realm) and not the Dharmakaya (causal Emptiness) and not the Svabhavikakaya (nondual Suchness). But once you plug the body into these higher stages and realms, they tend to reach down and literally transfigure the physical body itself. Why, who knows, you might even begin to glow in the dark. The body will take on a strange and haunting beauty, and in any event the body will be the transparent vehicle of the primordial Spirit that you eternally are.

Friday, August 15

Richard G. Young, one of the directors of The Center for Contemplative Christianity and the publisher of Pathways: A Magazine of Psychological and Spiritual Transformation, wrote a review of The Eye of Spirit for that magazine. It's very funny. In the middle is this: "Why am I such a devotee of this elusive iconoclast who never gives lectures or leads retreats, rarely grants interviews, and goes out of his way to discourage anyone from considering him a spiritual teacher? Simple. I'm hoping to *guilt* him into granting us an interview for Pathways."

I faxed Pathways—"Okay, okay."

Saturday, August 16—Denver

Marci and I spent the day in Denver, wandering around, shopping for some shoes for her, enjoying the ease of existence. Marci is an adorable, extraordinary soul. She works daily with developmentally challenged people; I have seen her interact with these innocents, who are loving and direct, but who do not know enough to know the terrible ways of civilized folks, and therefore need supervision. They slobber on her, they clutch at her, they demand her attention, they cry and shout and yell— and she never turns away, she never recoils. She holds them, and says it will be okay, and they believe her, they reach out to her, they trust her, and for very good reason: she is always there for them, and they know it.

She's been accepted for the Peace Corps, which she is due to enter this coming February. But she is having second thoughts, in part, no doubt, because of our relationship; but also, and just as decisive, she has been promoted to head of marketing for the organization that runs several care centers where she works. This was unexpected, and a superb opportunity. She would still be working in a service organization, which is what she wants, but this one will also allow her to pay off her student loans, etc. That means our relationship won't have to end in February; I'm selfishly delighted.

Love for a specific person is radiant when it arises in Emptiness. It is still love, it is still intensely personal, it is still very specific; but it is a wave that arises from an ocean of infinity. It is as if a great sea of love brings forth a wave, and that wave carries the force and thrill of the entire sea in its every breaking crest. The sensation is like watching an early morning sunrise in the desert: a vast open clear blue spaciousness, within which there arises, on the horizon, an intense red-yellow fire. You are the infinite sky of Love, in which a particular fire-ball of personal love arises.

One thing is certain: infinite love and personal love are not mutually exclusive—the latter is just an individual wave of an infinite ocean. When I lie awake, next to her, early in the morning, doing meditation, nothing really changes in the contemplation except this: there is a whole-body bliss, paradoxically faint but intense, that edges my awareness. It is sexual energy reconnected to its source in the subtle regions of the bodymind. I will often touch her lightly as I meditate; it definitely completes an energy circuit, and she can feel it, too.

But that is what men and women (as well as "butch/femme" pairings across sexual orientations) can do for each other, and that is the core claim of Tantra as well: in a very concrete, visceral way, the union of male and female is the union of Eros and Agape, Ascending and Descending, Emptiness and Form, Wisdom and Compassion. Not theoretically but concretely, in the actual distribution of prana or energy currents in the body itself. And this is why, in the very highest Tantric teachings (anuttaratantrayoga), the mere visualization of sexual congress with the divine consort is not enough for final enlightenment. Rather, for ultimate enlightenment, one must take an actual partner—real sex—in order to complete the circuits conducive to recognizing the already-enlightened mind.

Monday, August 18—Boulder

Just got off the phone with Professor Sara Bates, who is using Brief History and Eye of Spirit as texts for her classes on art and native cultures. She teaches at Florida State but is now visiting lecturer at San Francisco University, from which she phoned me. Sara is Cherokee Indian; she and two of her friends—one a Hopi, one a Mojave—have formed a discussion group concerned with issues of cultural studies, religion, art, and native societies. They are using my work, she says, because of its cross-cultural and integral nature.

"What do you think of this new interest in Native American spirituality?" she asked.

"I think that middle-class white people do some very strange things with Native beliefs."

"I'll say. This whole romanticizing of Native belief is sad. Because that romantic view just doesn't exist; certainly not now, and maybe not ever. But a lot of Indians now go along with it."

"Yes, it's strange. Many Natives are buying the white man's version of the Natives' spirituality. It's weird."

"I've had this experience," Sara said, "of communing directly and immediately with an inner Light. This is a common type of spiritual experience in my tradition. One of my colleagues said, 'Do you think you have to be a Cherokee in order to have this experience?' He thought, of course, that I would say 'Yes,' but I said, 'No, of course not!' "

Sara is referring to the fact that extreme postmodernism has now slipped into a rather sad essentialism: you have to be a woman to know anything about women; you have to be an Indian to say anything about Indians; you have to be gay before you can explain anything about homosexuality. In other words, there is a regression from worldcentric to ethnocentric—identity politics alone rule, and extreme pluralism means none of us have anything in common anymore.

In this regressive atmosphere, as David Berreby puts it, writing in The Sciences, "Americans have a standard playbook for creating a political-cultural identity. You start with the conviction that being a member of your group is a distinct experience, separating you from people who are not in it (even close friends and relatives) and uniting you with other members of the group (even if you have never met them). Second, you assume that your own personal struggles and humiliations and triumphs in wrestling with your trait are a version of the struggles of the group in society. The personal is political. Third, you maintain that your group has interests that are being neglected or acted against, and so it must take action—changing how the group is seen by those outside it, for instance." It's not that such action is bad. It's just that, taken in and by itself, it is massively alienating and fragmenting, a type of pathological

<u>pluralism</u> that astonishingly believes that acceptance of my group can be accomplished by aggressively blaming and condemning exactly the group from which I seek the acceptance.

True pluralism, on the other hand, is always <u>universal pluralism</u> (or integral-aperspectival): you start with the <u>commonalities</u> and <u>deep struc-tures</u> that <u>unite</u> human beings—we all suffer and triumph, laugh and cry, feel pleasure and pain, wonder and remorse; we all have the capacity to form images, symbols, concepts, and rules; we all have 208 bones, two kidneys, and one heart; we are all open to a Divine Ground, by whatever name. And <u>then</u> you add all the wonderful differences, surface structures, culturally constructed variants, and so on, that make various groups—and various individuals—all different, special, and unique. But if you start with the differences and the pluralism, and never make it to the universal, then you have only the aperspectival, not also the inte-gral—you have, that is, pathological pluralism, aperspectival madness, ethnocentric revivals, regressive catastrophes.

Of course it is fine to highlight any group that you feel is important. But it's becoming impossible to define that group as "oppressed," be-cause now <u>every</u> group claims to be oppressed, and none admit they are oppressors. White males used to be the bad guys, but now even they have caught the fever. White males are no longer a single group that can be blamed for oppression, because most of them now claim to belong to an oppressed or marginalized group themselves: they are drug addicts, physically handicapped, alcoholics, were sexually abused as a child, vic-tims of an absent father, abducted by aliens, or turned into "success objects" by women. They can't oppress anybody because they are too busy being oppressed themselves.

Besides, according to essentialism, you can't say anything about white males unless you are a white male. So we can ignore everything feminists say about white males, and ask the white males themselves if they are oppressors. They say no. So there it is: we are a nation of brutally op-pressed groups, but without a single oppressing group. This is a nifty trick.

It is, of course, simply another name for narcissism. Whatever my problems, they do not stem from me. They stem from the Other, who is the Bad Guy always. The real travesty here is that the cases of true oppression—a genuine case of a woman, a gay, a black, an Indian, a white male, getting held back due <u>solely</u> to <u>ethnocentric</u> or <u>group</u> preju-dice—those cases lose all their urgency because they are drowned out by a thousand other voices all screaming oppression to explain even the most trivial and often unavoidable disappointments of life.

So here is Sara taking the course of universal pluralism—not ethno-centric pluralism—and it is refreshing beyond belief.

"So I told him, 'No, I do not think you have to be a Cherokee to have this type of interior illumination.' I definitely do not think these inner experiences are culturally constructed, do you?"

"Not totally, no. Cultural construction is, at best, only one of the four quadrants [the Lower Left]. What I try to do is highlight the universal or <u>deep features</u> in these experiences—seeing an interior illumination, for example—which appear to be fairly similar wherever they appear. But they all have various <u>surface features</u> that do in fact vary from cul-ture to culture, so some cultural construction is indeed present, but not nearly what the extreme postmodernists say."

"But are those cultural surface structures present even at the point of the direct communion with this interior being of Light?"

"To some degree, yes, I think so. For example, when these experiences occur in the Tibetan tradition, the inner being never looks like Jesus of Nazareth. Likewise, if this experience occurs to a Christian, the inner being rarely has four arms, which is quite common with the Tibetan version, like Chenrezi."

"I see, so even at the moment of direct experience, the cultural back-ground is playing some sort of role."

"Yes, right up to complete cessation, but, as you say, you don't have to be a Cherokee to have these types of experiences. The fact that they are <u>partially</u> molded by culture does not mean they are <u>merely</u> a product of your culture or your group background. This extreme constructivist view is a terrible distortion of religious experience. It reduces all spiritual realities to nothing but human-created symbols. Humans do not create Spirit, Spirit creates humans! I think these people have it a little back-wards. Anyway, I think it's useful to highlight the universal or deep features of these experiences, as well as the cultural surface features and local variations. They are both very important."

"Well, that's what my friends and I are doing. We want to explain our traditions, but we want to fit them with other traditions as well."

And so the discussion went. Sara had some sharp criticism for ecopsy-chology ("it really does leave out the interior dimensions"), for art theory that actually ignores art ("they talk about everything except art"), for the sad state of extreme postmodernism ("fragments everywhere"), and for the devaluation of aesthetics in favor of it-language ("anthropology over art"). She is going to send me some of her writing in aesthetic theory, as well as some of her art. I really like her; am glad we have connected.

Tuesday, August 19

Inner Directions is bringing out a new edition of Talks with Sri Ramana Maharshi, which is the main source of the teachings of this extraordinary Realizer. They asked to me write a foreword, and I agreed. I don't think we could say that Ramana was an exemplary representative of an integral view; but his own Self-realization—or the recognition of the always-already truth of the Witness and its ever-present ground in One Taste—was unsurpassed.

In the foreword, I incorporated a few pointing-out instructions that I had given in one of the Naropa seminars, and somehow this seemed appropriate enough. The Naropa Institute was named after the renowned Indian teacher and mahasiddha Naropa (eleventh century CE), who was a central figure in the university of Nalanda—which at one time had over ten thousand students and was one of the truly great learning centers of the world. This was also the period—from the eighth to the eleventh centuries CE in India—during which occurred the greatest flowering of the Nondual tradition the world has ever seen. That Nondual vision—in the form of Vedanta, Shaivism, Mahayana and Vajrayana Buddhism—is the precious gift of India to the world, and it found its purest, most elegant, most brilliant expression in the simple sage of Arunachala.

THE SAGE OF THE CENTURY

I am often asked, "If you were stranded on a desert island and had only one book, what would it be?" The book you are now holding in your hands—*Talks with Sri Ramana Maharshi*—is one of the two or three I always mention. And the *Talks* tops the list in this regard: they are the living voice of the greatest sage of this century and, arguably, the greatest spiritual realization of this or any time.

One of the many astonishing things about these *Talks* is how remarkably unwavering is the tone and style, the voice itself—not in the sense that it is fixed and rigid, but rather that it speaks with a full-blown maturity from the first word to the last. It is as if—no, it is certainly the case that—Ramana's realization came to him fully formed—or perhaps we should say, fully formless—and therefore it needed no further growth. He simply speaks from and as the absolute, the Self, the purest Emptiness that is the goal and ground of the entire manifest world, and is not other to that world. Ramana, echoing Shankara, used to say:

> The world is illusory;
> Brahman alone is real;
> Brahman is the world.

This profound realization is what separates Ramana's genuine enlightenment from today's many pretenders to the throne—deep ecology, ecofeminism, Gaia revivals, Goddess worship, ecopsychology, systems theory, web-of-life notions—none of which have grasped the first two lines, and therefore, contrary to their sweet pronouncements, do not really understand the third. And it is exactly for all of those who are thus in love merely with the manifest world—from capitalists to socialists, from green polluters to green peacers, from egocentrics to ecocentrists—that Ramana's message needs so desperately to be heard.

What and where is this Self? How do I abide as That? There is no doubt how Ramana would answer those—and virtually all other— questions: Who wants to know? What in you, right now, is aware of this page? Who is the Knower that knows the world but cannot itself be known? Who is the Hearer that hears the birds but cannot itself be heard? Who is the Seer that sees the clouds but cannot itself be seen?

And so arises *self-inquiry*, Ramana's special gift to the world. I *have* feelings, but I am not those feelings. Who am I? I *have* thoughts, but I am not those thoughts. Who am I? I *have* desires, but I am not those desires. Who am I?

So you push back into the source of your own awareness—what Ramana often called the "I-I," since it is aware of the normal I or ego. You push back into the Witness, the I-I, and you rest as That. I am not objects, not feelings, not desires, not thoughts.

But then people usually make a rather unfortunate mistake in this self-inquiry. They think that if they rest in the Self or Witness, they are going to see something, or feel something, something really amazing, special, spiritual. But you won't see anything. If you see something, that is just another object—another feeling, another thought, another sensation, another image. But those are all objects; those are what you are *not*.

No, as you rest in the Witness—realizing, I am not objects, I am not feelings, I am not thoughts—all you will notice is a sense of Freedom, a sense of Liberation, a sense of Release—release from the terrible constriction of identifying with these little finite objects, the little body and little mind and little ego, all of which are objects that can be seen, and thus are not the true Seer, the real Self, the pure Witness, which is what you really are.

So you won't see anything in particular. Whatever is arising is fine. Clouds float by in the sky, feelings float by in the body, thoughts float by in the mind—and you can effortlessly witness all of them. They *all* spontaneously arise in your own present, easy, effortless awareness. And this witnessing awareness is not itself anything specific you can see. It is just a vast, background sense of Freedom—or *pure Emptiness*—and in that pure Emptiness, which you are, the entire manifest world arises. You *are* that Freedom, Openness, Emptiness—and not any little finite thing that arises in it.

Resting in that empty, free, easy, effortless witnessing, notice that the clouds are arising in the vast space of your awareness. The clouds are arising within you—so much so, you can taste the clouds, you are one with the clouds, it is as if they are on this side of your skin, they are so close. The sky and your awareness have become one, and all things in the sky are floating effortlessly through your own awareness. You can kiss the sun, swallow the mountain, they are that close. Zen says "Swallow the Pacific Ocean in a single gulp," and that's the easiest thing in the world, when inside and outside are no longer two, when subject and object are nondual, when the looker and looked at are One Taste. And so:

The world is illusory, which means you are not any object at all—nothing that can be seen is ultimately real. You are *neti, neti,* not this, not that. And under no circumstances should you base your salvation on that which is finite, temporal, passing, illusory, suffering-enhancing and agony-inducing.

Brahman alone is real, the Self (unqualifiable Brahman-Atman) alone is real—the pure Witness, the timeless Unborn, the formless Seer, the radical I-I, radiant Emptiness—is what is real and all that is real. It is your condition, your nature, your essence, your present and your future, your desire and your destiny, and yet it is always ever-present as pure Presence, the alone that is Alone.

Brahman is the world, Emptiness and Form are not-two. *After* you realize that the manifest world is illusory, and *after* you realize that Brahman alone is real, *then* can you see that the absolute and the relative are not-two or nondual, then can you see that nirvana and samsara are not-two, then can you realize that the Seer and everything seen are not-two, Brahman and the world are not-two—all of which really means, the sound of those birds singing! The entire world of Form exists nowhere but in your own present Formless Awareness: you can drink the Pacific in a single gulp, because the entire world literally exists in your pure Self, the ever-present great I-I.

Finally, and most importantly, Ramana would remind us that the pure Self—and therefore the great Liberation—*cannot be attained*, any more than you can attain your feet or acquire your lungs. You are *already* aware of the sky, you *already* hear the sounds around you, you *already* witness this world. One hundred percent of the enlightened mind or pure Self is present right now—not ninety-nine percent, but one hundred percent. As Ramana constantly pointed out, if the Self (or knowledge of the Self) is something that comes into existence—if your realization has a beginning in time—then that is merely another object, another passing, finite, temporal state. There is no reaching the Self—the Self is reading this page. There is no looking for the Self—it is looking out of your eyes right now. There is no attaining the Self—it is reading these words. You simply, absolutely, cannot attain that which you have never lost. And if you do attain something, Ramana would say, that's very nice, but that's not the Self.

So, if I may suggest, as you read the following words from the world's greatest sage: if you think you don't understand Self or Spirit, then rest in that which doesn't understand, and just that is Spirit. If you think you don't quite "get" the Self or Spirit, then rest in that which doesn't quite get it, and just that is Spirit.

Thus, if you think you understand Spirit, that is Spirit. If you think you don't, that is Spirit. And so we can leave with Ramana's greatest and most secret message: the enlightened mind is not hard to attain but impossible to avoid. In the dear Master's words:

> There is neither creation nor destruction,
> Neither destiny nor free-will;
> Neither path nor achievement;
> This is the final truth.

Wednesday, August 20

Got up a little earlier than usual so I could get the day's reading done before Mitch and his new love Freada arrive. For volume 2 specifically, I've now gone through around five hundred books, with as many more to go—on anthropology, ecology, feminism, postmodernism, cultural studies, postcolonial studies—and the vast majority of them are, alas, drudgery. To add insult to injury, the style is ponderously indecipherable; you can read entire chapters possessing not a single understandable sentence; the prose suffocates you with insignificance. The best it gets up to is a type of rancid torpor, where the prose drags its belly across the gray page, always on the verge of a near-life experience.

Thursday, August 21

Freada is a real sweetie. Attractive, very bright, very open, very perceptive. Mitchell just lights up around her, which makes me quite happy. We threw a party for Mitch Wednesday night; several people wanted to meet him and several others wanted to meet me, so I just invited them all, thus killing several birds with one party.

And now they are off. It was great seeing them together. I'm guessing it will last. Shiva and Shakti always find each other, and who would ever suspect?

Monday, August 25

Sara Bates called and left a message, inviting me to participate in a conference being sponsored by the San Francisco Art Commission and the

Society for American Indian Studies. She said the nicest thing: "You are the only person I have read recently who really has a complete understanding of cross-cultural integrative vision." Even better, she sent me some of her art, and it is deeply beautiful. The photos show large (twelve-foot) mandalas, lying on the ground, which Sara has constructed out of hundreds of different types of objects and materials, both natural and manmade. Her art is a type of integration and inclusion of modernist themes (abstract patterns), postmodern themes (multiperspectival), and traditional themes (in her case, Native American).

The Cherokee Nation has seven clans—Wolf Clan, Deer Clan, Red Pain Clan, Bird Clan, Twisters Clan, Blue Clan, and Wild Potato Clan. Sara is Wolf Clan, so she includes elements of this in her art. But what attracts me to her work is the way she embraces elements representative of a collective and interconnected humanity—again, not ethnocentric pluralism but universal pluralism. From one of her brochures: "Many artists draw from history to tell a story of their particular reality as an American Indian or a woman or an artist within the milieu of art history. They go to great pains to describe what sets them apart from other individuals [group-identity or ethnocentric pluralism]. Bates has chosen instead to use the history and philosophy of her heritage as an American Indian and, more particularly, a member of the Cherokee Nation to talk about how similar we are and to describe our *interconnectedness*"—worldcentric or universal pluralism. This is such balm for our fragmented souls, for the nightmare of identity politics, the politics of narcissism, the politics of self-pity. That Sara is expressing universal pluralism in her art—and fighting the fashionable but brutal trends of ethnocentric pluralism and extremist diversity—is absolutely wonderful.

Friday, August 29

There is a superb rock group called Live; its lead singer is Ed Kowalczyk. Their CD Throwing Copper sold over five million copies and is one of my favorites. They are giving a concert in the area and Ed called and wanted to know if he could drop by—Brief History apparently meant a lot to him. I said fine, come on over.

Ed is twenty-six, very bright, handsome, and actually quite sweet. He has a strong spiritually devotional side to him and wants increasingly to write music reflecting this. Both he and his fiancée, Erin, are altogether likeable, genuine people. The three of us spent the evening together, and I promised to follow his progress as he heads into more spiritual music.

Marci is visiting her folks in Pennsylvania, and as much as she said she was going to miss me, she was <u>really</u> upset she couldn't meet Ed.

Sunday, August 31

A TICKET TO ATHENS

PATHWAYS: Why does Spirit bother to manifest at all, especially when that manifestation is necessarily painful and requires that It become amnesiac to Its true identity? Why does God incarnate?

KW: Oh, I see you're starting with the easy questions. Well, I'll give you a few theoretical answers that have been offered over the years, and then I'll give you my personal experience, such as it is.

I have actually asked this same question of several spiritual teachers, and one of them gave a quick, classic answer: "It's no fun having dinner alone."

That's sort of flip or flippant, I suppose, but the more you think about it, the more it starts to make sense. What if, just for the fun of it, we pretend—you and I blasphemously pretend, just for a moment—that we are Spirit, that Tat Tvam Asi? Why would you, if you were God Almighty, why would *you* manifest a world? A world that, as you say, is *necessarily* one of separation and turmoil and pain? Why would you, as the One, ever give rise to the Many?

PATHWAYS: It's no fun having dinner alone?

KW: Doesn't that start to make sense? Here you are, the One and Only, the Alone and the Infinite. What are you going to do next? You bathe in your own glory for all eternity, you bask in your own delight for ages upon ages, and then what? Sooner or later, you might decide that it would be fun—just *fun*—to pretend that you were not you. I mean, what else are you going to do? What else *can* you do?

PATHWAYS: Manifest a world.

KW: Don't you think? But then it starts to get interesting. When I was a child, I used to try to play checkers with myself. You ever tried that?

PATHWAYS: Yes, I remember doing something like that.

KW: Does it work?

PATHWAYS: Not exactly, because I always knew what my "opponent's" move was going to be. I was playing both sides, so I couldn't "surprise" myself. I always knew what I was going to do on both sides, so it wasn't much of a game. You need somebody "else" to play the game.

KW: Yes, exactly, that's the problem. You need an "other." So if you are the only Being in all existence, and you want to *play*—you want to play any sort of game—you have to take the role of the other, and then *forget* that you are playing both sides. Otherwise the game is no fun, as you say. You have to pretend you are the other player with such conviction that you forget that you are playing all the roles. If you don't forget, then you got no game, it's just no fun.

PATHWAYS: So if you want to play—I think the Eastern term is *lila*—then you have to forget who you are. Amnesis.

KW: Yes, I think so. And that is exactly the core of the answer given by the mystics the world over. If you are the One, and—out of sheer exuberance, plenitude, superabundance—you want to play, to rejoice, to have fun, then you must first, manifest the Many, and then second, forget it is you who are the Many. Otherwise, no game. Manifestation, incarnation, is the great Game of the One playing at being the Many, for the sheer sport and fun of it.

PATHWAYS: But it's not always fun.

KW: Well, yes and no. The manifest world is a world of opposites—of pleasure versus pain, up versus down, good versus evil, subject versus object, light versus shadow. But if you are going to play the great cosmic Game, that is what you yourself set into motion. How else can you do it? If there are no parts and no players and no suffering and no Many, then you simply remain as the One and Only, Alone and Aloof. But it's no fun having dinner alone.

PATHWAYS: So to start the game of manifestation is to start the world of suffering.

KW: It starts to look like that, doesn't it? And the mystics seem to agree. But there is a way out of that suffering, a way to be free of the opposites, and that involves the overwhelming and direct realization that Spirit is not good versus evil, or pleasure versus pain, or light versus

dark, or life versus death, or whole versus part, or holistic versus analytic. Spirit is the great Player that gives rise to *all* those opposites
equally—"I the Lord make the Light to fall on the good and the bad
alike; I the Lord do all these things"—and the mystics the world over
agree. Spirit is not the good half of the opposites, but the ground of *all*
the opposites, and our "salvation," as it were, is not to find the good
half of the dualism but to find the Source of both halves of the dualism,
for that is what we are in truth. We are both sides in the great Game of
Life, because we—you and I, in the deepest recesses of our very Self—
have created *both* of these opposites in order to have a grand game of
cosmic checkers.

That, anyway, is the "theoretical" answer that the mystics almost always give. "Nonduality" means, as the *Upanishads* put it, "to be freed
of the pairs." That is, the great liberation consists in being freed of the
pairs of opposites, freed of duality—and finding instead the nondual
One Taste that gives rise to both. This is *liberation* because we cease the
impossible, painful dream of spending our entire lives trying to find an
up without a down, an inside without an outside, a good without an
evil, a pleasure without its inevitable pain.

PATHWAYS: You said that you had a more personal response as
well.

KW: Yes, such as it is. When I first experienced, however haltingly,
nirvikalpa samadhi—which means meditative absorption in the formless
One—I remember having the vague feeling—very subtle, very faint—
that I didn't want to be alone in this wonderful expanse. I remember
feeling, very diffusely but very insistently, that I wanted to share this
with somebody. So what would one do in that state of loneliness?

PATHWAYS: Manifest the world.

KW: That's how it seems to me. And I knew, however amateurishly,
that if I came out of that formless Oneness and recognized the world of
the Many, that I would then *suffer*, because the Many always hurt each
other, as well as help each other. And you know what? I was glad to
surrender the peace of the One even though it meant the pain of the
Many. Now this is just a little tongue taste of what the great mystics
have seen, but my limited experience seems to conform to their great
pronouncement: You are the One freely giving rise to the Many—to pain
and pleasure and all the opposites—because you choose not to abide as

the exquisite loneliness of Infinity, and because you don't want to have dinner alone.

PATHWAYS: And the pain that is involved?

KW: Is *freely* chosen as part of the necessary Game of Life. You cannot have a manifest world without all the opposites of pleasure and pain. And to get rid of the pain—the sin, the suffering, the *duhkha*—you must *remember* who and what you really are. This remembrance, this recollection, this anamnesis—"Do this in Remembrance of Me"—means, "Do this in Remembrance of the Self that You Are"—Tat Tvam Asi. The great mystical religions the world over consist of a series of profound practices to quiet the small self that we pretend we are—which *causes* the pain and suffering that you feel—and awaken as the Great Self that is our own true ground and goal and destiny—"Let this consciousness be in you which was in Christ Jesus."

PATHWAYS: Is this realization an all-or-nothing affair?

KW: Not usually. It's often a series of glimpses of One Taste—glimpses of the fact that you are one with absolutely all manifestation, in its good and bad aspects, in all its frost and fever, its wonder and its pain. You are the Kosmos, *literally*. But you tend to understand this ultimate fact in increasing glimpses of the infinity that you are, and you realize exactly why you started this wonderful, horrible Game of Life. But it is absolutely not a cruel Game, not ultimately, because you, and you alone, instigated this Drama, this Lila, this Kenosis.

PATHWAYS: But what about the notion that these experiences of "One Taste" or "Kosmic Consciousness" are just a by-product of meditation, and therefore aren't "really real"?

KW: Well, that can be said of any type of knowledge that depends on an instrument. "Kosmic consciousness" often depends on the instrument of meditation. So what? Seeing the nucleus of a cell depends on a microscope. Do we then say that the cell nucleus isn't real because it's only a by-product of a microscope? Do we say the moons of Jupiter aren't real because they depend on a telescope? The people who raise this objection are almost always people who don't want to look through the instrument of meditation, just as the Churchmen refused to look through Galileo's telescope and thus acknowledge the moons of Jupiter. Let them live with their refusal. But let us—to the best of our ability, and hopefully driven by the best of charity or compassion—try to convince them to look, just once, and see for themselves. Not coerce them, just invite them. I suspect a different world might open for them, a world that has been abundantly verified by all who look through the telescope, and microscope, of meditation.

PATHWAYS: Could you tell us. . . .

KW: If I could interrupt, do you mind if I give you one of my favorite quotes from Aldous Huxley?

PATHWAYS: Please.

KW: This is from *After Many a Summer Dies the Swan*:

> "I like the words I use to bear some relation to facts. That's why I'm interested in eternity—psychological eternity. Because it's a fact."
>
> "For you perhaps," said Jeremy.
>
> "For anyone who chooses to fulfill the conditions under which it can be experienced."
>
> "And why should anyone wish to fulfill them?"
>
> "Why should anyone choose to go to Athens to see the Parthenon? Because it's worth the bother. And the same is true of eternity. The experience of timeless good is worth all the trouble it involved."
>
> "Timeless good," Jeremy repeated with distaste. "I don't know what the words mean."
>
> "Why should you?" said Mr. Propter. "You've never bought your ticket for Athens."

PATHWAYS: So contemplation is the ticket to Athens?

KW: Don't you think?

PATHWAYS: Definitely. I wonder, could you tell us a little bit about your own ticket to Athens? Could you tell us a little about the history of your own experiences with meditation? And what is "integral practice" and what does it offer the modern spiritual seeker?

KW: Well, as for my own history, I'm not sure I can say anything meaningful in a short space. I've been meditating for twenty-five years, and I suspect my experiences are not terribly different from many who have tread a similar path. But I will try to say a few things about "integral practice," because I suspect it might be the wave of the future. The idea is fairly simple, and Tony Schwartz, author of *What Really Matters: Searching for Wisdom in America*, summarized it as the attempt to "marry Freud and Buddha." But that really just means, the attempt to integrate the contributions of Western "depth psychology" with the great wisdom traditions of "height psychology"—the attempt to integrate id and Spirit, shadow and God, libido and Brahman, instinct and Goddess, lower and higher—whatever terms you wish, the idea is clear enough, I suspect.

PATHWAYS: As an actual practice?

KW: Yes, the actual practice is based on something like this: Given the Great Nest of Being—ranging from matter to body to mind to soul to spirit—how can we acknowledge, honor, and *exercise* all of those levels in our own being? And if we do so—if we engage all of the levels of our own potential—won't that *better* help us to remember the Source of the great Game of Life, which is not other than our own deepest Self? If Spirit is the Ground and Goal of all of these levels, and if we are Spirit in truth, won't the whole-hearted engagement of all of these levels help us remember who and what we really are?

Well, that is the theory, which I realize I have put in rather dry terms. The idea, concretely, is this: Take a practice (or practices) from *each* of those levels, and engage whole-heartedly in all of those practices. For the physical level, you might include physical yoga, weightlifting, vitamins, nutrition, jogging, etc. For the emotional/body level, you might try tantric sexuality, therapy that helps you contact the feeling side of your being, bioenergetics, t'ai chi, etc. For the mental level, cognitive therapy, narrative therapy, talking therapy, psychodynamic therapy, etc. For the soul level, contemplative meditation, deity yoga, subtle contemplation, centering prayer, and so on. And for the spirit level, the more nondual practices, such as Zen, Dzogchen, Advaita Vedanta, Kashmir Shaivism, formless Christian mysticism, and so forth.

I hesitate to give that list, because, as you know, there are literally thousands of wonderful practices for all of those levels, and I shudder at excluding any of them. But please just focus on the general idea: take one or more practices from each of the levels of your own being—matter to body to mind to soul to spirit—and exercise *all of them* to the best of your ability, individually and collectively. Not only will you, on a mundane level, simply start to feel better, you will dramatically increase your chances of falling into your own radical Estate, which is Spirit itself, your own deepest identity and impulse.

PATHWAYS: Are there any teachers who are now doing this type of integral practice?

KW: Well, unfortunately, there are not many teachers, at this early time, who are doing this. In part, this type of integral practice is a union of East and West, and they have just recently been introduced to each other. But there are many *superb* teachers dealing with one or more of the many levels in your own being—and therefore, at this time, you simply have to "mix and match"—or choose the best teachers for you at each of the levels. Find a good physical exercise that works for you, and a decent nutritional program. Try to engage in a good psychotherapeutic practice—it could be as simple as writing down your dreams, or belonging to a discussion group. Try a good meditation practice, and engage in community service. I don't want to make this sound like it's a horrible fascist type of thing—but just try, as best you can, to engage all of you in order to awaken all of you.

PATHWAYS: Are there any teachers who are at least moving toward this integral practice?

KW: Yes. There are a few writers who today emphasize the importance of an integral approach, and although all of them are very preliminary, they are a good place to start. You might try Michael Murphy and George Leonard's *The Life We Are Given*; Tony Schwartz's *What Really Matters*; Roger Walsh and Frances Vaughan's *Paths Beyond Ego*; and my *The Eye of Spirit*.

But the idea is simple enough: practicing on only one level of your being will not enlighten all of you. If you *just* meditate, your psychodynamic "junk" will not automatically go away. If you *just* meditate, your job or your relationship with your spouse will not automatically get better. On the other hand, if you *only* do psychotherapy, do not think that you will be relieved from the burden of death and terror. Render unto Freud what is Freud's, and render unto Buddha what is Buddha's. And best of all, render unto the Divine all of yourself, by engaging all that you are.

Good grief, I sound like a commercial for the Marines: "Be all that you can be." But the point, really, is that the more of your own dimensions you engage in the quest to find the Source of this Game of Life, the more likely you are to discover the stunning fact that you are its one and only Author. And that's not a theoretical proposition, it is the very best chance we have to get our ticket to Athens.

SEPTEMBER

Tuesday, September 2

When bodymind drops, when I am nowhere to be found, there is such an infinite Emptiness, a radical Fullness, endlessly laced with luminosity. I-I open as the Kosmos, here where no object corrupts primordial Purity, here where concepts are too embarrassed to speak, here where duality hides its face in shame, and suffering cannot even remember its name. Nothing ever happens here, in the fullness of infinity, singing self-existing bliss, alive with self-liberating gestures, always happy to be home. Infinite gratitude meets utter simplicity in the openness of this moment, for there is just this, forever and forever and hopelessly forever.

Saturday, September 6

Both Princess Diana and Mother Teresa are dead. The two most famous women in the world, gone within a week. (The world's response to their deaths was a striking example of the pyramid of development—the greater the depth, the less the span.)

Diana, by all accounts, was a good person, caring, loving, and devoted; but more to the point, she was stunningly beautiful and glamorous. She really was the world's Princess. And in our flat and faded postmodern world, where everything is supposed to be drearily equal, a true Princess was promise that there can be more. In her own way, she was royally, divinely beautiful, and millions of people around the world loved her deeply and sincerely, because she evoked the beauty hidden in all of them as well. She was a ray of something more, and the world responded with adoration—it went quite beyond anything Diana was in person; but it was still through her person, and no other, that this wonderful ray shone forth. Watching her two sons, William and Harry, walk behind her funeral carriage, I began crying, like millions of others.

Mother Teresa was much closer to that divine ray, and practiced it more diligently, and without the glamour. She was less a person than an opening of Kosmic compassion—unrelenting, fiercely devoted, frighteningly dedicated.

I, anyway, appreciated them both very much, for quite different reasons, and there is considerably less light in the world this morning than there was yesterday.

Wednesday, September 10

Kate Olson and T George came over for dinner last night with Marci and me. T George is pretty amazing. He's what? Seventy-two years old? And still vital and alert and impressive. It's almost impossible to create a successful magazine—nine out of ten quickly fail—and yet T George has started two of them—Psychology Today and American Health, both still going strong. I'm convinced he'll make it three, with Spirituality and Health, but the odds are rather steep this time, because "spirituality" means so many things to so many people that it's hard to focus efforts and rally others to the cause.

The difficulty is exacerbated, of course, by the pre/trans fallacy: much of what people call "spiritual" is not transrational awareness but prerational feeling, and this is a real problem—which we spent much of the evening discussing. I used the diagram in figure 4 to suggest a few points.

Human growth and development generally unfolds from body to mind to soul to spirit—not as a linear ladder, but as nested waves, with each wave enveloping its predecessor(s)—if all goes well. But at almost any stage, the higher can repress the lower. Instead of enfold and em-

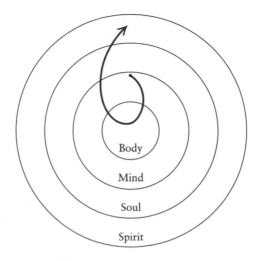

FIGURE 4. *The Curative Spiral*

brace, there is deny and reject. Instead of transcend and include, there is alienate and repress.

This is especially true of the relation between the mind and body. The first few years of life are basically sensorimotor, preverbal, and largely premental—the self is all body, feelings, and organic impulse. But starting around age 2, the symbolic and conceptual mind begins to emerge, and by age 6 or 7, the concrete operational mind emerges. Ideally the mind transcends and includes the previous bodily sensations, feelings, impulses, and drives. But more often than not—and this is Freud's great province—the mind (the ego-mind) represses or denies some previous bodily feeling, often sex or aggression. This repressed feeling does not simply go away, but rather reappears, in disguised forms, as painful neurotic symptoms.[18]

Thus, by the time most people reach young adulthood, they suffer various forms of mind/body dissociation: they are out of touch with their bodies, their feelings, their organic richness, their élan vital. This

---

18. This is not to deny the importance of brain neurochemistry and developmental neurobiology in the genesis of psychopathology. Every Upper Left (or psychological) event has an Upper Right (or material) correlate—in fact, all four quadrants have an interactive hand in every psychopathology. In this discussion I am simply focusing on the Upper Left component—the inner dissociation of conceptual mind and felt body.

has two specific consequences: one, it dulls life itself; two, it makes higher development harder and therefore much less likely to occur.

Thus, in order to both revitalize the present and allow higher growth to occur, it is often necessary to recontact the body. Many therapies are designed to do just this. Some of the body therapies approach the body directly (through sensory awareness, Rolfing, bioenergetics, etc.), while other therapies will actually engage in a type of regression to the awareness of early childhood. We temporarily regress back to the preverbal body, recontact and befriend it, and then reintegrate it with the mind (this is classically called "regression in service of the ego"). But in all these cases, the ultimate goal is to become fully in touch with both the body and the mind.

Once we have integrated the body and the mind, it is much easier—and more likely—that growth can then continue beyond the body and mind, into the realms of soul and spirit. In the diagram, these two general movements—regression in service of the ego, and then progression in transcendence of the ego—are indicated by the large spiral, which, for the typical adult, first moves down (regression) and then up (transcendence).

In the regressive part of this spiral, we are not, as maintained by the Romantics, recontacting a higher Ground that was lost, but simply a lower bodily feeling that was repressed.[19] We are not recapturing a transrational awareness that we had as an infant but then lost, but rather a prerational impulse that we unfortunately repressed. That repression is nonetheless painful and deleterious, and it can only be cured by recontacting and befriending the alienated impulses and bodily feelings (regression in service of ego, as a prelude to progression in transcendence of ego).

Now the problem with many forms of therapy, and most forms of alternative spirituality, is that we start along this healing spiral and then—caught in a pre/trans fallacy—we get stuck at the prerational, sensory, bodily stage. We regress back to feelings, emotions, sensations, bodily awareness—which itself is fine, and is the first leg of the jour-

---

19. Michael Washburn also speaks of a spiral in development, but we disagree on almost all aspects of this spiral movement. See *The Eye of Spirit*, chapter 6, for a full discussion of this topic.

ney—but then we simply stop there and call that transrational spirit, whereas it is nothing of the sort. Trying to go transrational, we end up prerational, and this is called liberation. This is a bit of nightmare.

Both T George and Kate seemed to agree with this analysis, and Kate jumped in. "I agree with that, but you are not saying that all feelings are prerational or egocentric, are you?"

"No, not at all. There are, as it were, levels of feeling, or levels of affect—moving from egocentric feelings to sociocentric feelings to worldcentric feelings to spiritual feelings—roughly, body to mind to soul to spirit."

"But how can you tell which feeling is which?" Marci wondered.

"If you are sitting around trying to get in touch with your feelings—if you are using sensory awareness, felt meaning, bodily focusing, somatic therapy, bioenergetics—then you are at the egocentric stage. This in itself is not bad. As a matter of fact, it is the foundation of all further practice. But if you stay there, you are in fact deeply regressed to a preconventional mode of awareness. Of course it feels good—initially—because you have abdicated the rigors of sociocentric awareness and mutual understanding. You are simply wallowing in you—constantly 'processing' your feelings and prodding your impulses—and this feels great for a little while, until—as Kierkegaard pointed out—it inevitably turns into despair, because you are cut off from the circle of sharing that exists outside of yourself."

"That circle of sharing is the next stage," T George pointed out.

"Yes, I think so. You move from egocentric feelings to sociocentric feelings—from Me to We—when you take your feelings and relate them to others in a dialogue aimed at mutual understanding, concern, and care. This is true for both men and women—Kohlberg called this moving from self-oriented to reciprocity, and Gilligan called it moving from the 'selfish stage' to the 'care stage.' Your feelings now expand to include a circle of sharing, caring, and mutual understanding. You are at least as concerned with how others feel as with how you feel. You have expanded from self to group."

"So what's the stage after group?" Kate wondered.

"All groups," said T George.

"Yes, worldcentric. You go from egocentric to sociocentric to worldcentric, from me to us to all of us. You are concerned not just with your tribe, your nation, your group—but instead with all groups, all peoples, everywhere, regardless of race, sex, or creed. And you feel this; it is not an abstraction. You ache for the world, silly as that sounds."

"I know exactly that feeling," said Kate. "It sometimes comes up when I am doing centering prayer. It's like the bodhisattva vow."

"Yes, and I think that is actually the next stage—worldcentric feelings give way to truly spiritual feelings, because all sentient beings as such are taken into account. But the wonder of this is that we can feel a deeply worldcentric/spiritual feeling of universal care and compassion. Schopenhauer said the only way we could feel this feeling is if we are all ultimately One Self, and I think that is definitely the case."

"But," Marci pointed out, "all of that universal compassion gets lost when all you do is try to contact your feelings, or stay in your body, or process your emotions. That happens at Naropa all the time. Everybody is trying to remain in their feelings—they call that 'spiritual'!—and so nobody transcends anything."

"Very true," I agreed, "but by no means confined to Naropa. In fact, being fixated to sensory or bodily modes is called bodyism, and bodyism is actually a hallmark of the modern and postmodern world. Bodyism is just another term for flatland, for the belief that only gross, sensory, empirical realities are real. And both the mainstream culture and the counterculture are equally dominated by bodyism, by flatland. We all recognize that scientific materialism is the dominant worldview of the mainstream. But look at the countercultural views: ecopsychology, deep ecology, body therapies, ecofeminism, the web of life, Great Mother religions, immanent spirituality, somatic therapy—they all have one thing in common: ultimate reality is the gross sensory world. In other words, bodyism—the same bodyism subscribed to by the mainstream. Welcome to flatland, to the purely Descended world of the modern and postmodern wasteland."

Both T George and Kate were curious as to why this bodyism has become so rampant. I suggested it was part of the downside of modernity.[20] For over a thousand years, the West was dominated by an Ascend-

---

20. For a fuller account of the historical rise of bodyism and flatland, see *A Brief History of Everything*. Bodyism is simply another term for subtle reductionism, for the belief that only entities with simple location are real, the belief that only Right-Hand realities are real.

ing ideal—God was purely otherworldly, merely transcendent, and his Kingdom was not of this world. But then, beginning with the Renaissance and culminating with the Enlightenment, this Ascending ideal was violently rejected, so much so that the baby of transcendental truth was tossed with tons of bathwater. The result was that the modern West ended up embracing a purely Descended worldview—gross, sensorimotor, empirical bodyism—in other words, flatland.

And so now, even when the countercultural movements claim that they are overthrowing or transgressing the old Enlightenment paradigm, they are, for the most part, still firmly caught in it. They are trapped in the purely Descended grid, with its intense bodyism and flatland holism and avid embrace of the merely gross realm, exactly like the "old paradigm" they so vocally condemn.

(I was also thinking of Joan Brumberg's The Body Project, which tracks girls and their bodies over the last two centuries. A typical diary entry in the late eighteen hundreds ran: "To work seriously. To be dignified. Interest myself in others." A typical entry today reads: "I will lose weight. Get new lenses, good makeup, new clothes and accessories." Brumberg comments: "Before the twentieth century, girls simply did not organize their thinking around their bodies. Today they believe that the body is the ultimate expression of the self." Brumberg, of course, tries to make this bodyism a feminist issue, when it is nothing of the sort; it is simply one of the definitions of flatland, affecting men and women equally—a regressive, narcissistic, leveling pull in consciousness—we have tried to cure repression of the body with regression to the body—we no longer deny the body, we are obsessed with it and totally fixated to it—and the result is a purely Descended, sensorimotor world.)

The idea, of course, is to integrate both the Ascending movement (from body to mind to soul to spirit) and the Descending movement (from spirit to soul to mind to body). But so far, all we really have are a few merely Ascending transcendental religions, and tons of totally Descended, flatland, bodyism movements. We are still awaiting a truly integral, nondual worldview, and although several people are working in this direction, there is still much work to do.

Friday, September 12

The galleys arrived for Sense and Soul; minor corrections and sent them back; we're close to the end.

When I was in New York, at the Four Seasons, during that two-day auction, talking to the various publishers, I always ended up saying the same thing, and I am convinced more than ever of its truth: There are two major dialogues in the modern world that I believe must take place, one between science and religion, and then one between religion and liberalism. Spirituality must first get through the eye of the needle of modern science—and showing how that might happen was a main theme of Sense and Soul. But once that happens, spirituality must then get through the eye of the needle of liberalism (and that is a main theme of the planned follow-up book to Sense and Soul).

The way it is now, the modern world really is divided into two major and warring camps—science and liberalism, on the one hand, and religion and conservatism, on the other. And the key to getting these two camps together is first, to get religion past science, and then second, to get religion past liberalism, because both science and liberalism are deeply antispiritual. And it must occur in that order, because liberalism won't even listen to spirituality unless it has first passed the scientific test.

In one sense, of course, science and liberalism are right to be antispiritual, because most of what has historically served as "spirituality" is now prerational—magic or mythic, implicitly ethnocentric, fundamentalist dogma. Liberalism traditionally came into existence to fight the tyranny of prerational myth—to fight traditional, parochial, ethnocentric religion—and that is one of its enduring and noble strengths (namely, the freedom, liberty, and equality of individuals in the face of the often hostile or coercive collective). And this is why liberalism was always allied with rational science as against fundamentalist, mythic, prerational religion (and the conservative politics that usually hung on to that religion).

But neither science nor liberalism is aware that, in addition to prerational myth, there is transrational awareness. There are not two camps here: liberalism versus mythic religion. There are three: mythic religion, rational liberalism, and transrational spirituality. Liberalism can be rightfully distrustful of prerational myth, and yet still open itself to transrational awareness. Its objections to mythic forms do not apply to formless awareness, and thus liberalism and authentic spirituality can walk hand in hand into a greater tomorrow. If this can be demonstrated to them <u>using terms they both find acceptable</u>, then we would have, I believe for the first time, the possibility of a <u>postliberal spirituality</u>, which combines the strengths of conservatism and liberalism, but moves beyond both in a transrational, transpersonal integration. I believe <u>Sense and Soul</u> is at least a good start for the first dialogue, and my hope is to follow that up with the second dialogue (spirituality and liberalism) within five years or so.

But one thing is absolutely certain: all the talk of a "new spirituality" in America is a complete waste of time unless those two central dialogues are engaged and answered. Unless spirituality can pass through the gate of science, then of liberalism, it will never be a significant force in the modern world, but will remain merely as the organizing power for the prerational levels of development around the world.

Monday, September 15

"What's a pandit?" Her name was Pritam. Tammi had brought Pritam and Matthew over for a long talk about several pressing matters. (Tammi Simon is the founder of Sounds True, one of the most successful audiotape companies in America, located here in Boulder. Tammi tapes everybody, from Thich Nhat Hanh to Carolyn Myss to the Dalai Lama. Her favorites she drags up to my house and we all have dinner.) Matthew, an assistant at Sounds True, and Tammi were editing the most recent book of Gangaji, an American woman spiritual teacher in the lineage of Vedanta. Pritam wanted to ask me questions about my work, and Tammi and Matthew were full of questions about Gangaji.

"I am a pandit, not a guru." And with that line, which I have used a hundred times in my life, the conversation moved, yet again, to this most difficult topic. "In India they make that important distinction. The main difference is that a guru accepts devotees, a pandit does not. Also, pandits are usually scholars of a particular tradition—in America we call them 'pundits'—whereas a guru may, or may not, be very knowledgeable about the tradition."

"So why does a pandit refuse to take disciples or devotees?"

"It's an entirely different profession, as it were. For a guru or master to take on a devotee is a very serious affair—almost like a psychotherapist taking on a client. This is nothing that either party should do lightly, because it means years, even decades, of the most personal, intimate, and intense work between them. Gurus have to wrestle, often in public, with the karma or conditioning of all those who come to them. This is a severe and demanding task."

"So pandits don't do that."

"No, they don't. A particular pandit may be more, or less, enlightened than a particular guru, but in any event, pandits usually confine their understanding to writing, or teaching (at say, a university), or in other fairly ordinary pursuits. But they do not usually engage in spiritual therapy with people. That's an entirely different ballgame."

"So how does the guru actually work?" wondered Tammi.

"Well, it depends on the guru. But there is a common thread among good gurus, and this is the basis of Guru Yoga. Namely, the guru eats the karma (or conditioning) of the devotee. This occurs when the compassion of the guru meets the devotion of the student. That, anyway, is how it is traditionally stated. Let's use a fairly noncontroversial example here, say Sri Ramana Maharshi. (Ramana is arguably the greatest Guru who ever lived, just as Plotinus was probably the greatest pandit.) You've seen pictures of Ramana, and although he is not what you would call handsome, he is incredibly beautiful. You can't take your eyes off him. He is radiating the Beauty of the Divine, which is not other than his own condition, and you are natively drawn to that condition. You want to be in its presence. The guru—the authentic guru—radiates the attractiveness of the Divine, and this helps to awaken you to your own inherent Beauty, your own spiritual essence."

"Can't pandits do that?"

"Many do. But the second part of Guru Yoga is, there is an intense bond formed between the guru and the devotee—like between therapist and client, only more so—and that bond is an important part of the devotee's transformation and awakening. I suppose it's some sort of subtle transference process at work. In classical Freudian transference, the client transfers or projects past relationships onto the therapist, and it is then through an analysis of this projection that the client comes to understand—and hopefully be relieved of—the neurosis.

"The same thing, but on a higher level, seems to go on in authentic Guru Yoga. You, the devotee, project not merely your shadow but your own True Self onto the guru. You see the guru, but not yourself, as possessing the Divine Reality. And this is why the devotee is absolutely fascinated with the guru, drawn to the guru, wants always to be with the guru. You fall in love with your own True Self, as projected onto the figure of the guru.

"Now an accomplished guru will use this transference to awaken devotees to their own True Self, their own true Godhood or Buddha-nature. Traditionally, there are two ways that this can occur. One is through an actual transmission from the guru, and one is through a meditative practice on the part of the student or devotee. In the first, you completely submit to the guru and that submission will reduce the ego, allowing the True Self to shine forth; in the second, you inquire into the source of the ego, and it will revert to its ground in the True Self. Either way will work—submission or inquiry—but the first depends upon how genuine and how potent the guru is."

"Okay, okay, one at a time," said Tammi. "In the first, the transmission route, is there actually something that is transmitted, like a force?"

"In my experience of this, yes, definitely. When a person is fairly enlightened, they can transmit—actually transmit—that enlightened awareness through a touch, a look, a gesture, or even through the written word. It's not as weird as it sounds. We are all 'transmitting' our present state to each other all the time. If you are depressed, it can be 'contagious,' depressing others around you. When you are happy, others tend to get happy. Just so with the higher states. In the presence of a psychic-level yogi, you tend to feel power. In the presence of a subtle-level saint, you tend to feel great peace. In the presence of a causal-level sage, you tend to feel massive equanimity. In the presence of a nondual siddha—these are often very ordinary people—you simply find yourself smiling a lot."

"But pandits can do that, too."

"Anybody can do that. We are all transmitting our own level of awareness all the time. What a guru does that nobody else does, is take a particular person as a devotee—as a 'client'—and work with them personally. And, since you were asking, that is something that I myself do not wish to do."

"Can that even be done in America?" asked Matthew.

"Well, that's a good point. I happen to believe that, when it is done right, Guru Yoga is the most powerful yoga there is. But in today's world it is almost impossible to do it right, for at least two reasons. One, Guru Yoga was invented in agrarian-feudal times. To completely submit to the guru—your money, your possessions, your body and mind and soul— was, if not exactly easy, nonetheless acceptable. But in today's democratic societies, this surrender is viewed as alarming, or even as a sign of pathology. Which is the second problem. In our egalitarian culture, where nobody is supposed to have any more depth than anybody else, the whole notion of the guru is frowned on. The thought that anybody is better than anybody else is profoundly offensive and officially taboo. We are a society of deeply entrenched egos, and if you threaten the ego with thoughts of submission or transcendence, you will be run out of town on a rail.

"So for all these reasons, doing Guru Yoga in this country is probably not a good idea, which is too bad. On the other hand, Guru Yoga, precisely because it is so strong, has more problems than . . ."

"Wait," said Tammi. "Why is it so strong?"

"Have you ever tried learning a foreign language? It's really quite hard to do, and takes a very long time, especially if you want to be proficient at it. But I have been told by many people that if you have a lover who speaks a foreign language, you can learn it much more quickly. Makes sense, doesn't it?, because the learning is driven by love. The same is true with Guru Yoga. With Guru Yoga, you fall in love— deeply and desperately in love—and that love is the vehicle through which you much more quickly learn the language of your own True Self. Precisely because this learning is driven by love, it happens more rapidly than sitting alone, in the corner, on your meditation mat, counting your breaths."

"I see. But that opens it to much abuse."

"Yes, that's what I was about to say. Precisely because Guru Yoga is so strong, it can also cause the most damage. The abuses are legion, and we hear about a new one almost every day. In any event, I honestly do not think that Guru Yoga—for some very good reasons, and for some truly pathetic reasons—can flourish in this country."

"So that is why you don't want to be a guru?"

"No, I don't want to be a guru because I do not want to enter into a therapist/client relationship with people. Whatever understanding I have I try to put into my writing—the transmission is in the written word—

and you can use that transmission as you wish, and judge for yourself whether it is true or not. But whenever I feel myself going down anything that even vaguely resembles a guru path, such as intentionally transmitting in person, I simply stop it. It's <u>not</u> that I think the guru principle is bad. It's just that there are no karmas in me to do this. I am not qualified to wrestle with people over their spiritual destinies. I have no desire to interfere with the course of anybody's life—whereas, if you are a therapist or a guru, you most certainly are going to interfere in the course of people's lives, even or especially if you are being nondirective. I totally applaud therapists, spiritual teachers, and good gurus—we need them all desperately—but they are not my calling."

"So you will never have any students?"

"Traditionally there is a gradation of increasing involvement with any teacher: student, disciple, and devotee. If you study any of my books, you are already a <u>student</u> of my work, and that's fine. I accept that particular teacher/student relationship. But because I have no plans to get involved with anybody's personal transformation, it looks like I will never have disciples, let alone devotees."

"So there are students of your <u>work</u>. Will there be any students of <u>yours</u>? I mean, you teach seminars every now and then. Will you do more of that?"

"In a seminar I can reach perhaps a hundred people. With a book, a hundred thousand. I really feel I have to concentrate on writing. On the other hand, I've always said that when I retire from academic writing, I'd like to teach, travel, and write bad novels. So who knows."

They all leave, and I am alone with the Alone, the simple Mystery of this moment, and this moment, and this.

Wednesday, September 17

Wonderful! Sara [Bates] was awarded the 1997 Foreman Institute of the Creative Arts Award. I'm so happy for her. But then some bad news: at a conference at Hartwick College, Sara fell and broke her leg in two places. "However, being strong in Spirit, I was able to a create a twelve foot Honoring circle [the type of art Sara specializes in] by rolling around on a mechanics creeper on the floor with a cast on my leg. The students were amazed and so was I. I didn't take any pain medication because I was afraid I wouldn't be able to focus. It took 48 hours of very focused work, but I think it is one of the most beautiful pieces I have ever made."

Now there is strong in Spirit.

Thursday, September 18

Had lunch with Nancy Levine, a wonderful woman, bright, beautiful, vivacious, who worked at Naropa until a few months ago, when she became the conference organizer for New Age magazine. She said that she and her staff read "A Spirituality That Transforms" and it really hit them hard, because "almost everything we do at New Age is merely translative." But we both agreed that translative spirituality has an important role to play, but it is, at best, introductory. My basic suggestion was, at the very least, don't lie about what you are doing. Don't present translative beliefs and label them as transformative. If New Age would simply start telling the truth about what it is doing, that in itself would be a move toward transformation.

Saturday, September 20

Early morning, Emptiness shines, the bodymind is the smallest ripple on this infinitely beautiful sea, the sea of just this. And now the sun, usurper of the throne of Luminosity, rises to shine its derivative light on a pitiful little Gaia, a small green speck on an infinite sea of unending tranquillity.

The great Zen Master Yasutani: "Now look. The whole phenomenal world is entirely oneself. Therefore the clouds, the mountains, and the flowers; the sound of a fart and the smell of urine; earthquakes, thunder, and fire are all the Original Self. Reading sutras and holding services, telling a pack of lies, slander and idle talk, ugliness and cuteness, everything altogether is supreme enlightenment. Everything is your Original Self that is perfectly without lack and is completely fulfilled in itself. Don't be surprised."

There is One Taste. There is the Big Self, and it includes "farts, the smell of urine, a pack of lies and slander." And likewise, until the ecologists understand that the ozone hole, pollution, and toxic wastes are all completely part of the Original Self, they will never gain enlightened awareness, which alone knows how to proceed with these pressing problems.

At the same time, the entire world can disappear—which it does in nirvikalpa—and the Original Self is still itself, full and complete, spaceless and therefore infinite, timeless and therefore eternal. This is not a doctrine of popular pantheism, which simply equates the manifest world with Spirit. The manifest world is not Spirit, it is a gesture of Spirit, as the waves are a gesture of the ocean. But the wetness of individual waves is identical to the wetness of the entire ocean—there is only One Taste to every wave, and that taste is Spirit itself. Spirit is the wetness of every wave in the entire universe, including, as Yasutani said, farts and lies and everything else, ozone hole and all.

We want to fix the ozone hole, not because it is hurting Spirit (or the Goddess), but because it is killing us. A true spiritual ecology does not equate the biosphere with Spirit—a horrible confusion of relative and absolute, finite and infinite, temporal and timeless (and itself just another version of bodyism)—but it does see the biosphere as a glorious manifestation of Spirit, and thus treats it with the respect that all God's children deserve, knowing, too, that these children are the manifestation of one's own deepest Self. You weep at the destruction of the biosphere, not because your God is dying, but because your children are.

Sunday, September 21

There is such a strange and radically paradoxical thing about One Taste: you never really enter or leave it. You have always known One Taste— literally, for fifteen billion years you have known this, and one day, sooner or later, you will admit it, and the Great Search will be undone. And then you will see that any state that can be entered is not One Taste.

Emptiness through all eternity, Fullness to all infinity. And it's just this, only this. It cannot be any more obvious, which is why it usually takes lifetimes to see. Too close to be grasped, too effortless to be reached, too present to be attained. The Buddhas never attained this; sentient beings never lost it. Who will believe this?

Monday, September 22

The International Cosmos Prize is an annual award given by a well-known Japanese foundation (Expo '90). It is known as the "Japanese

Nobel Prize" or sometimes the "Asian Nobel Prize." Its brochure states that "Its purpose is to honor those individuals who have, through their work, applied and realized a total context and stressed the need to understand our world as a single interdependent entity." The amount of the award is $500,000.

One can certainly applaud the aims of the Cosmos Prize; as their brochure puts it: "Of vital importance for research conducted now and in the future is the need to understand the character of the interdependent relationship among all things. The answers, however, cannot fully be attained with analytical and divisive methods that have served the mainstream science of the past. The necessity for new paradigms formed through *integrative* and *inclusive* approaches has been realized.

"The Foundation recognizes the importance of a holistic global perspective and wishes to extend its support to those dedicated to this approach. Therefore, it has decided to reward the endeavors of researchers and scientists all over the world who have shown their dedication in this respect, thus giving them the recognition they so greatly deserve. By so doing, not only are the ideals of the Foundation upheld, but also it is hoped that a new tide of values is promoted and its fruits shared with all of mankind."

They write that they would like to give me the Cosmos Prize. Before they do so, I must attend a few conferences, etc. This is very interesting, because all of its recipients so far have been Right-Hand-only theorists— that is, systems theorists or eco-theorists working mostly in third-person it-language, thus ignoring and devaluing the first and second (I and we) dimensions. In other words, they have been honoring exterior holism (Right Hand) but not interior holism (Left Hand), the world of consciousness, lived experience, rich awareness, interior illuminations, spiritual revelations.

This attempt to reduce interior to exterior (or Left to Right) is not gross reductionism, but subtle reductionism (flatland holism, systems theory, the empirical web of life, etc.—the reduction of I and we to systems of interactive its). This subtle reductionism or flatland holism— the reduction of art and morals to science—is the dominant mood of modernity, and taken in and by itself, this Right-Hand approach is actually very reductionistic and divisive, despite its vocal pronouncements.

As I have often said (paraphrasing Karl Krauss), systems theory is the disease for which it claims to be the cure.

Nonetheless, subtle reductionism (reducing all interwoven I's and we's to interwoven its) is infinitely preferable to gross reductionism (going even further and reducing all interwoven its to atomistic its). So the Expo Foundation has been doing a great service in at least rewarding a holistic approach, even if the holism has been exterior only.

But now, for them to nod in this direction means, I believe, that they recognize that a true holism must include both interior holism and exterior holism (i.e., all four quadrants). I think this means that "all-level, all-quadrant" might be an idea whose time has finally come One can at least hope that it signals the end of a mere flatland holism, a world of meaningless its roaming a network world possessing no depth, no within, no soul, no spirit.

Tuesday, September 23

THE NEW PERSON-CENTERED CIVIL RELIGION

Two sociological reports recently surfaced that have caused quite a stir. One is Paul Ray's "The Rise of Integral Culture," the other is Robert Forman's "Report on Grassroots Spirituality." Taken together they purport to show an extraordinary cultural revolution now underway, centered largely on the baby boomers. Paul Ray's conclusion is that a new, higher, more transformative culture—which he calls "Integral Culture," inhabited by what he calls "Cultural Creatives"—is now on the rise, and that it well might be one of the most significant cultural transformations of the last thousand years. In many ways these reports are not much different from the early boomer manifestos, The Aquarian Conspiracy, The Making of a Counter-Culture, The Turning Point, and The Greening of America. What sets them apart is an attempt at data collection and sociological methodology: they are presented as something of a social scientific conclusion, however preliminary. And the gist of both reports is that the presently occurring revolution is a deeply spiritual revolution. According to Paul Ray, the Cultural Creatives comprise 24% of the American population, or a staggering forty-four million people.

At the same time, it seems obvious that forty-four million mostly middle-class and upper-middle-class baby boomers are not undergoing profound transformative spiritual realization, even though at least half of them seem to be claiming that they are. What on earth is going on here?

What we have, I think, is a truly fascinating cultural phenomenon, which involves not primarily a new mode of transformative spirituality, but the emergence of a relatively new mode of translative spirituality. Not a new authenticity—or way to find actual transcendence of the self—but a new legitimacy—or way to give meaning to the self. Not a new and profound growth in consciousness, but a new way to feel good at one's present stage. Herein lies a tale.

In the late 1950s, a number of serious scholars (including Talcott Parsons, Edward Shils, and Robert Bellah) put forth the notion of civil religion. The idea was that many Americans had transferred a sense of the sacred from institutional religion (Church religion) to certain aspects of their own civil society. The result—a civil religion—tended to view certain American characteristics and historical events as being sacred, divine, or divinely inspired. The immigration to America was a new Exodus and Americans were the new Chosen People, meant to carry a spiritual epiphany to the rest of the world.

This civil religion was clearly translative, not transformative; it did not transcend the self, but it did connect the self to a sense of something bigger. It thus gave many Americans a sense of meaning and legitimacy to their lives. Meaning, because they were linked to something larger than themselves; legitimacy, because their lives were sanctioned by what they took to be sacred. And that is indeed what all translative spirituality does for the individual. Correlatively, for the society at large, legitimation is a crucial ingredient in cultural meaning and social cohesion. And the point that these scholars made was that the civil religion was now performing many of these crucial tasks (emotional expression and social cohesion) that the Churches were failing to do. Thus, many civil and secular institutions were imbued with a sense of the sacred that the Churches were not adequately offering, but always with the understanding that this sacredness was part of a special mission that these Americans were shouldering.

However, in the late 1960s, the secular and civil religion—along with many other American institutions—underwent a legitimation crisis. In A Sociable God, I discussed this legitimation crisis at length and concluded that three general outcomes were likely. As conventional legitimacy fragmented, individuals (and society itself) could: (1) avail themselves of the opportunity to grow in more postconventional directions, including, for a few, genuinely transpersonal, transrational, and spiritual modes; (2) regress to preconventional and egocentric modes; or (3) find a new civil religion, or comparable legitimating belief system, that would take the ordinary translations of the separate self and call them sacred.

It appears, in almost all ways, that the Integral Culture described by Ray is the new civil religion. There is little evidence that post-postconventional modes are operative in many of the Cultural Creatives; and although there is a fair amount of regressive narcissism, for the most part these individuals seem to be at about the same general level of development that their parents were. What we see, rather, is a new and novel form of translative legitimacy and translative spirituality, which operates not to transcend the separate self but to give it meaning, consolation, sanction, and promise.

Largely boomer driven, this new religion—which I will call Person-Centered Civil Religion—has all the characteristics of the general postmodern post-structuralist agenda that still dominates boomer academia. Namely, with a few exceptions, it is: antihierarchical, anti-institutional, anti-authority, antiscience, antirationality, and deeply subjectivistic [see November 23 for a discussion of these trends]. This is in sharp contrast to much of the old civil religion. However, like the old civil religion, the new believers no longer find the Church to be dispensing enough sacredness ("grassroots spirituality," according to Forman, believes in ABC: Anything But the Church). And also like the old civil religion, they generally believe they are the vanguard of a new spiritual realization, or, at the least, a new-paradigm; and many further believe that it will save or transform the world, heal the planet, heal America, etc.

The specific contents of the new Person-Centered Civil Religion (PCCR) can be traced to several influences, in my opinion. First and foremost is Romanticism—an emphasis on feeling instead of reason, on sentimental connection with others, and on the sacredness of nature as opposed to culture (the largest subset of the Cultural Creatives, according to Ray, are the Green Cultural Creatives). The second is the self-experiential therapies made popular in the sixties (Cultural Creatives, according to Ray, are the prime consumers of experiential workshops).

The third is new-age religion (which is one of the main ingredients of Integral Culture religion, according to Ray, even though many object to the name). The fourth is anything holistic (or, as Ray puts it, "holistic everything"—although, self-contradictorily, the actual details of this holism are never spelled out, since that would be "too controlling"—it's a holism with few specifics, although it sometimes relies on flatland systems theory). The fifth is globalism, or an intent to see their values shared by the rest of the world. The sixth is feminism and women's spirituality (60% of Cultural Creatives are women).

The emphasis on women's spirituality is interesting, I believe, and is a key to much of Person-Centered Civil Religion, both in positive and negative ways. Much of women's spirituality takes its cue from Deborah Tannen's and Carol Gilligan's research, which showed that females tend to emphasize communion, relationship, and care, whereas males tend to emphasize agency, rights, and justice. The former tend to be heterarchical (which means no position is privileged, but all perspectives are linked and joined); the latter tend to be hierarchical (which means wider and deeper perspectives are ranked). Women's spirituality has therefore taken a very strong antihierarchical stance and, indeed, tends to vociferously define itself that way.

What this unfortunately overlooks is Gilligan's actual findings, which is that women (like men) go through three major hierarchical (her word) stages of growth, which she calls selfish (egocentric or preconventional), care (sociocentric or conventional), and universal care (worldcentric or postconventional). Both males and females develop through that same hierarchy, but males do so with an emphasis on agency, women on communion. (And remember, hierarchy really means holarchy, because each higher stage transcends but includes—or envelops and nests—its juniors: a development that is envelopment, and this is true for both men and women.)

The fact that so much of women's spirituality, cultural creatives, and grassroots spirituality all aggressively deny a developmental hierarchy is probably one of the main reasons that so few of those movements seem to be genuinely transformative. Transformation means hierarchical growth, but if you deny holarchy in the first place, you have no compass, no way to find your direction, no way to find authenticity and transformation, and so you must settle for legitimacy and translation instead.

And that is what the new Person-Centered Civil Religion does. This anti-hierarchy stance is very likely destined to keep the PCCR a largely translative, not transformative, movement.

As Roger Walsh, reviewing movements such as the Integral Culture, concluded: "These movements are generally antithetical toward hierarchies. Yet the reality is that spiritual development does occur through levels and some people are more developed than others. Failure to recognize this can lead to such problems as an unwillingness to make essential discernments, a lack of critical thinking, and a pseudo-egalitarianism. To put it bluntly, the central question is to what extent integral culture or grassroots spirituality is actually fostering spiritual maturation and to what extent they are simply making people feel good. Much of what passes for spirituality at the present time seems to consist merely of intense feelings." [See July 5 for the "415 Paradigm," one of the most prominent versions of the PCCR.][21]

Still, there are many good things that can be said about Person-Centered Civil Religion as a translative, legitimate spirituality. It is the first translative religion to take ecological concerns seriously. It includes many previously marginalized groups, including most especially women (however, it is a largely white, middle- and upper-middle-class religion). It has a guarded but infectious social optimism. It highly values education, neighborhood building, and especially dialogue and small group discussion ("civil" means associations that lie between the family and the state; the PCCR values small, civic associations, but still focused on the person, hence the title). These are all quite positive, it seems to me, at least in a translative sense. And, of course, anybody at virtually any stage of growth can have a temporary peak experience—an authentic

---

21. Robert Forman is a gifted theorist and a superb editor; his research is not necessarily agreeing with the contents of his respondents, but simply reporting them. In Forman's excellent *The Problem of Pure Consciousness,* he advances the hypothesis that the state of formless absorption (or unmanifest cessation) is a near universal of profound mystical spirituality. I agree. So perhaps in his next round of research, Robert might pointedly ask all of his respondents, "Have you had a direct and prolonged experience of pure formless cessation? If so, please describe it." This would give Robert a better idea of the percentage of grassroots spirituality that is accessing this profound dimension, and, by subtraction, the percentage that is involved in lesser or merely translative spirituality (such as Person-Centered Civil Religion).

spiritual experience—and this certainly includes members of Person-Centered Civil Religion, so they are not without access to genuine glimpses of the Divine (but the same is true for all people, so this is nothing that sets the PCCR apart).

Tossed into that mix is an intense consumerism; a love of tourism (especially if labeled eco or spiritual); an obsessive interest in food and food consumption; the highest attendee rate at feeling-experiential workshops. They are the innovators for boutique beers, and are more likely to have at least five flavors of vinegar. They generally despise TV (which definitely leaves me out of the new Integral Culture; but then, I have always thought that if these authors watched more TV, they would never write books like The Aquarian Conspiracy or The Greening of America, because they would see what is actually going on out there).

In my opinion, 24% of the population is not engaged in deeply trans-formative, transpersonal spirituality. About 1% is—which is still several million people!—but not nearly the numbers claimed by the Aquarian Conspiracy or the Integral Culture. Aside from that 1%, the rest of the population seek their legitimacy through (1) traditional mythic (biblical) religion, which is still a huge force in this culture; (2) traditional republi-canism or civic humanism, closely allied, in America, with biblical mythic religion; (3) secular science, the religion of the educational elites; (4) political liberalism, closely allied with science; (5) regressive new-age movements; and (6) Person-Centered Civil Religion.

Whatever we might think about the Cultural Creatives, there is one item I especially appreciate about them (which means, about my genera-tion): we were the first generation to take seriously, on a very wide scale, the notion of transformative, authentic, spiritual liberation. We brought Eastern mysticism here in an unprecedented fashion; we insisted on Christianity and Judaism going back to their mystical roots (in every-thing from the Gnostics to Eckhart to Luria and Kabbalah); we de-manded direct spiritual experience, not mere dogma. We were a generation almost defined by Be Here Now. We had all of that as at least an idea of greater possibilities. We would, in the best and truest sense, subvert and transgress all conventions and thereby find a freedom that previous generations could only dream of.

Alas, all of that remained pretty much an idea only. It was one thing to drink coffee, smoke cigarettes, and talk endlessly about the Zen of this and the Zen of that, the Tao of this and the Tao of that. It was quite another to actually practice Zen, to spend at least six years in grueling meditation practice in order to truly transgress the world and subvert samsara. And thus, in the coming decades, we indeed dropped out, not of conventionality, but of true transgression, true transformative practice, and, with the help of Person-Centered Civil Religion, we reentered the marketplace, not from the tenth of the Zen Ox-Herding Pictures, but from the first. We in fact became yuppies, and carried out our self-obsession with a capitalistic fury; or we confined our spiritual impulses to the gross realm alone, turning poor Gaia into the only God we could find. In general, we took to Romanticism—a horizontal obsession with self—and abandoned real Idealism—a vertical transcendence of self. And with the help of the PCCR, we could rationalize the entire charade, and get on about the dirty business of nursing this self obsession through the long days and lonely nights.

But what I appreciate is the fact that, from that 24% of the population, which at least still has the <u>idea</u> that true transcendence is possible, comes most of the 1% of the population that is <u>actually</u> transcending, actually engaged not just in translative spirituality or the occasional peak experience, but in authentic practice, plateau experience, and permanent realization. The fact remains that 1% of a population—several million people—actually practicing authentic transcendence and compassionate embrace is extremely rare in any culture, and this just might turn out to be one of the true gifts my generation gives to the world.

At the same time, this sets an important educational agenda: how can we reach out and educate people as to the difference between mere translative beliefs and genuine transformative practices? How can we help turn that 1% into five, ten, twenty percent? As Jack Crittenden says, this is an elitism, but an elitism to which everyone is invited.

Wednesday, September 24

I'm a fan of the art of Anselm Kiefer; it is profoundly significant and moving. In one of those funny synchronicities, today I get the following letter from Marian Goodman, owner of the Marian Goodman Gallery in New York: "I have an art gallery representing a large group of some of the leading contemporary artists. One among them is an artist named

Anselm Kiefer, who has had many major one-man museum shows world-wide. I think it is safe to say that he is one of the most important contemporary artists working today, and probably the major European painter of his generation.

"Anselm Kiefer is German, born in 1945, with all the sense of struggle for meaning, so critical to his post-war generation. The subject of his work has evolved over time from the questioning of sources of the German catastrophe, through mythology, history, etc., to a wider reflection on man's capacity for good and evil. In recent years his work has taken an inward, more spiritual and transcendental turn.

"We will be giving a large exhibition of his paintings in mid-November. For this occasion we are planning to publish a book." She says that Anselm would like me to write the text for the book. I'll be glad to.

I was trying to remember where I had last read a review of Anselm's work. It was in Suzi Gablik's wonderful Has Modernism Failed?, a brilliant indictment of extreme postmodernism. (I also thoroughly enjoyed her Progress in Art, which demonstrates that art does indeed evolve or develop.) Gablik: "If the eclectic image-plundering of the Americans Julian Schnabel and David Salle never quite coalesce into commitment or meaning—and therefore seem more like a symptom of alienation than a cure—there are others, like the German Anselm Kiefer, whose imagery is engaged and even suggests a willingness to believe again. Kiefer, it seems to me, is one of the few artists working today who opens up the vision and ideal of apocalyptic renovation and makes the effort to regain the spiritual dignity of art. It is as if he were opening up the fenestra aeternitatis—the window onto eternity and spiritual clairvoyance— which in our society has been closed for a long time."

Friday, September 26

Roger and Frances are here for two days, hanging out with Marci and me. Frances, representing the Fetzer Foundation, will soon give a speech to the Arizona Center for the Study of Consciousness, which is heavily supported by Fetzer. I had written a long paper (for their associated journal, the Journal of Consciousness Studies), called "An Integral Theory of Consciousness," which stressed the need for an "all-level, all-quadrant" approach. The conclusion, put simply, is that we need to "you"

combine first-person ("I"), second-person ("we"), and third-person ("it") approaches to the study of consciousness: what we might call a 1-2-3 approach.

But Roger and Frances and I noticed, as we surveyed the field of consciousness studies, that almost everybody is still in their favorite quadrant, pushing one approach to the exclusion of others, and it's truly depressing. So Frances thought she might call the talk "The 1-2-3 of Consciousness Studies," and encourage a more integral approach. Roger had a fantastic idea, which he calls 20/20: each quadrant should have at least a 20% representation in the Center's activities. The chances of that are probably slim, but it's a fine notion, perhaps applicable elsewhere.

Monday, September 29

"It is not what a person says, but the level from which they say it, that determines the truth of a spiritual statement." He was a young professor, from a local college, and I had agreed to chat with him for an hour or so, late this afternoon.

"How do you mean that?" he asked.

"Well, anybody can say, 'All things are One,' 'All sentient beings possess Spirit,' 'All things are part of a great unified Web of Life,' or 'Subject and object are nondual.' Anybody can say those things. The question is, do you directly and actually realize that? Are you speaking with any sort of awakened authority, or are these just words to you?"

"What if they are just words? What does it matter?"

"Well, spiritual realities involve not merely statements about the objective world, but also statements of subjective facts, interior facts—and for those statements to be true when they come from your mouth, you must be directly in touch with those higher, interior facts, or else you are not being truthful, no matter how 'correct' the words might sound. It is the subjective state of the speaker, and not the objective content of the words, that determines the truth of the utterance."

"Yes, I see. But could you give some examples?" He was furiously scribbling, but I was not sure if he was taking notes or recording his own thoughts.

"Okay. Anybody can say 'All things are One,' so you have to determine the subjective state of consciousness—or the level of consciousness—of the person making the statement in order to judge its actual truth value, its truthfulness. We need to know the level of consciousness of the speaker in order to know what he or she actually means by 'All things.' Do they mean all gross-level things are one? All subtle-level things are one? All causal realities are one? Do they mean all of those taken together? You see, the simple statement 'All things are One' actually has a number of quite different meanings, and those meanings depend, not on the objective content of the words—which are the same in each case—but on the subjective level of consciousness of the speaker, which varies dramatically. You might be one with everything on a given level, but what if there are higher and deeper levels that you don't know about? You're not one with those, you see?"

"Yes. So how can you tell?"

"There are several tip-offs. Most of the books written about systems theory, Gaia, the Great Mother, ecopsychology, the new-paradigm, and so on, are all written with reference to the gross, waking state. You can easily tell this because they never mention any of the subtle realm phenomena—nothing about the various meditative states, samadhis, interior illuminations, the extraordinary states of dream yoga, archetypal illumination, and so on. Nor do they mention the even higher states of causal formlessness. So when they claim to be 'holistic' and 'nondual,' they really aren't, not in any full sense. At best, they are at the level of nature mysticism, where consciousness is confined to union with the gross, waking state. This is fine as far as it goes, it just doesn't go very far. It is the shallowest of the spheres of mystical Oneness in the Great Nest of Spirit."

"How can you tell if their consciousness extends beyond the gross realm?"

"Once consciousness becomes strong enough to persist from the waking state into the dream state—once you start to lucid dream, for example, or once you enter into various types of savikalpa samadhi (meditation with form)—an entirely new realm becomes available to you—namely, the subtle realm—and this is unmistakably reflected in your life, your writing, your theorizing, your spiritual practice. You are no longer confined to thinking about the gross sensorimotor realm— your god is no longer merely green—but rather an extraordinary interior landscape opens to the mind's eye. If you are a painter, you are no longer confined to painting bowls of fruit, nature landscapes, or nudes. You can paint the subtle interior scenes, as with Surrealism and Fantastic Realism, or the interior meditation objects, as with Tibetan thangka painting. But none of those subtle objects can be seen with the eye of flesh."

"So when somebody at that subtle level says 'All things are One,' they mean something different than when the gross-realm theorist says that."

"Yes, quite different. Usually, when someone whose access consciousness is confined to the gross realm says 'All things are One,' they mean something like systems theory or ecopsychology—they mean all empirical phenomena are aspects of a unified process. But when someone also has access to subtle-realm consciousness, they mean all empirical and all subtle phenomena are aspects of a unified process. This is a much deeper and wider realization, which transcends and includes the gross realm."

"So their consciousness is actually stronger."

"In a sense, yes. Their awareness does not blank out at the threshold of the dream state. Because of their own development and evolution of consciousness, they can remain 'awake' even as the dream arises—or they can enter profound states of savikalpa samadhi and not go blank. And this 'strength' of consciousness becomes even greater at the causal stage of development, because you reach a type of 'constant consciousness' or 'constant witnessing capacity,' which means you are 'awake' or conscious through all three major states—waking, dreaming, and deep sleep. So consciousness becomes stronger and stronger, persisting through more and more changes of state, and this is reflected unmistakably in your life, your work, your theorizing, and so on. These signs are hard to miss."

"Yes, I can see that. So if you are at the subtle stage, you have access . . . ?"

"At the subtle stage you have access to a variety of forms of deity mysticism—interior illuminations, nada, shabd, various samadhis or meditative states, saguna Brahman (Deity with Form), prayer of the heart, dream yoga, most of the bardo realms, and so on. This is the subtle realm of deity mysticism. Because the subtle-soul transcends but includes the gross-sensorimotor realm, at the level of deity mysticism you also have access to nature mysticism, so those are not exclusive. But the lower, nature mystics tend to think you're nuts."

"And the causal . . ."

"Is the home of formless mysticism—pure Emptiness, the Abyss, the Unborn, ayn, nirodh, nirvikalpa, jnana samadhi, classical Nirvana or cessation. This experience (or 'nonexperience') of cessation is unmistakable and indelible. And when somebody has directly experienced that state, and they are writing spiritual books, believe me, they will write about that! And you will intuitively feel that they know what they're talking about."

"You also mention the nondual."

"Yes, once you push through causal formlessness—which is the home of the pure Witness—then the Witness itself collapses into everything that is witnessed through all three states. Vedanta calls this sahaja, which means the spontaneous union of nirvana (emptiness) and samsara (form); the Tibetans call it One Taste, because all things, in all states, have the same flavor, namely, Divine; the Taoists call it tzu-jan, which means 'of itself so,' or perfectly spontaneous. So when a person here says 'All things are One,' they mean every single thing in the gross and in the subtle and in the causal has the same One Taste. And that is very different from somebody awake only in the gross realm saying 'All things are One.' "

"I see, yes. That's why you said that"—he glanced at his notes—"it is the subjective state of the speaker and not the objective content of the words that determines the truth of the utterance."

"Yes, that's right."

"So we have a type of Oneness at the psychic level, at the subtle, at the causal, and at the nondual."

"Basically, yes. And those cover just the transpersonal, transrational types of Oneness or Union. There are also the primitive, prerational, prepersonal forms of 'oneness' or fusion. There is archaic or pleromatic fusion, or oneness with the physical world (which is typical of the first year of life). There is magical animism, or the indissociation of emotional subject and object, a type of vital-level oneness (which is typical of 1–4 yrs). And there is mythic syncretism, or the oneness of symbolic fusions (typical of 4–8 yrs). Of course, as Jean Gebser emphasized, these primitive types of cognition—archaic, magic, and mythic—are still available to all of us, although nested by deeper developments. And then we reach the rational forms of Oneness, such as systems theory, which are achieved by mature reason (or vision-logic)."

"Could you just list them all?"

"Pleromatic fusion, magical animism, mythic syncretism, rational systems theory, psychic or nature mysticism, subtle or deity mysticism, formless or causal mysticism, and nondual One Taste."

"And all of those," he said, "can make statements like 'All things are One,' and yet they all mean something totally different."

"That's it."

"Yes, I see, I see." He continued scribbling.

"Look, here's the point," I suggested. "There have recently been a plethora of books about how all things are part of a unified whole, we are all strands in the web of life, all things are aspects of a great unified process, the world is an organic living system, and so on—all of which are variations on 'All things are One.' But that statement in itself is perfectly meaningless, as we have just seen. Its truth depends entirely on the level of consciousness of the person making the statement.

"And that means two things: First, when you read these books, try to judge as best you can the actual depth of the writer—anybody can say 'All things are One.' Most of the books written about 'oneness with the world' are written from, and about, magical animism, mythic syncretism, or, at best, a type of rational systems theory. So try to find a writer addressing the transrational, not just the rational or prerational, levels of awareness. And second, the writer should be giving you, first and foremost, practices to help you awaken to a higher level of Oneness in yourself. Not just a new objective description of the world—that's worthless in this regard—but a series of subjective practices to change the level of your own consciousness.

"So these writers should be awakened to a higher Oneness—psychic or subtle or causal or nondual—and they should be giving you practices to help you awaken as well. At the very least, these writers should be giving you, not merely new ways to translate the world, but new ways to transform your own consciousness. And if they don't directly give you these practices, they should make it clear how centrally important they are."

I made him a cup of green tea, and we silently watched the light slowly fade as the sun disappeared behind the mountains. He seemed lost in intense thought, as if wearing an invisible Walkman receiving a song only he could hear. "Thank you," he finally said, and I walked him to the door.

OCTOBER

And then there is the sense that in spite of Everything—*I sup-pose this is the Ultimate Mystical conviction—in spite of Pain, in spite of Death, in spite of Horror, the universe is in some way All Right, capital A, capital R. . . .*

—ALDOUS HUXLEY

There is no reaching the Self. If Self were to be reached, it would mean that the Self is not here and now but that it is yet to be obtained. What is got afresh will also be lost. So it will be impermanent. What is not permanent is not worth striving for. So I say that the Self is not reached. You are the Self; you are already That.

—SRI RAMANA MAHARSHI

Wednesday, October 1

I went to have dinner with Marci, stopping to pick her up at the developmental disabilities apartment where she works. One of the residents, Richard, is what, in a less sensitive time, would be called "retarded." But by whatever name, Richard is, nonetheless, awfully perceptive. He also has a big crush on Marci, so when we started dating, he wanted to know who this interloper was. Marci told him I was a writer, and showed him a few of my books. So today when I arrive, Richard is conspicuously walking around with a copy of Transformations of Consciousness.

"I can understand this book, you know. I read at a fourth-grade level."

Thursday, October 2

After twenty-five years of meditating in the lotus posture, I now often meditate in the yogic "corpse pose," which is on your back, feet together, arms slightly out at your sides, which is how I also sleep. So when I wake up and start meditation, there is often no movement at all. "But I can tell when you start to meditate," Marci said this morning. "How's that?" "Your breathing changes, becoming very regular but very subtle, sometimes stopping. And when you meditate all night long"—she means, when constant consciousness is present through all three states—"you breathe exactly like that all night long. I like it; it beats snoring."

Started writing the essay for Anselm's art book. It's called "To See a World—Art and the I of the Artist." Speaking of the corpse pose, in some of Anselm's recent paintings, there is a man depicted in the foreground, lying immobile on his back, in exactly the corpse pose— "corpse," because it represents the death of the ego, the death of the separate-self sense, and thus an opening to the transpersonal and superconscious. Art of the superconscious—there is the art of the future.

Friday, October 3

DEVELOPMENT AND REGRESSION
[Phone Conversation with a Study Group]

QUESTION: Since you are presenting a type of integral holism, why do you criticize so many other views, since everything is part of the whole. Shouldn't everything be accepted? Wouldn't a real holism embrace everything instead of criticizing so much of it?

KW: Well, that's exactly the central question for any type of holism, isn't it? You can read in the "new-paradigm" books—books on Gaia, systems theory, and ecology—that "everything is connected to everything else" and that "we are all equally inseparable parts of the web of life." So if everything is equally part of the inseparable whole, does that mean that we are to embrace the views of the Nazis? Aren't they equally part of the whole? Are we to make the Ku Klux Klan part of our inseparable whole? Are we to give equal weight to Mother Teresa and Jack the

Ripper? I'm not talking about the absolute view, where all things in their suchness are perfect manifestations of Emptiness and all things are equally Divine; I'm talking about the relative, finite, manifest world, where this holism and web of life are supposed to apply. You see the problem?

QUESTION: Not exactly. In the manifest world, if everything is equally part of the whole, why shouldn't we embrace everything?

KW: Everything is not equally part of the whole. Everything is part of a holarchy, and a holarchy is a ranking of degrees of wholeness—some things are more whole than others. Atoms are contained in molecules, which are contained in cells, which are contained in organisms. The wholeness of an atom is an amazing thing, but a molecule contains all of that wholeness plus its own more complex wholeness. And that molecule's wholeness, extraordinary as it is, is completely contained in the wholeness of a living cell. And so on up the Great Holarchy or Great Nest of manifest existence. Each senior level has more wholeness—is higher—precisely because it transcends but includes its juniors.

And notice, it is not vice versa. Molecules contain atoms, but atoms do not contain molecules. Each senior level embraces and includes its junior, but not vice versa—there is a ranking of wholeness here—and this ranking is intrinsic in the nature of holism. The only way you can get a holism is via a holarchy—otherwise you have heaps, not wholes.

QUESTION: So how do the Nazis and KKK fit in here?

KW: The Nazis and the KKK are indeed part of the holarchy of human development, but they are a particularly pathological version of a rather low level in it. Of course they are "part of everything," but they occupy a very low-level slot in that hierarchical "everything," and as such, they sabotage higher and deeper moral responses to the Kosmos.

QUESTION: But if they are so bad, why do they even exist? What possible part do they play in any sort of holarchy?

KW: Oh, everybody goes through some version of these lower and early stages—they are, so to speak, the atoms and molecules of moral development, upon which the higher cells and organisms are built. The Nazis and the KKK have a bad case of arrested development. They are at a lower level of wholeness. In the overall moral holarchy or moral sequence of growth—which moves from preconventional and egocentric, to conventional and ethnocentric, to postconventional and worldcentric, to post-postconventional and spiritual—the KKK and the Nazis have a twisted case of arrested development at the <u>ethnocentric</u> stage: their race, their group, their religion, their extended tribe is superior to all others, who deserve slaughter. The KKK and the Nazis are part of the Web of Life, all right, but a part we must <u>resist</u>, precisely because it is a <u>lower order</u> of wholeness, and therefore <u>less</u> moral.

QUESTION: So a true holism is actually very critical.

KW: Yes, that's right. And that's the important point. A true holism is based on holarchy—a ranking of <u>increasing</u> wholeness, inclusion, embrace, and care. A true holism involves levels of love, as it were, and in both directions: Eros reaching up and Agape reaching down. But a love that is, therefore, a "tough love," a true compassion, not an idiot compassion that "avoids ranking." In other words, a true holism contains an explicit <u>critical theory</u>.

QUESTION: That's why you're worried about regression in this country.

KW: Yes. We are seeing various trends that want to surrender the postconventional, worldcentric, liberal gains of the Enlightenment and regress to sociocentric and ethnocentric revivals, identity politics, racial essentialism, gender essentialism, blood and soil volkish movements, ecofascism, tribal glorification, and the politics of self-pity. (Not to mention even further regression to egocentric and narcissistic me-ism!) We are seeing, in short, a type of retribalization occurring not only around the world, where nations are disintegrating along racial/tribal lines, but also, most ominously, in this country, where we see back-to-the-noble-savage, back-to-nature, back-to-tribal revivals, all of which are bolstered by a flatland holism—"we're all equally inseparable parts of the great web"—which is not really holism but heapism. It encourages just this type of retribalization and fragmentation, precisely because it refuses to judge degrees of depth, since "everything is equally part of the whole."

This regressive disintegration is also, alas, rampant in academia—it is behind much of postmodernism and the extreme diversity and multicultural movements, where every cultural wiggle is included as part of the "rich diversity" of existence. Well, if we really want diversity, then by all means let us include the Nazis. If we want true multiculturalism, then we must include the KKK.

QUESTION: That's a failure to engage in judgment based on degrees of depth.

KW: Yes, that's right.

QUESTION: Is there anything beneficial in the diversity and multi-cultural movements?

KW: Oh, definitely. Those liberal movements are trying to express a non-ethnocentric or worldcentric stance, which is universal pluralism. The problem is that, in their understandable zeal, they emphasize the pluralism and forget the universal. But it is only from a postconventional, universal, worldcentric stance that we can embrace true pluralism and reject lesser stances, such as Nazism. And that means, if we really want to be genuinely pluralistic, we must support and encourage moral development as it moves from egocentric to ethnocentric to worldcentric. We must not sit back and say, Gee, all views are equally okay because we're celebrating rich diversity.

To the extent liberalism/postmodernism embraces that mindless diversity, it shoots itself in the foot. It undermines, even destroys, its own foundations. Liberalism is a very high, postconventional developmental stance which then turns around and says, Gosh, all stances are to be equally cherished, which completely eats away its own basis.

In other words, liberalism is now encouraging those positions which will destroy liberalism. Precisely because it refuses to make the moral judgment that not all stances are equal, that worldcentric is better than both ethnocentric and egocentric, then it ends up, by default, encouraging retribalization, regression to lesser stances, and a feeding frenzy of hyper-individual egocentric rights, all of which are tearing liberalism apart—and ripping the fabric of this society into almost unrecognizable shreds.

So that's the inherent contradiction—and self-destroying stance—of extreme liberalism and postmodernism. I'm obviously sympathetic with many of their goals—particularly universal pluralism—but I'm criticizing the self-defeating ways they are going at it.

QUESTION: So they need to embrace a real holarchy, which is a moral ranking that leads to universal pluralism, but it would be critical of lower moral stances.

KW: Yes. Everybody talks about holism, about the web of life, about being more inclusive, about compassion and embrace. But as soon as you really carry it through—and not just give some flatland, nebulous notion of the "web of life" and "equal diversity"—you will find that the real world, in all four quadrants, is holarchical (a nested hierarchy)—which is a <u>ranking</u> of value and depth and wholeness—and therefore <u>critical</u> in the best sense. A new critical theory is the call of a true holism.

STUDENT: Is that why you are sometimes polemical?

KW: No, you can be critical without being polemical. I am occasionally polemical for other reasons.

STUDENT: What?

KW: Well, too often in this field we have a type of sanctimonious stance—you know, we have the new-paradigm that will transform the world, or a new spirituality that will save the planet, and so on. You all know how smug and self-righteous this can get. We see it all the time, yes? Well, polemic is an old and honorable way, even or especially among spiritual teachers, to deflate some of the pomposity, and to really rattle the cage. It especially rattles idiot compassion. So I think a good dose of polemic every now and then is sorely needed, especially in this field, which, bless its heart, takes itself altogether too seriously.

Sunday, October 5—Denver

It's 86 degrees today, a record high for this time of year, so after a long morning's work, Marci and I head out to Denver to wander the air-conditioned malls. I feel slightly disconnected from it all. There is such a sharp difference between Witnessing and depersonalization. In the former you are nonattached; in the later, detached. In the former, you have a ground of equanimity from which you engage passionately in everything that arises; in the later, you are numb, unable to feel passion for anything. In the former, you see everything with intense clarity and bright luminosity; in the latter, it's like you are looking at the world through the wrong end of a telescope. I still have a mild but, for me, unusual dose of the latter, the latter, and the latter.

But enter the emptiness, and find Emptiness.

Monday, October 6—Boulder

His name is John; he is staying in one of the care facilities for which Marci does marketing and management. John is dying of AIDS, as did his wife recently. Over his bed—it is a small bed, in a small room, with four other small beds, each with nothing but a thin curtain to mark the space called mine—is a picture of him and his wife, the way they once were, healthy and strong, smiling and happy, both very handsome people. This photograph is all John has left of the life he once knew. The staff have given him perhaps two weeks to live, and John knows it.

"You said I would like this place, and I hate it," he says to Marci, who had arranged for him to be admitted to this facility. The sad fact is, this is by far the best of the options that John has available to him, and he's fortunate Marci got him in. But in times like this, it's hard to remember.

"I hate it! I hate it! I hate it! Look at me!" John pulls up his gown, and there are sticks where his legs used to be, white bones wrapped in parchment paper. "You lied to me, you lied to me. I'm dying, I only have a few weeks left, and look at me. I hate this place! And I hate the food, I especially hate the food. I don't want to die like this."

"John, listen to me. What kind of food do you like?"

And John begins a list of food that he says he wants, but is in fact a list of foods he used to want. He eats nothing now, no matter what.

"And especially I love Mexican burritos and a Coke."

Marci got up early this morning, and got him a burrito and Coke, and put it beside his bed, in his tiny little room, where he is dying.

Tuesday, October 7

Thinking of John, and it dawns on me, yet again, that all spiritual practice is a rehearsal—and at its best, an enactment—of death. As the mystics put it, "If you die before you die, then when you die, you won't die." In other words, if right now you die to the separate-self sense, and discover instead your real Self which is the entire Kosmos at large, then the death of this particular bodymind is but a leaf falling from the eternal tree that you are.

Meditation is to practice that death right now, and right now, and right now, by resting in the timeless Witness and dis-identifying with the finite, objective, mortal self that can be seen as an object. In the empty Witness, in the great Unborn, there is no death—not because you live forever in time—you will not—but because you discover the timelessness of this eternal moment, which never enters the stream of time in the first place. When you are resting in the great Unborn, standing free as the empty Witness, death changes nothing essential.

Still, every death is so very sad in its own way.

Wednesday, October 8—Denver

Dinner with Leo and our friends Paul and Cel at Morton's in the LoDo. Leo is an awfully nice person, very bright and gentle. Motorola is the only company to get into China without being forced to have the communist government as a partner; there are now 67,000 Motorola workers in China. Leo was just recently in Beijing, and Paul and Cel are headed over there on business for the last three weeks in November, so they traded travel tips.

Business obviously involves the production and selling of goods and services. But these Right-Hand products are originally created by Left-Hand consciousness, and so, as Leo pointed out, much of his job involves the interior development of managers—that's what originally put him on to my work. And this is why the three hot areas for the application of consciousness studies are education, political theory, and business.

It was an early evening, since Leo had to fly out at 8 P.M. Paul and Cel returned home, and Marci and I—we had earlier checked in at the Brown Palace—sat in the Roosevelt Room, had a martini, and disappeared in a romantic mist.

Friday, October 10—Boulder

Sam is back from France, where he taught meditation for a month, and Roger just left for a month's meditation retreat. As Frances's son, Bob, puts it, "In order to advance, Roger retreats."

Sunday, October 12

Marilyn Schlitz is in Boulder and came by for dinner with Marci and me, and the three of us just hung out. Marilyn is as bright as they come—she's on various directorial boards at Harvard, Stanford, National Institutes of Health, Arizona Center for Consciousness Studies, Esalen, IONS. . . . And most of all, she's a real sweetie. She's married to Keith Thompson; I like both of them a lot. Keith and I go back a long way. A protégé of Mike Murphy, Keith has written or edited several books; he has a beautiful writing style, very literate and elegant (which is extremely rare in this field, for some reason). Keith is now an editor at the Institute of Noetic Sciences (IONS), where Marilyn is director of research.

Marilyn is particularly interested, at this point, in researching the wisdom of indigenous cultures, but without the Romanticism that marks too much of that research (as she says, referring to one tribe, "Let's not forget these people are head-hunters"). This even-handed approach— acknowledging both wisdom and wretchedness—is one I wholeheartedly support.

Tuesday, October 14

Ever since the publication of Sex, Ecology, Spirituality—and particularly A Brief History of Everything—there has been increasing interest in my work in very conventional and orthodox areas, particularly politics, business, and education. The reasons for this are very interesting, I think.

The earlier phases of my work (what I described, in The Eye of Spirit, as wilber-1, wilber-2, and wilber-3) involve indelibly transpersonal and spiritual realms. If you want to use these models, you pretty much need to include the higher and transcendental levels. This severely limits the use of these models in the real world because few people are actually interested in, or evolved to, those higher levels. Few were the applications to business and education.

But with wilber-4 (the four quadrants, each with a dozen or so levels), there is an almost instant applicability to most endeavors, because the four quadrants cover a multitude of ordinary events. You do not have to include, or even believe in, the higher and transpersonal levels of each quadrant in order to find the quadrants themselves useful. And the quadrants are useful precisely because they give a simple, easily understood way to fight the flatland reductionism so prevalent in the modern and postmodern world. Since unmitigated reductionism is simply false, this reductionism will adversely affect or even cripple your efforts in any and all fields, from business to politics to education—and thus the four quadrants give you an immediate way to avoid this crippling. And that will pay off in everything from more responsible politics to more efficient education to increased profits.

I believe that is why this model is now being applied in so many different areas, theoretical as well as practical. A few examples:

Bill Godfrey, head of Greenhills School (levels 6–12) in Ann Arbor, Michigan, sent a long summary of "the application of the quadrant theory to our curriculum design process as well as our entire school model." It's a very impressive document, mapping out the overall goals and means of education using the four quadrants (and their developmental levels); these are now being implemented at Greenhills. Similarly, Ed McManis writes that the Denver Academy, a school for kids with learning disabilities, "has already implemented many of these ideas in our curriculum." I've received several dozen similar letters from educational facilities around the world.

Jeb Bush's people in Florida called and wanted to discuss these ideas in politics—an example from the conservative side—and Michael Lerner and his Politics of Meaning organization find them useful from the liberal (or postliberal) side, something that simply did not—and could not—happen when I was focusing mostly on "the further reaches of human nature." The four quadrants operate with the lower and middle reaches as well—which is where most of the action is in the real world.

Dr. Kenneth Cox, of NASA, sent "A Futurist Perspective for Space," which uses this model to outline future directions for NASA and space research. The report outlines the twenty tenets, the nature of holons, their four characteristics, etc., and concludes "Earth/Space is a holon and evolutionary patterns can be developed by investigating its whole/parts characteristics." I'd love to see NASA try to get funding from Congress by explaining the nature of holons. "Sorry, Colonel, but we're due back on planet earth."

Ron Cacioppe, business expert from Australia, is writing a text on business management using these ideas, and I am increasingly getting mail from business and organizational people (such as Leo Burke at Motorola). Daryl Paulson, founder of BioScience Laboratories, has written a paper on business management that is particularly striking. Daryl points out that there are four major theories of business management—Theory X (individual behavior), Theory Y (individual understanding), Systems Management (organization structure and function), and Cultural Management (management of shared values). These are, of course, precisely the four quadrants. This understanding, which Daryl develops and documents at length, allows us not only to integrate these four important management styles, but also plug business into a much larger "big picture" that gives meaning and substance to the endeavor itself.

This understanding is not merely theoretical or pie-in-the sky; it has very specific applications. Daryl published "Developing Effective Topical Antimicrobials" (i.e., antibacterial soap), which opens: "Because the goal is to introduce products into the market which will be successful, manufacturers must develop a product from a multidimensional perspective." Good point. "The holonic quadrant model states that at least four perspectives should be addressed: social, cultural, personal subjective, and personal objective. Let us look at the quadrant model in greater detail." He then proceeds to outline why and how the four quadrants offer a much better grasp of market requirements and successful market placement. (My work used to reach those interested in satori; now it reaches those interested in soap.)

Susan Campbell, who worked extensively with John Robbins (Diet for a New America), is interested in diet and overall well-being, especially for kids. She wrote The Healthy School Lunch, a critically acclaimed book on just that, and is now working on her second book, which uses the four quadrants to design a national nutrition program.

Dr. Thom Gehring (an authority in prison education) and his wife, Carolyn Eggleston, are "writing a book on the history of correctional education (prison education, education for inmates), describing the progress made in our field in each quadrant, by historical period." Thom makes a very interesting point: "I take the 'all quadrants, all levels' advice seriously, but I am currently unable to make the leap to the 'all levels' part of that advice in my presentation. I am therefore seeking to move from a beginner's 'all quadrant' understanding to a more mature 'all level' understanding. Does this strategy seem reasonable and workable?" Indeed it does, and that is rather my point: it is so much easier to start with the four quadrants, since they apply to virtually all endeavors, and <u>then</u> move to an "all-level" orientation that includes the higher, transpersonal realms.

Anyway, I've received several hundred examples now of what I take to be an increasingly widespread revolt against flatland reductionism. I'm glad my work has been a catalyst for some of this, but the deeper interest is in integrative and holistic approaches in general, which is very encouraging.

Wednesday, October 15

DEVELOPMENT AND REGRESSION
[Phone Conference, Continued]

QUESTION: You often say that each stage is adequate, but the next stage is more adequate. What does that mean?

KW: Well, you see, if you are going to have a genuinely <u>holistic</u> view, you have to find some way to fit <u>all</u> views into the holistic picture, but not all views are, or can be, <u>equally</u> significant. So you have to figure out some way to rank the importance of views, or else, as we were saying, you have to put Mother Teresa and Jack the Ripper on equal footing, and you have to invite Nazis to the multicultural banquet, since supposedly they are "all inseparable parts of the richly interwoven web." That's a real problem, yes?

This is where the idea of <u>development</u> becomes so crucial. Development supplies the key—or certainly, a key—to this extremely difficult problem. Because in virtually all types of development that we are aware of, each succeeding stage <u>transcends but includes</u> its predecessor(s), and this gives us a natural, inherent, intrinsic ranking—a ranking of wholeness and depth. We already saw the simple example of atoms to molecules to cells to organisms—each of those stages is whole, but each succeeding stage is "more whole." And this <u>developmental unfolding</u> of increasing wholeness and depth gives us a crucial key for understanding how <u>all</u> views can fit into the big picture, but some views are <u>better</u> than others because they have more depth.

QUESTION: Could you give some examples in human development?

KW: Let's use moral development, since we are already talking about that. Kohlberg's moral stages have now been tested in over forty different cultures—including Third World—and no major exceptions to his scheme have been found. Carol Gilligan suggested that women move through Kohlberg's stages "in a different voice" (namely, relationally rather than agentically), but she did not contest the three major stages themselves, which move from preconventional (what I want is what is right—egocentric) to conventional (what the group wants is right—sociocentric) to postconventional (what is right for all people, regardless of race, sex, or creed—worldcentric). So those are good examples to use.

The point is, we all start out at the preconventional stages, then develop the conventional, and then, with luck, the postconventional. None of those stages can be skipped or bypassed. Each succeeding stage builds upon certain features gained in the previous stage, then adds its own unique and emergent elements—just as, for example, you must have letters before you can have words, and words before sentences, and sentences before paragraphs. Nobody has ever gone from letters to sentences and skipped words.

This means that the lower stages are not simply wrong, or stupid, or misguided. The preconventional stages are the most moral you can be at those early stages. You can't yet take the role of other, you can't participate in mutual understanding, your worldview is magical and narcissistic, and so of course your moral stance is egocentric and preconventional. But because that is the best you can possibly be under those circumstances, those early moral stages are adequate enough; they are phase-specific and phase-appropriate.

But with the emergence of conventional morality, you learn to take the role of other, you can put yourself in another person's shoes, and so of course your moral response expands and deepens from me to we. This is a more adequate moral response, because it takes others into account. Of course, your moral response is then trapped in the view of the group—this stage is also called conformist—but again, the point is, you have no choice at this stage. This is the best that you can do with the limited equipment you have at that point. So it is also phase-specific, phase-appropriate, phase-adequate.

With the emergence of postconventional morality, you attempt to decide what is good and right, not just for my group or my tribe or my religion, but for all peoples, regardless of creed or sex or color. Your moral response once again expands and deepens to encompass more people—it is a greater wholeness—and therefore, even more adequate. And most of you know that, in my system, this is the gateway to a spiritual morality, which includes all sentient beings as such.

QUESTION: So that's adequate, more adequate, even more adequate. . . .

KW: Yes, that's right. Each stage is adequate, each succeeding stage is more adequate. And that's important because, again, it lets us fit all views into the big picture, but without giving all views equal weight.

QUESTION: Is the same thing true with worldviews?

KW: Oh, I think so, definitely. As most of you know, I trace several developmental worldviews, which move from archaic to magic to mythic to rational to existential to psychic to subtle to causal to nondual. Each of those views is important and adequate; each succeeding view is more important and more adequate.

The difficulty comes with regression, because then you are moving back to a view that was once phase-appropriate but is now outmoded. The magical worldview, for example, is not a sickness or a disease; it is the phase-appropriate and completely adequate worldview of the four-year-old. Age four is not a disease. Moreover, even for adults, magical cognition can play an important, if subsumed, role in various situations. But if you are an adult in a rational-pluralistic culture, and you regress to nothing but egocentric magic, then you have a real problem, you have an "emotional illness." In order to regress, several higher and complex structures have to come unglued, and this is catastrophic and very painful. The tectonic plates of your psyche separate and you fall through the cracks.

QUESTION: One last question, if you don't mind. You said that liberalism is based on a high developmental achievement, namely, the worldcentric stance of universal pluralism.

KW: Yes.

QUESTION: How can liberalism encourage that stance without imposing its beliefs on others?

KW: Are you in college?

QUESTION: Yes.

KW: Political theory by any chance?

QUESTION: Yes.

KW: I thought as much, because you just hit on the central problem
for liberalism. Liberalism is dedicated to the proposition that the State
cannot impose any notion of the Good life on its citizens. Individuals
should be free to choose their own religion, their own beliefs, and their
own paths to happiness (as long as they don't harm others or infringe
on their rights). The liberal State, in other words, has its moral foundations in postconventional, universal pluralism, and these worldcentric
principles are embedded in its laws and institutions so as to prevent
egocentric and ethnocentric responses from taking over.

But in democracies, laws are ultimately made and supported by the
people, and this means that the liberal State depends for its existence on
at least a good portion of its population developing to the postconventional level. It is only from the postconventional level that "rich diversity" can be tolerated, and yet if you only encourage rich diversity, you
will undermine the need to develop to the postconventional level in the
first place (because every response, including egocentric and ethnocentric, is to be "equally cherished," thus removing social incentives to
moral growth).

So there's the dilemma: how can the State encourage people to develop to a postconventional stance of universal pluralism, without imposing this on people? If liberalism doesn't figure out a way to do this,
liberalism and true multiculturalism will die.

QUESTION: That's my question.

KW: Well, here is one short response. It is true that individuals have
the right to "life, liberty, and the pursuit of happiness," but the State has
certain rights, too. And one of those rights is the right to demand of its
citizens certain basic skills necessary for the cohesion and survival of the
society. This is why we have long recognized that the State has the right
to wage war, to draft people to fight war, to demand that children receive vaccinations against contagious diseases, and—especially important here—the State has the right to demand compulsory education up
to a certain level of competence (barring disabilities).

Now traditionally, you see, a liberal education was exactly how the
liberal State in effect sneaked in the demand to grow, and imposed on
its citizens the demand to develop. Citizens must complete a certain level
of education. And the hope was, in being exposed to a liberal education,
the conditions would be set for the growth of a liberal morality—which

is to say, a postconventional, worldcentric, universal pluralism—by whatever name.

I happen to think that is a fine idea. Since you cannot <u>force</u> plants or people to grow, all you can really do is <u>set the conditions</u> that best allow the growth to occur (like water the plant). The State cannot demand the growth, but it can demand the conditions, and this it has traditionally done in the widely accepted demand for compulsory education.

QUESTION: So that puts a large part of the burden on the educational process.

KW: Definitely. Which is why the state of education in this country today is rather disturbing. Education today is often dominated by many extreme postmodern agendas—and therefore it often has some frighteningly regressive tendencies. On the one hand, the diversity and multicultural movements have enormously helped to ensure that universal pluralism is <u>genuinely</u> pluralistic by expanding the canon to include many previously marginalized groups. This is simply the culmination of the liberal doctrine of equal access for all, regardless of sex, color, creed—the culmination of worldcentric or universal pluralism—and in that regard I am an ardent fan of those postmodern movements, particularly in education.

But, as we were saying, they have, in their zeal, often gone to self-contradictory and self-defeating extremes. The whole point of a liberal/multicultural education is to provide certain basic skills and conditions within which moral development might, of its own accord, grow from egocentric to ethnocentric/sociocentric to worldcentric/pluralistic. But the New Left agenda has taken that to extremes and totally sabotaged its own higher goals. Middle and higher education in this country now actually <u>encourages</u> ethnocentric identity politics, gender essentialism, racial identity, and the politics of self-pity—all part of "rich diversity." History is being taught as self-esteem therapy: not what happened where and when, but what immoral slugs they all were compared to you. Using the values of the liberal Enlightenment, you condemn all previous history, including the liberal Enlightenment.

Even worse, it's not just that education often encourages regression from worldcentric to ethnocentric, it has astonishingly managed, on occasion, to encourage even further regression from ethnocentric to egocentric. Get rid of those nasty grades and give everybody a gold star.

There is no better or worse in others, which also means, there is no better or worse in yourself—development is completely undercut. This prepares the child for the future the same way the beggars in India used to prepare their children for a job: by breaking their legs, they gave them a reason and a means to beg.

So once again, liberalism—this time in education—is pursuing self-defeating goals. By emphasizing this flatland notion—this "equal diversity"—and by refusing to make judgments based on degrees of depth, liberal education is encouraging those trends which will destroy liberal education.

QUESTION: Is it your sense that education will correct itself?

KW: Well, the amazing thing about growth and evolution is that there is an Eros to the Kosmos, an intrinsic push to unfold higher and deeper wholes. The regressive trends—which I believe are driven by Thanatos, a type of death wish—sooner or later run into their own inherent painfulness. Across this country, in the last few years, we have seen a backlash, in the good sense, against these regressive agendas, and a call for some enforceable education standards. So, on balance, I'm cautiously optimistic.

All we're really talking about here is the traditional liberal education as an <u>unfolding of one's deepest and highest potentials</u>. And that means, in addition to self-esteem and accepting yourself the way you are now, you <u>also</u> need to meet yourself with real challenges and real demands— with real wisdom and real compassion—and therefore vow to grow, develop, and evolve into your own highest Estate. But we are not going to do that in lower, middle, or higher education if we meet ourselves with idiot compassion instead of real compassion.

Friday, October 17

Mike [Murphy] is in the middle of a book tour for <u>The Kingdom of Shivas Irons</u>, which took him through Denver and Boulder, and he made arrangements to stop by. Mike's book <u>The Life We Are Given</u> (coauthored with his friend George Leonard) outlines an excellent version of an integral transformative practice (ITP), and Mike reports that there are now around forty ITP groups that have sprung up around the country, which is good news indeed. There are now the same number of kw study groups around the country, so we discussed ways of perhaps getting them together. When Mike left, Marci said, "He sparkles. What exactly does 'endearing' mean?" "Adorably lovable." "Mike is adorably lovable."

Tony is, at this very moment, flying to Italy, because some Italian foundation or other has selected <u>What Really Matters</u> for some sort of big Italian award. It's a huge media event; Tony will give a speech (he wrote a quite impressive twelve-page statement of an integral approach to health and well-being, an approach that most of the time he actually follows) and get his picture in all the papers. Then he will spend a week in Italy, eating and drinking and—at least for this week—not practicing everything in his speech.

Tuesday, October 21

TO SEE A WORLD:
ART AND THE I OF THE BEHOLDER

It is not the object expressed, but the depth of the subject expressing it, that most defines art. And this shifts art and art criticism from irony to authenticity—a rather unnerving move, at least to today's eyes. Can art and art criticism survive the loss of irony, the loss of inauthenticity, as its central source? And if today's art abandons sardonic surfaces, where will it finally reside?

· · ·

We do not live in a pregiven world. One of the more remarkable tenets of the postmodern revolution in philosophy, psychology, and sociology is that *different worldviews exist*—different ways of categorizing, presenting, representing, and organizing our experiences. There is not a single, monolithic world with a single, privileged representation, but rather multiple worlds with pluralistic interpretations. Moreover, these worldviews often—indeed, almost always—change from epoch to epoch, and from culture to culture.

This insight need not be taken to extremes—there are plenty of common features in our various interpretations to prevent the world from falling apart. Indeed, scholars have discovered that there are at least some (and often many) universals in languages, in affects, in cognitive structures, and in color perception, to name a few. But these universal ingredients are woven together and organized in a rich variety of ways, resulting in a tapestry of multiple worldviews.

Although there are, in theory, an almost infinite number of worldviews, in the course of human history on this planet, there seem to be about a dozen that have had, or are still having, a widespread and significant influence. Investigated by scholars such as Jean Gebser, Gerald Heard, Jürgen Habermas, Michel Foucault, Robert Bellah, Peter Berger, and others, these major worldviews include: sensorimotor, archaic, magic, mythic, mental, existential, psychic, subtle, causal, and nondual. (The exact meaning of those terms will become more obvious as we proceed.)

It is not a matter of which of these worldviews is right and which is wrong; they are all adequate for their time and place. It is more a matter of simply cataloging, as carefully as possible, the very general characteristics that define each worldview, and "bracketing" (or setting aside), for the moment, whether or not they are "true"—we simply describe all of them as if they were true.

The *magic-animistic* worldview, for example, is marked by a partial overlap of subject and object, so that "inanimate objects" like rocks and rivers are directly felt to be alive or even to possess souls or subjective spirits. The *mythic* worldview is marked by a plethora of gods and goddesses, not as abstract entities but as deeply felt powers, each having a rather direct hand in the affairs of earthly men and women. The *mental* worldview—of which the "rational worldview" is the best known subset—is marked by a belief that the subjective realm is fundamentally set apart from the objective realm of nature, and how to relate these two realms becomes one of the most pressing problems in this worldview. The *existential* worldview possesses an understanding that multiple perspectives are built into the universe, so that not only are there no privileged perspectives, individuals must carve for themselves some sort of meaning from that frightening multitude of possibilities. The *subtle* worldview is marked by an apprehension of subtle forms and transcendental archetypes, primordial patterns of manifestation which are usually felt (and claimed) to be Divine. The *causal* worldview is marked by the direct realization of a vast unmanifest realm—variously known as emptiness, cessation, the Abyss, the Unborn, ayn, the *Ursprung*—a vast Formlessness from which all manifestation springs. And the *nondual* represents a radical union of the Formless with the entire world of Form.

Those various worldviews present a truly dizzying array of the many ways that our experiences can be organized and interpreted. Those are by no means the only worldviews, nor is the list fixed or predetermined—it is constantly unfolding with new possibilities. But without some sort of worldview, we remain lost in the blooming buzzing confusion of experience, as William James put it.

In other words, all of our individual perceptions are, to some extent, embedded in particular worldviews. Within those worldviews, we still possess abundant freedom of choice; but worldviews generally constrain what we will even consider choosing. We moderns do not, for example, often get out of bed with the thought, "Time to kill the bear." Each worldview, with its distinctive characteristics, stamps itself all over those born within it, and most individuals do not know, or even suspect, that their perceptions are occurring within the horizons of a given and rather specific worldview. Each worldview, operating for the most part collectively and unconsciously, simply presents the world as if it were the case. Few question the worldview in which they find themselves, just as a fish is unaware it is wet.

Nonetheless—and here the story takes a decidedly fascinating turn—research in both individual psychology and cross-cultural anthropology demonstrates rather convincingly that, under various circumstances, individuals have available to them *the entire spectrum of worldviews*. The human mind, it appears, comes with all of these worldviews—archaic to magic to mythic to mental to subtle to causal—as potentials in its own makeup, ready to emerge when various factors conspire to allow them to do so, rather like a seed awaiting water, soil, and sun to unfold.

So, even though certain epochs were especially marked by a particular worldview—foraging, by magic; agrarian, by mythic; and industrial, by mental-rational, for example—nonetheless, all of these major modes of interpreting our experience seem to be potentials of the human organism, and any of them can be brought forth in any individual under the right circumstances. To the question, "Which worldviews are available to us now?," the answer appears to be, "All of them."

Still, at any given time, and in any given culture, most adults tend to inhabit the landscape of one particular worldview. The reason is simple enough: each worldview is, indeed, a person's world. To lose that world is to experience a type of death-seizure. To surrender a worldview is a psychological earthquake somewhere around 7.0 on the internal Richter scale, and most people avoid this at all costs.

But sometimes, under exceptional circumstances . . . or in exceptional artists . . . higher or deeper worldviews break through the crust of our ordinary perceptions, and the world is somehow never quite the same again.

. . .

Artists express worldviews. Paleolithic artists, for example, painted the magical worldspace—objects overlapping each other, little perspectivism, animistic symbols, few constraints of space and time, wholes interchangeable with their parts. Medieval artists painted the mythic worldspace—an entire pantheon of angels, archangels, a God, a Son of that God, the Mother of that God, Moses parting the Red Sea—the themes were the endless possibilities of the mythic worldspace, all depicted, not as symbols, but as realities (precisely because, as we saw, all worldviews present themselves as simply true). With the rise of the very general movement of Modernity in the West—riding as it did on the mental worldview, with its separation of subjective mind from objective nature—we see a gradual replacement of mythic themes with themes dominated by nature, by realism, by impressionism, by subjective expressionism, and by abstract expressionism. And with the general rise of Postmodernism, we see those trends carried even further into the existential worldspace, where multiple perspectives, at first a source of endless creativity, soon became a paralyzing nightmare of infinite jest, met with infinite irony.

The existential worldview is called "integral-aperspectival" by Gebser—"aperspectival" because it presents multiple perspectives, none of which are privileged; and "integral" because nonetheless some sort of unity, coherence, or meaning has to be fashioned in the midst of multiplicity. In the previous worldview—the mental-rational, which Gebser also called "perspectival"—the single, rational subject tended to take up a single, fixed interpretation of the world, and this was evidenced in everything from science (Newton) to philosophy (Descartes) to portraiture (Van Eyck) to perspectivism (starting with Renaissance painting, especially Brunelleschi, Alberti, Donatello, Leonardo, Giotto). But with the shift to integral-aperspectival, the subject itself becomes part of the objective scene—the camera becomes part of the movie, the author's stream of thought becomes part of the novel, the painter's own operations show up conspicuously on the canvas. Multiple perspectives draw the subject into the world of objects, making it one object among many others, all lost in a dizzying regress of self-reflexivity, from which there is no escape.

Every worldview has its pathological expressions. The rational worldview's most notorious is "Cartesian dualism"—subject split from object, mind divorced from nature—a dualism against which, it seems, every thinking person of the last three hundred years has vocally declared war. But the postmodern, integral-aperspectival stance is not without its own major aberration, known generally as "aperspectival madness," the insane view that no view is better than another. Starting with the noble proposition that all of the multiple perspectives are to be treated fairly and impartially ("pluralism and rich diversity"), postmodernism slides, in its extreme forms, into the insidious notion that no perspective whatsoever is better than another, a confusion that results in complete paralysis of will, thought, and action. Madness it is indeed: it claims no view is better than another, except its own view, which is superior in a world where nothing is supposed to be superior at all. And worse: if no view is better than another, then the Nazis and the KKK are on the same moral footing as, say, art critics.

"Aperspectival madness" might fairly well describe much of the last two decades of art, art criticism, lit crit, and cultural studies. Irony is one of the few places you can hide in a world of aperspectival madness—say one thing, mean another, therefore don't get caught in the embarrassment of taking a stand. (Since, allegedly, no stand is better than another, one simply *must not commit*—sincerity is death). So skip sincerity, opt for sardonic. Don't construct, deconstruct; don't look for depth, just hug the surfaces; avoid content, offer noise—"surfaces, surfaces, surfaces is all they ever found," as Bret Easton Ellis summarized the scene. No wonder that David Foster Wallace, in a recent essay that received much attention, lamented the pervasiveness of the art of "trendy, sardonic exhaustion" and "reflexive irony," art that is "sophisticated and extremely shallow."

But if we do abandon irony and seek to make sincere statements, where do we begin? If we do surrender surfaces and look also for the depths, what exactly does that mean? And where are these "depths" to be found?

Wallace suggests that, instead of "reflexive irony," art should provide "insights and guides to value." A fine sentiment, but let us note immediately that *specific values exist only in specific worldviews.* The mythic worldview, for example, valued duty to a rigid social hierarchy, which few moderns find appealing. The mythic worldview also valued male dominance and female subordination, which most enlightened moderns regard as ignorant. All values exist in particular worldviews, and if trendy sardonic exhaustion is actually the exhaustion of the existential worldview, then the only possible conclusion is that we will have to look to other worldviews altogether if we are to escape aperspectival madness and its relentless insincerity.

. . .

The reason that art in the postmodern, existential world has reached something of a cul-de-sac is not that art itself is exhausted, but that the existential worldview is. Just as rational modernity previously exhausted its forms and gave way to aperspectival postmodernity, so now the postmodern itself is on a morbid death watch, with nothing but infinitely mirrored irony to hold its hand, casting flowers where they will not be missed. The skull of postmodernity grins on the near horizon, and in the meantime, we are between two worldviews, one slowly dying, one not yet born.

Whatever we may think about it—and volumes have been delivered—perhaps the best that can be said of the avant-garde is that it always implicitly understood itself to be riding the crest of the breaking wave of evolving worldviews. The avant-garde was the leading edge, the growing tip, of an evolving humanity. It would herald the new, announce the forthcoming. It would first spot, then depict, new ways of seeing, new modes of being, new forms of cognition, new heights or depths of feeling, and in all cases, new modes of perception. It would spot, and depict, the coming worldview, while breaking decisively with the old.

The story is familiar. Jacques-Louis David's art was part of the early rise of modernity (reason and revolution) that violently broke with the remnants of the mythic, aristocratic, hierarchical, rococo past. From neoclassicism to abstract expressionism, each succeeding growing tip became in turn the conventional, accepted norm, only to see its own form challenged by the next avant-garde. Even postmodernism, with its aperspectival madness, which first attempted to deconstruct the avant-garde altogether, intimately depended upon it for something to deconstruct; thus, as Donald Kuspit points out in *The Cult of the Avant-Garde Artist*, a type of "neo-avant-garde" art inevitably dogged postmodernism from the start.

Like huge successive waves crashing ashore, worldviews succeed one another, and the avant-garde, at its best, were the great surfers of these waves. And now that the postmodern wave is washing on the shore of its own demise, what new waves are forthcoming? What new worldviews surge from the ocean of the soul to announce a new perception? Where are we to look for the *contents* of the sincere artistic statements that will supplant irony and aperspectival madness? Standing on tiptoe, looking through the mist, can the vague outline of the face of tomorrow's art—and therefore, tomorrow's world—even be seen?

. . .

What worldviews, from those available, might carry the contours of tomorrow's art? Of course, some aspects of the coming landscape will be entirely new and original. "Creative advance into novelty," according to Whitehead, is the basic feature of the universe. But we also know, from extensive psychological and sociological research, that certain basic features of the dozen or so major worldviews, briefly summarized above, are potentials *already* available to the human organism, and instead of starting entirely from scratch, nature usually reworks what is at hand, before adding the finishing touches of novelty.

We know the worldviews that have been tried, toiled, worked, and exhausted: archaic, magic, mythic, mental-rational (modern), and existential-aperspectival (postmodern). The postmodern, of course, will continue its major influence for decades to come, on the way to its final resting place. It is simply that artistic productions, as canaries in the cultural mine shaft, are dropping dead in alarming numbers as the rotting gas of postmodernity first starts wafting down that tunnel. So the art world, more quickly than the sturdier herd mentality, seeks out new horizons; and thus, as we earlier noted, the dead-end of today's art is really the future endgame of the postmodern worldview in general. So what other horizons are available *right now*?

Three, at least. We already named them: subtle, causal, and nondual. The phenomenologists of worldviews (those who research and describe the contours of available worldviews) describe these three worldviews as being *transrational* or *transpersonal*, and they contrast them with the earlier worldviews, some of which are *prerational* or *prepersonal* (archaic, magic, and mythic), and some of which are *rational* or *personal* (mental and existential). This gives men and women, as potentials in their own organisms, a spectrum of available worldviews, ranging from prerational to rational to transrational, from prepersonal to personal to transpersonal, from subconscious to self-conscious to superconscious. Supposing that we have exhausted the dizzying rhetorical regress of self-reflexivity, there are only two ways to go: back into subconsciousness, or forward into superconsciousness—back to the infrarational, or beyond to the suprarational.

The distinction is important, because the transrational, transpersonal worldviews are what might be called "spiritual," yet they bear little relation to the traditional religious worldviews of the magic and mythic spheres. The transrational realms have nothing to do with external gods and goddesses, and everything to do with an interior awareness that plumbs the depths of the psyche. Nothing to do with petitionary prayer and ritual, and everything to do with expanding and clarifying awareness. Nothing to do with dogma and belief, everything to do with cleansing perception. Not everlasting life for the ego, but transcending the ego altogether.

When one exhausts the personal, there is left the transpersonal. There is, right now, simply nowhere else to go.

.   .   .

Not just different values, but different objects, exist in different worldviews. And artists can paint, depict, or express their particular perceptions of the objects in any of these realms, *depending on whether or not they are themselves alive to these realms.*

The *sensorimotor* world is familiar enough—those objects that can be seen with the senses: rocks, birds, bowls of fruit, nudes, landscapes. Artists can, and doggedly have, painted those objects, in everything from a glaringly realistic fashion to the softer tones of impressionism. The *magical* worldview is one of plastic displacement and condensation, the world of the dream, full of its own very real objects (when dreaming—when actually in that worldview—it appears absolutely real, as all worldviews do). Artists can paint those objects, as the Surrealists, among others, have demonstrated. The *mythic* worldview is full of gods and goddesses, angels and elves, disembodied souls, figures kind and cruel, helpful and malevolent. Artists can paint those objects, and, indeed, most artists around the world, from 10,000 BCE to 1500 CE, painted *nothing but* those objects. The *mental* worldview is crowded with concepts and ideas, rational perspectivism and abstract forms. Artists not only can represent those contents (conceptual art, abstract art), they can express them as well (abstract expressionism). The *existential* (aperspectival) worldview involves, among other things, the terror of the isolated subject confronting an alien world bereft of mythic consolations and rational pretensions. Artists in every medium have depicted this state of affairs, often overpoweringly (e.g., Edvard Munch, *The Scream*). But the aperspectival worldview is also, at its limits, a subject looking at itself as it tries to look at the world. Artists have attempted to depict this self-reflexive regress in a variety of ways, from deconstruction to ironic reflexivity to doubling (including the artist as part of the art)—all a dicey game, all headed eventually for self-strangulation.

Which leaves the transpersonal worldspaces with their contents, themes, and perceptions. All of these realms are, indeed, transpersonal, which simply means those realities that include, but go beyond, the personal and the individual—wider currents that sweep across the skin-encapsulated ego and touch other beings, touch the cosmos, touch spirit, touch patterns and places kept secret to those who hug the surfaces and surround themselves with themselves.

That these transpersonal worldspaces are available to us as great, potential houses does not mean they come with all the furniture. We supply that ourselves. We build, create, add, model, fashion, mold, bring forth, and compose, and here artists in every medium have traditionally led the way, avant-garde in the best and truest sense. So, on the one hand, we might look to the past for those rare occasions where a subculture plugged into the transpersonal realm and brought it forth in art and architecture, poetry and painting, crafts and compositions—the influence of Zen on Japanese aesthetics, for example. But we can look to the past only for hints, because the house of our tomorrow can only be decorated by those standing now on the threshold of that unfolding.

What will these furnishings look like? We are standing now in the open clearing, between two worlds, awaiting exactly that birth. But one thing is certain: it will come from the consciousness of men and women who stand open to the transpersonal in their own case, who bring forth, from the depths of the heart and spirit, those radiant realities that speak to us in unmistakable terms. For one thing we have seen: all of the major worldviews are available as potentials in the human bodymind. The deeper the awareness of individuals, the more worldspaces they can plumb. And that is why ultimately, profoundly, inescapably, it is the depth of the subject that provides the objects of art.

We have seen sensory objects, magic objects, mythic objects, mental objects, and aperspectival objects . . . and we have seen them all exhaust the play of their own significance. Who will show us now the objects of the transpersonal landscape? Who will open themselves to such depths that they can scale these new heights, and return to tell those of us silently waiting what they have seen? Who can stand so far aside from self and same, ego and shame, hope and fear, that the transpersonal comes pouring through them with such a force it rattles the world? Who will paint what reality looks like when the ego is subsumed, when settling into the corpse pose, it dies to its own wonderment and beholds the world anew? Who will paint that rising landscape? Who will show us that?

Saturday, October 25

Great rock groups of the last few years: Elastica, Pulp, The Crystal Method, Artificial Joy Club, the Chemical Brothers, No Doubt, Garbage, Fluffy, La Bouche, Lush, Rancid, Texas, Klover, the Muffs, Fastbacks, 60 Ft. Dolls, Belly, One Dove, Dance Hall Crashers, Superdrag,

En Vogue, Republica, Blackhawk, Goo Goo Dolls, the Fugees, NIN, The Goops, Nitzer Ebb, Sleeper, Bluetones, Offspring, De La Soul, Echo Belly, Midnight Oil, the Mavericks, Live, Wallflowers, Sleater-Kinney, London Suede.

Marc Jacobs at Louis Vuitton. It's really amazing the number of Anglo-Saxons taking over major Continental design houses—Galliano at Dior, McQueen at Givenchy, McCarthy at Chloe, Marc Jacobs at Vuitton, Rebecca Moses at Genny, and still my favorite, for women anyway, Tom Ford at Gucci.

Robert Isabell's bedroom: my idea of perfection in interior decorating, a type of Zen minimalist aesthetic, beautifully conceived.

I hear Atom Egoyan's The Sweet Hereafter won at Cannes, so it looks like he might finally break out.

L. A. Confidential is the best crafted film I've seen this year; it is brilliantly executed in every way by Curtis Hanson, and, so far, gets my vote for Oscar. The Japanese film Shall We Dance? is the most touching film I've seen in years. I'm still not sure exactly why it works, except for the deeply nuanced performance of Koji Yakusho; I sat teary-eyed for half the movie, laughed the other half. The African-American film love jones is probably the most literate film this year—a real sleeper. And Polish-born director Agnieszka Holland has turned in another exquisite effort, Henry James's Washington Square (in a world that denies consciousness, a novelist that dwells on it is a freakish relief. What did somebody say about the brothers William and Henry James? Something like, William James is a novelist disguised as a psychologist, and Henry James is a psychologist disguised as a novelist). Agnieszka's previous Europa, Europa is one of my all-time favorite films, deeply engrossing on several levels, beautifully wrought (and wasn't it one of Julie Delphy's first roles? Isn't that enough?).

The hippest film? Grosse Pointe Blank. John and sister Joan are two of my favorites, and Minnie is adorable. New music by Joe Strummer, so no surprise to see a Clash poster on Minnie's wall. Cusack plays a professional hit man, on his way to his tenth-year high-school reunion. Alan Arkin is Cusack's therapist, who is basically scared witless that if he screws up, Cusack will whack him. His standard advice is, "Have a good time, don't kill anybody." Cusack is worried that he won't have anything in common with anybody at the reunion. "What do I say? By the way, I killed the president of Paraguay with a fork. How have you been?" The reunion goes fine, except for that body they have to dispose of in the school's basement incinerator. And so on. But what makes the film work is the sizzling intelligence of the script. Along with Leaving Las Vegas (the Zen of self-destruction: when drinking, just drink), Shallow Grave, Trainspotting, Swingers, Bound, Flirting with Disaster, Kicking and Screaming, and a few others, it's one of my favorite recent releases.

And yet, I am constantly asked, why pay any attention to any of that? Isn't this middle-brow culture somehow not really spiritual? I hear the same thing about TV all the time: really serious scholars, let alone spiritual practitioners, shouldn't find any of it interesting.

What a small God, that. All forms are one with Emptiness, no exceptions. Why avoid those particular forms, or look down on them? Are they not equally manifestations of Spirit's ultimate delight, splashing in the effervescent waters of its own exuberance? Are they not equally ripples in the waterfall of One Taste, flavors of the very Divine, playing here and there? Must I worship the God of special interests only?

Sunday, October 26

The effects that different types of music have is fascinating. Rock music, no question, hits the lower chakras (perhaps 2 to 3, sex and power.)[22] Rap music is often street survival music (chakra 1). The best of jazz (say, Charlie Parker, Miles, Wynton) is 3 to 4.

The great romantic composers (Chopin, Mahler) are quintessential 4th chakra, all heart emotion, sometimes drippingly. Haydn, Bach, Mozart, later Beethoven, push into 5th to 6th, music of the spheres, or so it seems to me. You can actually feel your attention gravitate to various bodily centers (gut, heart, head) as these musical types play.

I find whenever I am writing about, say, Plotinus, Eckhart, or Emerson, the only music that doesn't disturb thought is Mozart and the later

---

22. The seven chakras of kundalini yoga are the archetypal presentation of the Great Chain, consisting of seven basic levels of consciousness, each correlated with a bodily location (because, as I would put it, every Left Hand or consciousness component has a Right Hand or objective-bodily correlate). The seven range from the lower chakras (in the gut), to the middle chakras (in the chest/heart), to the upper chakras (crown of the head and beyond).

Beethoven, some of Haydn. But when I'm doing the drudge work of bibliography, footnotes, etc., gimme rock and roll any day.

But the crucial point of kundalini yoga and the seven chakras is: all seven, without exception, are radiant forms of Shakti, the energy of the Goddess, in an eternal embrace with Shiva, the pure formless Witness. All Forms are one with Emptiness: Shakti and Shiva are eternally making love, bound to each other with a fierce devotion that time, turmoil, death, and destiny cannot even begin to touch.

In Dzogchen Buddhism, the same idea is expressed in the thangka of the Adi-Buddha (or the very highest Buddha), Samantabhadra, and his consort, Samantabhadri. Samantabhadra is depicted as a deep blue/ black figure, naked, seated in the lotus posture. On his lap, facing him, in sexual congress, is Samantabhadri, also naked, but a luminous bright white. Samantabhadra represents the Dharmakaya or radical Emptiness, which is completely formless and therefore "black" (as in deep dreamless sleep). Samantabhadri represents the Rupakaya, the entire world of Form, which is a brilliant white luminous display. Emptiness and Form, Consciousness and Matter, Spirit and the World. But the point is, they are making love; they are one in the ecstatic embrace of each other; they are united through all eternity by the unbreakable bond of a Love that is invincible. They are, to each other, One Taste.

This thangka, of Samantabhadra and Samantabhadri (Purusha and Prakriti, Shiva and Shakti, Emptiness and Form, Wisdom and Compassion, Eros and Agape, Ascending and Descending), is not merely a symbol. It is a depiction of a direct realization. When you settle back as I-I, and rest as the formless Witness, you literally are Samantabhadra, you are the great Unborn, the radically unqualifiable Godhead. You are a great black Emptiness of infinite release. And yet, in the space of that Emptiness that you are, the entire universe is arising moment to moment: the clouds are floating through your awareness, those trees are arising in your awareness, those singing birds are one with you. You, as formless Witness (Samantabhadra), are one with the entire World of Form (Samantabhadri), and it is forever an erotic union. You are literally making love to the entire world as it arises. The brutal, torturous gap between subject and object has collapsed, and you and the world have entered an intimate, sexual, ecstatic union, edged with bliss, radiant in release, the thunder and lightning of only One Taste.

It has always been so.

Monday, October 27

Marci is working hard to finish her master's thesis, which is on internal management in business. Leo Burke, the head of management training at Motorola, is coming to visit us this Wednesday, and I think Marci is really looking forward to the discussion. It's nice to have a business expert around to help stop me from making an idiot of myself, though I'm not sure even Marci is up to that task.

Friday, October 31

People make two common mistakes on the way to One Taste. The first occurs in contacting the Witness, the second occurs in moving from the Witness to One Taste itself.

The first mistake: In trying to contact the Witness (or I-I), people imagine that they will see something. But you don't see anything, you simply rest as the Witness of all that arises—you are the pure and empty Seer, not anything that can be seen. Attempting to see the Seer as a special light, a great bliss, a sudden vision—those are all objects, they are not the Witness that you are. Eventually, of course, with One Taste, you will be everything that you see, but you cannot start trying to do that—trying to see the Truth—because that is what blocks it. You have to start with "neti, neti": I am not this, I am not that.

So the first mistake is that people sabotage the Witness by trying to make it an object that can be grasped, whereas it is simply the Seer of all objects that arise, and it is "felt" only as a great background sense of Freedom and Release from all objects.

Resting in that Freedom and Emptiness—and impartially witnessing all that arises—you will notice that the separate-self (or ego) simply arises in consciousness like everything else. You can actually feel the self-contraction, just like you can feel your legs, or feel a table, or feel a rock, or feel your feet. The self-contraction is a feeling of interior tension, often localized behind the eyes, and anchored in a slight muscle tension throughout the bodymind. It is an effort and a sensation of contracting in the face of the world. It is a subtle whole-body tension. Simply notice this tension.

Once people have become comfortable resting as the empty Witness, and once they notice the tension that is the self-contraction, they imagine that to finally move from the Witness to One Taste, they have to get rid of the self-contraction (or get rid of the ego). Just that is the second mistake, because it actually locks the self-contraction firmly into place.

We assume that the self-contraction hides or obstructs Spirit, whereas in fact it is simply a radiant manifestation of Spirit itself, like absolutely every other Form in the universe. All Forms are not other than Emptiness, including the form of the ego. Moreover, the only thing that wants to get rid of the ego is the ego. Spirit loves everything that arises, just as it is. The Witness loves everything that arises, just as it is. The Witness loves the ego, because the Witness is the impartial mirror-mind that equally reflects and perfectly embraces everything that arises.

But the ego, convinced that it can become even more entrenched, decides to play the game of getting rid of itself—simply because, as long as it is playing that game, it obviously continues to exist (who else is playing the game?). As Chuang Tzu pointed out long ago, "Is not the desire to get rid of the ego itself a manifestation of ego?"

The ego is not a thing but a subtle effort, and you cannot use effort to get rid of effort—you end up with two efforts instead of one. The ego itself is a perfect manifestation of the Divine, and it is best handled by resting in Freedom, not by trying to get rid of it, which simply increases the effort of ego itself.

And so, the practice? When you rest in the Witness, or rest in I-I, or rest in Emptiness, simply notice the self-contraction. Rest in the Witness, and feel the self-contraction. When you feel the self-contraction, you are already free of it—you are already looking at it, instead of identifying with it. You are looking at it from the position of the Witness, which is always already free of all objects in any case.

So rest as the Witness, and feel the self-contraction—just as you can feel the chair under you, and feel the earth, and feel the clouds floating by in the sky. Thoughts float by in the mind, sensations float by in the body, the self-contraction hovers in awareness—and you effortlessly and spontaneously witness them all, equally and impartially.

In that simple, easy, effortless state—while you are not trying to get rid of the self-contraction but simply feeling it—and while you are therefore resting as the great Witness or Emptiness that you are—One Taste might more easily flash forth. There is nothing that you can do to bring about (or cause) One Taste—it is always already fully present, it is not the result of temporal actions, and you have never lost it anyway.

The most you can do, by way of temporal effort, is to avoid these two major mistakes (don't try to see the Witness as an object, just rest in the Witness as Seer; don't try to get rid of the ego, just feel it), and that will bring you to the edge, to the very precipice, of your own Original Face. At that point it is, in every way, out of your hands.

Rest as the Witness, feel the self-contraction: that is exactly the space in which One Taste can most easily flash forth. Don't do this as a strategic effort, but randomly and spontaneously throughout the day and into the night, standing thus always on the edge of your own shocking recognition.

So here are the steps:

Rest as the Witness, feel the self-contraction. As you do so, notice that the Witness is not the self-contraction—it is aware of it. The Witness is free of the self-contraction—and you are the Witness.

As the Witness, you are free of the self-contraction. Rest in that Freedom, Openness, Emptiness, Release. Feel the self-contraction, and let it be, just as you let all other sensations be. You don't try to get rid of the clouds, the trees, or the ego—just let them all be, and relax in the space of Freedom that you are.

From that space of Freedom—and at some unbidden point—you may notice that the feeling of Freedom has no inside and no outside, no center and no surround. Thoughts are floating in this Freedom, the sky is floating in this Freedom, the world is arising in this Freedom, and you are That. The sky is your head, the air is your breath, the earth is your skin—it is all that close, and closer. You are the world, as long as you rest in this Freedom, which is infinite Fullness.

This is the world of One Taste, with no inside and no outside, no subject and no object, no in here versus out there—without beginning and without end, without ways and without means, without path and without goal. And this, as Ramana said, is the final truth.

That is what might be called a "capping exercise." Do it, not instead of, but in addition to, whatever other practice you are doing—centering prayer, vipassana, prayer of the heart, zikr, zazen, yoga, etc. All of these other practices train you to enter a specific state of consciousness, but One Taste is not a specific state—it is compatible with any and all states, just as wetness is fully present in each and every wave of the ocean. One wave may be bigger than another wave, but it is not wetter. One Taste is the wetness of the water, not any particular wave, and therefore specific practices, such as prayer or vipassana or yoga, are <u>powerless</u> to introduce you to One Taste. All specific practices are designed to get you to a particular wave—usually a Really Big Wave—and that is fine. But One Taste is the wetness of even the smallest wave, so any wave of awareness you have right now is fine. Rest with that wave, feel the self-contraction, and stand Free.

But continue your other practices, first, because they will introduce you to specific and important waves of your own awareness (psychic, subtle, and causal), which are all important vehicles of your full manifestation as Spirit. Second, precisely because One Taste is too simple to believe and too easy to reach by effort, most people will never notice that the wave they are now on is wet. They will never notice the Suchness of their own present state. They will instead dedicate their lives to wave hopping, always looking for a Bigger and Better wave to ride—and frankly, that is fine.

Those typical spiritual practices, precisely by introducing you to subtler and subtler <u>experiences</u>, will inadvertently help you <u>tire of experience altogether</u>. When you tire of wave jumping, you will stand open to the wetness or Suchness of whatever wave you are on. The pure Witness itself is <u>not an experience</u>, but the opening or clearing in which all experiences come and go, and as long as you are chasing experiences, including spiritual experiences, you will never rest as the Witness, let alone fall into the ever-present ocean of One Taste. But tiring of experiences, you will rest as the Witness, and it is as the Witness that you can notice Wetness (One Taste).

And then the wind will be your breath, the stars the neurons in your brain, the sun the taste of the morning, the earth the way your body feels. The Heart will open to the All, the Kosmos will rush into your soul, you will arise as countless galaxies and swirl for all eternity. There is only self-existing Fullness left in all the world, there is only self-seen Radiance here in Emptiness—etched on the wall of infinity, preserved for all eternity, the one and only truth: there is <u>just this</u>, snap your fingers, nothing more.

NOVEMBER

The mystics are channels through which a little knowledge of reality filters down into our human universe of ignorance and illusion. A totally unmystical world would be a world totally blind and insane.

— *GREY EMINENCE*, ALDOUS HUXLEY

Sunday, November 2

Tony flew in today at noon. Marci picked him up at the airport, then went off to work on her thesis. Joyce Nielsen dropped by to say hello (it was the first time we had met). Then Marci joined us, and we all had dinner together. I cooked my world-famous vegetarian chili, of which nobody took seconds.

Tuesday, November 4

Charles "Skip" Alexander sent his latest dream/meditation research; it is as I expected it would be, and it confirms my little experiments on myself with an EEG machine. Namely, advanced meditators, during sleep, show "theta-alpha activity simultaneously with delta activity." The subjects report being "conscious" during sleep, and the EEG seems to support this, in that alpha (waking), theta (dreaming), and delta (deep sleep) patterns are <u>all simultaneously present</u>—this is "constant consciousness" through all three states.

What is so exciting about this type of research is that it gives us yet another empirical correlate of higher, transcendental states. There are several immediate applications. One, individuals could use this to help monitor their own progress in consciousness transformation. Spiritual growth would be less of a hit and miss affair. Two, this gives us one way to test the effectiveness of different "transformative practices." Divide students into various groups—let one group spend two years reading books like Ecopsychology, Return of the Goddess, and You Can Heal Your Life; let another group meditate; let another do shamanic drumming, another yoga, another contemplative prayer, etc., and measure the actual changes in brain wave patterns as a correlate of consciousness transformation.

The point, in other words, is practice, and this type of research is so important because it encourages people to practice diligently, not merely to think differently. Thinking (and reading) will only alter alpha and beta states (the gross realm); but profound meditative practice will take you into theta (the subtle realm) and delta (the causal), and then allow all three to be present simultaneously—constant consciousness through all three states, whereupon the Ground of all three states—nondual Spirit itself—will become as obvious as a glass of cold water thrown in your Original Face.

This is yet another call to let merely translative spirituality—which is well over 90% of the market—give way to genuinely transformative spirituality, which rewires your soul and plugs it directly into God.

Friday, November 7

UNITAS MULTIPLEX

Rented Nowhere, the last of Gregg Araki's nihilism trilogy (along with Doom Generation, which was even bleaker, and Totally Fucked Up, even stranger). It's appropriately named. The postmodern world has always found nihilism (and it's cousin skepticism) to be very cool, very hip, very "in." Nihilism is supposed to reflect accurately the relativism of cultural values, the socially constructed nature of all reality, the sliding nature of all signification, the deconstruction of moral guideposts, and the inherent uncertainty of all beliefs. The only "way cool" stance in the face of the real world is nihilism and a yawn.

But the joke is on the nihilists. They belabor the point that there is nothing to believe in. They accept no value system; embrace no vision;

believe no tenets. Yet they eat three times a day, so clearly they believe in food. They sleep at night, so they believe in resting. They seek out water, shelter, and warmth, so they deeply believe in physiological needs. Most of them certainly believe in sex. So here, in fact, are their major beliefs: food, shelter, physiological needs, sex. In other words, they do not lack values, they simply believe in a set of values that are shared with rabbits, rats, and weasels.

So much for nihilism. It's not just that the stance itself is deeply hypocritical—claiming no values, but in fact entrenched in the lowest (and as such, reduced to a value system shared by crustaceans)—but that the only "fun" of nihilism is tearing down somebody else's beliefs—this, after all, was the thrill that the boomers found in deconstruction. But if somebody else doesn't construct first, you can't deconstruct. No more fun, and so you have nothing else to do but go on about your life of ratty, weasel values. And truly, how fun can that be?

But, in just the last two or three years, I sense a real turning against this extreme postmodern nihilism—against extreme relativism, contextualism, and constructivism. As Jerome Bruner has pointed out, unitas multiplex is still the rule: there are various universal or deep features to human existence, as well as various local or surface features, and we have to honor both, instead of losing ourselves merely in the relative, constructed, diverse, and different.

Bruner: "Languages differ, but there are linguistic universals that make access into any language easy for any child. Cultures differ, but they too have universals that speak to the generality of mind and probably to some general features of its development. *Unitas multiplex* may still be the best motto."

This issue—the validity of unitas multiplex (or universal pluralism)—is crucial, not only for cultural studies in general, but for spirituality in particular. The standard argument of the constructivists—David Katz, for example—is that there can be no perennial philosophy, no transcendental Reality, no universal Spirit, because there is no universal anything, period. (Except, of course, for his own claim, which he maintains is universally true—the performative contradiction.)

I've gone through seemingly endless books for volume 2, and I decided not to discuss any of them in these pages, or else this would turn into nothing but a gigantic book review. But what I've noticed in all these books, across dozens of fields, in a stronger and stronger way, is an unmistakable revolt against relativity and constructivism. Scholars are increasingly recognizing that behind extreme relativism is nihilism, and behind nihilism is narcissism. If I see one more really good book nailing these issues (I have seen at least a dozen so far), I am going to declare my own personal national holiday.

Tuesday, November 11

Constant consciousness all last night; spontaneous wakefulness through the dream and deep sleep state, one with whatever arises. There is no I, but simply a primordial awareness or basic wakefulness—a very, very subtle awareness—that neither comes nor goes, but somehow is time-lessly so, One Taste in the dream and dream sleep state. When this oc-curs, morning meditation is no different from what went on during the night. There is simply One-Taste awareness in the causal itself (during deep formless sleep), and this tacit nondual awareness continues as the subtle arises out of the causal (and the dreaming state begins), and then the gross arises out of the subtle (with normal waking). Thus, when the gross state manifests (around three A.M.), there is no major change in primordial awareness or constant consciousness—there simply occurs within it a perception of the gross body, the bed, and the room. That is, the gross realm arises in the One Taste that I-I timelessly am. There is then nothing specifically called "meditation," since it is already inherent in this nondual awareness or very subtle constant consciousness.

Should constant consciousness not be noticed during the night, then when the gross realm arises, I specifically take up several meditative or contemplative practices, starting always with ultimate guru yoga, which is self-inquiry, or looking directly into the nature of the mind (e.g., "Who am I? What is this pure Empty Witness?"). The way I practice this is generally indistinguishable from the "capping exercise" [October 31]. As I wake up, I contemplate or feel the rise of the separate-self sense (i.e., I feel the tiny interior tension in awareness that is the separate self), and rest in the prior Emptiness of which the self-contraction is an unnecessary gesture. If this capping exercise is successful—that is, if it is done with no thought of success—then the separate-self sense relaxes into pure Emptiness, vast Openness, infinite Freedom—which is itself constant, timeless, nondual consciousness, or Infinite Spaciousness. The self uncoils in Emptiness, and I return to what I-I timelessly am. Then kw simply arises as a gesture of what I-I am, and to a great degree (which still varies considerably) I am not particularly identified with that one—kw is simply one among a billion vehicles of Spirit and its everlasting song, and I-I am that Song, not any particular note.

In any event, around four or five A.M. I do one or two hours of more typical meditative and contemplative practices. Even if constant consciousness is present, I try to do these practices, because they exercise and express that Song more beautifully than anything else I know. (Suzuki Roshi, when asked why we should meditate, always said the same thing: We do not meditate to attain Buddha-nature—because, being ever-present, it is literally unattainable—rather, we meditate to express the Buddha-nature that we always already are.) Although I have been meditating for around twenty-five years—and have tried dozens of different spiritual practices—most of those that I do at this time were received at the Longchen Nyingthig given by His Holiness Pema Norbu (Penor) Rinpoche, now head of the Nyingma school of Tibetan Buddhism. These especially include tigle gyachen and the shi tro (elaborate practices that include togyal and trekchod, the two major practices of Dzogchen or Maha-Ati Buddhism). Many of these practices were also initiated by my primary Dzogchen teacher, Chagdud Tulku Rinpoche.

I end this formal meditation with the practice known as tonglen, "taking and sending," which I also practice randomly throughout the day (probably more than any other practice). The basic form of tonglen is: you breathe in the suffering of the world, you breathe out whatever peace and happiness you possess—you take in suffering, you send out release. This profound practice undercuts the dualism between self and other, enemy and friend, subject and object, and constantly re-introduces you to your own primordial nature, pure Emptiness, pure Spirit.

The general outline of these various practices can be found in Grace and Grit. Although they are basically Buddhist, I honestly think I could be just as happy with any number of subtle, causal, and nondual practices, from any of the world's great nondual traditions, East or West, North or South. The whole point of authentic contemplation is simply to accelerate the growth, development, or evolution from the subconscious to the self-conscious to the superconscious dimensions of your own Being. We now have abundant evidence that meditation does not alter or change the basic stages of the development of consciousness, but it does remarkably accelerate that development.[23] Meditation speeds up evolution. It accelerates the remembering and the re-discovery of the Spirit that you eternally are. Meditation quickens the rate that acorns grow into oaks, that humans grow into God.

The zikr of Sufism, shikan-taza of Zen, devekut of Judaism, the Prayer of the Heart, vision quest of shamanism, self-inquiry of Ramana, vipassana of Theravada, chih-kuan of T'ien T'ai, centering prayer—the raja, jnana, hatha, karma, and kundalini yogas—the vast and stunning panoply of the contemplative practices of the world's great wisdom traditions—the whole point is to re-member, re-collect, and re-discover that which you always already are. And in that shattering realization, you will reawaken to a world where the Kosmos is your soul, the clouds your lungs, the raindrops the beat of your heart.

Thursday, November 13

Stuart Davis is a singer/songwriter, twenty-six years old, internationally recognized (The Dresdener News, Germany: "At the forefront of the talented young songwriters from the United States, Stuart Davis offers an insightful, painfully honest look into the social and personal components of life. A truly captivating performer with an equally powerful poetry"). But more than that, he has an outrageous sense of humor. His notes from his latest CD: "At the age of twenty-six, with five albums released in sixteen countries, Stuart Davis has earned an international reputation for his daring command of language and a knack for using it to conquer difficult subjects. On his latest release, Kid Mystic, he surveys nothing less than creation, the evolution of consciousness/spirit, and death (all in twelve catchy pop nuggets). Finally a collection of singable, danceable tracks that blend lyrical genius with topics like the direct apprehension of God, alien abduction, and suicide! Davis has put mysticism where it belonged all along, in the hook of a three-minute single."

Stuart wanted to drop by the house—he dedicated Kid Mystic to me—so I said sure. Marci got us Chinese takeout and we all spent the

---

23. See The Eye of Spirit for an in-depth discussion of this topic.

evening together. Stuart felt that he was at something of a crossroad in his life, moving more and more into transpersonal and spiritual dimensions (he's already meditating twice daily; I urged him to strengthen that practice). We talked at length about art and its capacity—at its best—to evoke higher realities; I showed him some of Anselm's work, and Alex's. Stuart was absolutely stunned, almost speechless, by Alex's art. This type of transpersonal message could be done in music as well, and since almost nobody is doing this, why shouldn't Stuart be one of the first?

We were then treated to a thirty-minute performance, Stuart singing the most beautiful and touching songs (Marci started crying at one point). He's performing tomorrow night at Mars lounge in Boulder; we've decided to go.

Friday, November 14

We were going to Stuart's performance, but we decided to dye Marci's hair as a prelude, and things went, um, well, slightly wrong.

I'm not sure "wrong" is the right word; depending on your tastes, it could be described as anything from "way cool" to "horrifyingly awful." Marci wanted to dye her hair platinum white, so we hit a local drugstore, realized that dark hair took at least two strong agents to dye white, bought both of them, and gave it a try.

Her hair turned bright orange.

I am now dating Ronald McDonald.

We did not go see Stuart perform.

Saturday, November 15

Marci made emergency calls to every hair salon in the area, begging them to get her in on short notice. I happen to like her hair—it's wild—but she'd like it toned down from outrageous orange to merely shocking white, and she finally found a place that would take her.

It worked fine; pure white hair; I'm no longer dating Ronald McDonald, I'm dating a Q-tip.

Sunday, November 16

Brant Cortright's <u>Psychotherapy and Spirit</u> just arrived, and it is quite disappointing, not least of which for the way it badly misrepresents my work. (I am sometimes accused of claiming too often that certain writers distort my work. You decide:)

In The Eye of Spirit, I divide my work into four main phases: wilber-1 was Romantic; wilber-2 was basically the Great Chain understood in developmental terms (a model first presented in The Atman Project); wilber-3 goes considerably further and suggests that there are numerous different developmental lines that progress relatively independently through the various levels of the Great Chain (a model first presented in Transformations of Consciousness and fleshed out in The Eye of Spirit); and wilber-4 sets those levels and lines in the context of the four quadrants (the psychological component of wilber-3 and wilber-4 are essentially the same, so I often refer to my latest psychological model as wilber-3, with the understanding that it is simply the Upper Left quadrant of wilber-4).

Cortright is still dealing mostly with wilber-2, not wilber-3 (let alone wilber-4), which is unfortunate. He anachronistically insists on seeing my position as a monolithic, single spectrum model, a clunky stepladder affair where you have to complete psychological development before spiritual development can occur. This misperception is so common—and inaccurate—that it led Donald Rothberg to go out of his way to emphasize, when summarizing my present (wilber-3) model: "Development doesn't somehow proceed in some simple way through a series of a few comprehensive stages which unify all aspects of growth. . . . The [different] developmental lines may be in tension with each other at times, and some of them do not show evidence, Wilber believes, of coherent stages. . . . There might be a high level of development cognitively, a medium level interpersonally or morally, and a low level emotionally. These disparities of development seem especially conditioned by general cultural values and styles." In other words, through the levels of the Great Chain, various developmental lines proceed relatively independently, so that you can be at a high level of development in some lines, medium in others, and low in still others.

The central inadequacy of Cortright's book is that he doesn't seem to grasp the basic issues of psychological and spiritual development. First of all, I make it very clear in The Eye of Spirit that you can think of these as two separate lines of development—the psychological and the spiritual—so that spiritual development can indeed occur alongside of psychological development (as I will explain in a moment). Cortright fully acknowledges that I say this, and then proceeds to completely ignore it. His discussion makes it clear that he has failed to grasp the central, haunting issue: even if spiritual development is a separate line (or lines), how can you define it? If spiritual development is a separate line of development (in addition to other lines, such as cognitive, moral, motivational, kinesthetic, affective, etc.), then you must be able to define the spiritual line in terms that do not include cognitive insight, morals, motivations, needs, ethical commitments, or affective love and compassion—because all of those already have their own separate lines of development. If "spirituality" is a separate line of development, you have to be able to describe it in specific, distinctive terms, which Cortright does not credibly do—a defect that cripples his entire approach. I happen to believe that some aspects of spiritual development refer to higher stages of various lines (such as higher affects or transpersonal love, higher cognition or transrational awareness, etc.), and that some aspects of spiritual development are themselves a separate, distinct line (such as concern and openness)—but you must spell these out carefully before you make grand pronouncements about "spiritual" development.

For example, even if we say that the higher stages of the various developmental lines are "spiritual," and the lower stages are "personal" or "psychological"—which many transpersonalists do—nonetheless, in my model (wilber-3), the various lines themselves develop relatively independently, and therefore a transpersonal or spiritual stage of development in one line (say, cognition) can occur simultaneously with a personal or psychological stage in another line (say, morality)—so that "spiritual" and "psychological" growth, in the various developmental lines, are occurring alongside of each other, and not stacked on top of each other like so many bricks (which Cortright maintains is my view). The idea that any of these lines must be fully completed before another can begin is silly—not even wilber-2 maintained that rigid a schedule.

Cortright, in a truly odd section of the book, says that my "middle levels" of development—concrete operational, formal operational, and vision-logic, as they have their own correlative self-pathologies—simply do not exist. If I understand him correctly, he thinks they can all be reduced to one level. Yikes. The evidence for the existence of these stages is massive, and all I have done is to suggest that wherever there is a real stage, there is something that can go wrong at that stage—hence the levels of pathology through these very real stages of development. Cortright ignores all of this evidence, and then moves into a politically correct broadside at my suggestion—following a vast amount of clinical evidence—that most forms of psychosis have a developmental (and/or genetic) lesion in the earliest stages of development. In a cookie-cutter fashion, I am lambasted for my moral insensitivity, as the author preens and prompts us to remember how wonderfully high-minded and moral he is. This is by far the most unbecoming section of the book.

Cortright's understanding of the world's great wisdom traditions seems pale, sometimes completely lacking; and the fact that he clearly misrepresents some of these traditions bodes poorly for the book as a whole. A few examples: Cortright says that the stage conception I present doesn't work for meditative development—e.g., "The Buddhist literature is full of many, many examples of people directly realizing the impersonal emptiness of the nondual." In fact, there are virtually no cases of such. He might have in mind the Zen mondos, where, after a brief and pithy exchange with a Zen Master, a student gets "total satori." But as any Zen teacher will tell you, that exchange occurred after an average of six years of intensive meditation, which itself proceeds through stages (e.g., the Ten Ox-Herding Pictures).

Cortright tries to give several examples to support his case, and they are all demonstrably inaccurate. "Ramana Maharshi, whom Wilber holds out as an exemplar of nondual realization, emerged directly into the nondual experience without 'passing through' either the psychic or subtle stages." In fact, Ramana's awakening was, as he clearly reported, a three-day ordeal, in which he passed through savikalpa samadhi (psychic and subtle forms) and nirvikalpa and jnana samadhi (causal formlessness), only then to awaken to sahaja (pure One Taste or nondual Suchness). That Cortright so confidently and cavalierly misreports this crucial event is typical, I'm afraid, of his reporting in general. He similarly misreports Aurobindo's model, and that of Vajrayana. He mentions Aurobindo as an "exemplar of this tradition," the tradition that, according to Cortright, does not believe in a specific sequence of spiritual development, overlooking Aurobindo's explicit statement that "The spiritual evolution obeys the logic of a successive unfolding; it can take a new decisive main step only when the previous main step has been sufficiently conquered: even if certain minor stages can be swallowed up or leaped over by a rapid and brusque ascension, the consciousness has to turn back to assure itself that the ground passed over is securely annexed to the new condition; a greater or concentrated speed [which is indeed possible] does not eliminate the steps themselves or the necessity of their successive surmounting" (Aurobindo, The Life Divine, II, 26).

Cortright likewise implies that Vajrayana Buddhism doesn't acknowledge these inherent developmental dimensions, thus overlooking the only in-depth study ever done on this topic—that by Daniel P. Brown, who carefully analyzed over a dozen major texts of Mahamudra meditation, only to find that they all, without exception, subscribe to a specific-stage model of development (stages that fit rather precisely what I have defined as psychic, subtle, causal, and nondual, as demonstrated in Transformations of Consciousness). Brown and Engler then tested this stage-conception against the typical Chinese meditative tradition and the vipassana tradition, and found that, in every case, it held up consistently. Cortright cheerfully ignores all of this evidence.

When it comes time to summarize the field of transpersonal therapy, Cortright incredibly sets up wilber-2 as the "old paradigm," and then presents wilber-3 as the "new-paradigm," while identifying my model as wilber-2 only. Well, what can I say?

Cortright gives the new-paradigm as follows: "All of this points to a view where psychological and spiritual development are composed of multiple, complex developmental pathways that sometimes intermingle, interpenetrate, and overlap, while other times remain discrete and more obviously separate. Sometimes growth is psychological, sometimes growth is spiritual, and at other times both are occurring together." That is precisely the wilber-3 model, as I just explained. What I think happened here is that Cortright had written much of his book before he read The Eye of Spirit, and instead of having to rewrite his entire book, he presents almost nothing but wilber-2 notions (which he had already written), and then, to cover himself (after reading The Eye of Spirit), he simply tacked on a few disclaimers (of the sort, "Wilber doesn't really believe this, but let's attack it anyway"). But wilber-3 identifies over a dozen separate developmental lines, such as cognitive, moral, affective, love, concern, attention, self-identity, defenses, interpersonal, artistic, and kinesthetic—some of which themselves are spiritual, and some of whose higher stages are spiritual—which allows us to track these various overlapping developments, all of them organized and coordinated by the self.[24] Cortright triumphantly presents a watered-down version of this wilber-3 model as the new breakthrough paradigm—but the version he offers lacks a real grasp of the developmental evidence, and especially lacks a sensitivity as to how we are honestly going to define "spirituality" in terms that do not merely repeat other developmental lines. (He likewise completely ignores the work of Jenny Wade, gives a strangely skewed interpretation of Hameed Ali, etc.)

Cortright fully embraces Huston Smith's Great Chain of Being, yet he rejects the so-called "monolithic" spectrum of consciousness, failing, apparently, to realize that they are basically identical. But what I have tried to do, with reference to the Great Chain, is go one step further and suggest that there are different developmental lines (or streams) that unfold independently through the different levels (or waves) of the Great Chain, and that only by recognizing that fact—levels and lines—can we integrate Eastern wisdom with Western knowledge. The four quadrants—or simply the Big Three of I, we, and it—are some of the most basic lines or streams, each of which develops through the levels or waves of the Great Chain [see figure 3, page 65]. Cortright thinks that this "levels and lines" concept terribly complicates the picture, whereas in fact it enormously simplifies a massive amount of data; and he thinks it confuses and weakens the Great Chain, whereas in fact it salvages it.

Here is a simple way to picture wilber-3, which involves the integration of the levels of the Great Chain with various developmental lines moving through those levels (or streams through those waves). Let's use a simple version of the Great Chain, with only four levels (body, mind, soul, and spirit); let's use only five lines (there are almost two dozen); and let's make spirituality both the highest development in each line and

---

24. Perhaps the dominant theory in cognitive science at this moment is that of *modules*—the idea that the brain/mind is composed of numerous, independent, evolutionary modules, from linguistic to cognitive to moral. These modules are, in many ways, quite similar to what I mean by relatively independent developmental lines or streams. The major difference is that the module theorists vehemently deny that there is any sort of transcendental self or unity of consciousness. And yet, according to their own theory and data, individuals are capable of being aware of these modules, and can in fact override them on occasion. If you can override a module, you are not just a module. QED.

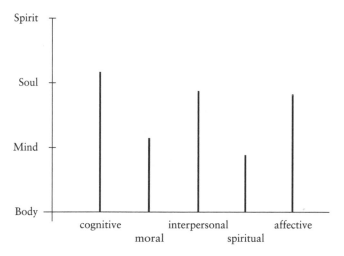

FIGURE 5. *The Integral Psychograph*

a separate line of its own, to cover both common definitions (see figure 5).[25]

Since "hierarchy" upsets many people, let's also draw that hierarchy in the way that it is actually defined, namely, as a holarchy (see figure 6). This is the identical concept, but some people are more comfortable with nice feminine circles (I prefer them myself, because they so clearly show the "transcend and include" nature of the Great Nest of Being).

The point of both of those diagrams—what I call an "integral psychograph"—is that you can track the different developmental lines (or streams) as they move through the various levels (or waves) of the Great Nest. You can be at a higher, transpersonal, or "spiritual" level in several lines, and at a lower, personal, or "psychological" level in others, so that both spiritual and psychological development overlap—and the separate spiritual line(s) can be relatively high or low as well.

All of these streams and waves are navigated by the self (or the self system), which has to balance all of them and find some sort of harmony in the midst of this mélange. Moreover, something can go wrong in any stream at any of its waves (or stages), and therefore we can map various types of pathologies wherever they occur in the psychograph—different

25. For a refined view of this model, see "Two Patterns of Transcendence," *Journal of Humanistic Psychology*, 30, no. 3 (Summer 1990) 113–36.

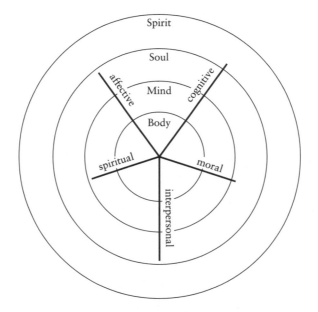

FIGURE 6. *The Integral Psychograph as a Holarchy*

types of pathologies occur at different levels or waves in each of the lines.

Even though we can say, based on massive evidence (clinical, phenomenological, and contemplative), that many of these developmental streams proceed through the waves in a stagelike fashion, nonetheless overall self development does <u>not</u> proceed in a specific, stagelike manner, simply because the self is an amalgam of all the various lines, and the possible number of permutations and combinations of those is virtually infinite. Overall individual growth, in other words, follows no set sequence whatsoever.

Finally, as suggested in the nested diagram (figure 6), because each senior dimension transcends but includes (or nests) the junior dimension, to be at a higher wave does not mean the lower waves are left behind. This is not (and never has been) based on a ladder, but on the model of: atoms, molecules, cells, and organisms, with each senior level enfolding or enveloping the junior—as Plotinus put it, a development that is envelopment. So even at a higher level, "lower" work is still occurring simultaneously—cells still have molecules, Buddhas still have to eat.

That's wilber-3 in a nutshell. While I'm on that topic, I'll give one last example of why I believe that this type of wilber-3 model is an improvement on the traditional Great Chain model (or wilber-2), which contains the various <u>levels</u> of Being but does not fully understand how and why different <u>lines</u> develop through those levels.[26] Huston Smith, we have seen, accurately summarizes the traditional Great Chain as body, mind,

---

26. For students of my work, the exact relation of wilber-3 with the Great Chain is as follows:

   1. I have expanded the traditional Great Chain from matter, body, mind, soul, and spirit, to include: matter (physical), body (sensation, perception, impulse, emotion), mind (image, symbol, concept, rule, formal, vision-logic), soul (psychic, subtle), spirit (causal, nondual). Those can still be subdivided; but even in this form it brings the lower levels of the Chain into accord with Western research.

   2. Most important of all, we note that the Great Chain *develops* or *evolves*, both individually (ontogeny) and collectively (phylogeny). This hinges on a paradox: Spirit is both the highest level of evolution, and the ground or suchness of all levels of evolution—it is *both* pure formless Emptiness, which does not evolve, and the entire world of Form, which does. Integrating the transcendental and the immanent aspects of Spirit is paramount. The *form of development* (outlined in *The Atman Project* and the Twenty Tenets in SES) is, to put it simply, *transcend and include.*

   3. Each of those fifteen or so levels I call the basic levels of consciousness or the *basic structures* of consciousness—or again, the *basic waves*. Once they emerge in development, they remain in existence, subsumed but still fully functioning. Each basic structure is a system of *relational exchange* with other holons at the *same level* of organization in its surroundings.

   4. Through those levels or waves of consciousness (through the expanded Great Chain) pass various developmental lines or streams, and they do so in relatively independent ways. These lines include cognitive, affective, moral, proximate self-identity or "ego development" (not to be confused with overall self development, which follows no set sequence), defenses (the standard hierarchy of defense mechanisms), interpersonal, artistic, concern, love, epistemic mode, joy (level of exuberance of existence), visual-spatial, death-seizure, logico-mathematic, psychosexual, self-needs, mode of spacetime, object relations, kinesthetic, deeper psychic, specific talents, creativity, witnessing capacity, altruism, and worldviews—to name those for which we have credible evidence.

   The majority of research (which I summarize in *The Eye of Spirit*) concludes that each of those lines grows and develops through a largely invariant sequence of stages, although they do so relatively independently of each other. Many researchers refer to these universal, invariant stages as preconventional ("precon"), conventional ("con"), and postconventional ("postcon"). I have suggested, based on cross-cultural evidence, that we must add at least a fourth major level or stage, the post-postconventional ("post-postcon"). Although substantial empirical evidence demonstrates that each line develops through these

soul, and spirit (correlative with realms he calls terrestrial, intermediate, celestial, and infinite). That model is fine as far as it goes, but the trouble is, it starts to fall apart under further scrutiny, and it completely collapses under the avalanche of modern psychological research.

To begin with, the traditional Great Chain tends to confuse the levels of Being and the types of self-sense associated with each level. For exam-

holarchical stages in an invariant sequence, nonetheless, because all two dozen of them *develop relatively independently*, overall growth and development is a massively complex, overlapping, nonlinear affair, following no set sequence whatsoever.

5. The largely universal, invariant, holarchical stages of precon, con, postcon, and post-postcon are none other than the Great Chain. Precon covers sensorimotor, vital body, and early body-bound mind (body); con refers to the middle mind (up to rule and early formal); postcon refers to the late mind (formal and vision-logic); and post-postcon refers to the spiritual/transpersonal (considered as the highest development, which does not preclude separate spiritual lines). They are simply another way of looking at the basic levels or basic waves of consciousness (the Great Chain itself), through which the various lines move. The reason researchers have found these waves to be largely invariant is because the Great Chain is largely invariant.

6. But only in its deep features. Each of the levels and lines, I have suggested, has both deep features and surface features. (I used to call them deep structures and surface structures, and I sometimes still do, but that terminology is often confused with Chomsky's formulations, which limits their meaning). The *deep features* of any level or line are those features that research indicates are largely universal; but these deep features are molded by local customs and cultures, resulting in various *surface features* that differ from culture to culture, and often from person to person.

7. Navigating the entire unfolding of streams and waves is the self (or self-system). The self has various important capacities, including identification, organization, will, defense, metabolism, and navigation.

8. As the self develops through the basic waves of consciousness, it generates different levels of self-identity (e.g., Loevinger), self-needs (e.g., Maslow), and self-morals (e.g., Gilligan), to name the most important. These *self-stages* (such as needs and morals) are some of the most important lines of development, simply because they so profoundly affect the individual.

9. But in addition to that—and just as important—the overall self has to juggle and balance all the other developmental lines, which are usually occurring at quite different rates of development. This "juggling act" is the key to the overall self's life drama.

10. As the self negotiates its own growth through the basic waves, it first identifies/fuses with a particular wave, then differentiates/transcends it, then includes/integrates it from the next higher wave. This 1-2-3 process is called a fulcrum of development.

ple, mind is a level of the Great Chain, but the ego is the self generated when consciousness identifies with that level (i.e., identifies with mind). The subtle is a level of the Great Chain, the soul is the self generated when consciousness identifies with the subtle. The causal/spirit is a level in the Great Chain, the True Self is the "self" associated with that level, and so on. So the sequence of levels in the Great Chain should be body, mind, subtle, and causal/spirit, with the correlative self stages of body-ego, ego, soul, and Self—to use the very simplified version. Although I often use the traditional terminology (body, mind, soul, spirit), I always have in mind the difference between the actual levels (body, mind, subtle, causal) and the self at those levels (bodyego, ego, soul, Self).

Here is where some of these distinctions start to pay off (and the usefulness of the move from wilber-2 to wilber-3 becomes more obvious). The traditions generally maintain that men and women have two major personality systems, as it were: the frontal and the deeper psychic. The traditional Great Chain theorists (and wilber-2) would simply say

---

11. At any stage of its own growth and unfolding, something can go wrong with the self. Something can go wrong at each fulcrum. The result is psychopathology, and there are as many levels of pathology as there are levels of growth. In my system, I usually give the Great Chain with nine or so levels, so I have outlined nine levels of pathology. These are not rigid distinctions, and there are always overlaps.

12. Different therapies, East and West, have evolved to deal with these nine levels of pathology, and a balanced approach to growth would include the entire spectrum, and not simply privilege one or two approaches.

13. One last definition. I mentioned that the basic structures or basic waves of consciousness are *enduring structures*—once they emerge, they remain (subsumed but functioning). But most of the developmental lines consist of *transitional structures* that are relatively temporary or phase-specific, and are *replaced* more than subsumed by subsequent stages in that line. This is an important distinction, because it allows us to determine what should remain in development, and what should be let go of. The need for food remains; the oral stage does not (barring fixation and pathology).

14. Finally, and most important of all, the Great Chain itself applies mostly to the Upper Left quadrant, and it (along with all its various levels and lines) must be set in the context of *the four quadrants*.

This system fully honors the traditional Great Holarchy of Being, in both its Ascending (Eros) and Descending (Agape) arcs, albeit in an expanded form; by further adding waves and streams, enduring and transitional structures, deep and surface features, the form of development, the self and its pathology, and the four quadrants, it allows us, I believe, to integrate the best of modern knowledge with the best of ancient wisdom.

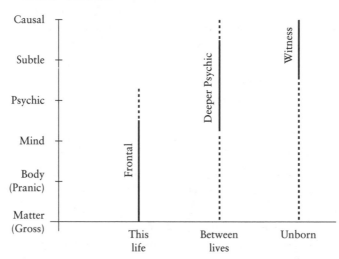

FIGURE 7. *The Development of the Frontal (or Ego), the Deeper Psychic (or Soul), and the Witness (or Self)*

that the frontal is the self associated with the body and mind, and the deeper psychic is associated with the soul, which would indeed be a type of ladder arrangement. But the frontal and the deeper psychic seem much more flexible than that; they seem to be, not different levels, but separate lines, of development, so that their development occurs alongside of, not on top of, each other. We can graph this as shown in figure 7 (for which I have reverted to a more accurate six levels.)[27]

The frontal being is the <u>gross-oriented personality</u>—in the widest sense, what we mean by "ego," or the personality that is oriented outwardly to the sensorimotor world. The frontal being begins its developmental line or stream with material conception, continues through the emotional-sexual or pranic stages, into the mental stages, and fades out at the psychic. <u>Frontal development</u> represents the evolution of the self

---

27. In Vedanta—the most traditional of the Great Chain models—there are five *levels* (matter, *prana, manomayakosha* or lower mind, *vijnanamayakosha* or higher mind, and *anandamayakosha* or bliss mind), divided into three major *realms* (gross, subtle, and causal). Matter is the gross realm, the bliss mind is the causal realm, and the three middle levels (body/*prana*, lower mind, and higher mind) are *all* the subtle realm. When I speak generally and simply of the three realms (gross, subtle, causal), I agree with that correlation. But I also use "the subtle" to mean the *highest* of the three subtle realms (the *anandamayakosha*). Context will indicate which is meant.

(or self-identity) through the lower-to-intermediate waves of the Great Nest of Being.

According to the traditions, while the frontal personality is that which develops in this life, the deeper psychic is that which develops between lives. It is, in the very widest sense, what we mean by the word "soul." At any rate, the deeper psychic is said to be present sometime from conception to midterm; in fact, some research suggests that prenatal, perinatal, and neonatal memories do in fact exist, and since these cannot be carried by the frontal personality and the gross brain (since they have not developed), the traditions would maintain that these memories are being carried by the deeper psychic being and are later lost as frontal development gets under way and submerges the early psychic being.[28] Likewise, past-life memories, if they are genuine, would be carried by the deeper psychic. Nonetheless, it is not necessary to believe in either prenatal memory or past lives in order to acknowledge the deeper psychic self, which is <u>primarily</u> defined by its access to higher consciousness, not by its access to past lives.

Although the deeper psychic is present from birth (or mid-prenatal), it plays a modest role until the <u>necessary</u> frontal development finishes its task of orienting (and adapting) consciousness to the gross realm. As the frontal personality begins to fade, the deeper psychic being comes increasingly to the fore. Just as the frontal personality orients consciousness to the gross realm, the deeper psychic orients consciousness to the subtle realm. And, as we saw, the self associated with the subtle realm is the "soul," which is why "deeper psychic" and "soul" are generally synonymous. But the deeper psychic, even though its roots are in the subtle realm per se, nonetheless has a development that reaches down to some of the earliest stages, culminates in the subtle, and disappears at the causal.

Already we can begin to see the advantage of making the frontal and the deeper psychic not discrete levels but overlapping lines; not different waves but often parallel streams. We can go one step further and note that there is a last major "personality," that of the Self, associated with the causal, but also, like the others, having developments that reach down into earlier stages. In other words, we can usefully treat the Self

---

28. In this case, in fig. 7 the lowest quarter inch of the "Deeper Psychic" line would also be solid. See *The Eye of Spirit* for a full discussion.

as a separate line or stream of development, even though its basic orientation is the causal.

The Self, or the transpersonal Witness, is not—like the ego or the soul—a "personality," since it has no specific characteristics whatsoever (it is pure Emptiness and the great Unborn), except for the fact that it is an Emptiness still separate from Form, a Witness still divorced from that which is witnessed. As such, the Self or Witness is the seat of attention, the root of the separate-self sense, and the home of the last and subtlest duality, namely, that between the Seer and the seen. It is both the highest Self, and the final barrier, to nondual One Taste.

Nonetheless, the power of Witnessing is the power of liberation from all lower domains, and the Witness itself is present, even if latently, at all previous stages. Each developmental stage "transcends and includes" its predecessor, and the "transcend" aspect, in every case, is the power of the higher to be aware of the lower (the soul is aware of the mind, which is aware of the body, which is aware of matter). And in each case, the "is aware of" is simply the power of the Witness shining through at that stage.

Although the Witness is present as the power of transcendental growth at every stage, it comes to its own fruition in the causal realm. As the ego orients consciousness to the gross, and the soul orients consciousness to the subtle, the Self orients consciousness to the causal. While all of them have their root dispositions in specific realms or waves of the Great Nest, they also have their own lines or streams of development, so they often overlap each other, as indicated in figure 6. And this is what I think so many meditation teachers and transpersonal therapists see in themselves and their clients, namely, that ego and soul and Spirit can in many ways coexist and develop together, because they are relatively separate streams flowing through the waves in the Great Nest of Being. And there can be, on occasion, rather uneven development in between these streams.[29]

---

29. This is why some early cultures apparently showed advanced psychic capacities but rather poor frontal development—which is why, whatever else their merits, they were not exemplars of integral culture, although we can admire much of their wisdom.

We all know fairly enlightened teachers (alive to the Unborn) who nonetheless still have "big egos," in the sense of strong, forceful, powerful personalities. But the presence of the ego is not a problem; it all depends upon whether the person is <u>also</u> alive to higher and deeper dimensions. As Hubert Benoit said, it is not the identification with the ego that is the problem, but the exclusive nature of that identification. When our self-identity expands beyond the ego, into the deeper psychic, then even into the Unborn and One Taste, the ego is simply taken up and subsumed in a grander identity. But the ego itself remains as the functional self in the gross realm, and it might even appropriately be intensified and made more powerful, simply because it is now plugged into the entire Kosmos. Many of the great enlightened teachers had a big ego, a big deeper psychic, and a very big Self, all at once, simply because these are the three functional vehicles of the gross, subtle, and causal domains, and all three vehicles were appropriately intensified in the great awakened ones.

Now—and this is what tends to confuse people—although the various developmental lines often overlap each other, and in no specific sequence, <u>the individual lines or streams themselves usually have their own invariant, universal, developmental sequence</u>—namely, to the extent that they unfold into consciousness, they must negotiate the levels or waves in the Great Nest, and in an order that is given by the Nest itself. For example, we have substantial evidence that cognition, morals, affects, kinesthetic skills, and interpersonal capacity, to name a few, all develop through preconventional, conventional, and postconventional waves.[30] In other words, the various streams seem to move through the levels in the Great Nest in a fashion that is determined by the universal Great Nest itself. Although all sorts of regressions and temporary leaps forward are possible, the empirical fact remains as Aurobindo said: individual streams obey the law of a successive unfolding (undulating through the waves of the Great Nest itself).

At the same time, I repeat: even though all developmental lines (including the frontal, the deeper psychic, and the capacity for witnessing) follow their own stages, the <u>overall</u> mixture of lines does not. The "over-

---

30. See *The Eye of Spirit* for a summary of this extensive research.

all self" is a juggling of some two dozen different developmental lines, and thus each individual's unfolding will be a radically unique affair.

Monday, November 17

Precisely because the ego, the soul, and the Self can all be present simultaneously, we can better understand the real meaning of "egolessness," a notion that has caused an inordinate amount of confusion. But egolessness does not mean the absence of a functional self (that's a psychotic, not a sage); it means that one is no longer exclusively identified with that self.

One of the many reasons we have trouble with the notion of "egoless" is that people want their "egoless sages" to fulfill all their fantasies of "saintly" or "spiritual," which usually means dead from the neck down, without fleshy wants or desires, gently smiling all the time. All of the things that people typically have trouble with—money, food, sex, relationships, desire—they want their saints to be without. "Egoless sages" are "above all that," is what people want. Talking heads, is what they want. Religion, they believe, will simply get rid of all baser instincts, drives, and relationships, and hence they look to religion, not for advice on how to live life with enthusiasm, but on how to avoid it, repress it, deny it, escape it.

In other words, the typical person wants the spiritual sage to be "less than a person," somehow devoid of all the messy, juicy, complex, pulsating, desiring, urging forces that drive most human beings. We expect our sages to be an absence of all that drives us! All the things that frighten us, confuse us, torment us, confound us: we want our sages to be untouched by them altogether. And that absence, that vacancy, that "less than personal," is what we often mean by "egoless."

But "egoless" does not mean "less than personal," it means "more than personal." Not personal minus, but personal plus—all the normal personal qualities, plus some transpersonal ones. Think of the great yogis, saints, and sages—from Moses to Christ to Padmasambhava. They were not feeble-mannered milquetoasts, but fierce movers and shakers—from wielding bullwhips in the Temple to subduing entire countries. They rattled the world on its own terms, not in some pie-in-the-sky piety; many of them instigated massive social revolutions that have continued for thousands of years. And they did so, not because they avoided the physical, emotional, and mental dimensions of humanness, and the ego that is their vehicle, but because they engaged them with a drive and intensity that shook the world to its very foundations. No doubt, they were also plugged into the soul (deeper psychic) and spirit (formless Self)—the ultimate source of their power—but they expressed that power, and gave it concrete results, precisely because they dramatically engaged the lower dimensions through which that power could speak in terms that could be heard by all.

These great movers and shakers were not small egos; they were, in the very best sense of the term, big egos, precisely because the ego (the functional vehicle of the gross realm) can and does exist alongside the soul (the vehicle of the subtle) and the Self (vehicle of the causal). To the extent these great teachers moved the gross realm, they did so with their egos, because the ego is the functional vehicle of that realm. They were not, however, identified merely with their egos (that's a narcissist), they simply found their egos plugged into a radiant Kosmic source. The great yogis, saints, and sages accomplished so much precisely because they were not timid little toadies but great big egos, plugged into the dynamic Ground and Goal of the Kosmos itself, plugged into their own higher Self, alive to the pure Atman (the pure I-I) that is one with Brahman; they opened their mouths and the world trembled, fell to its knees, and confronted its radiant God.

Saint Teresa was a great contemplative? Yes, and Saint Teresa is the only woman ever to have reformed an entire Catholic monastic tradition (think about it). Gautama Buddha shook India to its foundations. Rumi, Plotinus, Bodhidharma, Lady Tsogyal, Lao Tzu, Plato, the Baal Shem Tov—these men and women started revolutions in the gross realm that lasted hundreds, sometimes thousands, of years, something neither Marx nor Lenin nor Locke nor Jefferson can yet claim. And they did not do so because they were dead from the neck down. No, they were monumentally, gloriously, divinely big egos, plugged into a deeper psychic, which was plugged straight into God.

There is certainly a type of truth to the notion of transcending ego: it doesn't mean destroy the ego, it means plug it into something bigger. (As Nagarjuna put it, in the relative world, atman is real; in the absolute, neither atman nor anatman is real. Thus, in neither case is anatta a correct description of reality.)[31] The small ego does not evaporate; it remains as the functional center of activity in the conventional realm. As I said, to loose that ego is to become a psychotic, not a sage.

"Transcending the ego" thus actually means to transcend but include the ego in a deeper and higher embrace, first in the soul or deeper psychic, then with the Witness or primordial Self, then with each previous stage taken up, enfolded, included, and embraced in the radiance of One Taste. And that means we do not "get rid" of the small ego, but rather, we inhabit it fully, live it with verve, use it as the necessary vehicle through which higher truths are communicated. Soul and Spirit include body, emotions, and mind, they do not erase them.

Put bluntly, the ego is not an obstruction to Spirit, but a radiant manifestation of Spirit. All Forms are not other than Emptiness, including the form of the ego. It is not necessary to get rid of the ego, but simply to live it with a certain exuberance. When identification spills out of the ego and into the Kosmos at large, the ego discovers that the individual Atman is in fact all of a piece with Brahman. The big Self is indeed no small ego, and thus, to the extent you are stuck in your small ego, a death and transcendence is required. Narcissists are simply people whose egos are not yet big enough to embrace the entire Kosmos, and so they try to be central to the Kosmos instead.

But we do not want our sages to have big egos; we do not even want them to display a manifest dimension at all. Anytime a sage displays humanness—in regard to money, food, sex, relationships—we are shocked, shocked, because we are planning to escape life altogether, not live it, and the sage who lives life offends us. We want out, we want to ascend, we want to escape, and the sage who engages life with gusto, lives it to the hilt, grabs each wave of life and surfs it to the end—this deeply, profoundly disturbs us, frightens us, because it means that we, too, might have to engage life, with gusto, on all levels, and not merely escape it in a cloud of luminous ether. We do not want our sages to have bodies, egos, drives, vitality, sex, money, relationships, or life, because those are what habitually torture us, and we want out. We do not want to surf the waves of life, we want the waves to go away. We want vaporware spirituality.

---

31. See *Sex, Ecology, Spirituality*, chap. 14, n. 1, for an in-depth discussion of this topic.

The integral sage, the nondual sage, is here to show us otherwise. Known generally as "Tantric," these sages insist on transcending life by living it. They insist on finding release by engagement, finding nirvana in the midst of samsara, finding total liberation by complete immersion. They enter with awareness the nine rings of hell, for nowhere else are the nine heavens found. Nothing is alien to them, for there is nothing that is not One Taste.

Indeed, the whole point is to be fully at home in the body and its desires, the mind and its ideas, the spirit and its light. To embrace them fully, evenly, simultaneously, since all are equally gestures of the One and Only Taste. To inhabit lust and watch it play; to enter ideas and follow their brilliance; to be swallowed by Spirit and awaken to a glory that time forgot to name. Body and mind and spirit, all contained, equally contained, in the ever-present awareness that grounds the entire display.

In the stillness of the night, the Goddess whispers. In the brightness of the day, dear God roars. Life pulses, mind imagines, emotions wave, thoughts wander. What are all these but the endless movements of One Taste, forever at play with its own gestures, whispering quietly to all who would listen: is this not you yourself? When the thunder roars, do you not hear your Self? When the lightning cracks, do you not see your Self? When clouds float quietly across the sky, is this not your very own limitless Being, waving back at you?

Tuesday, November 18

Marci has been driving my Jeep for many months, because she doesn't really have a working car. She parked it in front of the Spearly Center, where she works, and it was stolen.

The police told us that there was about a 0% chance of getting it back, so yesterday I went out and bought a new Jeep. This morning I get a call: they recovered the Jeep. Apparently my poor ole Jeep—it's been around awhile—foiled its own theft by blowing a tire one block away, whereupon it was immediately abandoned.

But I don't need two Jeeps, so I gave the new one to Marci. She is major ecstatic. But, of course, "This too will pass," as all things do. Paraphrasing Buddha's last words, "Things that are put together fall apart. Work out your salvation with care." In other words, can you find the great Unborn, which, not being made of form, will never be stolen?

Wednesday, November 19

It's not quite right to describe One Taste as a "consciousness" or an "awareness," because that's a little too heady, too cognitive. It's more like the simple Feeling of Being. You already feel this simple Feeling of Being: it is the simple, present feeling of existence.

But it's quite different from all other feelings or experiences, because this simple Feeling of Being does not come or go. It is not in time at all, though time flows through it, as one of the many textures of its own sensation. The simple Feeling of Being is not an experience—it is a vast Openness in which all experiences come and go, an infinite Spaciousness in which all perceptions move, a great Spirit in which the forms of its own play arise, remain a bit, and pass. It is your own I-I as your little-I uncoils in the vast expanse of All Space. The simple Feeling of Being, which is the simple feeling of existence, is the simple Feeling of One Taste.

Is this not obvious? Aren't you already aware of existing? Don't you already feel the simple Feeling of Being? Don't you already possess this immediate gateway to ultimate Spirit, which is nothing other than the simple Feeling of Being? You have this simple Feeling now, don't you? And you have it now, don't you? And now, yes?

And don't you already realize that this Feeling is Spirit itself? Godhead itself? Emptiness itself? Spirit does not pop into existence: it is the only thing that is constant in your experience—and that is the simple Feeling of Being itself, a subtle, constant, background awareness that, if you look very closely, very carefully, you will realize you have had ever since the Big Bang and before—not because you existed way back when, but because you truly exist prior to time, in this timeless moment, whose feeling is the simple Feeling of Being: now, and now, and always and forever now.

You feel the simple Feeling of Being? Who is not already enlightened?

Thursday, November 20

Ah, but we humans don't just want Spirit, we want agitation as well. We don't just want the simple Feeling of Being, we want to feel . . .

something. Something special. We want to feel rich, or we want to feel famous, or we want to feel important; we want to stand out, make a mark, be a somebody. And so we divide up the simple Feeling of Being—we qualify it, categorize it, name it, separate it. We do not want to impartially witness the world as I-I and then be the world in the Feeling of One Taste. And so, instead of being the world, we want to be somebody. We want, that is, to suffer the lacerations of finite limitation, and this we do, horribly, when we become a somebody. Abandoning the simple Feeling of Being—where I-I am the world—we identify with a little body in a pitifully small space, and we want this little body to rise up over all other bodies and triumph: we will be somebody, by god.

But if I remain in the simple Feeling of Being, what does it matter if a friend gets a new house and I do not? Her joy is my joy, in the simple Feeling of One Taste. What does it matter if a colleague receives accolades and I do not? His happiness is my happiness, in the simple Feeling of One Taste. When there is but one Self looking out through all eyes, do I not rejoice in good fortune wherever it occurs, since it is the good fortune of my own deepest Self? And when suffering occurs anywhere in the universe, do I not also suffer, since it is the suffering of my own deepest Self? When one young child cries from hunger, do I not suffer? When one young husband delights in seeing his wife come home, do I not rejoice?

Traherne got it exactly: "The streets were mine, the temple was mine, the people were mine. The skies were mine, and so were the sun and moon and stars, and all the world was mine, and I the only Spectator [Witness] and enjoyer of it. I knew no churlish proprieties, nor bounds, nor divisions; but all proprieties and divisions were mine; all treasures and the possessors of them. So that with much ado I was corrupted and made to learn the dirty devices of the world, which I now unlearn. . . ."

In the simple Feeling of Being, where I-I am the world, jealousy and envy can find no purchase; all happiness is my happiness, all sadness is my sadness—and therefore, paradoxically, suffering ceases. Tears do not cease, nor do smiles—just the insane notion that I am somebody in the face of my own display. To cease being somebody—when "bodymind drops"—when I-I rests in Emptiness and embraces the entire world of Form: all of this is given in the simple Feeling of Being, the simple Feeling of One Taste. I simply feel Existence, pure Presence, nondual Isness, simple Suchness, present Thusness. I simply feel Being, I do not feel being this or being that—I am free of being this or being that, which are merely forms of suffering. But as I rest in the simple, present, effortless sensation of existence, all is given unto me.

You already possess the simple Feeling of Being. And so, again, please tell me: Who is not already enlightened?

Friday, November 21

Paul called from mainland China; he and Cel are having a wonderful trip, but they were taken aback by two things in Beijing: the horrible pollution, and the fact that everybody seems to smoke. Paul said the pollution is so bad they're probably using the cigarettes to filter the air.

Roger has finished his Seven Practices book—at least for this draft—and is now in the process of letting his agent shop it around. This is such a profound idea for a book—seven practices that the world's great wisdom traditions all share—but I fear for its fate in the marketplace, simply because practice seems to be the last thing people want to do when it comes to spirituality. We want simply to be told that we are the Goddess, or God, or one with eco-Gaia, read a few books, translate a little differently: but years of transformative practice? Well, Roger has written a book for people who are serious about awakening, which is to his everlasting credit, and the good fortune of those few who will engage such a liberating demand.

Saturday, November 22

Ann has been made the President of Random House.

"Is it a little crazy around there?"

"Hell's a poppin'. But it's fine now. It just happened very fast."

I couldn't be happier for her. Entertainment Weekly came out with its list of the hundred most powerful people in the entertainment business, and only two editors were on the list: Sonny Mehta and Ann Godoff. I suspect she just moved up several notches. But aside from all that, I simply like her enormously, and am very glad for her.

Sunday, November 23

Just read yet another book that dismantles the relativists, constructivists, and extreme postmodernists, so I am indeed going to declare my own personal national holiday.

The book is Thomas Nagel's <u>The Last Word</u>, and, in conjunction with so many other books (I've seen over a dozen), it really does look like the almost two-decades-long reign of the narcissists and nihilists (relativists and constructivists) has finally come to a close. There are some very important truths in postmodernism—which I have gone out of my way to champion and embrace, and will continue to do so—but the extremists have blown them all out of proportion in an attempt to deny any universal truths, any transcendental realities, and any common human ground, and they have done so in a tone that is often vicious, cranky, and mean-spirited.

The extreme relativists and constructivists—who maintain, for example, that all of reality is socially constructed, and thus relative from culture to culture—have already had their tenets decisively deflated by the likes of Jürgen Habermas and Karl Otto-Apel (who both show the performative self-contradiction hidden in the very center of the constructivists' claims), John Searle (who demonstrated that socially constructed realities must rest on objective truths or the construction can never get under way in the first place), Peter Berger (who relativized the relativizers, thus defeating their own claims), Charles Taylor (who showed that the relativists' antiranking was itself a ranking), among others. Nobody has taken these extremists seriously for many years—except the boomers and their "new-paradigms," which will "subvert" the old paradigms and replace them with new ones, which is possible because all realities are "socially constructed" and therefore capable of being "deconstructed." All of those notions, however well intentioned, are deeply confused, and Thomas Nagel is simply the last in a long line of theorists to demonstrate why.

Just as significant is the review of Nagel's book by Colin McGinn carried in <u>The New Republic</u>.[32] As a bastion of liberalism, TNR has itself often championed the extreme diversity, constructivism, and relativism that is part and parcel of the narcissism and nihilism of postmodernity. To have TNR come out so strongly in favor of Nagel's position is most illuminating.

McGinn starts by summarizing the extreme postmodernist conception of rationality. "According to this conception, human reason is inher-

---

32. Colin McGinn, "Reason the Need," *The New Republic*, August 4, 1997.

ently local, culture-relative, rooted in the variable facts of human nature and history, a matter of divergent 'practices' and 'forms of life' and 'frames of reference' and 'conceptual schemes.' There are no norms of reasoning that transcend what is accepted by a society or an epoch, no objective justifications for belief that everyone must respect on pain of cognitive malfunction. To be valid is to be taken to be valid, and different people can have legitimately different patterns of taking. In the end, the only justifications for belief have the form 'justified for me.' " (Note the narcissism or intense subjectivism.)

McGinn continues: "In such a view, objectivity, if it exists at all, is a function of social relations; a matter of social consensus, not of acknowledging truths and principles that obtain whether or not any society recognizes them. The norms of reasoning are ultimately like the norms of fashion."

Nagel shows, and McGinn agrees, that all of those claims are self-contradictory. This is the path also taken by Habermas, and, indeed, I extensively made the same argument in the Introduction to The Eye of Spirit (and earlier in SES, and again in chapter 9 of Sense and Soul [see July 9 for a short example of this]). But leave it to Nagel to nail it. McGinn: "The subjectivist holds that reason is nothing other than a manifestation of local and relative contingencies, and that its results have no authority beyond the parochial domain; in trying to go beyond the local, reason overreaches itself and produces empty assertions. This is clearly a theory about the nature of reason: it purports to tell us what reason is, what its place in the world amounts to. But the point is that this theory is offered as the *truth* about reason, as something that ought to command the assent of all rational beings. It is not offered as merely true for its propounder or his speech community. No, it is meant as a non-relatively true account of the very nature of reason. In propounding it, therefore, the subjectivist himself employs principles of reasoning and commitments to truth which are taken to have more than relative validity."

McGinn then drives to Nagel's inescapable conclusion: "But this is to presuppose the very thing that the subjectivist is claiming to call into question. There is a dilemma here: either announce the debunking account of reason as the objective truth, or put it forward as merely an instance of its own official conception of truth. In the former case, the subjectivist contradicts himself, claiming a status for his utterance that according to him no utterance can have; but in the latter case, the claim is merely true for him and has no authority over anyone else's beliefs. If the subjectivist's statement is true, then we can ignore it; if it is not, then it is false. In either case it is not a claim we can take seriously. And so subjectivism is refuted."

McGinn states that Nagel's argument "is absolutely decisive. Nagel applies his general anti-subjectivist argument in a number of areas, including language, logic, arithmetic and ethics. In each of these areas he argues convincingly that the content of the judgments involved cannot be construed in subjectivist fashion, but must be taken as affording objective reasons with universal prescriptive force."

My own view, of course, is that there are universal deep features with relative surface features—unitas multiplex, universal pluralism. The deep features are generally similar wherever we find them, while the surface features are local, culturally constructed, and relative, usually differing from culture to culture. But in making the culturally relative surface features the entire story, the extreme postmodernists have devastated human and spiritual understanding, which always includes a universal/transcendental component. "The case that Nagel presents should disturb all those who have been lulled, or bludgeoned, into the flabby relativism that is so rampant in contemporary intellectual culture. Richard Rorty comes in for some stern critical words from Nagel, and they are richly deserved."

McGinn says that "Nagel's argument is not only correct, it is also urgent." Why urgent? Because it is required to combat the rampant narcissism that is at the heart of the relativist/constructivist game, which claims for itself a truth that it denies to all others, or, at the very least, anchors all truth in subjectivist, egocentric preferences. "First-person avowals" are the only "truth" acknowledged. In this insane view, says Nagel, "Nothing is right, and instead we are all expressing our personal or cultural points of view. The actual result has been a growth in the already extreme intellectual laziness of contemporary culture and the collapse of serious argument throughout the lower reaches of the humanities and social sciences, together with a refusal to take seriously, as anything other than first-person avowals, the objective arguments of others." Narcissism and fragmentation have replaced truth and communication, and this is called cultural studies.

McGinn gets very close to the heart of the matter. "*The Last Word* is a book that should be read and pondered in this golden age of subjectivism [egocentrism, narcissism]. As to why such leanings exist and are so prevalent today . . . , I have a notion." And his notion is that universal truths, as opposed to subjectivist views, "clash with a popular and misguided ideal of freedom." Universal truth "constrains our thinking. We must obey its mandates. Yet people don't want to be constrained; they want to feel they can choose their beliefs, like beans in a supermarket. They want to be able to follow their impulses and not be reined in by impersonal [let alone transpersonal] demands. [This] feels like a violation of the inalienable right to do whatever one wants to do."

In plain language, universal truths curb narcissism; they constrain the ego; they force us outside of our subjectivist wishes, there to confront a reality not merely of our own making. It has become increasingly obvious that extreme social constructivism is the grand refuge of subjectivism/narcissism (which is precisely why it is so popular with my generation; if boomers have one reputation, it is for self-absorption). Wanting nothing to violate one's egocentric priorities—the "misguided ideal of freedom"—it is necessary to make facts plastic. Feminists don't like the relative advantage that males have in physical strength and mobility, so simply claim all biology is socially constructed. New-agers don't like conventional restraints, so claim they are socially constructed. Deep ecologists, ecofeminists, retro-Romantics, new-paradigmers, all would have recourse to social constructivism as a prelude to denying any realities they didn't happen to like and replacing them with ones of their own subjective choosing.

Many critics have harshly noted, therefore, that a boomer-driven, narcissistically based cultural studies would have these features: social constructivism (so I can deconstruct whatever I want), relativism (no universal truths to constrain me), equation of science and poetry (no objective facts to get in my way), extreme contextualism (no universal truths except my own), all interpretation is reader-response (I create all meaning), no meta-narratives or big pictures (except my own big picture about why all other big pictures are invalid), antirationalism (there is no objective truth except my own), antihierarchy (because there is nothing higher than me). This would be laughable were those not the exact characteristics of most academic cultural studies in America—and some of the central features of the Person-Centered Civil Religion (another reason the PCCR is so rarely transformative; it rests, in part, on a series of unfortunate self-contradictions, embedded in antihierarchism, relativism, and subjectivism, and thus it can't get any traction for transformation [See September 23]).

Just as SUNY Press is the purveyor of much of extreme postmodernism in this country, Blackwell is in Britain. So I was fascinated to see that its most recent A Dictionary of Cultural and Critical Theory, which one would expect to be chock full of postmodern post-structuralist tenets, in fact contains a Nagel-like attack on most postmodern theories of constructivism and relativism. "Therefore it follows, supposedly, that all truth talk, whether in the natural or more theory-prone human sciences, comes down to a choice of the right sort of metaphor (or the optimum rhetorical strategy) for conjuring assent from others engaged in the same communal enterprise. Scientists have understandably considered this an implausible account of how advances come about through the joint application of theory and empirical research. Hence the recent emergence of causal-realist or anti-conventionalist [universal and anti-subjectivist] approaches which offer a far better understanding of our knowledge of the growth of knowledge. After all, there seems rather little to be said for a philosophy of science that effectively leaves itself nothing to explain by reducing 'science' to just another species of preferential language game, rhetoric, discourse, conceptual scheme, or whatever. The current revival of realist ontologies betokens a break with this whole misdirected—as it now appears—line of thought."

While I am obviously in major agreement with these decisive attacks on extreme postmodernism (by Habermas, Otto-Apel, Ernst Gellner, Charles Taylor, Nagel, McGinn, among others), I have always taken a slightly different approach. These critics tend to simply demolish the extreme postmodernists altogether, and give them not an inch of ground on which to stand. My approach has been that there are some important but partial truths in postmodernism, and that what needs to be attacked is the extremist versions that take relativism, constructivism, and contextualism to be the only truths in existence—at which point they all become self-contradictory and unworthy of respect. But buried in the postmodern agenda are several noble impulses, I believe, yet in order to salvage them, they must themselves be placed in a larger context, which both limits their claims and completes their aims.

The noble impulses are those of freedom, tolerance, aperspectival embrace, and liberation from unnecessary or unfair conventions. The liberal/postmodern agenda has been to cherish cultural differences and multiple perspectives, including previously marginalized cultures and groups (women, minorities, gays, etc.). That stance—namely, universal pluralism—is a very high developmental achievement, coming into existence only at the worldcentric, postconventional level of growth. The liberal/postmodern stance, at its best, is generated at and from that high level of consciousness evolution.

But in their zeal to "transgress" and "subvert" conventional levels in favor of postconventional freedom, the extreme liberal/postmodernists ended up championing any and all stances (extreme diversity and multiculturalism), including many stances that are frankly ethnocentric and egocentric (since all stances are to be equally valued). This allowed, and often encouraged, regressive trends, a devolution from worldcentric to ethnocentric to egocentric—to a rampant subjectivism and narcissism, in fact, which then anchored the entire (and at this point completely misguided) agenda. Noble impulses horribly skewed—there is the best that can be said for liberal/postmodernism. The noble vision of universal pluralism was devastated, the universal part was completely ditched or denied, and rampant pluralism, driven by rampant narcissism, came to carry the sad day.

It is against this vulgar pluralism—which actually dissolves and destroys the liberal stance itself, destroys the demand for evolution to the worldcentric, postconventional levels which alone can support and protect the liberal vision—that the recent attacks have been directed. Habermas, Nagel, and crew are simply pointing out that the very claim of pluralism has, in fact, a universal component, and unless this universal component is acknowledged and included, the entire liberal/postmodern agenda self-destructs. I totally agree. But let us not forget the noble impulses hidden in that agenda, and let us not forget that those impulses can be redeemed, and the original liberal/postmodern vision can be fulfilled, if we retire pluralism and return to universal pluralism and unitas multiplex: universal deep features, local surface features. These universal features are accessed by empathy and compassion. And the liberal/postmodern vision itself can be protected <u>only</u> if it includes, in its own agenda, a cultural encouragement that individuals do their best to grow and evolve from egocentric to sociocentric to worldcentric, there to stand open to universal spiritual glories.

Freedom—the core of the liberal values—does not lie in egocentric or ethnocentric realms. Real freedom, true freedom, lies in the vast expanse of worldcentric awareness, which itself opens onto the infinite expanse of pure Spirit and primordial Self, a Self common in and to all sentient beings as such, and therefore a domain in which Freedom radiates in all directions. That is why we must move in a postliberal, not preliberal, fashion. So it is the irony of ironies that liberal/postmodernism, in searching for freedom for all, has championed modes of intense unfreedom: the egocentric is not free, for he is a slave to his impulses; the ethnocentric is not free, for he is a slave to his skin color; only in worldcentric awareness, which sets a mature individuality in the context of all individuals and moves easily in that vastly expanded space, does a real freedom begin to dawn, a freedom that opens onto pure Spirit in a timeless embrace of the All. Let liberalism continue to move that original direction, of progressive growth and evolution, and cease the self-contradictory and mindless championing of any subjectivist impulse that comes down the pike.

It is the narrow, misguided, narcissistic, relativistic sludge that is being so effectively demolished by these critics, and rightly so. <u>Make no mistake</u>: if postmodernism is right, there is and can be no Spirit whatsoever. If Spirit is anything, it is universal. If Spirit is anything, it is all-encompassing. If Spirit is anything, it is the Ground of manifestation everywhere, equally, radiantly. But if there is nothing universal—and that is the claim of the extreme postmodernists—then there is nothing genuinely spiritual anywhere in the universe, nor can there ever be. So while I hold open the noble impulses in the original vision—that of universal pluralism and unitas multiplex—I join in the attack on those who have forgotten the unitas and offer only the multiplex.

Monday, November 24

Roger, Frances, Kate, and T George have all convened in San Francisco for the annual conference of the American Academy of Religion, running the 22nd through the 25th. Roger, in particular, has attended these regularly in the past, mostly out of professional responsibility, but he always reports the same thing: these scholars are involved in almost nothing but translative spirituality, and then not even in an engaged fashion, but merely as an object of dreary, detached, desiccated study. Roger says to attend most of these talks is to take boredom into uncharted waters.

When I was a youngster, and being the mad scientist type, I used to collect insects. Central to this endeavor was the killing jar. You take an empty mayonnaise jar, put lethal carbon tetrachloride on cotton balls, and place them in the bottom of the jar. You then drop the insect—moth, butterfly, whatnot—into the jar, and it quickly dies, but without being outwardly disfigured. You then mount it, study it, display it.

Academic religion is the killing jar of Spirit.

Thursday, November 27

Marci cooked a huge Thanksgiving dinner, to which we invited Kate. The dinner was fabulous, though at first I thought the turkey was going to burn, it was so large and had to cook so long. Which reminded me of Gracie Allen's instructions on how to cook a chicken. "I always burn everything I cook. But I finally figured out how to cook a chicken correctly. You put a large chicken and a small chicken in a hot oven. When the small chicken burns, the large one is done."

Saturday, November 29

Marci took me to The Nutcracker, which was sweet. I feel truly fortunate to have her in my life. With love, the frontal gets an intense glow, the deeper psychic resonates with virtue, the Witness embraces all. But it's like the old Yiddish saying: "I've been rich and I've been poor; rich is better." Same with being in love.

Sunday, November 30

There are four major stages or phases of spiritual unfolding: belief, faith, direct experience, and permanent adaptation: you can believe in Spirit, you can have faith in Spirit, you can directly experience Spirit, you can become Spirit.

1. Belief is the earliest (and therefore, the most common) stage of spiritual orientation. Belief originates at the mental level, generally, since it requires images, symbols, and concepts. But the mind itself goes through several transitional phases in its own development—magic, mythic, rational, and vision-logic—and each of those is the basis of a type (and stage) of spiritual or religious belief.

Magic belief is egocentric, with subject and object often fused, thus marked by the notion that the individual self can dramatically affect the physical world and other people through mental wishes—voodoo and word magic being the most well-known examples. Mythic belief (which is usually sociocentric/ethnocentric, since different people have different myths that are mutually exclusive: if Jesus is the one and only savior of humankind, Krishna is kaput) invests its spiritual intuitions in one or more physically disembodied gods or goddesses, who have ultimate power over human actions. Rational belief—to the extent that reason chooses to believe at all—attempts to demythologize religion and portray God or the Goddess, not as an anthropomorphic deity, but as an ultimate Ground of Being. This rationalization reaches its zenith with vision-logic belief, where sciences such as systems theory are often used to explain this Ground of Being as a Great Holistic System, Gaia, Goddess, Eco-Spirit, the Web of Life, and so forth.

All of those are mental beliefs, usually accompanied by strong emotional sentiments or feelings; but they are not necessarily direct experiences of supramental spiritual realities. As such, they are merely forms of translation: they can be embraced without changing one's present level of consciousness in the least. But as those merely translative gestures begin to mature, and as direct emergence of the higher domains increasingly presses against the self, mere belief gives way to faith.

2. Faith begins, if at all, when belief loses its power to compel. Sooner or later, any mental belief—precisely because it is mental and not supramental or spiritual—will begin to lose its forcefulness. For example, the mental belief in spirit as the Web of Life will begin to pale in its power to persuade: no matter how much you keep believing in the Web of Life, you still feel like a separate, isolated ego, beset with hope and fear. You try to believe harder; it still doesn't work. Mere belief might have pro-

vided you with a type of translative meaning, but not with an actual transformation, and this slowly, painfully, becomes obvious. (It might even be worse if you are involved in magic or mythic beliefs, because not only do these not usually transform you, they often act as a regressive force in your awareness, moving you not toward, but away from, the transrational.)

Still, there is often a genuine, spiritual, transmental intuition behind the mental belief in Gaia or the Web of Life, namely, an intuition of the Oneness of Life. But this intuition cannot be fully realized as long as belief grips consciousness. For all beliefs are ultimately divisive and dualistic—holistic beliefs are ultimately just as dualistic as analytic beliefs, because both make sense only in terms of their opposites. You are not supposed to think the All, you are supposed to be the All, and as long as you are clinging to beliefs about the All, it will never happen. Mere beliefs are cardboard nutrition for the soul, spiritually empty calories, and sooner or later they cease to fascinate and console.

But usually between letting go of belief, on the one hand, and finding direct experience, on the other, the person is carried only by faith. If the belief in Oneness can no longer offer much consolation, still the person has faith that Oneness is there, somehow, calling out to him or her. And they are right. Faith soldiers on when belief becomes unbelievable, for faith hears the faint but direct call of a higher reality—of Spirit, of God, of Goddess, of Oneness—a higher reality that, being beyond the mind, is beyond belief. Faith stands on the threshold of direct supramental, transrational experience. Lacking dogmatic beliefs, it has no sense of security; not yet having direct experience, it has no sense of certainty. Faith is thus a no-man's-land—a thousand questions, no answers—it possesses only a dogged determination to find its spiritual abode, and, pulled on by its own hidden intuition, it might eventually find direct experience.

3. Direct experience decisively answers the nagging questions inherent in faith. There are usually two phases of direct experience: peak experiences and plateau experiences.

Peak experiences are relatively brief, usually intense, often unbidden, and frequently life-changing. They are actually "peek experiences" into the transpersonal, supramental levels of one's own higher potentials. Psychic peak experiences are a glimpse into nature mysticism (gross-level oneness); <u>subtle</u> peak experiences are a glimpse into deity mysticism (subtle-level oneness); <u>causal</u> peak experiences are a glimpse into emptiness (causal-level oneness); and <u>nondual</u> peak experiences are a glimpse into One Taste. As Roger Walsh has pointed out, the higher the level of the peak experience, the rarer it is. (This is why most experiences of "cosmic consciousness" are actually just a glimpse of nature mysticism or gross-level oneness, the shallowest of the mystical realms. Many people mistake this for One Taste, unfortunately. This confusion is epidemic among eco-theorists.)

Most people remain, understandably, at the stage of belief or faith (and usually magical or mythical at that). Occasionally, however, individuals will have a strong peak experience of a genuinely transpersonal realm, and it completely shatters them, often for the better, sometimes for the worse. But you can tell they aren't merely repeating a belief they read in a book, or giving merely translative chitchat: they have truly seen a higher realm, and they are never quite the same.

(This is not always a good thing. Someone at the concrete-literal mythic level, for example, can have a peak experience of, say, the subtle level, whereupon the authority of the subtle is injected into their concrete myths, and the result is a reborn fundamentalist: their particular mythic god-figure is the <u>only</u> figure that can save the entire world, and they will burn your body to save your soul. Someone at the vision-logic level can have a psychic-level peak experience, and then their "new eco-paradigm" is the <u>only</u> thing that can save the planet, and they will gladly march lock-step in eco-fascism to save you from yourself. Religious fanaticism of such ilk is almost impossible to dismantle, because it is an intense mixture of higher truth with lower delusion. The higher truth is often a very genuine spiritual experience, a true "peek" experience of a higher domain; but precisely because it is a brief, temporary experience—and not an enduring, steady, clear awareness—it gets immediately snapped up and translated downward into the lower level, where it confers an almost unshakable legitimacy on even the ugliest of beliefs.)

Whereas peak experiences are usually of brief duration—a few minutes to a few hours—<u>plateau experiences</u> are more constant and enduring, verging on becoming a permanent adaptation. Whereas peak experiences can, and usually do, come spontaneously, in order to sustain them and turn them from a peak into a plateau—from a brief <u>altered</u>

state into a more enduring trait—prolonged practice is required. Whereas almost anybody, at any time, at any age, can have a brief peak experience, I know of few bona fide cases of plateau experiences that did not involve years of sustained spiritual practice. Thus, whereas belief and faith are by far the most common types of spiritual orientation, and while peak experiences are rare but authentic spiritual experiences, from this point on in spiritual unfolding, we find only those who are involved in sustained, intense, prolonged, profound spiritual practice.

Plateau experiences, like peak experiences, can be of the psychic, subtle, causal, or nondual domains. I will give one example, taken from Zen, that covers all four. Typically, individuals practicing Zen meditation will start by counting the breaths, one to ten, repeatedly. When they can do that for half an hour without losing count, they might be assigned a koan (such as the syllable mu, which was my first koan). For the next three or four years, they will practice several hours each day, concentrating on the sound mu and attempting not to drop it (there is, simultaneously, an intense inquiry into "What is the meaning of mu?" or "Who is it that is concentrating on mu?"). Several times each year, they will attend seven-day sesshins or intense practice sessions, where they will be encouraged to practice throughout the day and into the night.

The first important plateau experience occurs when students can uninterruptedly hold on to mu for most of their waking hours. Mu has become such a part of consciousness, such a part of you—in fact, you become mu—that you can hold it in awareness, in an unbroken fashion, all day, literally. In other words, a type of witnessing awareness is now a constant capacity throughout the gross-waking state. Students are then told that if they truly want to penetrate mu, they must continue working on it even during their sleep. (When I first heard this, I thought it was a joke, a type of macho initiation humor, of the sort, "If you want to be part of the fighting First Infantry, mister, you have to eat three live snakes." I thought they were just trying to scare me; they were actually trying to help.) Another two or three years, and dedicated students do indeed continue a subtle concentration on mu right into the dream state. There is now a constant witnessing awareness even in the subtle-dream realm.[33] At this point, as students approach the causal unmanifest (or pure absorption), they are on the verge of the explosion known as satori,

---

33. Of course, the dream state is only one of the many types of subtle-realm phe-

which is a breakthrough from the "frozen ice" of pure causal absorption to the Great Liberation of One Taste. At first, this One Taste is itself a peak experience, but it, too, will become, with further practice, a plateau experience, then a permanent adaptation.[34]

4. Adaptation simply means a constant, permanent access to a given level of consciousness. Most of us have already adapted (or evolved) to matter, body, and mind (which is why you have access to all three of

---

nomena; the classic subtle state is *savikalpa samadhi*, "nondual absorption with form," which introduces one to the subtle realm while awake. The dream state is said to be a subclass of the subtle, in that there are no gross material phenomena in the dream state (only images and forms). Thus, to enter the dream state consciously has always been seen as an analog of *savikalpa samadhi*, since in both there is alpha-waking and theta-dreaming present simultaneously. The effect on the evolution of conscious is quite similar in both cases: you have to some degree objectified the subtle—consciously seen it as an object, while awake—and thus it has lost its power over you: you have transcended it, and thus can begin to move into causal development.

Nirvikalpa samadhi is the classic state of causal consciousness: formless, unmanifest, pure cessation (one type of emptiness), which introduces you to the causal domain while awake (*nirvikalpa* matures into *jnana samadhi*, or radically pure formlessness, and in some traditions, into *nirodh*, or the complete extinction of objects altogether). Just as *savikalpa* and pellucid dreaming are analogs, so maintaining awareness during deep dreamless sleep and *nirvikalpa* are analogs. In both *nirvikalpa* and pellucid deep sleep, alpha-waking and delta-formlessness are present simultaneously: you have brought consciousness even into the formless realm, thus freeing consciousness from that realm, and opening it to the nondual. The causal has been transcended, and *nirvikalpa/jnana* (gnosis) gives way to *sahaja*, or effortless, spontaneous, ever-present One Taste.

In order to make a good deal of progress, one does not necessarily have to be able to pellucid dream or pellucid deep sleep. *Savikalpa samadhi* and *nirvikalpa samadhi* can be adequately attained during the waking state. It is just that, when practitioners gain competency of *savikalpa*, they often begin to pellucid dream—precisely because those are analogs. Likewise, a mastery of *nirvikalpa* is often accompanied by pellucid deep sleep. And conversely, pursuing one's meditation into the dream and deep sleep state is a dramatic and extremely effective way to enter *savikalpa* and *nirvikalpa*, and thus more easily stand open to *sahaja*. The Yoga of the Dream State has always been held to be one of the fastest, most efficient ways of reaching a plateau experience of subtle and causal realms, thus quickly opening the door to stable adaptation at—and transcendence of—those realms.

34. The stages of adaptation leading from causal/nirvikalpa/nirvana to One Taste are known as *post-nirvanic* stages, of which three or four are usually given. There are several variations on these stages, but they all center around constant consciousness, or the unbroken access to witnessing awareness through all three states—first as a plateau, then an adaptation—and then the disappearance of

them virtually any time you want). And some of us have had peak experiences into the transpersonal levels (psychic, subtle, causal, or nondual). But with actual practice, we can evolve into plateau experiences of these higher realms, and these plateau experiences, with further practice, can become permanent adaptations: <u>constant access</u> to psychic, subtle, causal, and nondual occasions—constant access to nature mysticism, deity mysticism, formless mysticism, and integral mysticism—all as easily available to consciousness as matter, body, and mind now are. And this is likewise evidenced in a constant consciousness (sahaja) through

---

witnessing into nondual One Taste—first as a peak, then as a plateau, then an adaptation.

Once One Taste has been stabilized as an *adaptation*, the *post-enlightenment* stages unfold. These are said to result in *bhava samadhi*, or the complete bodily translation of the human into the Divine; or, alternatively, "the complete extinction of all things into the *dharmata*"; or, another alternative, the achievement of a permanent light body. (See *The Eye of Spirit* for a discussion of post-nirvanic and post-enlightenment stages of development.)

The *post-nirvanic* stages (the essence of Mahayana and Vajrayana, which do not merely embrace Formlessness—nirvana—but integrate that with the entire world of Form—samsara) have always made sense to me; and, based on my own experience, I can testify to the existence of constant consciousness and One Taste, both of them as prolonged and recurrent plateau experiences, sometimes lasting uninterruptedly 24–36 hours (although, in one case, constant consciousness persisted day and night for eleven days). Neither is a permanent adaptation in my case, but there are several teachers I have met who, I believe, are in such, and the literature is replete with them. All of these post-nirvanic stages inherently make sense because they are, after all, simply the stages of adapting to nonduality (the stages of integrating nirvana and samsara, Spirit and manifestation, Emptiness and Form). Moreover, with the EEG data now being gathered by Alexander and others, we seem to have hard corroborating evidence that such stages do in fact exist.

But the *post-enlightenment* stages have never made much sense to me, nor have I ever met anybody who was believably at those stages. Those stages, as they are described, have always struck me as a holdover from magic—they always include items such as one's body going up in light, being able to perform extraordinary miracles of transformation, etc.—none of which has any credible, reproducible evidence. As for the notion of "the extinction of all things into the *dharmata*," this sounds indistinguishable from *jnana* or *nirodh*—a regression from One Taste, not a development beyond it. I am not saying these stages do not exist; I am saying that, compared with all the other stages that the traditions offer (and that I briefly outlined above, including the post-nirvanic stages), the post-enlightenment stages have the least amount of evidence—possibly because they are so rare, possibly because they are not there.

all three states—waking, dreaming (or savikalpa samadhi), and sleeping (or nirvikalpa samadhi). It then becomes obvious why "That which is not present in deep dreamless sleep is not real." The Real must be <u>present in all three states</u>, including deep dreamless sleep, and pure Consciousness is the only thing that is present in all three. This Fact becomes perfectly obvious when you rest as pure, empty, formless Consciousness and "watch" all three states arise, abide, and pass, while you remain Unmoved, Unchanged, Unborn, released into the pure Emptiness that is all Form, the One Taste that is the radiant All.

. . .

Those are some of the major phases we tend to go through as we adapt to the higher levels of our own spiritual nature: <u>belief</u> (magic, mythic, rational, holistic); <u>faith</u> (which is an intuition, but not yet a direct experience, of the higher realms); <u>peak experience</u> (of the psychic, subtle, causal, or nondual—in no particular order, because peak experiences are usually one-time hits); <u>plateau experience</u> (of the psychic, subtle, causal, and nondual—almost always in that order, because competence at one stage is generally required for the next); and <u>permanent adaptation</u> (to the psychic, subtle, causal, and nondual, also in that order, for the same reason).

Several important points:

· You can be at a relatively high level of spiritual development and still be at a relatively low level in other lines (e.g., the deeper psychic can be progressing while the frontal is quite retarded). We all know people who are spiritually developed but still rather immature in sexual relations, emotional intimacy, physical health, and so on. Even if you have constant access to One Taste, that will not make your muscles grow stronger, will not necessarily get you that new job, won't get you the girl, and won't cure all your neurosis. You can still have deep pockets of shadow material that are not necessarily dug up as you advance into higher stages of spiritual practice or meditation (precisely because meditation is <u>not</u>, contra the popular view, primarily an uncovering technique; if it were, most of our meditation teachers wouldn't need psychotherapy, whereas most of them do, like everybody else. Meditation is not primarily <u>uncovering</u> the repressed unconscious, but allowing

the emergence of higher domains—which usually leaves the lower, repressed domains still lower, and still repressed.)

So even as you advance in your own spiritual unfolding, consider
combining it with a good psychotherapeutic practice, because spiritual
practice, as a rule, will not adequately expose the psychodynamic unconscious. Nor will it appropriately exercise the physical body—so try
weightlifting. Nor will it exercise the pranic body—trying adding t'ai chi
ch'uan. Nor will it work with group or community dynamic, so add . . .
Well, the point, of course, is to take up integral practice as the only
sound and balanced way to proceed with one's own higher development.

• This is especially important because the Person-Centered Civil Religion (and the 415 Paradigm) is anchored predominantly in the stage of
holistic belief. In order for most people to move beyond those mental
translations, a genuine transformative practice is required. Integral practice is very likely the most effective. It emphasizes transformation not
just in the I, but in all four quadrants—or the Big Three of I, we, and
it—transformative practices in the self, with relationships and community, and with nature [see June 18], not merely as a change in type of
belief but in level of consciousness.

• Even though I have described higher stages whose access usually
takes at least five or six years of arduous practice (and whose highest
stages often take thirty years or more), don't let that put you off if you
are a beginner. Simply begin practice—five or six years will go by in a
blink, but you will be reaping the abundant rewards. On the other hand,
if you listen to those teachers who are selling nothing but beliefs (magic,
mythic, rational, or holistic), you will be nothing but five or six years
older. (Holistic beliefs are fine—and quite accurate—for the mental
realm. But spirituality is about the transmental realm, the supramental
realm, the superconscious realm, and no amount of mind translations
will help you transcend the mind. And no amount of Person-Centered
Civil Religion will deliver you from yourself.) Rather, you must take up
a contemplative, transpersonal, supramental practice. So no matter how
daunting practice seems, simply begin. As the old joke has it: How do
you eat an elephant? One bite at a time.

• The fact is, a few bites into the elephant and you will already start
gaining considerable benefits. You might begin, say, twenty minutes a

day of centering prayer as taught by Father Thomas Keating. Many people report almost immediate effects—calming, opening, caring, listening: the heart melts a little bit, and so do you. Zikr for a half hour; vipassana for 40 minutes; yoga exercises twice a day, worked into your schedule; Tantric visualization; prayer of the heart; counting your breaths for 15 minutes each morning before you get out of bed. Any of those are fine; whatever works for you, just take the first few bites. . . .

· We need to be gentle with ourselves, it is true; but we also need to be firm. Treat yourself with real compassion, not idiot compassion, and therefore begin to challenge yourself, engage yourself, push yourself: begin to practice.

· As any of these practices start to take hold, you might find it appropriate to attend an intensive retreat for a few days each year. This will give you a chance to extend the little "peeks" of practice into the beginning plateaus of practice. The years will go by, yes, but you will be ripening along with them, slowly but surely transcending the lesser aspects of yourself and opening to the greater. There will come a day when you will look back on all that time as if it were just dream, because in fact it is a dream, from which you will soon awaken.

· The point is simple: If you are interested in genuine transformative spirituality, find an authentic spiritual teacher and begin practice. Without practice, you will never move beyond the phases of belief, faith, and random peak experiences. You will never evolve into plateau experiences, nor from there into permanent realization. You will remain, at best, a brief visitor in the territory of your own higher estate, a tourist in your own true Self.

DECEMBER

This self-luminous, vividly clear, present wakefulness and
*   awareness,*
In which Form and Emptiness are nondual,
Is the consciousness in which the three states [waking, dream,
*   sleep] are spontaneously present.*
Maintain it day and night in a continuous practice, my heart
*   children.*
This is how nonduality is the natural freedom.
                                    —TSOGDRUK RANGDROL

Tuesday, December 2

Marci has finished her thesis, so we celebrate for the day. Rented Lone-
some Dove ("The only education you're gonna get is listening to me
talk"), drank wine, floated downstream.

Wednesday, December 3

Spirit is not an altered state of consciousness (ASC) or a nonordinary
state (NOSC). There is no alternative to it. There is only Spirit, within
which the world rolls out. There is only One Taste, within which different states arise. But One Taste itself neither comes nor goes; it is beyond
motion and stillness, commotion and quiet, movement or rest. Look to
the ends of the world, you will only find One Taste. Let your mind
wander to the edge of the universe, you will only find One Taste. Let
your awareness expand to infinity, you will still only find One Taste.

So where is this amazing One Taste? Well, who is reading this page? Who is looking out from those eyes? Who is hearing with those ears? Who is seeing this world right now? That Seer, that ever-present Witness, which is your own immediate Self, stands on the edge of the nondual revelation in this and every moment. Rest as your very own Self; rest as the clear seeing of this page, this room, this world; rest as the vast pure Emptiness in which the entire world is arising . . . and then see if that world isn't one with that Self. For in this moment of simple resting as the Witness, notice that the feeling of the Witness and the feeling of the world are one and the same feeling ("When I heard the bell ring, there was no I and no bell, just the ringing"). In the simple Feeling of Being, you are the World.

Look! It's just this.

And once you taste One Taste, no matter how fleetingly at first, an entirely new motivation will arise from the depths of your very own being and become a constant atmosphere which your every impulse breathes, and that atmosphere is compassion. Once you taste One Taste, and see the fundamental problems of existence evaporate in the blazing sun of obviousness, you will never again be the same person, deep within your heart. And you will want—finally, profoundly, and most of all— that others, too, may be relieved of the burden of their sleep-walking dreams, relieved of the agony of the separate self, relieved of the inherent torture called time and the gruesome tragedy called space.

No matter that lesser motivations will dog your path, no matter that anger and envy, shame and pity, pride and prejudice will remind you daily how much more you can always grow: still, and still, under it all, around it all, above it all, the heartbeat of compassion will resound. A constant cloud of caring will rain on your every parade. And you will be driven, in the best sense of the word, by this ruthless taskmaster, but only because you, eons ago, made a secret promise to let this motivation rule you until all souls are set free in the ocean of infinity.

Because of compassion, you will strive harder. Because of compassion, you will get straight. Because of compassion, you will work your fingers to the bone, push at the world until you literally bleed, toil till the tears stain your vision, struggle until life itself runs dry. And in the deepest, deepest center of your Heart, the World is already thanking you.

Friday, December 5

I was sorry to see that Leon Forrest died (cancer, age sixty). Forrest used a type of stream-of-consciousness writing to delve into the African-American experience. <u>Divine Days</u> left a deep and unsettling impression on me—seven or eight days in southside Chicago.

The slavery issue in this country is tragic. Of the dozens—more like hundreds—of different ethnic cultures that came to this country, only one was brought against its will. Only one was boiled and fried in the melting pot. Bereft of background culture and supporting social contexts, African-Americans have had to fight a brutal uphill battle to gain meaning, roots, self-determination, and economic power. The wonder is that African-Americans have accomplished the extraordinary amount that they have. It is often said that there are only two original American art forms: jazz and tap dance. Both, we note, are black inventions. In the arts, in sports, in politics, in academia, African-Americans have made profound contributions.

The issue of blame, however, is a dead-end. Historically, slavery was often practiced by Africans on Africans, and Africans sold Africans to white slave traders. Nobody has anything to be proud of in this particular regard. Moreover, the real issue of culpability lies elsewhere, for the most part. <u>All</u> types of pre-industrial societies had slavery, with no exceptions—foraging (hunting and gathering), herding, horticultural, maritime, and agrarian. Up to 90% of some societal types—herding and horticultural, for example—had slavery. Only with industrialization does the rate of slavery drop to 0%. In fact, in a one-hundred-year period, roughly 1770–1870, sanctioned slavery was eradicated from every industrialized nation on the face of the planet. It was America's ill fortune to have come of age when that transition was being made—the transition from a mythic-agrarian structure (which happily sanctions slavery) to a rational-industrial structure (which is abhorred by it).

What I find so unfortunate in the "race debate" is how cheaply each side tries to make points, without a certain sensitivity to the historical growth of consciousness itself. The values that liberal Westerners tend to share, the values of the Enlightenment (the values of rational-industrialism)—namely, liberty, equality, and freedom—were simply <u>not</u> the values of <u>any</u> other societal type, <u>ever</u>. Foragers occasionally had a type of diffuse egalitarianism, but physical strength in fact determined a covert male dominance. Horticultural societies—about a third of which were matrifocal, with Great Mother mythologies—had an 84% rate of slavery, one of the very worst in all of history. With the agrarian structure—which was almost entirely patriarchal—the percentage of societies engaged in slavery drops to around 54%. And with patriarchal industrialization, the rate drops to 0%—with the concomitant values of equality, liberty, and freedom—the first time, anywhere in history, where these values were implemented on a large scale, as part of the organizing principles of society.

Although whites engaged in slavery—as every pre-industrial race and societal type did—nonetheless, whites set in motion those ideas (the Enlightenment) and those structures (industrialism) that would, within one century, eradicate slavery for the first time in the history of the human race.

The difficulty is that both sides of the debate (by which I mean, roughly, liberal and conservative) get caught up with the wrong sides of the equation. Liberals tend to think that slavery is simply something that mean white people did to nice black people, failing to see that in pre-industrial societies, pretty much everybody did it to pretty much everybody else. The structures of pre-industrial societies simply were not strong enough to dispense with forced human labor. We are shocked that Thomas Jefferson—a deeply agrarian mind—could condone slavery, but this is, in fact, no surprise whatsoever. What is lamentable is how pompously liberals can climb on their high-horses and apply today's rational-industrial values to yesterday's agrarian ruminations. (This is also what is so profoundly confused and misleading about Spielberg's Amistad—a deeply liberal look at a deeply agrarian time, brutally misinterpreting the context.)

Conservatives fare no better. Modern liberalism came into existence with the rational Enlightenment, and shares its rational-industrial values: liberty, equality, freedom. But conservatism reaches back much further, with its roots thoroughly sunk in the soil of mythic-agrarian values: civic, hierarchical, aristocratic, ethnocentric, with a mythic-fundamentalist belief in a patriarchal God—and a belief in the rightness of slavery. And so even with today's typical conservative, you often get the sense that they think blacks simply deserved it: they were weaker, we were stronger, that's the way it goes. And indeed, that is the way it goes to the mythic-agrarian mind.

Well, a pox on both the liberals and conservatives in this particular regard. Whites are not to blame for slavery; pre-industrial conditions are to blame for slavery. And African-Americans certainly did not "deserve" any such treatment (nor did any other race on the face of the planet, including whites, that were enslaved by others). But it is only with rational-industrialism that machines could do the labor that men otherwise would force other men to do.

What I find so deeply sad about the African-American experience is not just the slavery, but the diaspora. After all, in many cases of slavery, you moved next door; horrible as it was, you were still in your own culture. But to be dispossessed of freedom and culture simultaneously is as brutal an insult as any can endure. But there, I think, is also the beginning of the extraordinary strength of the African-American soul. Starting in the death ships, Africans—they were not yet African-Americans—reached deep into their collective soul and brought forth a thing of brilliance and beauty, sharing and caring, strength and courage, the likes of which history has rarely seen.

What an extraordinarily rich addition to American culture. Muhammed Ali famously said, "I'm glad my great-great-granddaddy caught that ship." It will be a happy day when, on the other side of the color divide, more white Americans share that sentiment.

Sunday, December 7

Transcendence restores humor. Spirit brings smiling. Suddenly, laughter returns. Too many representatives of too many movements—even very good movements, such as feminism, ecology, and spiritual studies—seem to lack humor altogether. In other words, they lack lightness, they lack a distance from themselves, a distance from the ego and its grim game of forcing others to conform to its contours. There is self-transcending humor, or there is the game of egoic power. But we have chosen egoic power and politically correct thought police; grim Victorian reformers pretending to be defending civil rights; messianic new-paradigm thinkers who are going to save the planet and heal the world. No wonder Mencken wrote that "Every third American devotes himself to improving and lifting up his fellow citizens, usually by force; this messianic delusion is our national disease." Perhaps we should all trade two pounds of ego for one ounce of laughter.

Monday, December 8

Speaking of humor, Marci and I want to go see Bobbie Louise Hawkins, who writes brilliantly funny essays, stories, and poetry. She often teaches and performs at Naropa. She is not, alas, taken as seriously as is her due, precisely because she can be so funny. The ego wears grimness around its neck like a garland of garlic to ward off the evils of transcendence and humorous release. Bobbie wrote a very funny piece about funny pieces not being taken seriously, but it wasn't taken seriously.

Tuesday, December 9

Marci has her thesis presentation and defense this Saturday, and she is very nervous and apprehensive, in an endearing sort of way. She can't sleep, so she watches me meditate during the night, and I am aware of her doing so. It's very sweet.

Midnight in the Garden of Good and Evil, the film. Well, I liked it. "This place is like Gone with the Wind on mescaline. Everybody is heavily armed and drunk. New York is boring. I'm staying."

Rented Coldblooded, a very dark comedy, about a young hit man apprentice. "You've never had a girlfriend?" "No, never. I have been seeing the same hooker for a while." "Doesn't really count." But, of all things, he is saved by a good woman and . . . yoga.

Wednesday, December 10

THE STORY OF THE LOST AND FOUND GOD
A Theoretical Play of Political Redemption and Release,
in Three Acts with an Important Postscript

ACT I

Scene 1

In 1712, in Geneva, Jean-Jacques Rousseau's mother died giving him birth. He was abused and beaten by his father, then abandoned at age ten. By age sixteen he had made it to Savoy, where he was tutored in the ways of the mind, and the body, by Madame de Warens; by age thirty, Rousseau was in Paris, a minor figure in the philosophical circle of Diderot and d'Alembert, editors of the Encyclopédie, bastion of Enlightenment thought. Within a decade he had so alienated his former friends—including David Hume and Voltaire—that he fled city life for the countryside, where, for much of the next twenty years, until his death, he lived with Thérèse Levasseur, an unschooled laundry maid. They had five children, each of which they abandoned to orphanages. Isaac Kramnick tells us that Rousseau "wore shabby, thread-bare and often bizarre clothing; he was tactless and direct, oafish and vulgar." Hume called him "absolutely lunatic." Diderot said, "That man is insane." Sir Isaiah Berlin labeled him "the most sinister and most formidable enemy of liberty in the whole history of modern thought."

Scene 2

Rousseau's legacy is profound, paradoxical, and often contradictory. In modern times, he was the first great retro-Romantic; the first influential deep ecologist; the first major totalitarian; and the first great glorifier of narcissistic self-absorption. He was also the first great advocate of a more democratic society, geared to the many rather than the few; a compelling arguer for justice, but also for greatness; he condemned the inequalities of culture, even though he championed those of nature.

Perhaps the most commonly remembered—and influential—proclamation of Rousseau is the opening line of chapter 1 of The Social Contract: "Man is born free, and is everywhere in chains." Rousseau's thought on this matter was actually quite complex, but the general idea—at least as it entered popular imagination—is simply this: people are born good, but that natural goodness is slowly suffocated and buried by the forces of society. Nature is good, culture is suffocating; nature is authentic, society is artificial. The notion—which is the central tenet of Romanticism—is that we start out in a type of natural unity and wholeness, but that wholeness is fractured, broken, and repressed by the world of culture, speech, and reason. Thus our task is to recapture the prior wholeness and goodness, perhaps in a "more mature" form, or "on a higher level," but recaptured nonetheless.

Scene 3

"They're going to hunt you tomorrow," said the twins. So begins the last chilling incident in William Golding's classic novel, <u>Lord of the Flies</u>. A group of young boys, aged six to twelve, have been stranded on an uninhabited island. Left to their own devices, their true natures begin to emerge, and it is a progressive descent into savagery. By the end of the novel, the boys are naked, filthy, painted with crude designs . . . and hunting, in order to kill and roast, the only two remaining boys who will not join their "natural" displays.

Scene 4

The life of men and women in the state of nature is "solitary, poor, nasty, brutish, and short." With those five famous words, three of which most people remember, Thomas Hobbes staked out, more or less exactly, the opposite of the Romantic view. Hobbes believed that children are born concerned only with themselves. It is the job of education and training to widen their interests to include a concern for others, and perhaps, eventually, for all of humankind. But most people, he believed, only manage to extend the circle of care from themselves to their families.

Such is exactly the importance of civil society, according to Hobbes. It is only by subsuming the state of nature—where self-survival rules— that men and women can join together, beyond mere self-survival, and create a greater good, marked by moral virtues which lead to a peaceful and stable coexistence. We start out wretched, but we can join together and grow into goodness. Otherwise, "They're going to hunt you tomorrow," said the twins.

ACT 2

Scene 1

These two points of view—let us call them "recaptured goodness" and "growth to goodness"—have proven to be two of the most durable, and apparently incompatible, notions of the direction of human growth: devolution, or a downhill slide from a paradisiacal state, a slide that must be reversed in some sense; and evolution, or growth and unfolding from a lesser to a greater good.

The first view almost always uses the metaphor of <u>healing</u>; the second, that of <u>growth</u>. Healing, because the recaptured-goodness school be- lieves that we were once whole—in childhood, in the noble savage, in Eden—but this wholeness was fractured, broken, buried, or torn, and thus we are in need of healing. <u>Healing implies that health was once present, but then was lost</u>, and it needs to be recaptured or restored. The metaphor of healing almost always signals a hidden, or not so hidden, retro-Romantic viewpoint.

Growth, on the other hand, implies not that we are attempting to recapture anything we had yesterday, but that we are <u>evolving to our own higher possibilities</u>. The acorn becomes an oak, not by recapturing something it had yesterday, but by growing. The metaphor of growth almost always signals a developmental or evolutionary view.

The first school often uses the metaphor of <u>uncovering</u>; the second, that of <u>emergence</u>. Uncovering, because the goodness that we need was once present but was buried, and thus all that is required is to scrape off the layers of civilization to retrieve it. Emergence, because the goodness that we need was never present, but will emerge only if higher growth and development occurs.

In short, for the first school, we start out good, become bad, and must recapture that goodness in order to heal ourselves and heal the world. For the second, we start out, if not bad, then lacking good, a goodness that can only emerge if we grow and develop our fullest potential.

Scene 2

The first school, or natural goodness, is one of the prime ingredients in political <u>liberalism</u>; the second, or natural nastiness, of political <u>con- servatism</u>. The liberal notion is that children start out good, and the job of social institutions is to not disturb that natural goodness. Institutions are usually repressive, oppressive, or stifling of the natural goodness present in children, and these artificial conventions should not be al- lowed to get in the way of innate goodness. If they do—if social in- stitutions interfere with the natural goodness of people—then a revolutionary liberation is required—a subverting, a transgression, a freeing from the stifling limitations that society has placed on nature and natural goodness.

The conservative notion is that children start out selfcentric, and the job of institutions is to curb their primitive ways, or, we might say, expand their narrow views. When institutions break down, the savage breaks out. "Conservative" usually means the opposite of "progressive"; but in this case, the conservative view is progressive from childhood to adulthood (i.e., children must develop into moral goodness, because it is not given by nature or at birth), whereupon the conservative view indeed becomes <u>very</u> conservative: once this fragile growth to adult moral goodness has occurred, don't meddle with the social institutions that precariously hold it in place.

For the first school, social institutions often repress or oppress natural goodness, and they should be quickly abandoned if they become burdensome. Abandoning social institutions is not inherently problematic, according to this view, because under these artificial institutions there is only natural goodness awaiting us. For the second school, social institutions are not "artificial"; they are the means whereby we rise above the nasty, brutish, and short state of nature, and tampering lightly with these institutions is more likely to unleash the beast than the best.

Scene 3

Each school has its representative extremes. Rousseau, at least to many, has stood as the figure sanctioning reckless subversion and rebellion, always in the name of a natural goodness and recaptured innocence. The classic example, of course, is the French Revolution itself, where, as Simon Schama reports, "Their faith was the possibility of a collective moral and political revolution in which the innocence of childhood might be preserved into adulthood." Not figuratively, literally. The result, equally as certain, was the Reign of Terror, where those not innocent enough were simply beheaded by the newly invented guillotine, and the world watched in horror as natural goodness and noble savages ran riot through the streets of Paris. "They're going to hunt you tomorrow," said the twins.

And today as well. Most Marxists—radical liberals—believe in a primitive communism that would be recaptured in the post-proletariat world. More than one scholar (e.g., Cranston) has seen Rousseau as the father of the student rebellions of the sixties, indiscriminately tearing down institutions because institutions per se "restricted" their "natural freedom"—failing, as all Romantics do, to see that there is a massive difference between preconventional license (where you are a slave to your impulses) and postconventional freedom (where you are liberated into moral depth); the former belongs to nature, the latter, to culture.

Most recently, Ted Kaczynski, the Unabomber, lived the life of Rousseau—in a shack, alone, communing with nature, fighting "restrictive" institutions, and—as his manifesto made clear—"The positive ideal we propose is Nature." Kirkpatrick Sale, the little Robespierre to the Unabomber's Rousseau, wrote that "Unless [the Unabomber's] message is somehow heeded . . . we are truly a doomed society hurtling toward a catastrophic breakdown." Joe Klein, in an essay called "The Unabomber and the Left," correctly points out how much this message is essentially that of liberalism—namely, culture represses our natural goodness, so we must throw culture overboard and embrace nature, or else. . . . Eco-terrorism is just one of a dozen variations on the Reign of Terror that is inherently let loose when humans head in the preconventional direction in search of their "natural goodness."

If Rousseau is the extreme figure of natural goodness, back to nature, the noble savage, and the overthrow of restrictive culture, so Nietzsche is the extreme figure of growth and evolution, leading to the superman. Nietzsche railed against the notion that if you scrape off a social institution, all you will find is natural goodness underneath; he tore into those "political and social visionaries who with fiery eloquence demand a revolutionary overthrow of all social orders in the belief that the proudest temple of fair humanity will then at once rise up as though of its own accord. In these perilous dreams there is still an echo of Rousseau's superstition, which believes in a miraculous primeval but as it were *buried* goodness of human nature and ascribes all the blame for this burying to the institutions of culture in the form of society, state and education. The experiences of history have taught us, unfortunately, that every such revolution brings about with it the resurrection of the most savage energies in the shape of a long-buried dreadfulness." Rather, Nietzsche believed, we have to grow, evolve, into our own highest estate, not go treasure hunting in the regressive past.

Just as Rousseau, rightly or wrongly, was causally implicated in the Reign of Terror, so Nietzsche, rightly or wrongly, was appropriated by the Nazis. It turns out, historians agree, quite wrongly, but you can see how inviting it was for National Socialism to embrace evolution to the superman as one of their reigning ideals. Wherever there is a growth model, as opposed to a recapture or regressive model, then you must work hard for a future that is not yet, and not simply slide back into (or regain) a past that once was. Work, not permissiveness, pervades the growth agenda. The fascists, everybody agreed, got the trains to run on time.

Extreme liberalism, ending in communism enforced with terror, on the one hand; and extreme conservatism, ending in fascism, also enforced with terror, on the other. These two extremes exist precisely because both of these views—recaptured goodness, growth to goodness—are half right, half wrong, and if the half wrong aspect of either view is pressed into widespread action, hellish nightmares await. Communism, or extreme liberalism, sacrifices excellence for the lowest common denominator; it scrapes off the top of the pyramid of growth in order to feed the bottom, with the ultimate permissive society demanding no individual growth whatsoever, for all are to be equally and fully cherished, which in effect lets all equally rot. Fascism does precisely the reverse—it kills the bottom to feed the top—and as it works hard for a growth toward the superman, the gas chambers await those who are, rightly or wrongly (always wrongly), perceived to be subhuman.

ACT 3

Scene 1

Aside from the extremes, there clearly are merits to both schools—the extremes showing starkly what happens if the two approaches are not integrated and balanced. There is much truth to the growth-to-goodness notion, for not all goods are given at birth. And there is much truth to the idea of a recaptured goodness, because during growth itself, many potentials are lost that need to be regained. This translates as well quite directly to liberalism and conservatism, both of which have strengths to embrace, weaknesses to reject.

If we were only dealing with the arc of human evolution—both phylogenetically and ontogenetically—then the issues, if not the solutions, are fairly clear. But in the area of spiritual studies, we are also dealing, in some sense, with the arc of involution, whereupon things become much more complicated.

To start with evolution (and let us focus on ontogeny, or the growth of the individual). As it turns out, this issue has already been generally decided. As leading researcher Larry Nucci puts it, "Developmental psychologists have, since the 1960s, reached a measure of agreement on the process by which children acquire moral and social values."[35] And that agreement is: growth to goodness.

On the one hand, it is true that children come biologically prepared to make moral distinctions as they socially interact. Children as young as age two have a conception of right and wrong, based largely on emotional responses, and even young children show a capacity for a certain type of emotional empathy and remorse. Nonetheless, all of those will be enriched and expanded dramatically as cognitive, social, and moral growth proceed through their various stages. The child's major capacities, barring pathology, become more and more encompassing, not less and less. Summary: children are what Nucci calls emerging moral agents, and the growth-to-goodness, not recaptured-goodness, rather decisively takes the debate.

The sequence egocentric to sociocentric to worldcentric is still a good, simple summary of this growth to goodness, not as rigid stages, but as unfolding waves and capacities. Research has continued to confirm that boys and girls both develop through that same general hierarchy, but boys do so with an emphasis on justice, girls on care. Reasons for this, however, are hotly debated, some feeling it is due to biological factors, others cultural conditioning. (My sense is that it has a strong biological grounding, molded by culture.)

Just as pioneers Piaget and Kohlberg thought that the deep features of moral growth-to-goodness are universal, not relative, so leading contemporary researchers, such as Nucci and Turiel, agree. "Turiel has found that, unlike standards regarding dress, etiquette, and the like, standards regarding harm and justice are shared by children from a wide range of cultural backgrounds, suggesting that the development of these moral principles, including their differentiation from social conventions, is universal." There are, of course, enormous local variations in content, so that, once again, "unitas multiplex" is still the best motto: universal deep features, but culturally relative surface features, are what we find in the growth to goodness.

---

35. This is from an essay in *The Sciences*. Nucci also uses the example of Rousseau versus *Lord of the Flies*. I had long been using these as prime examples of the two opposing views, and Nucci does so wonderfully.

It's the narrowness of the child's cognitive and interpersonal world that makes the child, if not quite the savage some imagine, nonetheless lacking a depth of goodness. As only one example, research has demonstrated that, as David Berreby summarizes it, "Direct learning has less to do with the way racial thinking develops than is often imagined. Substantial aspects of children's racial cognitions do not appear to be derived from adult culture." Put bluntly, it appears children are born racists.

And born narcissists. And born lacking a capacity to take global concerns into account: born lacking a love of Gaia, lacking a global depth, lacking a capacity to take the role of other, lacking a true compassion and love—and locked instead into the narrow, tight, suffocating world of their own sensations. Dear Rousseau, in this regard, got it exactly backwards: You are not born free and everywhere end up in chains; you are born in chains and everywhere can evolve into freedom.

Scene 2

Nonetheless, the Romantic view is very true in this regard: at each stage of growth and development to goodness, something can go wrong. Whatever goodness emerges at any stage, just that can indeed be repressed, and that repressed good needs to be uncovered and reintegrated. (This, incidentally, is why Freud has been classified as both a Rationalist and a Romantic, which has confused many people because it seems so contradictory, but really isn't: he was a Rationalist in that he believed fundamentally in a growth to goodness out of the primitive, natural id; but if, in this growth, we too harshly deny the id, repress it and distort it—if we become our own little fascists—then we must relax the repression barrier, undergo Romantic regression in service of the ego, recapture these lost or repressed aspects of ourselves, and reintegrate them with the ego, thus facilitating our continued growth to goodness).

So, even in the evolutionary arc itself, we want to balance the growth-to-goodness model and the recaptured-goodness model, both of which have much to offer. In practical terms, with the child's development, we do not want to be excessively permissive (liberal), because little Johnny isn't the saint, full of natural goodness, that many parents (and Rousseau) like to imagine. Mere permissiveness—no demands, no constraints, so Johnny can stay close to his natural goodness—actually lets little Johnny rot, and he will eventually unleash an interior Reign of Terror as he wallows in his natural self. He will fail altogether to engage the demanding growth toward goodness; he will behead his own greater future; he will unleash the Unabomber on his own being.

At the same time, we do not want to be excessively authoritarian (conservative), and try to pipe in "family values" and "build character" for little Johnny, because character building is largely a developmental process that occurs as much on the inside as the outside, of its own unfolding accord, and trying to force this is like trying to make a plant grow by yelling at it. The result of excessive authoritarianism is that Johnny will become his own little interior fascist, repressing those aspects of himself that don't live up to the excessively high ideals and standards of the little Hitlers called his parents. And with this internal repression, little Johnny will send to the gas chambers aspects of his own self, lost and repressed potentials that will actually cripple his own growth to goodness.

Scene 3

But what of involution? And the Romantic intuition, not that we have lost some lower potential, but that we have lost, quite literally, our awareness of union with Spirit?

Well, indeed we have incurred such loss, according to the perennial philosophy. But this loss occurred, not at the beginning of evolution—or during the early years of life—but at the beginning of involution—or what happens to us prior to our birth in time. Those Romantic souls who intuit this horrible loss of Spirit are quite right; they have simply confused the date of its occurrence. And if we must think of this loss in historical or temporal terms, then the perennial philosophy gives three related definitions of when it occurred, which are simultaneously three related definitions of involution: the loss occurred prior to the Big Bang; prior to your individual conception; prior to your next breath.

Involution means, roughly, the movement from a higher to a lower—in this case, the movement from spirit to soul to mind to body to matter. Each step down renders the senior level "unconscious" (or involved and absorbed in the lower), so that the final result is a Big Bang that blows the material world into existence, a material world out of which evolution will then proceed in the reverse or recapitulating order, matter to body to mind to soul to spirit, with each step unfolding (evolving) that which was previously enfolded (involved), not in any rigidly set pattern or clunk-clunking of stages, but as unfolding atmospheres of subtler possibilities, unfolding waves of being in the Kosmos.

The perennial philosophy, particularly its Eastern and early Western form, maintains that this basic cycle of involution/evolution also occurs with individual souls as they transmigrate. Upon death, one evolves, if one has not already, into the higher levels of soul and spirit; if these are consciously recognized, then the forced cycle of rebirth is ended. If not, then involution occurs, from spirit to soul to mind to body, whereupon one is conceived, as a material body, in a womb, from there to commence one's own personal evolution and development, body to mind to soul to spirit.

Finally, this general involution/evolution sequence is also said to be the very structure of this moment's experience (this is the most important meaning of all, and the only one that is required to penetrate the sequence). In each moment, we start out nakedly exposed to One Taste in all its purity, but in each moment most of us fail to recognize it. We contract in the face of infinity and embrace our separate selves, whereupon we become involved with the stream of time, destiny, suffering, and death. But in each moment, we can recognize One Taste and bring the entire cycle to rest. We then cease the torment of life and death, being and nonbeing, existing and perishing, simply because we rest in the timeless, birthless, deathless moment, prior to time and cycles altogether.

In each of those three definitions of the "loss" of the awareness of Spirit, the loss occurs in early involution—it occurs as soon as Spirit "steps down" into souls and minds and bodies. It does not occur in early evolution, where bodies are starting to climb back or evolve to Spirit. By the time bodies show up on the scene, the entire loss has already occurred. In fact, according to the perennial philosophy, the early stages of evolution are the most alienated, because they are farthest from a conscious recognition of Spirit.

Yet the Romantics imagine that the early stages of evolution (both phylogenetic and ontogenetic) are a great paradisiacal state, the state of "natural goodness" that will be subsequently, horribly lost, and thus must be recaptured. But all that is actually lost is an unconscious whole-ness (or fusion) with the material world and bodily domains, the lowest dimensions in the Great Nest of Being. Those lowest stages of evolution are a type of "unity" or "fusion," but a fusion with the basement—precisely the shallowest identity that <u>must</u> be differentiated and tran-scended if growth to goodness is to occur.

But once again, let us appreciate the importance of both the Romantic (recaptured goodness) and the evolutionary (growth to goodness) mod-els. The Romantics are absolutely right: we did once walk with God and the Goddess, and bathe in the garden of eternal delights. But that garden didn't actually or historically exist <u>yesterday</u>. We did not lose Spirit when we went from foraging to horticulture, or from horticulture to agrarian—we did not lose Spirit at <u>any</u> point in evolution, time, or his-tory. We "lost" Spirit in involution, which is what happens when Spirit steps down into time in the first place. And when did that occur? Prior to the Big Bang; prior to your own birth; but most importantly, prior to the point right now where you recoil from infinity. Growth to goodness is indeed a <u>recaptured</u> goodness, but a goodness lost in involution, not evolution. With that simple understanding, both views can be honored.

AN IMPORTANT POSTSCRIPT

Here follows a set of ironies.

I described today's typical conservative as subscribing to a growth-to-goodness view, and that is generally true; but equally typically, that growth only extends from preconventional nature to conventional soci-ety, and does not easily continue into postconventional, worldcentric domains. Much of typical conservatism has its roots in the mythic-agrar-ian age, whose values were civic, aristocratic, hierarchical, militaristic, ethnocentric, patriarchal, and usually sunk in a context of a mythic-concrete God(s). As dismal as we moderns might find that type of soci-ety, nonetheless it arose around the globe, ubiquitously, for a five-thou-sand-year period, where it served its purposes, and served them quite well.

When the Rational-Industrial Age dawned, with its postconventional, worldcentric moral atmosphere, a new political vision became available to men and women: that of the liberal Enlightenment. In many ways this was a decisive break with the mythic and monarchical past: rationality would fight mythology, democracy would fight aristocracy, equality would fight hierarchy, and freedom would fight slavery. That, at its best, was the vision of modernity, and liberalism was the political agenda that captured those lofty ideals.

But modernity, critics have noted, was not always, and certainly not only, lofty. There was a downside to modernity—many downsides, perhaps, but all summarized in the notion of "flatland." Due largely to a rampant scientific materialism, coupled with material industrialism, all forms of holarchy—even the good, beneficial, and spiritual forms, such as the Great Nest of Being—were collapsed into a flat and faded view of the world, composed of nothing but systems of interwoven objects, interwoven its, with no I's and no We's to speak of. Gone was soul and gone was mind and gone was spirit, and in their place an unending flatland of material bodies, which alone were thought to be real (bodyism). The disenchantment of the world, one-dimensional man, the disqualified universe, the desacrilization of the world . . . were a few of the famous phrases critics used to summarize this dreary state of affairs.

Liberalism, too, as a child of modernity, was thoroughly caught in this collapse, and therefore instead of coming to an accurate self-understanding of its own interior foundations (namely, in the growth from egocentric to ethnocentric to worldcentric, liberalism represents worldcentric awareness), liberalism instead became the political champion of flatland. Instead of interior growth and development (Left Hand), liberalism came to advocate almost solely exterior, Right Hand, economic development as a means of freedom. Since, according to flatland, there are no interiors—and since morals are interior realities—then in succumbing to the modern flatland, liberalism abdicated its basic moral intuition (that of worldcentric freedom, a stance from which all are treated fairly, but a stance to which all should be encouraged to grow).

Sadly, inevitably perhaps, liberalism abdicated its moral voice and settled for demanding exterior, material, economic freedom alone, failing to realize that without interior freedom (found, as Kant knew, only in postconventional awareness), exterior freedom is largely meaningless. Left Hand development was abandoned, Right Hand development alone remained. And as for the interiors: since there are none, none can be better than others, and so permissiveness is fine, extreme diversity is fine, extreme multiculturalism is fine—all bask in the same natural goodness that a demand for growth only corrupts.

And so it came about that liberalism, representing a higher level of collective growth, was caught in the first great modern pathology: flatland. Flatland liberalism was thus a sick version of a higher level of collective evolution.

This left the conservatives—whose values, embracing the mythic-agrarian age, did not easily submit to the modern collapse—holding the interior domains: of religion, of values, of meaning, of a demand for interior growth-to-goodness. The only problem was, these were, for the most part, mythic-agrarian values: the religion was (and is) mythological, the growth-to-goodness reaches only to the conventional/sociocentric stages (and actively fights worldcentric, postconventional modes), the values are agrarian through and through (aristocratic, patriarchal, militaristic, often ethnocentric, often biblical-fundamentalist). These values were quite healthy, for the most part, during the mythic-agrarian era: they were the best to which one could aspire under the conditions of those times.

So there are our political choices in today's world: a healthy lower level (conservative) versus a sick higher level (liberal).

A refurbished, postliberal awareness is therefore, I believe, the only sane course to pursue. This would combine the very best of the conservative vision—including the need for growth to goodness, the importance of holarchical relationships and therefore meaning (self, family, community, nation, world, Spirit), the stress on equal opportunity instead of mindless equality. But all of those conservative values need to be raised up into a modern, postconventional, worldcentric awareness.

This means, likewise, that liberalism itself must abandon any remnant of a return to "natural goodness," and again become progressive, evolutionary. The irony here is that permissive liberalism (and extreme postmodernism) is actually and deeply reactionary, because it fails to engage the difficult demand for growth to postconventional goodness. The only place we can protect true diversity and multiculturalism is from the postconventional, worldcentric stance, and unless liberalism can encourage growth to that stance, it sabotages its own agenda. Idiot compassion, advocated by liberalism, is killing liberalism.

In short, liberalism must become truly progressive, not just in exterior, flatland, economic terms, but in the interior growth of consciousness, from egocentric to sociocentric to worldcentric, preconventional to conventional to postconventional (there to stand open to post-postconventional). Not as a state-sponsored agenda (the state shall neither favor nor sponsor a particular version of the good life), but as an atmosphere of encouragement—in its theoretical writings, in the example of its leaders, in the vision to which it calls us all, in its heart and mind and soul.

As it is now, liberalism, with its background belief in natural goodness and its foreground belief in extreme diversity, is simply fostering an atmosphere of regression—in everything from identity politics to ethnocentric revivals to egocentric license. I am not suggesting that liberals legislate against that (people are free to do whatever they want, bar harming others); I am simply suggesting that they stop encouraging it under the demonstrably false notion of natural goodness and the utterly self-contradictory theory of egalitarianism (which maintains that egalitarianism itself is better than the alternatives, when all are supposed to be equal). Those two pillars of liberalism are unquestionably false, and certainly indefensible, and at the very least, ought to be quietly dropped, while liberalism goes on about the postliberal task of finding ways to foster an atmosphere of growth to goodness.

And, of course, it is my own belief that this postconservative, postliberal vision would open us to post-postconventional awareness, by any other name, Spirit. The debate, truly, has been decided: You are born in chains, and can everywhere grow into freedom, finding, finally, your own Original Face.

Thursday, December 11

The sleep cycle is fascinating. The body goes to sleep, and that leaves the subtle (mind and soul) and the causal (formless Witness). So as the body goes to sleep, the subtle mind and soul appear vividly in dreams, visions, images, and occasionally archetypal illuminations—the typical dreaming state. At some point the subtle then also goes to sleep—the mind goes to sleep, the soul goes to sleep—and that leaves only formlessness, or deep dreamless sleep, which is actually the Witness or primordial Self in its own naked nature, with no objects of any sort. (This procession from gross to subtle to causal is one version of the evolutionary or ascending arc.)

At some point during the deep dreamless state, the soul stirs, awakens, and emerges from its sleep in formlessness, and dreaming once again begins. Since the limitations and restrictions of the gross body are not present in the dream state, the subtle mind and soul (the deeper psychic) can express their deepest wishes (to merely think or wish a thing is to see it materialize instantly in the dream)—which is why prophets, saints, sages, and depth psychologists have always given so much attention to dreams: a deeper self is speaking here, so for goodness' sake pay attention. Shankara, Freud, and Jimminy Cricket all agree: "A dream is a wish your heart makes, when you're fast asleep."

As the dream state comes to a close (there are often several cycles between subtle-dreaming and causal-dreamless), then the gross body begins to stir, and the subtle mind is slowly submerged as the gross egoic orientation and the gross body awaken from their slumber. The body wakes up, the ego wakes up (the gross ego and gross body are interlinked)—in short, the frontal personality wakes up—and the person remembers very little, if anything, of the extraordinary tour that just occurred. (That movement from causal to subtle to gross—from Unborn to deeper psychic to frontal, from Self to soul to ego—is one version of the involutionary or descending arc.)

Each "waking up" in that descending arc is accompanied, in the usual individual, with a forgetting, an anamnesis. In the deep dreamless state, individuals revert to their pure formless Self, but when the subtle arises, they forget the Self and identify with the soul, with luminosities and images and ecstatic visions—they are lost in the dream state, already mistaking it for reality. Then, as the gross ego-body awakens from its slumber in the dream, it generally forgets most of that subtle state itself, unless it struggles to remember a particular dream, which is only a fragment of the wonders of the subtle. Instead, the gross ego-body looks out upon the sensorimotor world—the smallest world of all—and takes that for ultimate reality. It has forgotten both its causal Self and its subtle soul, and it sees merely the gross and the sensorimotor. It has lost its Spirit and lost its soul and damn near lost its mind, and what is left it proudly calls reality.

(Incidentally, that sequence—gross dissolving into subtle dissolving into causal, upon which, if there are karmas present, causal giving rise to subtle giving rise to gross, whereupon one "awakens" to find oneself trapped in a gross body in a gross world—is the same sequence described in the Tibetan Book of the Dead, for that sequence is said to be identical in the process of death [gross dissolves into subtle dissolves into causal] and rebirth [causal gives rise to subtle gives rise to gross, with a "forgetting" at each step]. To consciously master the waking-dreaming-sleeping cycle is therefore said to be the same as being able to consciously choose one's rebirth: to master one is to master the other, for they are identical cycles through the Great Nest of Being, gross to subtle to causal and back again. Even so, that cycle, however exalted, is nothing but the cycle of samsara, of the endless rounds of torturous birth and death. Mastering that cycle is, at best, an aid to the ultimate goal: the recognition of One Taste. For only in One Taste does one step off that brutal cycle altogether, there to rest as the All. Neither gross nor subtle nor causal are the ultimate estate, which is the simple Feeling of Being, the simple Feeling of One Taste.)

Most individuals, then, have forgotten their own higher states—forgotten their soul, forgotten their Self, forgotten the One and Only Taste. But as consciousness becomes a little stronger—through growth, through meditation, through evolution—then the transitions between the three great states are not met with blacking out or forgetting or anamnesis. With constant Witnessing, you gain your first real Release from the world, because you are no longer its victim but its Witness. With One Taste you recognize a deeper Release, which is that you are free of the entire world because you are the entire world. Even the smallest glimmer of One Taste and you will never be the same. You will inhale galaxies with every breath and sleep as the stars all night. Suns and moons and glorious novas will rush and rumble through your veins, your heart will pulse and beat in time with the entire loving universe. And you will never move at all in this radiant display of your very own Self, for you will long ago have disappeared into the fullness of the night.

Friday, December 12

Tomorrow Marci gives her thesis presentation and defense. Then there is a big celebration for the graduates. This is the start of the party season. Goodbye Witness, hello cruel world.

Saturday, December 13

Marci passed her defense with flying colors. She used a developmental hierarchy (including Maslow's) and applied it to "internal management" in business, or how a company can "sell itself" to its employees by offering services that allow and encourage their own growth in the workplace—thus making employees happier and more productive in their jobs and the company more attractive to new employees—a superb win-win situation. As an unbiased and objective onlooker, I found it brilliant, provocative, novel, compelling, and utterly absorbing.

Then out for a big celebration.

Monday, December 15

BELL HOOKS: "I'm so disturbed when my women students behave as though they can only read women, or black students behave as though they can only read blacks, or white students behave as though they can only identify with a white writer. I think the worst thing that can happen to us is to lose sight of the power of empathy and compassion."

MAYA ANGELOU: "Absolutely. Then we become brutes. Then we risk being consumed by brutism. There's a statement which I use in all my classes, no matter what I'm teaching. I put on the board the statement, "I am a human being. Nothing human can be alien to me." Then I put it down in Latin, "Homo cum humani nil a me alienum puto." And then I show them its origin. The statement was made by Publius Terentius Afer, known as Terence. He was an African and a slave to a Roman senator. Freed by that senator, he became the most popular playwright in Rome. Six of his plays and that statement have come down to us from 154 BCE. This man, not born white, not born free, said *I am a human being.*"

—Discussion in the *Shambhala Sun*, January 1998

Neither hooks nor Angelou (nor Sara Bates) is denying differences or downplaying them, but simply setting our rich cultural differences in a universal context of a common humanity, accessed, as bell beautifully says, by empathy and compassion: postconventional worldcentric awareness, universal pluralism, unitas multiplex.

"Unitas multiplex" is actually a good motto for my work, and there are signs that it is itself an idea whose time has truly come. After modernity went through a period of rigid universalism or uniformitarianism (which denied any significant cultural differences by seeing the world only through the lens of the propertied white male), and after postmodernity went through a period of chaotic diversity amounting to glorified fragmentation (which denied any universal truths at all, except its own), we are in a position to take the best of both worlds: universal pluralism, unitas multiplex. And we are seeing signs of this new, integral understanding across the board—in psychology, philosophy, business, economics. . . .

The July issue of Wired, for example, has a superb interview with Larry Summers, Clinton's chief advisor on international trade, called "The Integrationists vs. the Separatists," which spells out the disasters of protectionism and separatism in world trade. The title pretty much says it all, but if it needs any explanation, the same issue contains a positively brilliant article, "The Long Boom," by my old acquaintance Peter Schwartz and Peter Leyden. They point out that five waves of technology, now already in motion (personal computers, telecommunications, biotechnology, nanotechnology, and alternative energy), will have several almost inevitable consequences, among which may be a fully integrated world by roughly the year 2020. This interconnected, networked, integral world, they point out, will not, contrary to critics, deny local cultural differences but embrace and cherish them. It will be a truly multicultural, inclusive world—a unitas multiplex. "We're entering an age where diversity is truly valued—the more options the better. Our ecosystem works best that way. Our market economy works best that way. Our civilization, the realm of our ideas, works best that way, too." But only if all of them are firmly set in a truly integrated world, not a world where diversity, by itself, is championed—that is the way of the "separatist," clearly the bad guy in their scenario.

They also point out that this growth toward an integral world, although driven in part by technology, depends equally on several interior values, particularly those of openness and tolerance, without which technology can (and will) be put to the most heinous uses. In other words, Right Hand factors alone will not carry the day; certain Left Hand values and awareness are mandatory if technology is not to be used to increase alienation and separation. Openness and tolerance—universal pluralism—are values of the postconventional, worldcentric level of development. The conclusion is obvious: if we are indeed to reach an integrated world—the long boom of prosperity, ecological sustainability, and cultural tolerance—then in addition to the exterior waves of technology that the authors outline, humanity will have to commit itself to the interior waves of development from egocentric to sociocentric to worldcentric awareness, there to find the openness and tolerance that can cherish individual differences and prevent technology from spelling doom instead of boom.

There are massive, irreversible forces now developing the exterior waves; who will speak for the interior development that alone will divert catastrophe?

Tuesday, December 16

Another Christmas party, this time for the staff and residents of the Developmental Disabilities Center. Marci and I were some of the main dance partners for the residents, and we spent about three hours dancing, if that's the right word. Allen stood in the middle of the floor and didn't move a muscle; but he was smiling. Tavio spun his wheelchair in circles. Sandy bobbed back and forth at a terrifying rate; I tried to keep up with her, but she was too fast for me. Tom jumped up and down, swirling his arms like helicopter blades, also too fast for me. There were perhaps one hundred residents present, about half of whom danced, often simultaneously. Holding hands in a circle and kicking up our feet seemed to be the group dance of choice, when we could get everybody facing the same direction.

I have often written about what I think are the three main types of value in the world: intrinsic value, extrinsic value, and Ground value. Intrinsic value is the value a thing has in itself. Extrinsic value is the value a thing has for others. And Ground value is the value that all things have by virtue of being manifestations of Spirit.

Intrinsic value is ranked according its degree of inclusiveness and wholeness. A molecule, for example, has more intrinsic value than an atom, because molecules contain atoms. Molecules, being more inclusive, contain more being in their own makeup, and thus their intrinsic value is greater. Cells have more intrinsic value than molecules; organisms, more than cells; and so on. Likewise, worldcentric has more intrinsic value than sociocentric, which has more than egocentric, because the former, in each case, has more depth and more wholeness.

But to say a cell has more intrinsic value than a molecule is <u>not</u> to say the molecule has no value at all. It's a sliding scale, depending upon how much of the universe is <u>embraced</u> in a holon. The more being that is internal to a holon, the more intrinsic value it has. The greater the depth, the greater the wholeness, the greater the intrinsic value.

Extrinsic value is pretty much the opposite of intrinsic. An atom has more extrinsic value than a molecule, because more holons depend for their existence on atoms than on molecules. Molecules themselves depend for their existence on atoms—but not vice versa—so atoms have more extrinsic value, or value for others.

It's pretty easy to see: the higher a holon is on the Great Holarchy, the more intrinsic value it has. The lower a holon is on the Chain, the more extrinsic value it has. Both are absolutely mandatory, because they can't exist without each other. Without the higher, the lower would have no meaning; without the lower, the higher would have no manifest existence.

Intrinsic value is the value a thing has by virtue of being a <u>whole</u> with <u>agency</u> (and the greater the depth of the whole—or the more levels it contains—then the greater its intrinsic value, or the more of the universe it embraces and enfolds in its own being). Extrinsic value, on the other hand, is the value a thing has by virtue of being a <u>part</u> in <u>communion</u> (and the more things it is a part of, the greater its extrinsic value). Agency concerns <u>rights</u> (we are individual wholes with individual rights, grounded in justice); communion concerns <u>responsibilities</u> (we are also parts or members of many relationships, grounded in care). All things are wholes that are also parts (all holons, without exception, are agency-in-communion), and thus all holons have <u>both</u> intrinsic and extrinsic value, both rights and responsibilities.

Intrinsic and extrinsic are relative values; Ground value is absolute. Ground value is the value that each and every holon has by virtue of being a radiant manifestation of Spirit, of Godhead, of Emptiness. All holons, high or low, have the <u>same</u> Ground value—namely, One Taste. Holons can have greater or lesser intrinsic value (the greater the depth, the greater the value), but all holons have absolutely equal Ground value: they all share equal Suchness, Thusness, Isness, which is the face of Spirit as it shines in manifestation, One Taste in all its wonder.[36]

Whenever I am with dear people who have been so cruelly disadvantaged in their own growth and development—crippled in their own depth—I am so much more easily reminded of their Ground value, green emeralds each and all, perfect in their glory. I am reminded that intrinsic and extrinsic fall away in One Taste, where all Spirit's children equally shine in the infinity that they are. I know this for a fact, because last night I spent three hours dancing with buddhas, and who would dare deny that?

Thursday, December 18

Twenty years ago, when Buddhism was first making headway in this country, you couldn't even broach the topic of combining meditation with psychotherapy, because Buddhism was maintained to be a "complete system," so therapy wasn't needed if you were doing Buddhism correctly. A similar reluctance has beset virtually every religion in the modern world: only believe in Christ, and all will be well; pray, and your psyche will heal; zikr will cure all; davening will suffice; yoga says it all. The clear implication is that if you have enough faith or spiritual practice, you would never need psychotherapy of any sort; and conversely, if you need therapy, something is seriously wrong with your faith. The relation of spirituality to science in general, and psychotherapy in particular, is the pressing issue for spirituality in the modern world, and most religions are not, it seems, handling this very well.

Even though my actual practice has mostly been Buddhist (and Vedantic), nonetheless my works have usually been looked upon with suspicion in Buddhist circles: that Wilber fellow is implying that Buddhism alone isn't enough. Many Buddhists refused to read anything I had written, and several told me so in quite un-Buddhist terms.

Twenty years later, it's a different story. By now almost every well-known American Buddhist teacher has, in fact, undergone considerable psychotherapy (although many of them still lamentably hide this fact

---

36. See *A Brief History of Everything* for a further discussion of this topic.

from their students). But most of them realize, at least privately, that there are issues that meditation simply does not (and cannot) address. The same might be said for centering prayer, satsang, zikr, yoga, and so on. The fact is, spiritual practice and psychological practice are, in part, different streams in the great waves of consciousness, and if you are having trouble in one it does not necessarily mean you are a wretch in the other. Neurosis is not a sin.

So, a year ago, when the Shambhala Sun (a major Buddhist magazine) approached me with an interview offer, I was reluctant. Nonetheless, one wants to support contemplative magazines of integrity, so I consented. The interview began with the standard "How can you say Buddhism isn't a complete path?," but it quickly moved in a more fruitful direction. And even though this discussion is specifically about Buddhist practice, I would emphasize exactly the same points with any other spiritual practice, Christian to Jewish to Islamic to Taoist. Followers of other faiths can translate the following sentiments directly into their own practice, for the issues here are absolutely crucial, I believe, in getting religion and therapy to talk to each other.[37]

SUN: I read your ideas about the evolution of consciousness in a pair of your most recent books that seem to go together: *Sex, Ecology, Spirituality* is the big one, 800 pages. *A Brief History of Everything* seems to be a summary written for the common man and woman. Who did you write that book for?

KW: Yes, *Brief History* is much shorter and more accessible. At least I hope it is. The common man and woman? Well, anybody reading this magazine is already very uncommon, wouldn't you say? I wrote the book for the same not so common people, I guess, nut cases like you and me who are interesting in waking up and other silly notions like that. This book is not going to knock Deepak off the charts. I suppose it's more for anybody who is looking for something like an overall world philosophy, an approach to consciousness and history that takes the best of the East and the West into account, and attempts to honor them both.

---

37. The following is a slightly condensed version of the original, for which see "Big Map: The Kosmos According to Ken Wilber," *Shambhala Sun*, September 1996.

SUN: And what effect do you hope to have? What can knowing your philosophy do for the advancement of consciousness?

KW: Not very much, frankly. Each of us still has to find a genuine contemplative practice—maybe yoga, maybe Zen, maybe Shambhala Training, maybe contemplative prayer, or any number of authentic transformative practices. That is what advances consciousness, not my linguistic chitchat and book junk.

But if you want to know how your particular practices fit with the other approaches to truth that are out there, then these books will help you get started. They offer one map of how things fit together, that's all. But none of this will substitute for practice.

SUN: But what if I am, say, a hardcore, born-again Buddhist, who doesn't use other systems of self-development or self-transformation. I get the idea from *Brief History* that I must be leaving something out of my self-culture. You have Buddhism listed in only one of four squares, so I must be leaving something out. When I gain enlightenment, won't it be incomplete according to you?

KW: If by "enlightenment" you mean the direct and radical recognition of Emptiness, no, that won't leave anything out at all. Emptiness doesn't have any parts, so you can't leave some of it behind. But there is absolute bodhichitta and there is relative bodhichitta [roughly, absolute and relative truth], and although you might have direct recognition of the absolute, that does not mean you have mastered all the details of the relative. You can be fairly enlightened and still not be able to explain, say, the mathematics of the Schroedinger wave equation. My books deal more with all these relative details, some of which are not covered by Buddhism, or any of the world's wisdom traditions, for that matter. But for the direct recognition of radical Emptiness and spontaneous luminosity, Buddhism is right on the money, yes?

SUN: Then why do I need your history of consciousness when I've got all the Buddhist teachings to play with?

KW: You don't. Unless you happen to find it interesting, or fun, or engaging. Then you'll do it just to do it. The Buddhist teachings don't specifically cover Mexican cooking, either, but you still might like to take that up.

SUN: We could also put it this way: What do you know that the Buddha doesn't?

KW: How to drive a Jeep.

SUN: As you note in *Brief History*, there are already plenty of progressive theories of history and theories of spiritual evolution. Sometimes your theory sounds like Hegel's dialectic, sometimes like Darwin, sometimes like various Asian views of world mind theory. What makes it different from these other systems?

KW: Well, that's sort of the point. It sounds like all of those theories because it takes all of them into account and attempts to synthesize the best of each of them. That's also what makes it different, in that none of those other theories take the others into account. I'm trying to pull these approaches together, which is something they are not interested in.

SUN: You don't divide up your world into atoms, or elements, or psychological states, but rather into units you call *holons*. These sound a lot like the *dharmas* of Buddhist Abhidharma. How influential was Buddhist Abhidharma in your theory?

KW: Well, I'm a long-time practicing Buddhist, and many of the key ideas in my approach are Buddhist or Buddhist-inspired. First and foremost, Nagarjuna and Madhyamika; pure Emptiness and primordial Purity is the "central philosophy" of my approach as well. Also Yogachara, Hua Yen, a great deal of Dzogchen and Mahamudra, and yes, the fundamentals of Abhidharma. The analysis of experience into *dharmas* is also quite similar to Whitehead's actual occasions. My presentation of holons was influenced by all of those. Again, I'm trying to take the best from each of these traditions and bring them together in what I hope is a fruitful fashion.

SUN: Your own worldview is complicated enough. Meditators might just say, "Why do I need to have a global-historical view at all? Leave me alone to just meditate." What would you say to them?

KW: Just meditate.

SUN: You have some interesting criticisms of conventional modernism and postmodernism. You seem to accept their positions and yet at the same time to transcend them, to put them in their place. Can you explain that?

KW: Yes, the idea is that all of the various approaches and theories and practices have something important to tell us, but none of them probably has the whole truth in all its details. So each approach is true but partial, and the trick is then to figure out how all of these true but partial truths fit together. Not, who's right and who's wrong, but how can they all be right? How can they all fit together into one rainbow coalition? So that's why I both accept these positions, but also attempt to transcend them, or "put them in their place," as you say. Whether or not I have succeeded remains to be seen.

SUN: You use the word "Kosmos" instead of "cosmos." Why?

KW: *Kosmos* is an old Pythagorean term, which means the entire universe in all its many dimensions—physical, emotional, mental, and spiritual. *Cosmos* today usually means just the physical universe or physical dimension. So we might say the Kosmos includes the physiosphere or cosmos, the biosphere or life, the noosphere or mind, all of which are radiant manifestations of pure Emptiness, and are not other to that Emptiness.

One of the catastrophes of modernity is that the Kosmos is no longer a fundamental reality to us; only the cosmos is. In other words, what is "real" is just the world of scientific materialism, the world of "flatland," the flat and faded view of the modern and postmodern world, where the cosmos alone is real. And one of the things these two books try to do is rehabilitate the Kosmos as a believable concept.

SUN: You write of the Kosmos as "the pattern that connects" all domains of existence. This reminds me of Gregory Bateson's *Mind and Nature: A Necessary Unity*. How did these modern, sort of New Age movements in the social sciences influence your thought?

KW: Not very much, I must say. I don't find Bateson a very useful theorist, although I know many bright people who do. But the book you mention is what I would call a very "flatland" book, monological, it-language, one-dimensional—not very good, frankly. But that's just my opinion.

SUN: Do you think Foucault, Derrida, and company were getting at points that Asian absolutists had already articulated in some way? Or have their post-structuralist approaches been completely fresh?

KW: The post-structuralist approaches are both more novel or fresh, and much less profound. The great Eastern traditions are, in essence, profound techniques of transformation, of liberation, of release in radical Emptiness. The post-structuralists have none of that; they simply offer new ways of *translation*, not *transformation*. They are interesting twists on relative truth, not a yoga of absolute truth. But within the relative truth, the post-structuralists have a few similarities with the relative aspects of some of the Eastern traditions, such as nonfoundationalism, the contextuality of truth, the sliding nature of signification, the relativity of meaning, and so on.

These are interesting and important similarities, and I try to take them into account, but they are all quite secondary to the real issue, which is *moksha, kensho, satori, rigpa, yeshe, shikan-taza*: none of that will you find in Foucault, Derrida, Lyotard, and company.

SUN: Does the Tibetan Buddhist cosmological thought play any special role in the development of your philosophy? Sometimes it reminds me of the apocalyptic approaches of the Kalachakra school.

KW: Vajrayana in almost all of its forms has been very important to me personally, and yes, to the overall view I have outlined. Kalachakra, as anuttaratantra, is very profound; also the Ati teachings, semde, longde, and upadesa. But really, I feel a great sympathy with all of the schools.

SUN: You want to integrate Freud with the Buddha, or, as you call them, "depth psychology" with "height psychology." Why is this necessary? Do you think that without this integration both systems are incomplete?

KW: Well, I think everything is incomplete, because the Kosmos keeps moving on. New truths emerge, new revelations unfold, new Buddhas keep popping up, it is endless, no? Freud and Buddha are just two examples of some very important truths that can benefit from a mutual dialogue. Emptiness does not depend on either of them; but the manifest world is a big place, plenty of room for both of these pioneers. And yes, I think they can each help the other's path proceed more rapidly.

SUN: Do you think, indeed, that the ancient systems of spiritual transformation are inadequate in modern times, since they leave out so much of the material you include in your synthesis?

KW: Inadequate? Not in absolute truth, no; in relative manifestation, sure, simply because Emptiness keeps manifesting in different forms, doesn't it? You can't find instructions for operating a computer in any of the Sutras or Tantras. You can't find out about DNA or medical anesthesia or kidney transplants in those texts, either. Likewise, the West has contributed a thing or two to psychological and psychotherapeutic understanding, and these contributions are altogether beneficial and helpful, and they don't have many parallels in any of the ancient teachings.

But it's not really a matter of inadequacy; it's a matter of making use of whatever is available. If your practice is working for you, excellent. If it seems to be stuck, maybe a little therapy might help. I myself don't think either side has to be threatened by this. It's a really big universe, very spacious, plenty of room for Freud and Buddha.

SUN: While we're on this topic, what do you think of the inner tantras, such as kundalini yoga and what we Buddhists do with *prana, nadi,* and *bindu* [certain interior spiritual visions]? The reality upon which they rely is not admitted by science and yet it occupies two higher levels in your system, the subtle and the causal. This is confusing, because a lot of spiritual practitioners never admit the existence of those levels and never do those practices. Yet you make them seem to be a necessity of higher development. Or am I misunderstanding you?

KW: I don't think they are a necessity. It's rather that, at those two higher stages that you mentioned (the subtle and causal), these types of processes may occur. Or they may not. It depends on the type of practice, among other things. It's just that, at a certain point in your own meditative practice, various gross processes tend to be replaced by subtle and then very subtle phenomena, and these sometimes include energy currents, *prana, bindu,* and so on. But in other cases it might simply be an increase in clarity and panoramic awareness. I was simply cataloging all the different types of meditative phenomena that can occur as meditation itself unfolds from gross to subtle to very subtle consciousness. Much of what I include here is pretty standard stuff in the traditions.

SUN: Why do some spiritual practitioners seem to make advances in some ways and still be primitive assholes in other ways?

KW: Well, one of the things I try to do with the developmental model of consciousness is outline two different things, which we can call streams and waves. The streams are the different developmental lines, such as cognitive development, emotional development, interpersonal development, spiritual development, and so on. Each of these streams goes through various stages or waves of its own development. What research indicates is that, one, these different streams can develop fairly independently of each other: you can be advanced in one stream, such as the spiritual, and "retarded" in others, such as emotional or interpersonal. And two, even though these streams develop independently, they all share the same basic stages or waves of development. For example, they all go from preconventional to conventional to postconventional forms.

So we have numerous different streams of development, yet each traverses the same general waves or stages of consciousness unfolding. And people can definitely be advanced in one stream and a "primitive asshole" in others. (I summarize this research in *The Eye of Spirit: An Integral Vision for a World Gone Slightly Mad.*)

But about your point, yes, development can be rather uneven. Most of the great wisdom traditions train people for higher or postconventional awareness and cognition, and for higher or postconventional affect, such as love and compassion. But they tend to neglect interpersonal and emotional development, especially in the conventional domains. We all know advanced meditators who are, well, unpleasant people. This, of course, is where Western psychotherapy excels—although it goes to the other extreme and almost completely neglects and leaves out the higher or transpersonal waves, another reason we need to get Freud and Buddha together.

SUN: Every old-timer in the contemplative game knows this is true—that growth is usually uneven. But some say the neurotic bits are actual regressions: a person made a real advance in meditation but then, seduced by samsara, abandoned it and thus got caught up in samsaric neurosis. Others say that meditation actually scoops up hidden, compacted neuroses in the advanced practitioner, making him or her suddenly and mysteriously become a jerk. Do you think there is any truth in such views, or is your view altogether different?

KW: No, I think each of those points you mentioned is sometimes true. People often do make real progress in meditation, only to abandon it because the demands are too great, and when they return to their "old" ways, their neurosis is even worse, because they have the same ole problem but now their sensitivity is increased, so it simply hurts even more.

And your second scenario is also common. Particularly at advanced stages of meditation, the really deeply buried complexes start to become exposed to awareness. Advanced practitioners can become very exaggerated people, because they have already worked through all the smooth and easy problems, and all that is left are the karmas from when you murdered twenty nuns in your last lifetime. I'm sort of kidding, but you get the idea: some really deep-seated problems can rush to the surface in advanced practice, and this can confuse people, because this does not look like "progress." But it's sort of like frostbite: at first you don't feel anything, because you're frozen. You don't even think you have a problem. But then you start to warm up the frozen part, and it hurts like hell. The cure, the warming up, is horrible. Advanced meditation is especially a fast warming up, a waking up, and it usually hurts like hell.

SUN: But you have some other scenarios as to why things can "go bad" in meditation.

KW: Yes, the idea is that, as we were saying, development consists of several different streams that develop through the basic stages or waves of consciousness unfolding. The great wisdom traditions tend to emphasize two or three of these streams, such as the cognitive (awareness), the spiritual (and moral), the higher affect (love and compassion). But they tend to neglect other streams, such as emotional, interpersonal, relationships, and conventional interactions.

Thus, as you tend to make progress in some of these streams—perhaps the meditative/cognitive—you can become a little "unbalanced" in your overall development. Other developmental lines become neglected, withered, atrophied. Your psyche is saddled with one giant and a dozen pygmies. And the *more* your meditation practice advances, the *worse* the imbalance becomes. You start to get very weird, and you are told to *increase* your meditative effort, and pretty soon you come apart at the seams like a cheap suit. Yes?

So one of the things that we might want to look at are ways to bring a more integral practice to bear on our lives, an integral practice that includes the best of ancient wisdom and modern knowledge, and blends the contemplative with the conventional. I don't have the answers here, but these books are, I hope, a way to begin this dialogue in good faith and good will.

SUN: When you earlier said that meditators could "just meditate," was that perhaps being just a little glib? Because it doesn't seem that you really think that meditation alone is enough.

KW: Well, you didn't ask if I thought meditation alone was enough. You asked what I would tell somebody who said "Leave me alone to just meditate." I'd say, Just meditate. I have no desire to interfere with anybody's practice. But if you asked instead, "What other practices do you think meditators could use to facilitate their growth?," then I would answer more or less as I just did. In other words, a judicious blend of Eastern contemplative approaches with Western psychodynamic approaches is an interesting and I think healthy way to proceed. And if you want a more comprehensive worldview in general, including both absolute and relative truths, then certainly there are numerous items that the West will bring to the feast. Any of those approaches taken in and by themselves are demonstrably partial by comparison.

Incidentally, if you're put off by all this, you don't have to come. But everybody has an invitation to this dance, I think. It's a real Shambhala Ball. Seriously. Chögyam Trungpa's Shambhala vision, as I understand it, was a secular and integral weaving of the Dharma into the vast cultural currents in which it finds itself. *A Brief History of Everything* outlines many of those currents, and suggests one way that the Dharma can enrich—and be enriched by—those currents. This is very simple, I think.

SUN: Fair enough. What I would like to do now is to ask a few very technical questions. Okay?

KW: Okay.

SUN: One of the most confusing things about being a practitioner of Asian mystical traditions is the fact that before the Enlightenment the West had a thousand-year tradition of a civilization based on a highly mystical religion: Christianity. And yet in *Sex, Ecology, Spirituality* you characterize this thousand-year period as one that promised but did not deliver genuine transcendence. Why do you say that? How could a whole civilization miss the point for so long when it had expressions of the idea in Plato, the Corpus Hermeticum, Neoplatonism, mystical Christianity, and so on?

KW: Imagine if, the very day Buddha attained his enlightenment, he was taken out and hanged precisely because of that realization. And if any of his followers claimed to have the same realization, they were also hanged. Speaking for myself, I would find this something of a disincentive.

But that's exactly what happened with Jesus of Nazareth. "Why do you stone me?" he asks at one point. "Is it for good deeds?" And the crowd responds, "No, it is because you, being a man, make yourself out

God." The individual Atman is not allowed to realize that it is one with Brahman. "I and my Father are One"—among other complicated factors, that realization got this gentleman crucified.

The reasons for this are involved, but the fact remains: as soon as any spiritual practitioner began to get too close to the realization that Atman and Brahman are one—that one's own mind is intrinsically one with primordial Spirit—then frighteningly severe repercussions usually followed. Of course there were wonderful currents of Neoplatonic and other very high teachings operating in the background (and underground) in the West, but wherever the Church had political influence—and it dominated the Western scene for a thousand years—if you stepped over that line between Atman and Brahman, you were in very dangerous waters. Saint John of the Cross and his friend Saint Teresa of Ávila stepped over the line, but couched their journeys in such careful and pious language they pulled it off, barely. Meister Eckhart stepped over the line, a little too boldly, and had his teachings officially condemned, which meant he wouldn't fry in hell but his words apparently would. Giordano Bruno stepped way over the line, and was burned at the stake. This is a typical pattern.

SUN: You say the reasons are complicated, and I'm sure they are, but could you briefly mention a few?

KW: Well, I'll give you one, which is perhaps the most interesting. The early history of the Church was dominated by traveling "pneumatics," those in whom "spirit was alive." Their spirituality was based largely on direct experience, a type of Christ consciousness, we might suppose ("Let this consciousness be in you which was in Christ Jesus"). We might charitably say that the Nirmanakaya of each pneumatic realized the Dharmakaya of Christ via the Sambhogakaya of the transformative fire of the Holy Ghost—not to put too fine a point on it. But they were clearly alive to some very real, very direct spiritual experiences.

But over a several-hundred-year span, with the codification of the Canon and the Apostle's Creed, a series of necessary *beliefs* replaced actual *experience*. The Church slowly switched from the pneumatics to the *ekklesia*, the ecclesiastic assembly of Christ, and the governor of the *ekklesia* was the local bishop, who possessed "right dogma," and not the pneumatic or prophet, who might possess spirit but couldn't be "controlled." The Church was no longer defined as the assembly of realizers but as the assembly of bishops.

With Tertullian the relationship becomes almost legal, and with Cyprian spirituality actually is bound to the *legal office* of the Church. You could become a priest merely by ordination, not by awakening. A priest was no longer holy (*sanctus*) if he was personally awakened or enlightened or sanctified, but if he held the office. Likewise, you could become "saved" not by waking up yourself, but merely by taking the legal sacraments. As Cyprian put it, "He who does not have the Church as Mother cannot have God as Father."

Well, that puts a damper on it, what? Salvation now belonged to the lawyers. And the lawyers said, basically, we will allow that one megadude became fully one with God, but that's it! No more of that pure Oneness crap.

SUN: But why?

KW: This part of it was simple, raw, political power. Because, you know, the unsettling thing about direct mystical experience is that it has a nasty habit of going straight from Spirit to you, thus bypassing the middleman, namely, the bishop, not to mention the middleman's collection plate. This is the same reason the oil companies do not like solar power.

And so, anybody who had a direct pipeline to God was thus pronounced guilty not only of *religious heresy*, or the violation of the legal codes of the Church, for which you could have your heavenly soul eternally damned; but also of *political treason*, for which you could have your earthly body separated into several sections.

For all these reasons, the summum bonum of spiritual awareness—the supreme identity of Atman and Brahman, or ordinary mind and intrinsic spirit—was officially taboo in the West for a thousand years, more or less. All the wonderful currents that you mention, from Neoplatonism to Hermeticism, were definitely present but severely marginalized, to put it mildly. And thus the West produced an extraordinary number of subtle-level (or Sambhogakaya) mystics, who only claimed that the soul and God can share a *union*; but very few causal (Dharmakaya) and very few nondual (Svabhavikakaya) mystics, who went further and claimed not just a union but a supreme *identity* of soul and God in pure Godhead: just that claim got you toasted.

SUN: As for some of these more profound currents that became marginalized. What is the relationship between Plato's concept of "remembering" and enlightenment? Ever since I read the *Meno* I've thought there was one. But I couldn't quite figure out what it was.

KW: Yes, I think there is a very direct relationship. If we make the assumption, pretty safe with this crowd, that every sentient being has Buddha-mind, and if we agree that with enlightenment we are not attaining this mind but simply acknowledging or recognizing it, then it amounts to the same thing if we say that enlightenment is the remembering of Buddha-mind, or the direct recognition or re-cognition of pure Emptiness.

In other words, we can't attain Buddha-nature any more than we can attain our feet. We can simply look down and notice that we have feet, we can remember that we have them. It sometimes helps, if we think that we do not have feet, to have somebody come along and point to them. A Zen Master will be glad to help. When you earnestly say, "I don't have any feet," the Master will stomp on your toes and see who yells out loud. Then he looks at you: "No feet, eh?"

These "pointing-out instructions" do not point to something that we do not have and need to acquire; they point to something that is fully, totally, completely present right now, but we have perhaps forgotten. Enlightenment in the most basic sense is this simple remembering, recognizing, or simply noticing our feet—that is, noticing that this simple, clear, ever-present awareness is primordial Purity just as it is. In that sense, it is definitely a simple remembering.

SUN: And you think Plato was actually involved in that type of recognition?

KW: Oh, I think so. It becomes extremely obvious in the succeeding Neoplatonic teachers, and in these areas, the apples rarely fall far from the tree. Plato himself says that we were once whole, but a "failure to remember"—*amnesis*—allows us to fall from that wholeness. And we will "recover" from our fragmentation when we *remember* who and what we really are. Plato is very specific. I'll read this: "It is not something that can be put into words like other branches of learning; only after long partnership in a [contemplative community] devoted to this very thing does truth flash upon the soul, like a flame kindled by a leap-

ing spark." Sudden illumination. He then adds, and this is very important: "No treatise by me concerning it exists or ever will exist."

SUN: Purely wordless.

KW: Yes, I think so. Very like, "A special transmission outside the
scriptures; Not dependent upon words or letters; Direct pointing to the
mind; Seeing into one's Nature and recognizing Buddhahood." We have
to be a little careful with quick and easy comparisons, but again, if all
sentient beings possess Buddha-mind, and if you are not yet going to be
crucified for remembering it, then it is likely enough that souls of such
caliber as Parmenides and Plato and Plotinus would remember who and
what they are in suchness. And yes, it very much is a simple remembering, like looking in the mirror and going "Oh!" As Philosophia said to
Boethius in his distress, "You have forgotten who you are."

SUN: I'd like to ask you a specific question about the connection
between ultimate and relative truth. You said that the Buddha's teachings are completely adequate for the realization of Ultimate Truth, but
that relative manifestation keeps on changing because "Emptiness takes
on different forms." But really in Buddhist teachings there is just one
intelligence. The Ati tantras call it *rigpa*. It's basically supposed to be
the same as *vipashyana* or *prajña*. I'm wondering if you agree about this
one intelligence? Is this the same intelligence that understands calculus?
Is it the same intelligence that discovers quantum physics? Is it the same
intelligence that microbiologists use to map the human genome?

KW: And you ask because . . . ?

SUN: They are supposed to be the same "one intelligence" but they
don't look the same. These scientific and philosophical teachings of the
West seem to be examples of relative truth that were not discovered in
Asia. You obviously believe that the Asians were the world's experts on
finding or identifying the mind that cognizes Emptiness. But how can we
reconcile this if there is only one intelligence? Put succinctly, why didn't
rigpa discover calculus or quantum physics or human DNA?

KW: Because there is not simply one intelligence, not the way you
mean it. Remember, even in the Madhyamaka, where we have the Two
Truths doctrine, there is a corresponding Two Modes of Knowing—
samvritti, which is responsible for the relative truths of science and philosophy, and *paramartha*, or the recognition of pure Emptiness.
Whatever relative manifestation there is, it is illumined or lit by *rigpa*,

as the one intelligence in the entire universe, which is true enough. But within that absolute space of Emptiness/*rigpa*, there arise all sorts of relative truths and relative objects and relative knowledge, and Emptiness/*rigpa* lights them all equally. It does not choose sides, it doesn't "push" anything. It doesn't push against anything because nothing is outside it.

SUN: Could this be summarized by saying whether there is one intelligence or not?

KW: One intelligence that flashes in many different forms. As the Christian mystics put it, we have the eye of flesh, the eye of mind, and the eye of contemplation—all of which are ultimately lit by *rigpa*, or one intelligence, or Big Mind, but each of which nonetheless has its own domain, its own truths, its own knowing. And, most important, mastering one eye does not necessarily mean you master the others. As we were saying, these are relatively independent streams.

SUN: So the eye of contemplation is capable of disclosing absolute truth or Emptiness, whereas the eye of mind and the eye of flesh can disclose only relative truth and conventional realities.

KW: Yes, I think that is a fair summary of what are after all some very complex issues.

The traditional analogy is the ocean and its waves, which is a really boring analogy, but bear with me. The wetness of the water is Suchness (or Spirit). All waves are equally wet. One wave isn't wetter than another. And thus, if I discover the wetness of any wave, I have discovered the wetness of all. When I directly recognize Suchness or Emptiness, or the wetness of my own being, right here, right now, then I have discovered the ultimate truth of all other waves as well. Emptiness is not a Really Big Wave set apart from little waves, but is the wetness equally present in all waves, high or low, big or small, sacred or profane—which is why Emptiness cannot be used to prefer one wave over another.

Enlightenment is thus not catching a really big wave, but noticing the already present wetness of whatever wave I'm on. Moreover, I am then radically liberated from the narrow identification with this little wave called me, because I am fundamentally one with all other waves—no wetness is outside of me. I am *literally* One Taste with the entire ocean and all its waves. And that taste is wetness, suchness, Emptiness, the utter transparency of the Great Perfection.

At the same time, I do not know all the details of all the other waves: their height, their weight, the number of them, and so on. These relative truths I will have to discover wave by wave, endlessly. No *Sutra of Wetness* will tell about that, nor could it. And no *Tantra of the Soggy* will clue me in on this.

That's why I earlier said that contemplation is sufficient for ultimate truth: it will directly show you the wetness of all waves, the radical suchness of all phenomena, the Emptiness in the Heart of the Kosmos itself, the primordial purity that is your own intrinsic awareness in this moment, and this moment, and this. But meditation will not, and really cannot, tell you about all the details of all the various waves that nevertheless arise as the ceaseless play of Emptiness and spontaneous luminosity. As you say, it will not automatically give you calculus, or the human genome, or quantum physics. And historically, it definitely did not, which should tell us something right there.

SUN: I have a question about the Great Chain of Being, and it dawned on me that the Great Chain might be related to what you are saying about manifestation and relative truth.

KW: Yes, they are very similar notions. In other words, the Great Chain theorists—from Yogachara and Vedanta in the East to Neoplatonism and Kabbalah in the West—maintain that Emptiness (or the "One," meaning the Nondual) manifests as a series of dimensions, or levels, or *koshas*, or *vijnanas*—or "waves"—a spectrum of being and consciousness. The spectrum of levels is the relative or manifest truth, and the vast expanse in which the spectrum appears is Emptiness or absolute truth. Ultimately the absolute and the relative are "not two" or nondual, because Emptiness is not a thing apart from other things but the suchness of all things, the wetness of all waves. And *rigpa* is the flash, the recognition, of that nondual isness, the simplicity of your present, clear, ordinary awareness—the opening or clearing in which the entire universe arises, just so.

But, of course, that is not merely an abstract concept. One Taste is a simple, direct, clear recognition, in which it becomes perfectly obvious that you do not see the sky, you are the sky. You do not touch the earth, you are the earth. The wind does not blow on you, it blows within you. In this simple One Taste, you can drink the Pacific Ocean in a single gulp, and swallow the universe whole. Supernovas are born and die all within your heart, and galaxies swirl endlessly where you thought your head was, and it is all as simple as the sound of a robin singing on a crystal clear dawn.

SUN: The different forms of Emptiness, the different waves of the Great Perfection.

KW: Yes, in the relative world, new truths are constantly emerging; they emerge within Emptiness, within this brilliantly clear opening that is your own awareness in this moment. And whether what arises in the vast expanse of your own primordial awareness is calculus, physics, pottery, or how to make yak butter, will depend on a thousand relative truths and relative forces, none of which individually can be equated with Emptiness, and yet all of which arise as gestures of the Great Perfection or Emptiness itself—that is, all of which arise in this simple, clear, ever-present awareness, the wetness or the transparency of your very own being.

So within "one intelligence" or "Big Mind," all sorts of small minds and stepped-down intelligences arise—that's the Great Chain—and those relative truths, like the clouds in the sky and the waves in the ocean, have an appointment with their own relative karmas and a date with their own destinies.

The West has its relative truths, the East has its relative truths. And mostly in the East we further get a clear understanding of absolute truth, because the toaster was not your fate for dabbling therein. And definitely, my theme is that a judicious blend of relative truths, East and West, set in the primordial context of radical Emptiness, is a very sane approach to the human situation.

Sunday, December 21

Several late-breaking news items on the national astrology debate.

Ivan Kelly sent me a copy of his paper "Modern Astrology: A Critique," and I must say, it is fairly devastating. We last left the debate with astrology hanging, definitely but weakly, by nothing but the Gauquelin thread. Will Keepin tried to also point to the anecdotal evidence collected by Tarnas and Grof, but Roger pointed out that those studies are "uncontrolled (that is, employ no control subjects), not blind (that is, the experimenters usually know the identity of the subjects), retrospective (assessed after the fact), and without reliability tests of the measurement procedures." The Grof/Tarnas studies, in other words, are lacking proof or even corroboration, and will remain biased and anecdotal until the controls Roger outlines are diligently applied.

The Gauquelin studies, on the other hand, were compelling to believers and nonbelievers alike, and were the only studies to be so. On the basis of that <u>evidence</u>—and since we must always follow the evidence—I suggested a theory to account for the Gauquelin effects. Contrary to Will's suggestion—that the astral effects were emanating from the World Soul (the psychic level) and, via downward causation, effecting individual minds (or character traits)—I suggested that they were emanating from a merely physical level (geomagnetic, gravitational) and, via upward causation, having a small but discernible effect (via hormonal or neuronal interactions) on individual minds (or character traits). I still maintain that hypothesis, but if and only if the Gauquelin data base is sound. If it is not, then astrology in all forms is simply kaput, as far as the evidence is concerned, and we need no explanatory hypothesis at all.

From Kelly's paper I learn that P. Seymour recently "attempted to strengthen the case for the Gauquelin planetary-occupation findings by proposing a mechanism based on . . . the response of our neural networks to fluctuations in the earth's geomagnetic field which, in turn, interacts with the gravitational fields of the planets." Similar to my suggestion.

But, Kelly points out, although those are plausible hypotheses, the data has not supported them, and worse, they all rest on the reliability of the original Gauquelin data base, which, far from being an invincible edifice, is under sharp attack. Among others, the Dutch mathematician Nienhuys has apparently delivered an effective challenge to the very foundation of the Gauquelin effects.

I am still willing to follow the evidence, but I must say, the total web of evidence at this point is crushingly against astrology in any form. If the Gauquelin data base holds up, I will revert to my original geomagnetic hypothesis; but at this point, it appears astrology is a belief without corroborating evidence.

What I see people yearning for, when they turn to astrology, is a sense of connection to the cosmos. But they would do better to turn to the Kosmos. That is, instead of plugging into the gross dimension of physical planets connected to their personal egos, let their awareness rise gently into the transpersonal realms. Not merely a horizontal connection to physical planets, but a vertical connection to soul and spirit, subtle and causal, ultimate and nondual. The spiritual impulse hidden in astrology and diverted into the cosmos needs to be released into the Kosmos, released into that ultimate Embrace which holds the planets in the palm of its hand, and spins galaxies in its stride. Not psyche and cosmos, but psyche and Kosmos, holds the secret to the connection long sought.

Thursday, December 25

Marci and I spent the day alone, wonderfully.

Monday, December 29

The year is coming to a close—is dying, as tradition has it. Death: the mystics are unanimous that death contains the secret to life—to eternal life, in fact. As Eckhart put it, echoing the mystics everywhere: "No one gets as much of God as those who are thoroughly dead." Or Ramana Maharshi: "You will know in due course that your glory lies where you cease to exist." Or the Zenrin: "While alive, live as a dead person, thoroughly dead."

They don't mean physically dead; they mean dead to the separate-self sense. And you can "test" your own spiritual awareness in relation to death by trying to imagine the following items:

1. A famous Zen koan says, "Show me your Original Face, the Face you had before your parents were born." This is not a trick question or a symbolic question; it is very straightforward, with a clear and simple answer. Your Original Face is simply the pure formless Witness, prior to the manifest world. The pure Witness, itself being timeless or prior to time, is equally present at all points of time. So of course this is the Self you had before your parents were born; it is the Self you had before the Big Bang, too. And it is the Self you will have after your body—and the entire universe—dissolves.

This Self existed prior to your parents, and prior to the Big Bang, because it exists prior to time, period. And you can directly contact the Self you had before your parents were born by simply resting in the pure

Witness <u>right now</u>. They are one and the same formless Self, right now, and right now, and right now.

By "imagining" what you were like before your parents were born, you are forced to drop all identity with your present body and ego. You are forced to find that in you which actually goes beyond you—namely, the pure, empty, formless, timeless Witness or primordial Self. To the extent you can actually rest as the timeless Witness ("I am not this, not that"), then you have died to the separate self—and discovered your Original Face, the face you had before your parents were born, before the Big Bang was born, before time was born. You have found, in fact, the great Unborn, which is <u>just this</u>.

2. Similarly, imagine what the world will be like a hundred years after you die. You don't have to imagine specific details, just realize that the world will be going on a century after you are gone. Imagine that world without you. So many things will have changed—different people, different technologies, different cars and planes. . . . But <u>one thing will not have changed</u>; one thing will be the same: Emptiness, One Taste, Spirit. Well, you can taste that <u>right now</u>. One and the same formless Witness will look out from all eyes, hear with all ears, touch with all hands . . . the same formless Witness that is your own primordial Self right now, the same One Taste that is yours, right now, the same radiant Spirit that is yours, right now.

Were you somebody different a thousand years ago? Will you be somebody different a thousand years from now? What is this One Self that is forever your own deepest being? Must you believe the lies of time? Must you swallow the insanity that One Spirit does not exist? Can you right now show me your Original Face, of which there is One and Only One in all the entire World?

Listen to Erwin Schroedinger, the Nobel Prize–winning cofounder of quantum mechanics, and how can I convince you that he means this <u>literally</u>?

> Consciousness is a singular of which the plural is unknown.

> It is not possible that this unity of knowledge, feeling, and choice which you call *your own* should have sprung into being from nothingness at a given moment not so long ago; rather, this knowledge,

feeling, and choice are essentially eternal and unchangeable and nu-
merically *one* in all people, nay in all sensitive beings.

The conditions for your existence are almost as old as the rocks.
For thousands of years men have striven and suffered and begotten
and women have brought forth in pain. A hundred years ago
[there's the test], another man sat on this spot; like you he gazed
with awe and yearning in his heart at the dying light on the glaciers.
Like you he was begotten of man and born of woman. He felt pain
and brief joy as you do. *Was* he someone else? Was it not you yourself?

WAS IT NOT YOU, YOUR PRIMORDIAL SELF? Are you not humanity
itself? Do you not touch all things human, because you are its only Witness? Do you not therefore love the world, and love all people, and love
the Kosmos, because you are its only Self? Do you not weep when one
person is hurt, do you not cry when one child goes hungry, do you not
scream when one soul is tortured? You <u>know</u> you suffer when others
suffer. You already know this! "*Was* it someone else? Was it not you
yourself?"[38]

3. By thinking of what you were like a thousand years ago or a thousand years hence, you drop your identity with the present body and ego,
and find that in you which goes beyond you—namely, the pure, formless, timeless Self or Witness of the entire World. And once every twenty-
four hours you completely drop your egoic identity, not as a mere imaginative exercise but as a fact. Every night, in deep dreamless sleep, you
are plunged back into the formless realm, into the realm of pure consciousness without an object, into the realm of the formless, timeless
Self.

This is why Ramana Maharshi said, "That which is not present in
deep dreamless sleep is not real." The Real must be present in all three
states, including deep dreamless sleep, and the <u>only</u> thing that is present
in all three states is the formless Self or pure Consciousness. And each
night you die to the separate-self sense, die to the ego, and are plunged
back into the ocean of infinity that is your Original Face.

---

38. I have edited the Schroedinger quote without including ellipses. See *Quantum
Questions* for the full quotations.

All three of those cases—the Self you had before your parents were born, the Self you will have a hundred years from now, and the Self you have in deep dreamless sleep—point to one and the same thing: the timeless Witness in you which goes beyond you, the pure Emptiness that is one with all Form, the primordial Self that embraces the All in radical One Taste. And That, which is just this, has not changed, will not change, will never change, because it never enters the corrupting stream of time with all its tears and terror.

The ultimate "spiritual test," then, is simply your relation to death (for all three of those cases are examples of death). If you want to know the "ultimate truth" of what you are doing right now, simply submit it to any of those tests. Practicing astrology? If it is not present in deep dreamless sleep, it is not real. Running with wolves? If it is not present a hundred years from now, it is not real. Care of the Soul? If it is not present in deep dreamless sleep, it is not real. Healing your inner child? If it was not present prior to your parents' birth, it is not real. You remember your reincarnated past lives? If it is not present in deep dreamless sleep, it is not real. Using diet for spiritual cleansing? If it is not present a hundred years from now, it is not real. Worshipping Gaia? If it is not present in deep dreamless sleep, it is not real.

All of those relative practices and translative beliefs are fine, but never forget they are secondary to the great Unborn, your Original Face, the Face of Spirit in all its radiant forms, the forms of your very own being and becoming, now and again, now and forever, always and already.

"*Was* it someone else? Was it not you yourself?"

Wednesday, December 31—Denver

Marci and I spent New Year's Eve at our favorite local hideaway, the Oxford Hotel in the LoDo district, Denver. Dinner at Jax's, drinks at the Cruise Bar, a midnight embrace, kiss the year goodbye.

Thursday, January 1, 1998—Boulder

A year ago today I was wondering what to do with Sense and Soul. It's been a wild ride, this year. In two weeks I go to Manhattan to meet with major book reviewers, all arranged by Ann. Then in March I'll do a six-city book tour, small but unprecedented for me. I will still, I trust, be in love with Marci, one of the most beautiful women and dearest souls I have ever known. I will be editing the <u>Collected Works</u>, and will be plowing through the reading for volume 2. I will be nine months away from my fiftieth birthday.

And none of that, of course, is present in deep dreamless sleep, or present a thousand years from now, or prior to my parents' birth, or in the formless realm itself, where I-I alone shine, where IAMness fills the timeless world to all infinity and back. None of it, in other words, touches the purest Emptiness that alone is Real, that bathes my being in delight and sends my mind to heaven. Yet all of that is a compassionate gesture of my very Self, the Self of each and every being without lack or limitation, the Self of all that truly is and truly ever shall be.

It is always already undone, you see, and always already over. In the simple feeling of Being, worlds are born and die—they live and dance and sing a while and melt back into oblivion, and nothing ever really happens here, in the simple world of One Taste. A thousand forms will come and go, a million worlds will rise and fall, a billion souls will love and laugh and languish fast and die, and One Taste alone will embrace them all. And I-I will be there, as I-I always have been, to Witness the rise and miraculous fall of my infinite easy Worlds, happening now and forever, now and forever, now and always forever it seems.

And then again, I might just stay here, and watch the sunset one more time, through the misty rain that is now falling, quietly all around.

INDEX

formless mysticism, causal realm of, 116, 241; I AMness in, 80, 108, 370; I-I in, 121, 150–51, 161, 370; judgements and, 101; "just this" of, 105–06, 112, 141, 160, 161, 190, 227–28; love for a specific person and, 197; not other than Form of, 135; One Taste and, 70, 82, 126, 158, 160, 203–04, 302; pop culture and, 271; pure consciousness and, 125–26; Witnessing and, 59, 88, 113, 158, 203–04, 273–76, 296
Enduring structures, waves of consciousness as, 293n
Eros. *See* Ascending current
Esalen Institute, 61
Essence, in Diamond Approach to psychospiritual growth, 169–73
Essential Gay Mystics, The (Harvey), 21–22
Essential Joy, 171–73
Euthanasia movement, 131
Evans, Harry, 40–41
Ever-present awareness, 125, 137–39, 159–60, 274–75
Evolution: Great Chain of Being, lack of understanding of, 119–20; higher stages emerging via Eros and, 119
Existential worldview, 261, 263–64, 265, 268
Exotica (film), 42
Experiential: awareness and, 191; of body and mind, 191–92; Witness and, 192
Exterior-collective quadrant. *See* Lower right (social) quadrant
Exterior-individual quadrant. *See* Upper right (behavioral) quadrant
Extrinsic values, 346–48
Eye, of flesh, mind, and spirit, 6, 91
Eye to Eye (Wilber), 85, 110
Eye of Spirit, The (Wilber): always-already truth concept in, 89; art and interpretation of, 90; in collected works series, 86; Crittenden forward to, 15–19; developmental psychology addressed in, 89, 284–85, 295n; Diamond Approach critiqued in, 169; Emerson and Plotinus

discussed in, 167; function of religion focus of, 27; Great Nest of Being concept in, 117n; hermeneutics in, 90, 90n. 8; integral approach of, 104–05, 106, 129, 213, 284–85; Integral Feminism concept in, 83; nature mysticism critiqued in, 167; perennial philosophy in, 57n, 58n; pre/trans fallacy concept in, 111n; "The Integral Vision" Introduction to, 153; universal truths and, 308
Eysenck, Hans, 178

Fadiman, Jim, 140, 182
Fame, 4
Family Viewing (film), 42
Faulkner, William, 11
Feeling of Being, 302–04
Fetzer Institute, 61–62, 65, 168–69
Fetzer, John, 61–62
Fichte, Johann, 136
5280 magazine, 112
Fitzgerald, F. Scott, 11
Five Ages of Man, The (Heard), 11
Flatland: as integral practice obstacle, 133; of Modernism, bodyism, 219–20, 219n, 220, 229–30; Warhol as artist of, 68
Ford, Tom, 97
Forest, Leon, 324
Forgotten Truth, The (Smith), 57
Form: Emptiness one with all Form and, 59, 88, 113, 125, 158, 203–04, 273–76; formless mysticism, causal realm of and, 116, 123, 165, 241, 341–43; not other than Emptiness of, 135
Forman, Robert, 230, 234n
Formless mysticism, 116, 123, 165, 241, 341–43
Fortress of science, 145
Foster, E. M., 9
Foucault, Michel, 261
"415 Paradigm", 156, 234
Freedom from the Known (Krishnamurti), 13
Freud, Sigmund: contributions of, 194, 216, 342, 353; as Rationalist and Romantic, 335; reductionist nature of, 110